IF YOU THINK YOU'VE HEARD IT ALL, YOU PROBABLY HAVEN'T HEARD THIS...

RUBBER BAND BALL: The world's largest rubber band ball, constructed by John J. Bain, weighed 3,120 lbs. (1,415.2 kg) when measured on October 22, 2003, in Delaware, U.S.A. It has a circumference of 15 ft. 1 in. (4.59 m).

HULA HOOPS: MOST HOOPED SIMULTA-NEOUSLY: Alesya Goulevich of Belarus was able to sustain three full revolutions with 99 hula hoops between her shoulders and her hips at the Big Apple Circus Big Top on April 26, 2004, in Massachusetts, U.S.A.

HEAVIEST AIRCRAFT PULLED: David Huxley pulled a Boeing 747-400 weighing 412,260 lbs. (206 tons) a distance of 298 ft. 6 in. (91 m) in 1 min. 27.7 sec. on October 15, 1997, in Sydney, Australia.

Accreditation

Guinness World Records Limited has a very thorough accreditation system for records verification. However, while every effort is made to ensure accuracy, Guinness World Records Limited cannot be held responsible for any errors contained in this work. Feedback from our readers on any point of accuracy is always welcomed.

Abbreviations & measurements

GUINNESS WORLD RECORDS LIMITED uses both metric and imperial measurements (metric in parenthesis). The sole exceptions are for some scientific data where metric measurements only are universally accepted, and for some sports data. Where a specific date is given, the exchange rate is calculated according to the currency values that were in operation at the time. Where only a year date is given, the exchange rate is calculated from December of that year, "One billion" is taken to mean one thousand million. "GDR" (the German Democratic Republic) refers to the East German state, which unified with West Germany in 1990. The abbreviation is used for sports records broken before 1990. The USSR (Union of Soviet Socialist Republics) split into a number of parts in 1991, the largest of these being Russia. The CIS (Commonwealth of Independent States) replaced it and the abbreviation is used mainly for sporting records broken at the 1992 Olympic Games.

Guinness World Records Limited does not claim to own any right, title or interest in the trademarks of others reproduced in this book.

General Warning

Attempting to break records or set new records can be dangerous. Appropriate advice should be taken first and all record attempts are undertaken entirely at the participant's risk. In no circumstances will Guinness World Records Limited have any liability for death or injury suffered in any record attempt. Guinness World Records Limited has complete discretion over whether or not to include any particular records in the book. Being a Guinness World Record holder does not guarantee you a place in the book.

GUINNESS

WORLD RECORDS 2006

BANTAM BOOKS
NEW YORK • TORONTO • LONDON • SYDNEY • AUCKLAND

ISBN-10: 0-553-58906-7
ISBN-13: 978-0-553-58906-1

Printed in the United States of America
Published simultaneously in Canada

www.bantamdell.com

OPM   10 9 8 7 6 5 4 3 2 1

GUINNESS WORLD RECORDS

2006

MANAGING EDITOR
Claire Folkard

CONTENTS

INTRODUCTION

Welcome to Guinness World Records 2006—The Most Exciting Edition We've Produced Yet...

It's been a busy 12 months for record-breaking America—a quick search of our ever-growing database reveals that over 14,818 claims were made from the U.S.A. over the past year: an average of 40 record attempts every day!

In terms of the world league table of record claims, America continues to claim the top spot. In every key area of record-breaking achievement, the U.S.A. makes a considerable impression: the **fastest human being on the planet** (Tim Montgomery) is American, as is the pilot of the **first private manned spaceflight** (Mike Melvill), the winner of the **most X Games medals for skateboarding** (Tony Hawk), and the **first person to fly around the world without refueling** (Steve Fossett).

RECORD-BREAKING AMERICANS
Among the thousands of record holders from the U.S.A. are:

Will Smith (p. 299)
(most personal appearances by a movie star in one day)

Lance Armstrong (p. 484)
(most Tour de France wins)

OutKast (p. 322)
(most weeks at both No. 1 and No. 2 on the U.S. singles chart)

Gwen Stefani (p. 321)
(biggest selling download single in a week in the U.S.A.)

Hilary Duff (p. 310)
(highest annual earnings by a child actress)

David Copperfield (p. 369)
(largest illusion ever staged)

Jessica Simpson (p. 310)
(highest annual earnings for a reality TV star)

Usher (p. 324)
(longest time spent at No. 1 on the U.S. singles chart in a year)

Ashrita Furman (p. 50)
(fastest time to pogo stick up the CN Tower)

But you don't need to be a world-class athlete or NASA astronaut to get your name in the *Guinness World Records* book! A flick through this year's edition reveals the likes of Gary Duschl, who this year celebrates his 40th anniversary of making the **longest gum-wrapper chain,** "Banana" George Blair, who marked his 90th birthday by being the **oldest barefoot water-skier,** and Gary Thuerk, sender of the **first spam e-mail!**

So, thanks to everyone whose sense of adventure, humor, and optimism helps make the book such a success. I'd also like to say thank you to those who took time out of their busy schedules last year to help us celebrate our golden anniversary. The party at the Parker Meridien Hotel, New York City, was the highlight of our year—where else would a man who holds snakes in his mouth (Jackie Bibby, **most rattlesnakes held in the mouth**) rub shoulders with a speedy balloon artist (John Cassidy, **fastest balloon sculptor)** and an architect who builds super-structures using playing cards (Bryan Berg, **tallest card tower)** but at a Guinness World Records party?!

As enjoyable as the anniversary year was, it left us with a real challenge:

David Hasselhoff—star of *Baywatch,* the most widely viewed TV show in history—gets a sneak preview of the 2006 book during his exclusive interview with Guinness World Records. Find out what it's like to be the most watched leading man in TV history on p. 308.

Her Majesty Queen Elizabeth II—a multiple record holder—receives a copy of the golden anniversary edition of *Guinness World Records* from Chief Operating Officer Alistair Richards during her visit to the company's London headquarters.

how do we follow the success of a sell-out 50th edition? Well, we've added an all-new **Sports Reference** section (p. 560). And we've committed ourselves to monitoring more categories than ever, so look out for up-to-date features on subjects such as **digital music** (p. 317), **computer games** (p. 369), **magic & illusion** (p. 363), and the **X Games** (p. 337). We're also looking at more ways in which *you* can become a record holder. Look out over the next year for **Guinness World Records** in your home town. Check out our website—**www.guinnessworldrecords.com/usa**—for upcoming record attempts and events. And don't be surprised if we turn up at your school or a local event!

You'll find everything you need to know on how to become a record breaker on p. xix. But if that sounds a bit too much like hard work, just settle back and dip into the **biggest selling copyright book of all time**—remember, at least 40 other people in the U.S.A. will be taking up a record-breaking challenge today. In the meantime, I hope you find this year's record-breaking record book packed full of inspiration...

Craig Glenday
Editor

TV host Regis Philbin receives his Guinness World Records certificate from adjudicator Stuart Claxton for **most hours spent on television.**

Adjudicator Stuart Claxton congratulates Donald Trump on his record-breaking achievement. "To be in this book for me was very special," he told us. "I must be honest with you, I never thought I'd make it—but I made it!" Find out more about his new record—the highest annual earnings for the host of a reality TV show—on p. 310.

Danny Way shows off his Guinness World Records certificate at the summer X Games X, 2004. He holds the records for the **longest skateboard ramp jump** and the **highest skateboard air** off a quarter-pipe.

WHAT'S NEW IN 2006? Look out for these exciting new features:

★ NEW RECORD
Every new category is identified with a ★ —so too are newly researched records that have just been added to our archive

☆ UPDATED RECORD
This refers to records that have been published in the past but have been recently broken or updated

CROSSHEADS
Where necessary, we've organized records under subheadings to make it even easier to find your favorite records

COMPARISONS
Compare the size of record breakers with simple, at-a-glance artwork

RECORD-BREAKING TV

The past 12 months have seen Guinness World Records travel to television screens around the globe...

Since *Guinness World Records* hit our TVs back in 1998, it has been seen in over 95 countries. Most recently, *Ultimate Guinness World Records* has been distributed to over 35 countries, from Russia to Indonesia—and a lot of places in between!

Guinness World Records TV becomes a firm favorite everywhere it's seen—often leading to a frenzy of record attempts by fans of the shows in a bid to get themselves into the internationally famous book. And as it continues to spread across the globe, Guinness World Records TV goes from strength to strength, covering ever more extraordinary feats and incredible achievements by truly remarkable people worldwide.

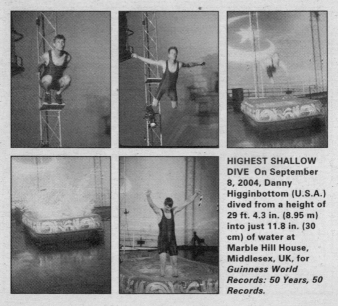

HIGHEST SHALLOW DIVE On September 8, 2004, Danny Higginbottom (U.S.A.) dived from a height of 29 ft. 4.3 in. (8.95 m) into just 11.8 in. (30 cm) of water at Marble Hill House, Middlesex, UK, for *Guinness World Records: 50 Years, 50 Records.*

AUSTRALIA

As part of GWR TV's golden anniversary celebrations, Seven Network aired *Guinness World Records: 50 Years, 50 Records,* a series of 50 awe-inspiring record attempts hosted by Grant Denyer and Jamie Theakston.

This one-off extravaganza proved so successful that Seven went on to commission a 13-part series of one-hour shows—entitled simply *Australia's Guinness World Records*—for screening in late 2005. Grant Denyer returns as host, this time with the help of Shelley Craft (both pictured). "It's sure to be an impressive new showcase for Australian record-breaking talent," says Grant from the set of the new show.

Record-Breaking TV

Dwayne Black (Australia) sheared a single sheep in 45.41 seconds on the set of TV show *Australia's Guinness World Records* on April 17, 2005.

UNITED KINGDOM

The UK marked the golden anniversary of this famous book with its own version of *Guinness World Records: 50 Years, 50 Records*. This glittering two-hour live celebration of record breaking was hosted by Jamie Theakston, who introduced the prime-time audience to no fewer than 50 remarkable record attempts.

Additionally, popular GMTV host Jamie Rickers took Challenge TV viewers on a 40-episode journey through the world's most awesome record attempts in *Ultimate Guinness World Records*.

And never standing still, Guinness World Records is currently developing a new celebrity-based, record-breaking TV format for UK and US audiences. New prime-time spectaculars will also be screened on RTL, Germany, in 2005 and 2006.

HIGHEST ALTITUDE BALLOON SKYWALK On September 1, 2004, Mike Howard (UK) walked on a beam between two balloons at an altitude of 21,400 ft. (6,522 m) near Yeovil, Somerset, UK, for *Guinness World Records: 50 Years, 50 Records*.

LONGEST TIME SPENT IN FULL-BODY ICE CONTACT Wim Hof (Netherlands) spent 1 hr. 8 min. in direct, full-body contact with ice on the set of *Guinness World Records: 50 Years, 50 Records* at the London Television Studios, UK, on September 11, 2004.

FRANCE

Guinness World Records' most ambitious TV show to date is *L'Été De Tous Les Records* (pictured on page xviii). This *live* outdoor extravaganza of smashed records and astonishing bravery takes place every weekday for nine weeks. It's presented by French hosts Pierre Sled, Emma Kostic, and "extreme" records expert Taïg Khris. They are all overseen by the huge (and hugely popular) former NBA star Barry White—our firm-but-fair judge.

Now in its third successful year, *L'Été De Tous Les Records* continues to see records smashed in a number of categories, ranging from extreme wall climbing to death-defying wakeboarding and skateboarding.

★MOST CONSECUTIVE INDIE FLIPS ON A SKATEBOARD On June 29, 2004, Terence Bougdoir (France) completed an incredible 10 consecutive indie flips on the set of *L'Été De Tous Les Records* in Biscarrosse, France.

BE A RECORD BREAKER

If you think you've got what it takes to be a Guinness World Record holder, then read on...

If you want to be a record breaker, there are thousands of records to choose from, but you could also make a suggestion for a new record. We're looking for new categories that are inspiring, interesting, require an element of skill, and that are likely to attract subsequent challenges from people worldwide.

1. SUBMIT AN APPLICATION

Making a record attempt takes time and requires patience. You need to **contact us before you make any attempt**—do not send us any evidence or documentation until we've assessed your proposal. Every Guinness World Record is governed by a unique set of rules that **must be followed.** You need to apply for these rules before you can submit an attempt.

The easiest and fastest way to submit an application is via our website. Simply go to **www.guinnessworldrecords.com,** click on the link that says "Make a Record Attempt" and follow the instructions.

If you have a **new record idea,** you need to find out if we will accept your proposal before you attempt the record. Give us as much relevant information as possible. If we like your idea, where appropriate, we'll draw up rules specifically for your attempt in order to set a standard for all subsequent challenges.

Once you've filled in the application, you'll be asked to choose a password, which we'll send you with a membership number. This gives you access to our new tracking system, which you can use to monitor the progress of your claim or ask any questions about your record attempt.

You'll also be asked to print and sign an agreement form, which you must send to us by mail or fax immediately. **We're unable to process any proposals until we've received the signed agreement form.**

Please note that all Guinness World Records must be **approved at our UK headquarters in London.** No one else has the authority to distribute rules or approve records on our behalf—despite any claim to the contrary— so please **do not send any correspondence, or requested evidence, to any address other than our London office.** (Note, also, that **we cannot return any evidence,** so please make sure you have taken copies of any valued photographs and video footage before sending us the originals.)

If your record proposal needs urgent consideration, we offer a premium fast-track service. This means a researcher is assigned to your proposal as soon as we've received your signed agreement and we'll respond within three working days after this. Please note that fast track is a chargeable

Guinness World Records' Nicola Savage times a jelly-bean sorting record attempt at the Southampton Road Show on October 30, 2004. At the same event, Steve Bugdale (UK) attempts the world record for the most push-ups in one minute using the back of the hands, under the watchful eye of adjudicator Chris Marais.

service and does not guarantee a positive response (more information is available on the website).

INVIGILATION

Most people don't have a Guinness World Record representative at their event—they just send in their documentation afterwards for verification. Invigilation is a premium service that we offer for a fee, dependent on whether we have a relevant invigilator available at the time. Please check the invigilation box on your application if you want further information on this.

2. WAIT TO HEAR FROM US

Once we've received your agreement form, your application will be reviewed by one of our specialized researchers. If it's accepted as a new category (or an existing one) we'll contact you with the corresponding **rules and regulations** that must be strictly adhered to. If we reject your idea, we'll reply to you detailing why it was not acceptable.

Although we'll reply as soon as we can, please note that it may take up to eight weeks during busy periods.

3. ORGANIZE YOUR ATTEMPT

Once we've sent you the guidelines, it is up to you to organize the event. As long as there is no violation of the rules, the attempt can be arranged in any way you choose.

Keeper of the Records, Stewart Newport, and Sophie Whiting from Guinness World Records attended the world's **biggest simultaneous handshake** on February 11, 2005, at the Deira City Centre shopping mall, Dubai, UAE.

After the attempt, you have to send us a package with all the verification documents. All evidence must be **marked with your claim identification number** (which will have been provided in prior correspondence).

If your claim passes all inspections, including final scrutiny from the Keeper of the Records (and providing a new record has not been set in the interim), you'll be declared a Guinness World Record holder!

Please bear in mind that with over 60,000 claims coming in every year, it can take between two weeks and three months to process a claim. Please be patient—we will get back to you as soon as we can.

The world's **biggest pair of cowboy boots** are 4 ft. 6.75 in. (1.38 m) tall and 3 ft. 11 in. (1.19 m) long.

4. RECEIVE YOUR CERTIFICATE

All Guinness World Record holders receive a certificate to commemorate their achievement. However, we can't guarantee that any specific record will appear in our book—but your certificate remains the proof that you are the world record holder.

Steve Fossett (U.S.A., middle) receives his GWR certificate for the first solo circumnavigation by an aircraft without refueling, accompanied by Sir Richard Branson (left) and adjudicator David Hawksett (right).

Susan Morrison presents Blair Morgan (Canada) with his certificate at the Winter X Games in January 2005 for the most **Winter X Games Snocross medals**, with seven in total.

On January 17, 2005, a record 31 arm-linked people stood up simultaneously at an event organized by UK Radio Aid and adjudicated by Della Torra Howes (holding book).

PHOTOGRAPHING YOUR RECORD

PHOTOGRAPHY TIPS

1. Avoid "camera shake"—try to keep the camera as still as possible. If you have a tripod, use it.

2. Keep the sun behind you. If you're outside, avoid shooting into bright light—position yourself so that the sun is behind you. (On the other hand, make sure your subject isn't squinting because the light is too strong!)

3. Keep it simple. Whatever you're shooting, don't clutter up the shot with stuff we don't need to see. Shooting against a white background often helps.

4. Focus on what matters. If you're photographing your dog because it's very long, for example, make sure the whole dog fits into the frame. But if you're photographing your dog's long eyelashes, get in close—we don't need to see its entire body. Feel free to send us more than one photo, but make sure that at least one of them shows clearly what's going on.

5. Capture the action. If you're shooting a mass participation event, make sure the people in the shot are actually doing the record. We don't want to see everyone after the event—we want action! (For example, if it's a mass pillow fight, we want to see lots of people hitting each other with pillows!)

6. Show a sense of scale. If you've made something that is very small (or very large), photograph it next to something of recognizable size to show the scale (see the big boots pictured above together with regular-size boots).

A person is often the best thing for reference, so ask a friend to photograph you next to what you've built. If the subject is really tiny, a coin is a great clue to its size. You could even place a ruler in the shot.

7. Get the whole picture. Make sure you get the whole record object in shot. If it's a "Largest" record, get both the top and bottom of the object in the frame.

8. Use your flash. Most cameras have an automatic flash setting, but to make sure, don't trust the camera—switch the flash on—even if you (or the camera) think there's enough light! If your camera has red-eye reduction, use it too.

PRINT PHOTOGRAPHY

Please send prints from the lab. Please DO NOT send laser or bubble jet prints or any photocopies.

DIGITAL PHOTOGRAPHY

Always use the highest quality setting. Often images are taken at the low setting and the resolution (dpi) is not high enough to print. Our minimum print size is 6 × 4 in. (15 × 10 cm) at 300 dpi. Please use this as a standard.

YOUNG ACHIEVERS

★**Longest school attendance without absences for a family**
Sharon (b. May 14, 1967), Neil (b. September 28, 1968), Honor (b. October 18, 1969), Howard (b. September 16, 1972), Olivia (b. March 26, 1977), Naomi (b. June 17, 1981), and Claire Stewart (b. January 14, 1983) of Markethill, Armagh, UK, completed their education from the ages of four to 16 without being absent from their schools—Markethill County Primary and High School—for a single day.

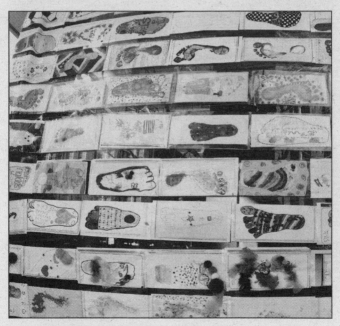

★**LONGEST LINE OF FOOTPRINTS** A single, unbroken line of 10,932 footprints from children all over the world was created by readers of *National Geographic Kids* magazine and unveiled at the National Geographic Society in Washington, D.C., U.S.A., on November 9, 2004. In total, the prints measured 9,969 ft. 8 in. (3,038.75 m). They were created from various materials—including paint, glitter, seashells, dried rice, mud, and tar—and were submitted from countries as far afield as Mongolia and Australia.

☆ **YOUNGEST TV HOST** Luis Tanner (Australia, b. May 9, 1998) currently hosts his own TV show, *Cooking for Kids with Luis* (Nickelodeon). The first episode in this weekly show was aired on October 25, 2004, when Luis was just 6 years 168 days old.

★**Largest class with perfect attendance** In 1984–85, 23 pupils in the class of Melanie Murray at David Barkley Elementary School, San Antonio, Texas, U.S.A., were never once absent from class.

★**Fastest time to push a soapbox cart 1,000 km** In September 2001, 30 pupils from the Laeveld Primary School in Nelspruit, South Africa, pushed an unpowered soapbox cart a distance of 621 miles (1,000 km) in 62 hr. 43 min. on the first leg of their 1,280-mile (2,061-km) journey between Komatipoort and Cape Town, South Africa. The attempt was part of an event called the NICRO Race Against Crime and Time.

★**Largest single-site egg-and-spoon race** A total of 859 students from Raynes Park High School, London, UK, took part in an egg-and-spoon race on October 24, 2003.

★**Longest balloon chain** OMR Heerbrugg School in Switzerland created a chain of 30,000 balloons measuring a total of 6,586 ft. 5.4 in. (2,007.55 m) on September 19, 2003.

Ryan Sheckler (U.S.A.) became the youngest X Games gold medalist after securing first place in the Skateboard Park event at the age of 13.

How old were you when you started skating? At 18 months old, I picked up my dad's board and started pushing around on my knees. By the age of four, I was trying to ollie off furniture around the house!

How does it feel to have won gold at such a young age? Oh yeah, I love skateboarding and the way it feels to be where I am right now. I still have a great vibe going. I'm still hungry for it and I'm still really, really excited to skate.

You must get a lot of respect being able to compete against these older skaters. I'm accepted with these guys, and I'm doing what they're doing. I guess they recognize that and give me credit for it.

What's your next goal? Keep on skating, come back next year and win X Games again, and have fun with all these guys!

How does it feel to get into the *Guinness World Records* book? It's crazy! When I was in fifth grade, we'd always go to the library and look through the book and check out all the people in there. I thought how cool it would be if I could get in there… I'm finally there, so I'm psyched.

☆**Largest bottle-cap mosaic** On October 23, 2003, students from Akiba Junior High School in Yokohama, Japan, created a mosaic spelling out "Love & Peace" using a record 150,480 bottle caps.

☆**Fastest mile of pennies** A mile of 79,200 pennies worth £792 ($1,224) was laid in 2 hr. 42 min. 29 sec. by members of The Willows School in Stratford-upon-Avon, Warwickshire, UK, on October 19, 2002.

☆**Longest drinking-straw chain** A chain of drinking straws measuring 20,417 ft. 8.8 in. (6,223.33 m) and consisting of 41,996 straws was made by 16 students from the Hayground School, Bridgehampton, New York, U.S.A., on June 11, 2004.

☆**Longest can chain** A chain of aluminum drinking cans measuring 4.77 miles (7.69 km) long and using 66,129 cans tied together with string was created by Hillcrest Primary School in Kloof, KwaZulu-Natal, South Africa, on November 29, 2003.

★**Largest song and dance routine (multiple sites)** Organized by the North London Performing Arts Centre, a total of 7,596 children from across north London, UK, danced and sang to the song "To the Show" for five minutes on March 22, 2002.

★**Longest line of dancers** Other than a conga, the longest continuous single line of dancers was made up of 331 children at Seathorne Primary School, Skegness, Lincolnshire, UK, on July 9, 2004. The children danced for six minutes to the Steps song "5, 6, 7, 8" in a line that measured 475 ft. (145 m) long.

★**Largest macarena dance** A total of 1,712 students of St. Bede's School, Redhill, Surrey, UK, danced the Macarena for at least five minutes on March 9, 2004. The event helped to raise money for charity.

★**YOUNGEST COMPOSER OF A MUSICAL** Adám Lőrincz (Hungary, b. June 1, 1988) was 14 years 76 days old when his 92-minute musical, *Star of the King,* was performed on August 16, 2002, in Szekesfehervar, Hungary. The musical is a tribute to singer Elvis Presley and features 23 performers. It has been performed at numerous locations throughout Hungary.

★Largest twist dance On April 30, 2004, a total of 1,691 staff and students from St. Aidan's Church of England High School and St. John Fisher Catholic High School in North Yorkshire, UK, danced for five minutes to Chubby Checker's "The Twist."

★Most leapfrog jumps in one minute On September 29, 2004, schoolboys Marius Martinsen Benterud and Christel Ek Blanck (both Norway) achieved 59 leapfrog jumps in one minute at the Jetix Challenge in Ski, Norway.

☆Most people brushing teeth simultaneously A total of 31,424 pupils at 261 schools in Hessen, Germany, brushed their teeth at the same time for at least 60 seconds—after being given the start signal via the radio station IIR1—on May 21, 2003.

Most consecutive soccer passes Members of the McDonald's Youth Football Scheme based in Tsing Yi, Hong Kong, China, achieved a record 557 consecutive soccer passes on May 4, 2002. About 1,250 children took part in the event.

WANT TO BE A RECORD BREAKER?
FIND OUT HOW ON P. XIX

HUMAN BODY

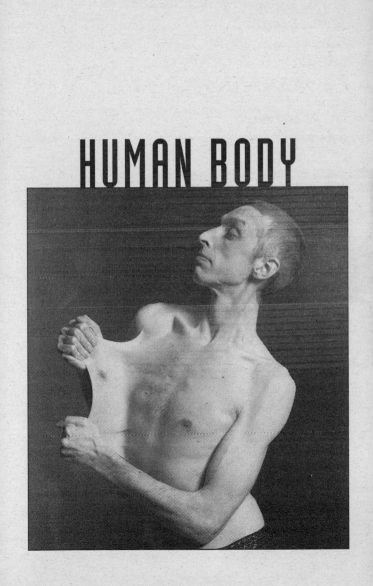

CONTENTS

EXTREME BODIES

TALLEST . . .

Living man After seven measurements taken over April 22–23, 1999, in Tunis, Radhouane Charbib's (Tunisia) height was averaged at 7 ft. 8.9 in. (2.35 m).

Man The **tallest man** for whom there is irrefutable evidence is Robert Pershing Wadlow (U.S.A., 1918–40), who, when last measured on June 27, 1940, was 8 ft. 11.1 in. (2.72 m) tall. His size was the result of an overactive pituitary gland, source of the growth hormone somatotrophin.

Woman Zeng Jinlian (China, b. June 26, 1964) of Bright Moon Commune, Hunan Province, China, measured 8 ft. 1.75 in. (2.48 m) when she died on February 13, 1982. This figure represented her height with assumed normal spinal curvature because she suffered from severe scoliosis (curvature of the spine) and could not stand up straight.

★TRIPLETS—LIGHTEST BIRTHS Peyton (1 lb. 4.6 oz.; 585 g), Jackson (14.8 oz.; 420 g), and Blake (13.4 oz.; 380 g) Coffey (all U.S.A.) became the lightest triplets to survive when born in Charlottesville, Virginia, U.S.A., on November 30, 1998.

★ LIGHTEST AND HEAVIEST BIRTHS ★

LIGHTEST	WEIGHT	HOLDER
Birth	10 oz. (283 g)	Marian Taggart (née Chapman, UK)
Twins	30.33 oz. (860 g)	Roshan and Melanie Gray (Australia)
		Anne and John Morrison (Canada)
★Triplets	3 lb. 0.8 oz. (1,385 g)	Peyton, Jackson, and Blake Coffey (U.S.A.)

HEAVIEST	WEIGHT	HOLDER
Birth	23 lb. 12 oz. (10.8 kg)	Born to Anna Bates (Canada)
Twins	27 lb. 12 oz. (12.58 kg)	Patricia Jane & John Prosser Haskin (U.S.A.)
Triplets	24 lb. (10.9 kg)	Born to Mary McDermott (UK)
Quadruplets	22 lb. 15.75 oz. (10.426 kg)	Born to Tina Saunders (UK)

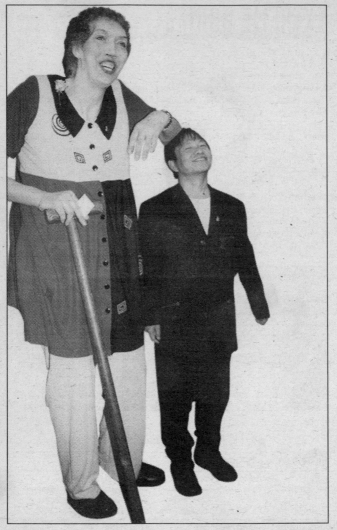

TALLEST LIVING WOMAN Sandy Allen (U.S.A.) was last found to measure 7 ft. 7.25 in. (2.317 m). She currently weighs 314 lb. (142 kg) and wears size 22 shoes. She gets her sneakers secondhand from the 7-ft. 4-in. (2.235-m) Indiana Pacers basketball star Rick "The Dunking Dutchman" Smits.

Living female twins Ann and Claire Recht (U.S.A.) were measured both horizontally and vertically three times on June 19, 2003, in Oregon, U.S.A., and were found to have an average overall height of 6 ft. 6 in. (1.98 m) and 6 ft. 5.9 in. (1.97 m), respectively.

Living male twins Michael and James Lanier (U.S.A.) of Troy, Michigan, U.S.A., both stand 7 ft. 3.9 in. (2.23 m). Their sister Jennifer is 5 ft. 2 in. (1.57 m) tall.

SHORTEST . . .

Living man Younis Edwan (Jordan) is believed to be 25.5 in. (65 cm) tall. (He has not been officially measured by GWR.) The **shortest man** ever was Gul Mohammed (India, 1957–97), who was examined at Ram Manohar Hospital, New Delhi, India, on July 19, 1990, and found to be just 22.5 in. (57 cm) tall.

Woman Pauline Musters was born in Ossendrecht, the Netherlands, on February 26, 1876, and measured 12 in. (30 cm) at birth. She died of pneumonia with meningitis on March 1, 1895, in New York, U.S.A., at the age of 19. A postmortem examination showed "Princess Pauline," as she was known, to be exactly 24 in. (61 cm).

Twins Matyus and Béla Matina of Budapest, Hungary, who later became naturalized U.S. citizens, both measured 30 in. (76 cm). The **shortest living twins** are also the **shortest identical male twins;** find out how they compare on p. 18.

Living identical female twins Dorene Williams and Darlene McGregor (both U.S.A.) each stand 4 ft. 1 in. (124.4 cm).

★**Baby** Nisa Juarez (U.S.A.) was born on July 20, 2002, and measured just 9.44 in. (24 cm) long at the Children's Hospital and Clinic in Minnesota,

SHORTEST LIVING WOMAN Madge Bester (South Africa) is only 25.5 in. (65 cm) tall. She suffers from *Osteogenesis imperfecta* (brittle bones and other deformities of the skeleton) and is confined to a wheelchair. Her mother Winnie is not much taller, measuring 27.5 in. (70 cm), and is also confined to a wheelchair.

U.S.A. She was born 108 days premature, weighed only 11.3 oz. (320 g) and was discharged from the hospital on December 6, 2002.

The **longest baby** was delivered by Anna Bates (née Swan, Canada, 1846–88) at her home in Seville, Ohio, U.S.A., on January 19, 1879. At 30 in. (76 cm), the baby was born taller than Gul Mohammed (India), the world's **shortest ever man.**

HEAVIEST . . .

Man In March 1978, Jon Brower Minnoch (U.S.A.) was admitted to University Hospital, Seattle, U.S.A., where consultant endocrinologist Dr. Robert Schwartz calculated that Minnoch must have weighed over 1,400 lb. (635 kg), much of which was water accumulation owing to congestive heart failure.

Minnoch's wife Jeanette (U.S.A.) weighed just 110.2 lb. (50 kg), making theirs the **greatest weight differential for a married couple** at about 1,289.7 lb. (585 kg).

Woman Rosalie Bradford (U.S.A.) peaked at 1,200 lb. (544 kg) in January 1987. After a health scare, she reduced her daily intake to 1,200 calories and began to exercise by clapping her hands. Five years later, she had lost the equivalent weight of seven people and claimed another record: the **greatest weight lost by a female.**

Twins In November 1978, Billy Leon and Benny Loyd McCrary, alias McGuire (both U.S.A.), weighed 743 lb. (337 kg) and 723 lb. (328 kg) respectively.

ARE YOU THE WORLD'S HEAVIEST PERSON?

Although we are aware of living people who weigh in excess of 1,120 lb. (508 kg), we have been unable to fully authenticate the record for **heaviest living person**—mostly owing to claimants' unwillingness to be weighed under controlled conditions.

While we do not encourage overeating, if you wish to put yourself forward for this category we ask that you fulfill these two simple requirements:

1. **Medical notes** of the measurements made by suitably qualified individuals must be submitted along with a statement from a qualified medical doctor.

2. A **copy of the birth certificate** must be submitted with the record claim.

LARGEST CHEST MEASUREMENT In February 1958, shortly before his death at the age of 32, Robert Earl Hughes (U.S.A.) weighed 1,067 lb. (484 kg) and had a chest measurement of 10 ft. 4 in. (3.15 m). At the age of six, he weighed 203 lb. (92 kg), and by the age of 10 he weighed 378 lb. (171 kg); at age 25, he reached 896 lb. (406 kg).

MEDICAL MARVELS

TRANSPLANTS

☆**Longest lived lung transplant survivor** On September 15, 1987, Wolfgang Muller (Canada) underwent a single lung transplant at Toronto General Hospital in Ontario, Canada. On July 19, 2004, he became the longest surviving lung transplant recipient at 16 years 307 days.

☆**Longest lived heart transplant survival** Derrick Morris (UK) underwent a heart transplant operation on February 23, 1980, at Harefield Hospital in Greater London, UK. The operation gave him a heart that had belonged to a 26-year-old woman.

★**Longest surviving heart-lung-liver transplant patient** Mark Dolby (UK) received a triple transplant (heart-lung-liver) on August 21, 1987, at Harefield Hospital in Greater London, UK. On June 4, 2004, 16 years 288 days later, he was confirmed as the longest-lived survivor of a triple operation.

★**Oldest kidney transplant recipient** Carroll Basham (U.S.A.) had a kidney transplant operation at the age of 77 years 185 days on October 2, 2002, at the Methodist Specialty and Transplant Hospital, San Antonio, Texas, U.S.A. His stepdaughter, Nancy Hildenburg, donated the kidney.

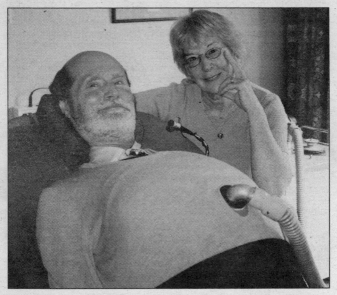

LONGEST SURVIVING IRON-LUNG PATIENT John Prestwich (UK) has been paralyzed since being struck by polio on his 17th birthday. Since November 24, 1955, he has been entirely dependent on a negative-pressure respirator ("iron lung") to breathe. An iron lung is an airtight shell that alters the pressure in the chest, forcing the lungs to inflate and allowing patients with no control of their breathing muscles to breathe.

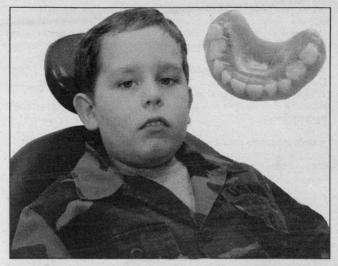

★YOUNGEST PERSON TO WEAR DENTURES Alexander Stone (U.S.A.) became the youngest recipient of a full set of dentures on June 7, 2001, at the age of 4 years 301 days. Alexander suffers from a hereditary condition called dentinogenesis imperfecta, which weakens and discolors the teeth, removing the pulp. He had his dentures fitted by family dentist Dr. Joseph E. Morton.

★First heart-lung transplant After two years of experiments, Dr. Bruce Reitz (U.S.A.) performed the first successful combined heart-lung transplant, at Stanford Medical Center in Stanford, California, U.S.A., in 1981.

Least blood transfused during a transplant In June 1996, a transplant team at St. James University Hospital, Leeds, UK, performed a liver transplant on 47-year-old Linda Pearson (UK) without any blood being transfused. Such an operation usually requires up to 6 pints (3.5 liters) of blood, but as a Jehovah's Witness, Pearson is unable to accept blood that is not her own.

OPERATIONS

★**Longest surviving triple-heart-bypass patient** Richard Smith (UK) underwent a triple-heart-bypass operation on February 8, 1978, at Papworth Hospital, Cambridge, UK, becoming the longest survivor of such a procedure on May 12, 2004, 26 years 93 days later.

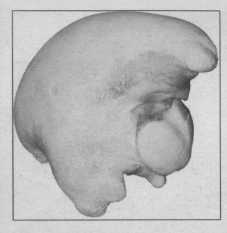

★**LARGEST KIDNEY STONE** Peter Baulman (Australia) had a kidney stone weighing 12.5 oz. (356 g) and measuring 4.66 in. (11.86 cm) at its widest point removed from his right kidney in December 2003 at The Gold Coast Hospital, Southport, Queensland, Australia.

★**Longest surviving open-heart-surgery patient** Sadie Purdy (UK), who was born in 1924 with a hole in her heart, had open-heart surgery on December 4, 1941, aged 17. The six-hour operation, performed at St. Bartholomew's Hospital, London, UK, by Oswald Tubbs, was still experimental, but has now extended her life by 63 years.

Largest gallstone A gallstone weighing 13 lb. 14 oz. (6.29 kg) was removed from an 80-year-old woman by Humphrey Arthure (UK) at Charing Cross Hospital, London, UK, on December 29, 1952.

☆**Largest appendix** The appendix removed from a 55-year-old man at the Pakistan Institute of Medical Sciences, Islamabad, Pakistan, on June 11, 2003, measured 9.2 in. (23.5 cm) in length—wider than this page!

★**Largest tumor at birth** A 2-lb. 9-oz. (1.2-kg) benign cystic hygroma was removed from the neck of a baby boy by a team led by Palin Khundongbam (India) at Shija Hospitals and Research Institute, Imphal, Manipur, India, on March 17, 2003. The tumor represented 40% of the child's body weight.

LARGEST OBJECT REMOVED FROM A STOMACH A hair ball weighing 5 lb. 3 oz. (2.53 kg) was removed from the gut of a 20-year-old female compulsive swallower in the South Devon and East Cornwall Hospital, UK, on March 30, 1895.

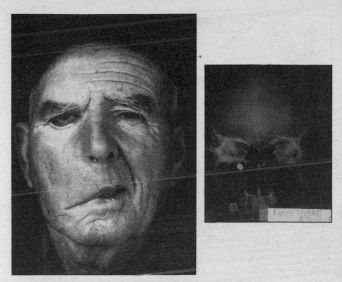

★**LONGEST TIME WITH A BULLET IN HEAD** Kolyo Tanev Kolev (Bulgaria) accidentally shot himself behind his right ear with a pistol in 1942, aged 17. X-rays taken on July 5, 2003 show the bullet lodged at the base of the skull, 61 years later.

MISCELLANEOUS

★**Youngest wisdom tooth extraction** Matthew Adams (U.S.A., b. November 19, 1992) had two wisdom teeth removed at Midland Oral and Maxillofacial Surgery, Michigan, U.S.A., on October 24, 2002, aged just 9 years 339 days.

Highest blood sugar level Alexa Painter (U.S.A.) survived a blood sugar level 20.7 times above average at 139 mmol/L (2,495 mg/dl) when treated for severe diabetic ketoacidosis at the Community Hospital of Roanoke, Virginia, U.S.A., on December 30, 1991. Normal blood sugar is 4.4–6.6 mmol/liter (80–120 mg/dl).

Most blood donated Maurice Creswick (South Africa) donated his 336th unit of blood on July 9, 2003, the equivalent of 49 gal. (188.9 liters).

Having given blood since his 18th birthday in 1944—59 consecutive years to 2003—he also holds the record for ☆**most blood donated over consecutive years.**

RECIPIENT OF MOST BLOOD The average human body contains about 10 pints (5.5 liters) of blood. But while undergoing open-heart surgery at the Michael Reese Hospital in Chicago, Illinois, U.S.A., in December 1970, Warren C. Jyrich (U.S.A.), a 50-year-old hemophiliac, required 2,400 donor units of blood—equivalent to 285 gal. (1,080 liters) or nearly 15 full bathtubs of blood!

GOLDEN OLDIES

OLDEST . . .

★**Woman to fly in zero gravity** On July 22, 2004, Dorothy Simpson (U.S.A., b. November 27, 1924) took part in a zero-gravity flight on an Ilyushin IL-76, aged 79 years and 237 days.

The flight was organized by Space Adventures (U.S.A.).

★**Reigning monarch** Taufa'ahau Tupou IV (b. July 4, 1918) became the king of Tonga when his mother, Queen Salote Tupou III, died in 1965, and has reigned ever since.

He is also the world's **heaviest monarch.** In September 1976, he weighed 462 lb. (209.5 kg). By 1985 he was reported to have slimmed down to 307 lb. (139.7 kg), in early 1993 he was 279 lb. (127.0 kg), and by 1998 he had lost more weight due to a fitness program.

★**Royal** Princess Alice, Duchess of Gloucester (UK, b. Lady Alice Christabel Montagu Douglas Scott, 1901–2004) became the oldest known

MALE STRIPPER Bernie Barker (U.S.A., b. July 31, 1940) began his career as a male stripper in 2000—at the age of 60—as a way to get in shape while recovering from prostate cancer. Since leaving his previous job of selling real estate, the "Silver Tom Selleck" has won more than 40 stripping contests and is a regular performer at clubs in Las Vegas, Nevada, U.S.A.

royal ever when she reached the age of 101 years and 69 days on September 20, 2003. She died on October 29, 2004.

★**Married couple** Thomas Morgan (UK, b. May 4, 1786) married Elizabeth (UK, b. January 17, 1786) in Caerleon, Wales, on May 4, 1809. They remained married for 81 years 260 days until Elizabeth's death on January 19, 1891. At this time, Elizabeth was aged 105 years 2 days and Thomas was 104 years 260 days, a total of 209 years 262 days. (Meet the **oldest living married couple** on p. 242.)

★ **BRIDESMAID** Flossie Bennett (UK, b. August 9, 1902, pictured far left) was matron of honor at the wedding of Leonard and Edna Petchey (both UK) on February 6, 1999, at St. Peter's Church, Holton, Suffolk, UK, at the age of 97 years 181 days. The oldest recorded bride is Minnie Munro (Australia), aged 102, who married Dudley Reid (Australia), aged 83, at Point Clare, Australia, on May 31, 1991.

★ **Unsupported trekker to the South Pole** Simon Murray (UK, b. March 25, 1940) completed a trek to the South Pole at the age of 63 years 309 days. He left the Antarctic coastline near Hercules Inlet on December 2, 2003, and arrived at the pole with his trekking partner, Pen Hadow (UK), on January 28, 2004. The trek covered a distance of about 683 miles (1,100 km).

★ **Honorary degree recipient** Bridget Dirrane (Ireland, b. November 16, 1894) received an honorary degree from the National University of Ireland, Galway, on May 18, 1998, aged 103 years 183 days. The award followed publication of a book that explored her perceptions of life over the span of a century.

Actress Jeanne Louise Calment (France, 1875–1997) portrayed herself at the age of 114 in the movie *Vincent and Me* (Canada, 1990)—a fantasy about a girl who travels through time to meet Dutch painter Vincent van Gogh. Calment, the **oldest person ever,** whose age of 122 years 164 days has been fully authenticated, is thought to have been the last living person to have known van Gogh.

★ **Regular newspaper columnist** Simon Blumenfeld (UK, b. November 25, 1907), a.k.a. Sidney Vauncez, has written a column for the performing arts and entertainment trade paper *The Stage* since June 1994.

CHORUS-LINE DANCER The oldest "showgirl" who is still regularly performing in a chorus line is Beverly Allen (U.S.A., b. November 4, 1917) of Santa Maria, California, U.S.A. A member of The Fabulous Palm Springs Follies, her jitterbug routine—in which her partner lifts her over his head to spin her "head-over-heels"—has become an audience favorite.

★**Dominoes player** Alf Hill (UK, b. August 31, 1908) became the oldest competitive dominoes player at the age of 92 in 2000. He plays for the Jolly Carter pub team and has been a member of the Lowton and District Darts and Dominoes League for over 25 years.

Base jumper James Talbot Guyer (U.S.A., b. June 16, 1928) parachuted off the 486-ft.-high (148-m) Perrine Bridge near Twin Falls, Idaho, U.S.A., on August 2, 2002, aged 74 years 47 days.

★**Opera singer** Luo Pinchao (China, b. June 19, 1912) began his singing career in 1930 and still regularly performs Cantonese opera. He celebrated his 93rd birthday by performing at the Guandong Cantonese Opera Grand Artistic Theater, Guangzhou, China, on June 20, 2004.

★**Nun** Sister Julia (France, b. Augustine Teissier) was born on January 2, 1869, in Florensac, France, and died aged 112 years 66 days on March 9, 1981, in Nîmes, France.

★**Ballerina** Charin Yuthasastrkosol (U.S.A., b. Thailand, December 30, 1930) began ballet lessons at the age of 47 and performed regularly through her senior years. Her most recent performance was for Sakthip Krairikish, Thailand's ambassador to the U.S.A., in New Mexico, U.S.A., on July 21, 2002, at the age of 71 years 203 days.

☆**Mountain climbers** Carl F. Haupt (U.S.A., b. April 21, 1926) reached the summit of Mount Kilimanjaro, Tanzania, on August 30, 2004, aged 78 years 131 days. The oldest person to climb Mount Everest is Yuichiro Miura (Japan, b. October 12, 1932), who reached the summit aged 70 years 222 days on May 22, 2003.

★**OLDEST PERFORMING CLOWN** Andrew Beyer (U.S.A., b. March 4, 1918) has been performing as Bumbo the Clown since 1952 and was recognized as the oldest clown still working at the age of 86 years 250 days on November 9, 2004.

Many clowns have lived and performed to a great age. Grock (Germany, 1880–1959) and Otto Griebling (Germany, 1896–1972) worked until the age of 74. Lou Jacobs (Germany, 1903–92) carried on until 82, and Charlie Rivel (Spain, 1896–1983) retired at the age of 85.

Human Body

☆**Licensed drivers** Fred Hale Sr. (U.S.A., 1890–2004) was issued with a driver's license in February 1995, and drove until it expired on his 108th birthday in 1998. He became the **oldest living man** in the world and died aged 113 years 354 days on November 19, 2004.

Layne Hall (U.S.A., b. December 24/25, 1884 or March 15, 1880) was issued with a license on June 15, 1989, when he was either 104 (according to his death certificate) or 109 (according to his driver's license). It was valid until his birthday in 1993, but he died on November 20, 1990.

Maude Tull (U.S.A.), the **oldest female driver,** who took to driving aged 91 after her husband died, had her license renewed on February 5, 1976, aged 104.

FAMILIES

★ RECORD-BREAKING MOTHERS ★

NAME	RECORD
Maddalena Granata (Italy, 1839–1886)	**Most sets of triplets** Gave birth to 15 sets of triplets.
Mrs. F. Vassilyev (Russia, 1707–ca.1782)	**Most prolific mother ever** In 27 confinements, gave birth to 69 children (16 pairs of twins, 7 sets of triplets, and 4 sets of quadruplets). This means that she also holds the record for the **most sets of quadruplets** and the **most sets of twins** born to one mother.
Merryl Thelma Fudel (née Coward, Australia, b. 1942)	**Oldest mother to have quadruplets** Gave birth to three girls and one boy on April 18, 1998, at the age of 55 years and 286 days.

SIBLINGS

★**Most siblings to reach retirement age** Seven sons and five daughters were born to John Zacher Sr. (Canada, 1877–1968) and his wife Elizabeth (Canada, 1886–1981) from 1907 to 1929, all of whom were claiming a state pension in 1999. Their ages ranged from 70 to 92 years.

All 12 daughters born to Albert Scott (UK, 1889–1977) and his wife Edith (UK, née Chittenden, 1889–1978) from 1910 to 1931 were claiming a state pension in November 2002. Their ages ranged from 71 to 92 years.

☆**Most albino siblings** Of the eight children born to George and Minnie Sesler (U.S.A.), the four oldest of their five sons were all born with the rare genetic condition, albinism. Identical twins John and George, Kermit and Kenneth were all born with translucent skin, pinkish-blue eyes, and white hair.

SHORTEST LIVING TWINS John and Greg Rice (U.S.A.) are identical twins, born on December 3, 1951. They both measure 2 ft. 10 in. (86.3 cm) in height.

The **tallest living twins** are Michael and James Lanier (both U.S.A.), who stand 7 ft. 3.9 in. (2.235 m) tall.

All four children of Mario and Angie Gaulin—Sarah, Christopher, Joshua, and Brendan (all Canada)—were born with the rare genetic condition oculocutaneous albinism. Their father also has the condition and their mother carries the gene.

★ **MOST SETS OF TWINS BORN ON THE SAME DAY** There are only two verified examples of a mother producing two sets of twins with coincident birthdays. The first is that of Laura Shelley (U.S.A.), who gave birth to Melissa Nicole and Mark Fredrick Julian Jr. on March 25, 1990, and Kayla May and Jonathan Price Moore on the same date in 2003 (left, top). The second is that of Caroline Cargado (U.S.A.), who gave birth to Keilani Marie and Kahleah Mae on May 30, 1996, and Mikayla Anee and Malia Abigail on the same date in 2003 (left, below).

MOST SIBLINGS TO COMPLETE A MARATHON The 11 Flaherty siblings—Terence, Kathleen, Dennis, Michael, David, Kevin, Brian, Margaret, Patricia, Gerard, and Vincent (all UK)—completed the London Marathon on April 18, 2004.

★**Longest separation of siblings** William James Pring (UK) was re-united with his sister Elsie May Ashford (UK, née Pring) on November 20, 1988, through the agency of the Salvation Army. They were reunited in London, UK, by Major Colin Fairclough exactly 81 years after their separation.

★**Most siblings to serve in World War II** The nine brothers Albert, Jim, Harry, Arthur, Bill, Tom, Dick, Sid, and Wally Windsor (all UK) all served in World War II.

This record is shared with the Lewtas brothers—Edward, Robert, William, Charles, George, Harry, Matthew, Thomas, and Christopher (all UK)—who served in various divisions of the military from 1939 to 1945.

FAMILY TREES

Longest family tree The lineage of K'ung Ch'iu or Confucius (China, 551–479 B.C.) can be traced back further than that of any other family. His great-great-great-great-grandfather Kung Chia is known from the 8th century B.C. Kung Chia has 86 lineal descendants.

Most descendants In polygamous countries, the number of a person's descendants can be incalculable. At the time of his death on October 15, 1992, the monogamous Samuel S. Mast (U.S.A.), then aged 96, had 824 living descendants: 11 children, 97 grandchildren, 634 great-grandchildren, and 82 great-great-grandchildren.

☆ **MOST CHILDREN TO SURVIVE FROM A SINGLE BIRTH** Bobbie McCaughey (U.S.A.) gave birth to septuplets on November 19, 1997, at the Blank Children's Hospital, Des Moines, Iowa, U.S.A., via caesarean section. Named Kenneth, Nathaniel, Brandon, Joel, Kelsey, Natalie, and Alexis, they weighed between 2 lb. 5 oz. and 3 lb. 4 oz. (1,048 g and 1,474.3 g).

On January 14, 1998, four boys and three girls were born prematurely to Hasna Mohammed Humair (Saudi Arabia) at the Abha Obstetric Hospital, Aseer. The smallest baby weighed just under 2 lb. (907 g).

Furthest traced descendant by DNA Adrian Targett (UK) is a direct descendant, on his mother's side, of Cheddar Man, a 9,000-year-old skeleton, one of the UK's oldest complete skeletons. This link stretches back 300 generations.

★ **Most generations alive at once** The greatest number of generations from a single family to be alive at the same time is seven. The **youngest great-great-great-grandmother** is Augusta Bunge (U.S.A.) aged 109 years 97 days, followed by her daughter aged 89, her granddaughter aged 70, her great-granddaughter aged 52, her great-great-granddaughter aged 33, and her great-great-great-granddaughter aged 15 on the birth of her great-great-great-great-grandson on January 21, 1989.

ADOPTION

★**Oldest adoptive parent** Frances Ensor Benedict (U.S.A., b. May 11, 1918) was aged 83 years 329 days when she officially adopted Jo Anne Benedict Walker (U.S.A.) on April 5, 2002, in Putnam County, Tennessee, U.S.A.

★**Oldest adoption** Jo Anne Benedict Walker (U.S.A.) was 65 years 224 days when she was officially adopted by Frances Ensor Benedict (U.S.A.) on April 5, 2002, in Putnam County, Tennessee, U.S.A.

**HOW OLD WAS THE WORLD'S OLDEST BRIDE?
FIND OUT ON PAGE 14**

BODY PARTS

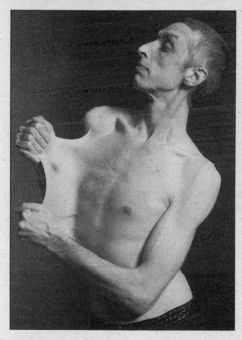

STRETCHIEST SKIN
Garry Turner (UK) can stretch his skin to a length of 6.25 in. (15.8 cm) owing to a medical condition called Elhers-Danlos Syndrome, a disorder of the connective tissues affecting the skin, ligaments, and internal organs. It also accounts for his success in another Guinness World Record category—☆ most clothespins clipped on a face—as Garry can attach 159 wooden pins to the skin of his face.

LARGEST...

Breasts Annie Hawkins-Turner (U.S.) has an under-breast measurement of 43 in. (109.22 cm) and an around-chest-over-nipple measurement of 70 in. (177.8 cm). She currently wears a U.S. size 52I bra, although needs a 48V bra, which is not manufactured.

Feet Robert Wadlow (U.S.A.), the **tallest man ever,** wore U.S. size 37AA shoes, equivalent to 18.5 in. (47 cm) long. Excluding cases of elephantiasis, then the **largest feet on a living person** are those of Xi Shun (b. 1951) of Inner Mongolia, China, at 13 in. (33 cm) long, as a result of measurements taken at the Millennium Hotel, London, UK, on September 21, 2005.

★ Gape J. J. Bittner (U.S.A.) is able to open his mouth to a width of 3.4 in. (8.4 cm). The gape is measured from the incisal edge of his maxillary central incisors to the incisal edge of his mandibular central incisors (that is, from the tips of his incisor teeth).

LONGEST . . .

Beard Shamsher Singh's (India) beard measured 6 ft. (1.83 m) from the end of his chin to the tip of the beard, as of August 18, 1997. The **longest beard on a female** belongs to Vivian Wheeler (U.S.A.) and last measured 11 in. (27.9 cm) from the follicle to the tip of the hair.

★**Stretched earlobes** Monte Pierce (U.S.A.) can stretch his earlobes to a length of 5 in. (12.7 cm) for his left lobe and 4.5 in. (11.43 cm) for his right. For the **longest earlobes,** see the tribes of southeast Asia on p. 90.

RECORD-BREAKING BODY PARTS

HEAVIEST BRAIN The brain of a 30-year-old U.S. male was reported to weigh 5 lb. 1.1 oz. (2.3 kg) by Dr. George T. Mandybur (U.S.A.) of the University of Cincinnati, Ohio, U.S.A., in December 1992. A normal brain weighs 2.8–3 lb. (1.3–1.4 kg).

★**LONGEST EYEBROW HAIR (3.078 in; 7.81 cm)** A single hair growing on the left eyebrow of Franklin Ames (U.S.A.) was measured on February 26, 2004, to have reached a length of 3.078 in. (7.81 cm).

FURTHEST EYEBALL POPPER (0.43 in; 11 mm) Kim Goodman (U.S.A.) can pop her eyeballs to a protrusion of 0.43 in. (11 mm) beyond her eye sockets.

★**LONGEST EYELASH (1.57 in; 4 cm)** Mark Gordon (U.S.A.) has a white eyelash on his left eyelid which, when measured on June 4, 2004, in Batavia, Ohio, U.S.A., was found to be 1.57 in. (4 cm) long.

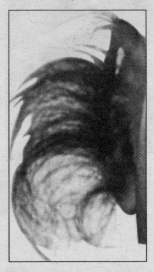

LONGEST EAR HAIR (5.19 in; 13.2 cm) Radhakant Bajpai (India) has hair sprouting from the center of his outer ears (middle of the pinna) that measures 5.19 in. (13.2 cm) at its longest point.

Hands Robert Wadlow's (U.S.A.) hands were 12.75 in. (32.3 cm) from wrist to tip of middle finger.

★Tooth A tooth extracted from Mark Henry (Canada) in January 2005 measured 0.47 in. (1.2 cm) wide.

Waist Walter Hudson (U.S.A.) had a waistline that measured 119 in. (302 cm) at his peak weight of 1,197 lb. (545 kg).

☆Hair The world's longest documented hair belongs to Xie Qiuping (China), and measured 18 ft. 5.54 in. (5.627 m) on May 8, 2004. She has been growing her hair since 1973, when she was 13.

★MILK TOOTH Daniel Valdes (U.S.A.) had three milk teeth removed on April 9, 2004, in Westlake, Ohio, U.S.A., the longest of which measured 0.66 in. (1.69 cm) long, having a crown length of 0.19 in. (0.5 cm).

ACTUAL SIZE

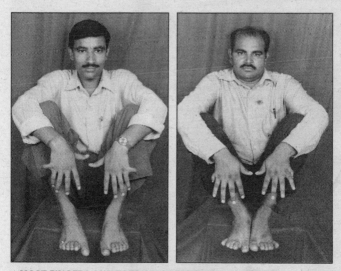

☆MOST FINGERS AND TOES ON A LIVING PERSON Brothers Tribhuwan and Triloki Yadav (both India) have the condition polydactylism, whereby each of their hands has five fingers and a thumb, and each foot has six toes.

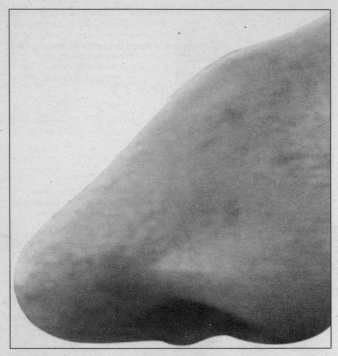

LONGEST NOSE ON A LIVING PERSON (3.46 in; 8.8 cm) Mehmet Ozyurek (Turkey) has a nose that was 3.46 in. (8.8 cm) long from the bridge to the tip when measured in his hometown of Artvin on January 31, 2001.

LONGEST NOSE (7.5 in; 19 cm) There are historical accounts that Thomas Wedders, who lived in England during the 1770s and was a member of a traveling circus, had a nose measuring 7.5 in. (19 cm) long.

★**LONGEST NIPPLE HAIR (3.5 in; 8.89 cm)** Christopher Tyler Ing (Canada).

★**LONGEST ARM HAIR (3.18 in; 9.7 cm)** David Hruska (U.S.A.).

LEG HAIR (4.88 in; 12.4 cm) Tim Stinton (Australia).

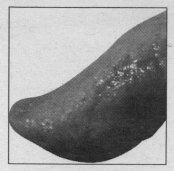

LONGEST TONGUE (3.7 in; 9.4 cm)
Stephen Taylor (UK) has a tongue
that measures 3.7 in. (9.4 cm) from
the tip to the center of his closed
top lip. It was measured at
Westwood Medical Centre,
Coventry, Warwickshire, UK, on
May 29, 2002.

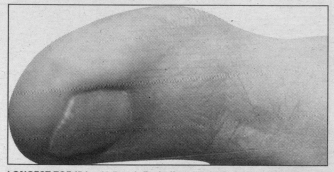

LONGEST TOE (5 in; 12.7 cm) Excluding cases of elephantiasis, the
longest toes are 5 in. (12.7 cm) long and belong to Matthew McGrory
(U.S.A.), who also holds records for the **largest feet for a living
person** and **tallest actor.**

HUMAN
ACHIEVEMENTS

CONTENTS

EPIC JOURNEYS

WHEN WAS THE FIRST CIRCUMNAVIGATION OF THE WORLD? FIND OUT ON P. 41

FARTHEST

☆**Longest driven journey** Since October 16, 1984, Emil and Liliana Schmid (Switzerland) have covered over 364,745 miles (587,000 km) in their Toyota Land Cruiser, crossing more than 150 countries and territories.

LONGEST JOURNEY BY WHEELCHAIR Rick Hansen (Canada), who was paralyzed from the waist down in 1973 as a result of a car accident, wheeled his wheelchair 24,901 miles (40,075 km) through four continents and 34 countries. He started his journey from Vancouver, British Columbia, Canada, on March 21, 1985, and arrived back there on May 22, 1987.

★Longest journey pushing a wheelbarrow Bob Hanley (Australia) started pushing his wheelbarrow around Australia on April 24, 1975, and finished on May 6, 1978—some 9,000 miles (14,500 km) later. He started and finished in Sydney, via Townsville, Alice Springs, Perth, Adelaide, and Melbourne.

☆Farthest distance on a snowmobile on water Tory Allan (Canada) traveled 15.7 miles (25.26 km) on Last Mountain Lake, Saskatchewan, Canada, nonstop on a standard snowmobile on September 3, 2004.

☆Longest journey by tractor Vasiliy Hazkevich (Russia) covered 3,425 miles (5,512 km) on an unmodified agricultural tractor from June 12 to July 5, 2004, starting and finishing in Novosibirsk, Russia.

Longest journey by skateboard In July 1976 and again in July 1984, Jack Smith (U.S.A.) skateboarded just under 3,000 miles (4,830 km) between Lebanon, Oregon, and Williamsburg, Virginia, U.S.A.

★Longest coastal journey by aquabike Paul Fua, Lynden Parmenter, and Randall Jones (all Australia) circumnavigated Australia—a total of 10,239 miles (16,478 km)—in 106 days, from August 20, 2000, on personal watercrafts (PWCs).

Longest bicycle journey by an individual Itinerant lecturer Walter Stolle (Germany) amassed a mileage of over 402,000 miles (646,960 km) in a bicycle tour from January 24, 1959 to December 12, 1976. He visited 159 countries, starting from Romford, Essex, UK.

LONGEST LIFEBOAT JOURNEY After his ship, the *Endurance,* stuck fast in Antarctic sea ice, Sir Ernest Shackleton (UK) and his crew of 28 set course for Elephant Island, about 100 miles (160 km) to the north, in three lifeboats. With five of his men, he then set off in their largest lifeboat for a whaling station in South Georgia—800 miles (1,300 km) away—reaching the island after 17 days, on May 19, 1916. Ten days later, they reached the whaling station on foot. All the men on Elephant Island were later rescued.

★ **LONGEST JOURNEY BY HAND-CRANKED CYCLE** David Abrutat (UK) completed a journey of 3,368.67 miles (5,421.34 km) around the coastline of the UK on a hand-cranked bicycle from May 10 to August 5, 2002, starting and finishing at Tower Bridge, London. A former Royal Air Force serviceman, he was partially paralyzed in a car accident in 2000.

FASTEST . . .

Circumnavigation by car The record for the first and fastest man and woman to have circumnavigated the earth by car covering six continents under the rules applicable in 1989 and 1991, embracing more than an equator's length of driving (24,901 road miles, or 40,075 km), is held by Saloo Choudhury and his wife Neena Choudhury (both India). The journey took 69 days 19 hr. 5 min. from September 9 to November 17, 1989. The couple drove a 1989 Hindustan "Contessa Classic" starting and finishing in Delhi, India.

★ **Journey on foot across Australia** David Parker (UK) walked across the Australian continental mainland from Cottesloe Beach, Perth, Western Australia, to Bondi Beach, Sydney, New South Wales, in 69 days 11 hr. 28 min. from July 1 to September 8, 1998.

★ **Unicycle ride across Australia** From June 30 to August 20, 1985, Hanspeter Beck (Australia) unicycled a total of 3,876.1 miles (6,237.96 km)

Note: Because of road safety reasons, Guinness World Records no longer monitors claims for point-to-point driving on public roads.

MEANS OF TRAVEL	NAME OF CRAFT	HOLDER
Aquabike/PWC	-	Alavaro de Marichalar (Spain)
Powerboat	*Destriero*	Cesare Fiorio (Italy)
Aircraft	SR-71 *Blackbird*	Maj. J. Sullivan & N. Widdifield (both U.S.A.)
Commercial aircraft	BA Concorde	Leslie Scott (UK)
Yacht	*PlayStation*	Steve Fossett (U.S.A.)
Monohull yacht	*Mari-Cha IV*	Robert Miller (UK)
Windsurfer	-	Sergio Ferrero (Italy)
"Walking" (on floats)	-	Remy Bricka (France)

from Port Hedland, Western Australia, to Melbourne, Victoria, in 51 days 23 hr. 25 min.

★**Underwater English Channel swim** On July 28, 1962, Simon Paterson (UK) swam underwater from France to England with an air hose attached to his pilot boat. He covered the distance—in excess of 22 miles (35 km)—in 14 hr. 50 min.

Journey on foot via the Pan-American Highway From January 26, 1977 to September 18, 1983—a total of 2,426 days—George Meegan (UK) walked 19,019 miles (30,431 km) in a journey that took him from the southernmost point of South America, at Ushuaia, Argentina, to the northernmost point of North America, at Prudhoe Bay in Alaska, U.S.A.

★**FASTEST CROSSING OF THE ENGLISH CHANNEL BY AMPHIBIOUS VEHICLE** Sir Richard Branson (UK) "drove" a street-legal Gibbs Aquada between Dover, UK, and Calais, France, in 1 hr. 40 min. 6 sec. on June 14, 2004.

ROUTE	DATE	TIME
Canary Islands—Antigua	05/04–21/2002	17 days 1 hr. 11 min.
New York (U.S.A.)—Cornwall (UK)	08/06–09/1992	2 days 10 hr. 32 min.
New York (U.S.A.)—London (UK)	09/01/1973	1 hr. 54 min. 56 sec.
JFK (New York)—Heathrow (London)	02/07/1996	2 hr. 52 min. 59 sec.
New York (U.S.A.)—Cornwall (UK)	10/10/2001	4 days 17 hr. 28 min.
New York (U.S.A.)—Cornwall (UK)	10/02–09/2003	6 days 17 hr. 52 min.
Canary Islands—Barbados	06/06–30/1982	24 days
Canary Islands—Trinidad	04/02–05/31/1988	59 days

★ **Cape-to-Cairo bicycle journey** Chris Evans, David Genders, Michael Kennedy (all UK), Paul Reynaert (Belgium), Jeremy Wex, Steve Topsham, Scotty Robinson, Andrew Griffin (all Canada), and Sascha Hartl (Austria) bicycled from Cairo, Egypt, to Cape Town, South Africa, in 119 days 1 hr. 32 min. from January 18 to May 17, 2003, during the inaugural Tour d'Afrique. The race covered 6,808 miles (10,957 km).

EXPLORATION

EVEREST & K2

Fastest ascent of Mount Everest by the north side Hans Kammerlander (Italy) completed the climb from base camp to the summit in 16 hr. 45 min. on May 23–24, 1996.

☆ **Fastest ascent of Mount Everest by the south side** Pemba Dorje Sherpa (Nepal) climbed from base camp to the summit in a time of 8 hr. 10 min. on May 21, 2004, the **fastest ever ascent** of the world's tallest mountain.

MOUNTAIN OF MOUNTAINS

With steeper and more technical climbing routes and more extreme weather, K2 is generally regarded as being a far tougher challenge than Everest. While over 1,200 people have climbed Everest, only around 200 have conquered K2. No wonder climbing legend Reinhold Messner dubbed it the "Mountain of Mountains."

★K2: FIRST ASCENT BY A WOMAN
Wanda Rutkiewicz (Poland) reached the summit of K2, the world's second highest mountain, on June 23, 1986, becoming the first woman to climb the 28,251-ft.-high (8,611-m) peak.

Most conquests of Mount Everest
Apa Sherpa (Nepal) reached the summit for the 14th time on May 17, 2004.

First solo climb of Mount Everest Reinhold Messner (Italy) reached the summit of Everest on August 20, 1980. The solo climb, without bottled oxygen, took him three days from his base camp at 21,325 ft. (6,500 m).

★Most siblings to have climbed Mount Everest By March 2003, Nepalese brothers Nima Gombu Sherpa and Mingma Tsiri Sherpa had each reached the summit eight times. Their siblings Ang Tsering Sherpa and Nima Temba Sherpa (both Nepal) had each made one ascent by the same date.

DRIVING TO THE HIGHEST ALTITUDE A standard Volkswagen Toureg SUV was driven to an altitude of 19,950 ft. (6,081 m) by Rainer Zietlow and Ronald Bormann (both Germany) on the slopes of the volcano Ojos del Salado on the Chile-Argentina border on January 29, 2005. The height they reached is higher than Everest base camp (around 18,045 ft., or 5,500 m) and Mt. Kilimanjaro, the tallest peak in Africa at 19,340 ft. (5,895 m).

★**First ascent of K2** Achille Compagnoni and Lino Lacedelli (both Italy) scaled the world's second highest mountain at 28,251 ft. (8,611 m) on July 31, 1954. Both men were members of an Italian expedition led by Ardito Desio (Italy). K2 is situated in the Karakoram range on the Pakistan-China border.

NORTH POLE & ARCTIC

★**Fastest ski journey to the North Pole by a woman** Catherine Hartley and Fiona Thornewill (both UK) skied to the North Pole (with support in the form of resupplies along the way) in 55 days from March 11 to May 5, 2001, after having set out from Ward-Hunt Island, Northwest Territories, Canada.

First solo expedition to the North Pole Naomi Uemura (Japan) became the first person to reach the North Pole in a solo trek across the Arctic sea ice on May 1, 1978. He traveled 450 miles (725 km), setting out on March 7, from Cape Edward, Ellesmere Island, northern Canada.

★**Fastest solo unsupported trek to the North Pole** Børge Ousland (Norway) skied his way to the North Pole from the Severnaya Zemlya archipelago in the Russian Federation without any external assistance in 52 days from March 2 to April 23, 1994. He was also the **first person to make a solo and unsupported journey to the North Pole from land.** He did not use any form of motorized transportation or parafoil kites.

★**Fastest unsupported crossing of the Arctic** Torry Larsen and Rune Gjeldnes (both Norway) crossed the Arctic Ocean via the North Pole in 109 days without assistance. They set out from the Siberian Severnaya Zemlya archipelago, Russian Federation, on February 15, 2000, and arrived at Ellesmere Island, Northwest Territories, Canada, on June 3, 2000.

★**Fastest unsupported North Pole trek by a woman** Tina Sjögren and her husband Thomas Sjögren (both Sweden) made the journey in 68 days from March 22 to May 29, 2002. They set off from Ward-Hunt Island in Canada's Northwest Territories and received no external support.

SOUTH POLE & ANTARCTICA

Fastest solo crossing of Antarctica Børge Ousland (Norway) completed the 1,671-mile (2,690-km) trek on January 18, 1997, 64 days after setting out on November 15, 1996. He dragged his 408-lb. (185-kg) supply sled from Berkner Island in the Weddell Sea to Scott Base in McMurdo Sound.

★ **YOUNGEST PERSON TO TREK TO THE SOUTH POLE** Sarah Ann McNair-Landry (U.S.A./Canada, far left) was 18 when she arrived at the Pole on January 11, 2005, without the use of dogs or motorized vehicles. She made the 683-mile (1,100-km) kite-assisted trip as part of an unsupported expedition led by her mother Matty McNair (right), a polar trekking guide. The expedition also included her brother Eric (middle), who was 20.

★ **Youngest Antarctic solo trekker** Ola Skinnarmo (Sweden) arrived unaided at the Scott Base in Antarctica on December 20, 1998, aged 26, after a 47-day, 746-mile (1,200-km) trek on skis across the frozen continent. He pulled a sled that weighed about 264 lb. (120 kg) laden, yet still finished 10 days earlier than expected.

★ **Fastest unsupported journey to the South Pole (kite assisted)** Børge Ousland (Norway) traveled to the South Pole on skis, with assistance from a parafoil kite, in 34 days from November 15 to December 19, 1996. The journey was solo and unsupported, meaning that he received no outside assistance.

★ **Fastest overland journey to the South Pole** Adventurer Shinji Kazama (Japan) traveled to the South Pole from the Patriot Hills on the Antarctic coastline on a specially modified Yamaha motorcycle in 24 days from December 10, 1991, to January 3, 1992. He was supported by a snowmobile that carried emergency supplies and offered occasional assistance over rough terrain.

WHAT IS THE FARTHEST DISTANCE TRAVELED ON ANOTHER WORLD? FIND OUT ON P. 203

Human Achievements

FASTEST SOLO UNSUPPORTED SOUTH POLE TREK Fiona Thornewill (UK) walked and skied her way to the South Pole from Hercules Inlet at the edge of the Antarctic continent in 41 days 8 hr. 14 min. from November 30, 2003, to January 10, 2004. She started pulling a 285-lb. (130-kg) supply sled—which weighed 9 lb. (45 kg) by the time she reached the pole—and averaged 17 miles (27.3 km) a day.

CIRCUMNAVIGATION

★**Fastest unpowered around-the-world trip along the equator**
Mike Horn (South Africa) circumnavigated the Earth along the equator by bicycle, dugout canoe, sailing trimaran, and on foot in 513 days from June 2, 1999, to October 27, 2000. His journey started and finished near Libreville in the west African state of Gabon and proceeded in six legs that included sailing across the Atlantic, Pacific, and Indian oceans, and crossing the Amazon and central Africa.

OLDEST AROUND-THE-WORLD YACHT RACE The quadrennial Volvo Ocean Race is the oldest regular around-the-world sailing race. It was first held in 1973 when it was called the Whitbread Round the World race, and was known by that name until the 2001/02 event. The last Volvo Ocean Race began in November 2005 in Vigo, Spain, and concludes in Goteborg, Sweden, in June 2006.

☆**FASTEST SOLO-SAILING CIRCUMNAVIGATION** Ellen MacArthur (UK) sailed solo and nonstop around the world in 71 days 14 hr. 13 min. 33 sec. from November 28, 2004, to February 7, 2005, in the trimaran *B&Q*. She started off from Ushant, France, rounded the Cape of Good Hope (South Africa), sailed south of Australia, and rounded Cape Horn (Argentina) before heading back up the Atlantic to Ushant.

BY BOAT

☆**Fastest around-the-world trip by a crewed sailing vessel** A crew of 14, captained by Bruno Peyron (France), sailed around the world in 50 days 16 hr. 20 min. 4 sec. in the maxi catamaran *Orange II* from January 24 to March 16, 2005. The journey started and finished off the coast of Ushant, France.

First circumnavigation of the world This record was first accomplished on September 9, 1522, when the Spanish vessel *Vittoria,* under the command of the Spanish navigator Juan Sebastian de Elcano, reached Seville in Spain. The ship had set out along with four others as part of an expedition led by the Portuguese explorer Ferdinand Magellan in 1519 and had rounded Cape Horn, crossed the Pacific via the Philippines, and returned to Europe after sailing around the Cape of Good Hope. *Vittoria* was the only ship to survive the voyage.

★**Longest series of sailing circumnavigations** Jon Sanders (Australia) completed a series of three nonstop single-handed circumnavigations in the 45-ft. (13.9-m) sloop *Parry Endeavour* in 657 days from May 25, 1986, to March 13, 1988. Starting and finishing in Fremantle, Western Australia, he made one circumnavigation westabout and two eastabout.

Longest solo nonstop yachting race The Vendée Globe Challenge starts and finishes at Les Sables d'Olonne, France. The distance currently sailed without stopping is 22,500 nautical miles (25,881 miles; 41,652 km). The race is for boats 50–60 ft. (15–18 m) in size, sailed single-handed.

BY AIR

★**First solo around-the-world balloon trip** Steve Fossett (U.S.A.) circumnavigated the globe in *Bud Light Spirit of Freedom,* a 140-ft.-tall (42.6-m) mixed-gas balloon, from June 19 to July 2, 2002. He took off from Northam, Western Australia, and landed at Eromanga, Queensland, Australia, after covering 20,626 miles (33,195 km).

★**Most flights around the world** Cosmonaut Sergei Avdeyev (Russia) has completed 11,968 orbits of the Earth during his career. He also holds the record for **most time spent in space** (see page 214).

★**Fastest aerial circumnavigation by a propeller-driven aircraft** Joe Harnish and David Webster (both U.S.A.) piloted a Gulfstream Commander 695A twin turboprop around the world at an average speed of 304.8 mph (490.51 km/h) from March 21 to 24, 1983, starting and finishing at Eckhart, California, U.S.A.

★**Fastest aerial circumnavigation via both poles** A Boeing 747 SP piloted by Captain Walter H. Mullikin (U.S.A.) achieved this record in 54 hr.

7 min. 12 sec. (including refueling stops) from October 28 to 31, 1977. The journey started and finished in San Francisco, U.S.A.

STEVE FOSSETT

Steve Fossett (U.S.A.) is the first person to fly around the world nonstop without refueling. He started and finished at Salina, Kansas, U.S.A., taking 67 hr. 1 min., from March 1 to 3, 2005. The Virgin Atlantic *GlobalFlyer* (below) was built by Scaled Composites (U.S.A.). It was powered by a single turbofan jet engine and carried nearly 11,000 lb. (5,000 kg) of fuel.

What was the first world record you broke? It was sailing around the coast of Ireland in September 1993—the previous record was 72 hours and I did it in 45!

What do you do to prepare yourself for these high-endurance record attempts? I do a lot of running and try to get some exercise every day. Sometimes I need acclimatization to altitude. For *GlobalFlyer* I went on a low-residue diet before the flight.

What's your next challenge? To fly a glider into the stratosphere—I'll have to wear a space suit, and once again I'm cooperating with NASA. The current altitude record for gliders is 49,000 ft. (15,000 m).

Who are your heroes? The great polar explorers. My favorite is Shackleton—and also Nansen, who carried out the first crossing of Greenland and never lost a man.

When has your life been in most danger? In August 1998, my balloon was ruptured by a thunderstorm at an altitude of 29,000 ft. (8,800 m). I plummeted into the Coral Sea and was just barely able to slow the balloon down enough to survive.

What record are you most proud of? The first solo balloon flight around the world. I worked on it for eight years and six attempts. It was something I was uniquely qualified to do—the combination of the hardship of flying solo and the knowledge of ballooning.

☆**Fastest circumnavigation by scheduled flights, visiting six continents** Michael Quandt (Germany), travel editor of the newspaper *Bild am Sonntag,* flew around the world via six continents on scheduled flights in a time of 66 hr. 31 min. from July 6–8, 2004. The journey started and finished in Singapore and covered Sydney (Australia), Los Angeles (U.S.A.), Houston (U.S.A.), Caracas (Venezuela), London (UK), Cairo (Egypt), and Kuala Lumpur (Malaysia).

STRENGTH & STAMINA

Most tires lifted Gary Windebank (UK) managed a freestanding "lift" of 96 tires weighing 1,440 lb. (653 kg) in February 1984. The tires used were Michelin XZX 155 × 13.

★**HEAVIEST WEIGHT LIFTED WITH TONGUE** Thomas Blackthorne (UK) lifted 24 lb. 3 oz. (11.025 kg) on the set of *Guinness World Records: 50 Years, 50 Records* at the London Television Studios, UK, on September 11, 2004.

☆**Greatest height attained on a climbing machine in one hour** Neil Rhodes (UK) climbed 7,345 ft. (2,238.75 m) while carrying a 40-lb. (18-kg) pack at Cannon's Health Club, Yeovil, Somerset, UK, on November 2, 2004.

★**Highest beer keg toss (female)** Heini Koivuniemi (Finland) threw a 27.1-lb. (12.3-kg) beer keg over a bar at a height of 11 ft. 4.2 in. (3.46 m) on August 9, 2001.

Juha Rasanen (Finland) threw a 27.1-lb. (12.3-kg) beer keg over a bar at a height of 22.73 ft. (6.93 m) on September 21, 2001, the **highest beer keg toss by a man.**

★**Heaviest weight lifted with ear** Zafar Gill (Pakistan) lifted gym weights of 113 lb. 15 oz. (51.7 kg) by using a clamp attached to his right ear and held it for seven seconds on May 26, 2004, at Lahore, Pakistan.

☆**Longest crucifix hold (10 kg)** Yannick Ollivier (France) held a 22-lb. (10-kg) dumbbell in each of his hands at arm's length and at a 90° angle to his body for 1 min. 18 sec. on the set of *L'Été De Tous Les Records* in Bénodet, France, on August 3, 2004.

Most bench presses—own body weight Michael Williams (UK) achieved 1,438 repetitions of lifting his body weight of 147.7 lb. (67 kg) in one hour by bench presses at Don Styler's Gymnasium, Gosport, UK, on April 17, 1989.

☆**Fastest time to run 100 miles on a treadmill** Arulanantham Suresh Joachim (Sri Lanka) ran 100 miles (161 km) on a treadmill in a time of 13 hr. 42 min. 33 sec. at Square One, Mississauga, Ontario, Canada, on November 28, 2004.

★**Greatest height climbed on a 5-m rope in one minute** Using just his hands and from a seated position, Stéphane Bock (France) climbed a 16-ft. 4.8-in. (5-m) rope to a height of 50 ft. (15.44 m) on July 27, 2004.

★ PUSH-UPS TABLE ★

EVENT	TIME	RECORD
One finger	consecutive	124
One arm	one minute	120
★One arm	one hour	1,777
One arm, back of hand	one hour	441
☆Two arms, back of hand	one minute	95
☆Two hands	one minute	138
Two hands	one hour	3,416
★Vertical	one minute	37

HEAVIEST AIRCRAFT PULLED David Huxley (Australia) pulled a Boeing 747–400 weighing 412,260 lb. (206 tons) a distance of 298 ft. 6 in. (91 m) in 1 min. 27.7 sec. on October 15, 1997, in Sydney, Australia. Huxley pulled his first aircraft, a Boeing 737 weighing 81,570 lb. (40 tons), in 1991. He progressed to pulling a 231,485-lb. (115-ton) Concorde 469 ft. (143 m) and eventually to the 747 at the age of 39.

☆**Fastest iron-bar-bend into suitcase** The fastest time to bend an iron bar 19.6 ft. (6 m) long and with a diameter of 0.47 in. (12 mm), and then fit it into a suitcase with dimensions 19.6 × 27.5 × 7.87 in. (50 × 70 × 20 cm), is 29 seconds by Les Davis (U.S.A.) in Dothan, Alabama, U.S.A., on July 17, 2004. He bent the bar a total of 11 times.

NAME	NATIONALITY	DATE
Paul Lynch	UK	April 21, 1992
Yvan de Weber	Switzerland	October 23, 2001
Doug Pruden	Canada	October 22, 2004
Bruce Swatton	UK	May 12, 2003
Steve Bugdale	UK	November 13, 2004
Roy Berger	Canada	February 28, 2004
Roy Berger	Canada	August 30, 1998
Murad Gadaborchev	Russia	July 20, 2004

★Most chin-ups in one hour Stéphane Gras (France) performed 445 chin-ups in an hour in Artix, France, on April 26, 2004.

★Most consecutive chin-ups Lee Chin-Yong (Korea) performed a total of 612 consecutive chin-ups at Jongmyo Park, Seoul, South Korea, on December 29, 1994.

Most bricks lifted side by side Russell Bradley (UK) lifted 31 bricks—which were laid side by side—off a table, raised them to chest height, and held them there for two seconds on June 14, 1992.

Most car lifts in one hour The greatest number of times the rear of a car has been lifted clear of the ground (i.e. so that the rear wheels do not touch the ground) in one hour is 580 by Mark Anglesea (UK) at The Hind, South Yorkshire, UK, on October 3, 1998. The car was a Mini Metro weighing 1,785 lb. (810 kg).

☆Full-body ice-contact endurance Wim Hof (Netherlands) endured contact with ice for 1 hr. 8 min. on the set of *Guinness World Records: 50 Years, 50 Records* at the London Television Studios, UK, on September 11, 2004. Wim uses meditation and yoga to overcome the dangers inherent in these activities.

☆FASTEST TIME TO RUN UP THE EMPIRE STATE BUILDING At the 26th Annual Empire State Building Run-Up, New York City, U.S.A., on February 4, 2003, Paul Crake (Australia, pictured) ran up the 1,576 steps in 9 min. 33 sec.

The fastest woman to achieve the feat is Belinda Soszyn (Australia), with a time of 12 min. 19 sec. in 1996.

☆**Most telephone books torn in three minutes** Edward Charon (U.S.A.) ripped 39 telephone books from top to bottom, each with 1,004 numbered pages, in three minutes in Roseburg, Oregon, U.S.A., on August 14, 2004.

Greatest laborer There are two contenders for this title. Miner Alexei Stakhanov (Ukraine) claimed to have hewn 204,000 lb. (102 tons) of coal in six hours in August 1935. Steel worker Henry Noll (U.S.A.) lifted and loaded 91,400 lb. (45.7 tons) of pig iron onto open railroad freight cars every day for weeks at a time in the winter of 1899.

MARATHON FEATS

★**Air hockey** Jaron Carson and Jordan Ouanounou (both Canada) played an air-hockey marathon continuously for 20 hours at Dave & Busters, Toronto, Ontario, Canada, on August 26–27, 2003.

Blackjack dealing The longest time spent dealing blackjack is 51 hr. 33 min. by Stephen De Raffaele (Malta) from August 24 to 27, 2001, at the Oracle Casino, Qawra, Malta.

Card playing Gareth Birdsall, Sonia Zakrzewski, Gad Chadha, Finn Clark, Sebastian Kristensen, Simon MacBeth, Tim West-Meads,

LONGEST DANCE PARTY The Heart Health Hop—a dance-party marathon organized by St. Joseph Aspirin and Rowland Communications Worldwide and held at the Rock and Roll Hall of Fame and Museum, Cleveland, Ohio, U.S.A.—began on July 29, 2003, at 5:10 a.m. with 42 dancers, 41 of whom completed the marathon after 52 hr. 3 min. on July 31, 2003.

LONGEST KISS Louisa Almedovar and Rich Langley (both U.S.A.) kissed continuously for 30 hr. 59 min. 27 sec. at the television studios of *Ricki Lake,* New York City, U.S.A., on December 5, 2001. The couple remained standing, without rest breaks, throughout the attempt.

and David Gold played a continuous game of bridge for 72 hr. 9 min. at St. John's Wood Bridge Club, London, UK, from October 31 to November 3, 2003. A total of 1,012 hands of bridge were played.

☆**CPR** Two teams of two people—consisting of Ray Edensor and Emma Parker and Paul Gauntlett and Mark Brookes (all UK) from the Staffordshire Ambulance Service—completed a CPR (cardiopulmonary resuscitation—15 compressions alternating with two breaths) marathon of 151 hours at Asda Superstore, Stafford, UK, from January 9–25, 2004.

Hula hooping Kym Coberly (U.S.A.) hula hooped for 72 hours in Denton, Texas, U.S.A., from October 17 to 29, 1984.

Ironing Eufemia Stadler (Switzerland) completed 40 hours of ironing. She continuously ironed 228 shirts while standing at an ironing board from September 16 to 18, 1999.

HOW MANY TELEPHONE BOOKS WERE TORN FROM TOP TO BOTTOM IN 3 MINUTES? FIND OUT ON P. 47

Lecturing Errol E. T. Muzawazi (Zimbabwe) talked on the subject of democracy for 62 hr. 30 min., from December 12 to 15, 2003, at a student residence of Politechnika Wrocklawska, Wrocklaw, Poland.

Mah-jongg Chris Pittenger, Betty Vance, Doris Natale, Mary Ann Blansett, Rosemarie Cannon, Judy Burt, Ann Wells, and Doris MacKenzie (all U.S.A.) played two games of mah-jongg simultaneously for 25 hours, in two groups of four people. The attempt took place at Sun City Hilton Head, Bluffton, South Carolina, U.S.A., from February 28 to March 1, 2003.

☆**Movie watching** Timothy Weber (Germany) watched 32 films for 70 hr. 1 min. at an event organized by CinemaxX Würzburg, Würzburg, Germany, from December 16 to 19, 2003. The attempt ended 49 minutes into the 33rd film, *Finding Nemo* (U.S.A., 2003).

★**Poker playing (individual)** Larry Olmsted (U.S.A.) played poker nonstop for 72 hr. 2 min. at Foxwoods Resort & Casino, Manshantucket, Connecticut, U.S.A., from June 10 to 13, 2004.

☆**Punching-bag** Ron Sarchian (U.S.A.) hit a punching-bag continuously (i.e. striking once every two seconds) for 36 hr. 3 min. at Premier Fitness, Encino, California, U.S.A., from June 15 to 17, 2004.

Quiz questions Quizmaster Gavin Dare (UK) asked a total of 3,668 general knowledge questions continuously at The Goff's Oak Public House, Hertfordshire, UK, for 32 hr. 15 min. on October 25–26, 2003.

☆**Reading aloud (individual)** Adrian Hilton (UK) recited the complete works of Shakespeare in a "Bardathon" lasting 110 hr. 46 min. at the Shakespeare Festival, South Bank, London, UK, and Gold Hill Baptist Church, Chalfont St. Peter, Buckinghamshire, UK, from July 16 to 21, 1987.

☆**Reading aloud (team)** A team made up of Amy White, Kristy Wright, Brian Jones, Michael Dahl, Jeanette Dean, and Georgina Konstana (all Australia) read aloud for 81 hr. 15 min. at the Sutherland Library, Sydney, Australia, from May 24 to 27, 2004. The record was held to celebrate Australian Library week, and raised money for various youth charities.

★ TOP SIX LONGEST MARATHONS ★

EVENT	HOURS	RECORD HOLDER(S)	DATE
Trampolining	1,248	Team of 6 (U.S.A.)	June 24 to August 15, 1974
Swimming	240	Team of 6 (U.S.A.)	August 14–24, 1979
☆ Ice hockey	203	Sudbury Angels (Canada)	April 3–11, 2004
Roller coaster	192	Richard Rodriguez (U.S.A.)	August 20–28, 2003
★ Snowboarding	180 hr. 34 min.	Berhard Mair (Austria)	January 9–16, 2004
Skiing	168	Christian Flühr (Germany)	March 8–15, 2003

GREATEST DISTANCE TRAVELED ON A POGO STICK Ashrita Furman (U.S.A.) jumped 23.11 miles (37.18 km) on a pogo stick in 12 hr. 27 min. on June 22, 1997, at Queensborough Community College Track, New York, U.S.A. He also holds the record for the ★**most pogo-stick jumps in 1 minute** (156), the **fastest mile on a pogo stick** (12 min. 15 sec.), and the **fastest time to travel up the CN Tower on a pogo stick** (57 min. 51 sec.).

The record for the most consecutive jumps on a pogo stick is held by Gary Stewart (U.S.A.), who completed 177,737 jumps in Huntington Beach, California, U.S.A., on May 25–26, 1990.

Ring-board Joe Norman, Robert Norman, Paul Harkes, Faye Savill, Marion Daly, Betty Murphy, Hazel Gannon, and Dennis Curtis (all UK) played ring-board for 24 hours at Silver Hall Social Club, Rainham, Essex, UK, on July 12–13, 2003.

☆**Rope skipping (individual)** Jed Goodfellow (Australia) skipped a rope for 27 hours at Oasis Shopping Mall, Broadbeach, Queensland, Australia, on December 5–6, 2003.

★**Square dance calling** Dale F. Muehlmeier (U.S.A.) called for 28 hours for the American Cancer Society at a Wal-Mart parking lot, Norfolk, Nebraska, U.S.A., on May 26–27, 2000.

★**Foosball** Andre Raison, Ghislain De Broyer, Rudy Mortier, and Daniel Vanbellinghen (all Belgium) played table foosball for 24 hr. 1 min. at the Young Band Brass Pub in Lembeek, Belgium, on October 19–20, 2002.

★**Steel toboggan riding** Michael Kinzel (Germany) rode the steel summer toboggan at Panorama Park in Kirchhundem, Germany, for 56 hours from May 4 to 6, 2002. A summer toboggan is a combination of a bobsled and a toboggan.

Trading-card-game playing William Stone, Bryan Erwin, and Christopher Groetzinger (all U.S.A.) played *The Lord of the Rings* trading card game for 128 hours from December 27, 2002, to January 1, 2003, at The Courtyard, Colorado Springs, Colorado, U.S.A.

☆**TV watching** Terrye Jackson (U.S.A.) watched NBC's Olympic coverage at Pat O'Brien's bar, Orlando, Florida, U.S.A., for 50 hr. 7 min. from August 15 to 17, 2004.

HOW LONG WAS THE LONGEST KARAOKE SESSION? FIND OUT ON P. 350

MASS PARTICIPATION

LARGEST . . .

★**Ceilidh** The Great Glengoyne Ceilidh was held on June 17, 1997, at various locales throughout Scotland simultaneously, catering for 6,568 people.

☆**Cheerleading cheer** A total of 435 cheerleaders from The Cheerful Dance Company performed a cheer in full uniform on the field of Bedworth United Football Club, Bedworth, Warwickshire, UK, on July 4, 2004.

★**MOST PEOPLE WEARING BALLOON HATS** At an event organized by Sentosa Leisure Management (Singapore), 1,039 participants designed, made, and wore hats constructed from balloons at the Sentosa Balloon Hats Festival held at Palawan Beach, Sentosa, Singapore, on March 13, 2004.

☆**Christmas cracker pulling** On November 16, 2003, 986 people participated in a simultaneous Christmas cracker pull in Culver Square, Colchester, Essex, UK.

☆**Game of leapfrog** A group of 1,100 people participated in the largest game of leapfrog at the Virgin Group summer party held in Kidlington, Oxfordshire, UK, on September 4, 2004.

WHERE DID THE LARGEST BREAKFAST IN THE WORLD TAKE PLACE? FIND OUT ON P. 256

Group hug On April 23, 2004, a crowd of 5,117 students, staff, and friends from St. Matthew Catholic High School hugged each other for at least 10 seconds in Orleans, Ontario, Canada. The hug was in support of The Force, a local cancer charity.

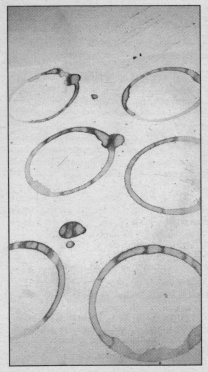

Human centipede A total of 2,026 people—made up of Nagoya Otani High School students and their parents and teachers—created the world's largest human centipede at Tsuruma Track and Field Stadium, Nagoya, Japan, on June 13, 2001.

The ankles of all participants were firmly tied to the ankles of those people next to them; the centipede successfully moved 98 ft. (30 m) without any mishaps.

☆**COFFEE MORNING** Macmillan Cancer Relief (UK) broke their own record set the previous year for the largest coffee morning with 576,157 people attending over 26,000 meetings simultaneously, across the UK, on September 26, 2003.

Human Achievements

☆ **HUMAN RAINBOW** The Polytechnic University of the Philippines (PUP) organized a human rainbow consisting of 30,365 participants at the Quirino Grandstand, Rizal Park, Manila, Philippines, on September 18, 2004.

Human domino line On September 30, 2000, 9,234 students aged 18–21 from the NYAA–Poly Connects project formed a human domino chain stretching 2.6 miles (4.2 km) across Siloso Beach, Sentosa Island, Singapore. It was arranged by the National Youth Achievement Award (NYAA) Council, in collaboration with the combined polytechnics of Singapore.

Human logo On July 24, 1999, 34,309 people gathered at the National Stadium of Jamor, Lisbon, Portugal, to create the Portuguese logo for Euro 2004. The event was part of the successful Portuguese bid to UEFA to hold soccer's 2004 European Championships.

Human national flag The world's largest human national flag was made up of 10,371 spectators. They formed the shape and colors of the German flag in the south grandstand at the Scotland v. Germany European Championships qualifying soccer match in Westfalenstadion, Dortmund, Germany, on September 10, 2003.

Marching band A total of 11,157 people in 317 bands, including a flag team of 1,092, marched at the Japan International Exposition Memorial Grand in Osaka, Japan, on May 11, 1997, to celebrate the 60th anniversary of the Music for Wind Instruments League in Kansai.

☆ **Martial arts display** On April 10, 2004, a group of 30,648 people performed wushu shadow-boxing for 16 min. 40 sec. at the opening ceremony of the 22nd Luoyang Peony Festival in Henan Province, China.

☆**Pillow fight** The largest pillow fight involved 2,773 participants and took place in Dodgeville, Wisconsin, U.S.A., on September 29, 2004.

☆**Ring-around-a-rosy rhyme** A group of 1,953 schoolchildren joined hands for the largest ring-around-a-rosy at The People's Park, Waterford, Ireland, on April 20, 2004.

The song was repeated for a total of six and a half minutes, with all of the participants falling down and getting up again in unison.

☆**Scottish reel** A Scottish country dance involving a group of 1,254 pupils from Ellon Academy, Ellon, Aberdeenshire, UK, took place on September 21, 2004.

☆**Rope skip** On May 25, 2004, a group of 2,350 schoolchildren skipped rope simultaneously at Redlands Sports Ground, Weymouth, Dorset, UK.

Snowball fight A snowball fight involving a group of 2,473 participants (in two teams, divided 1,162 against 1,311) took place in Triel at the ski resort of Obersaxen-Mundaun in Graubunden, Switzerland, on January 18, 2003.

☆**Teeth brushing** A total of 10,240 students brushed their teeth simultaneously for at least 60 seconds at Ai Guo Road, Luohu District, Shenshen City, China, on September 20, 2003.

The event was organized by the Health Bureau of Luohu District, the

MOST SURFERS A group of 38 surfers rode the same wave simultaneously at Manly Beach, Sydney, New South Wales, Australia, on December 1, 2002.

MOST EGGS BALANCED Students from Brigham Young University, Utah, U.S.A., balanced 1,290 eggs in 6 hr. 30 min. at the Wilkinson Student Center, Provo, Utah, U.S.A., on March 15, 2003.

Education Bureau of Luohu District, and the Chamber of Commerce of Luohu District and sponsored by Colgate-Palmolive (Guangzhou) Co. Ltd.

★**Tire roll** In an event sponsored by Michelin, a total of 138 employees of the Nationwide Building Society MAA division simultaneously rolled car tires over a distance of 328 ft. (100 m) at their head office in Swindon, UK, on July 2, 2004.

LARGEST TEA PARTY A simultaneous tea party that featured 11,760 participants was held as part of the Largest Tea and Buns event organized by Emergency Role of Sheltered Housing (ERoSH) at various locations across the UK on June 11, 2004.

LARGEST SIMULTANEOUS JUMP At 11:00 a.m. on September 7, 2001, 559,493 people began jumping up and down for one minute to mark the launch of Science Year in the UK. There were actually 569,069 participants—the extra numbers represent disabled pupils who contributed to the seismic activity by dropping objects onto the ground.

LARGEST AEROBICS CLASS In total, 48,188 participants took part in an aerobics class at the Quirino Grandstand, Luneta Park, Manila, Philippines (pictured), on February 16, 2003.

The ★largest ever simultaneous aerobics display (multiple sites) occurred on September 27, 2003, and involved 4,845,098 people throughout Kazakhstan.

Walk The New Paper Big Walk 2000 involved 77,500 participants, starting from the National Stadium, Singapore, on May 21, 2000. It was organized by The Singapore Press Holdings, The Singapore Amateur Athletic Association, and The Singapore Sports Council.

☆**Water balloon fight** A balloon fight involving 993 participants, who threw 8,000 balloons altogether, took place at the Peace River Bible Institute, Sexsmith, Alberta, Canada, on October 1, 2004.

☆**Whoopee cushion sit** The Quad City Mallards, members of the United Hockey League, achieved a simultaneous whoopee cushion sit involving 3,614 participants in Moline, Illinois, U.S.A., on March 19, 2004.

FASTEST . . .

★**Bandage relay** A total of 114 arm slings were applied in one hour by a St. John Ambulance relay team made up of Tony Lazell, Neil Fitch, Dawn Kemp, John Mowles, Rob Perris, Sheila Scott, and Bert Wilkins (all UK), working in pairs at the Felixstowe Leisure Center, Suffolk, UK, on June 27, 2004.

Time to build a bridge A team of British soldiers from 35 Engineer Regiment based at Hameln, Germany, successfully constructed a bridge across a gap 26 ft. 3 in. (8 m) wide using a five-bay single-story MGB (medium girder bridge) in a record time of 8 min. 19 sec. at Hohne, Germany, on November 12, 1998.

Coal-shoveling The record time for filling a 1,120-lb. (508-kg) hopper with coal using only a "banjo shovel" by a team of two is 15.01 seconds. Brian McArdle and Rodney Spark (both Australia) achieved their feat at the Fingal Valley Festival in Fingal, Tasmania, Australia, on March 5, 1994.

31-Legged race over 50 m Students from Sugikami Elementary school in Kumamoto Prefecture, Japan, ran a 31-legged race covering a total of 164 ft. (50 m) in 8.94 seconds at Yokohama Arena, Japan, on November 23, 2002.

★**Flying disc relay** A team of five threw and caught a flying disc down and back a 65-ft. 7-in. (20-m) course in 16 seconds on August 4, 2004. The record was set by Emmanuelle Tartoue, Yoann Greau, Michel Affile, Vincent Levievse, and Amaury Guerin (all France) on the set of *L'Été De Tous Les Records,* Bénodet, France.

★ **Monkey-bar relay** Jean-Philippe Causse, Nicolas Bec, and Guillem Briancon (all France) completed a monkey-bar relay in 1 min. 23 sec. on the set of *L'Été De Tous Les Records,* St.-Pierre-la-Mer, France, on September 8, 2003.

MOST . . .

★**Skiers towed behind an aquabike** A single Yamaha GP1300R WaveRunner towed 10 members of the H2O Entertainment water-ski team in Cockle Bay, Sydney, Australia, on September 4, 2004.

☆**Faces painted in an hour (team)** A team of five teachers from Szczecin Primary School Number 1, Szczecin, Poland, painted the faces of 351 different people, using a minimum of three colors per face, in a single hour on October 2, 2004.

People skipping on the same rope simultaneously A team at the International Rope Skipping Competition, Greeley, Colorado, U.S.A., achieved a total of 220 people skipping on the same rope simultaneously on June 28, 1990.

MISCELLANEOUS

Greatest distance to push a bath in 24 hours On March 11–12, 1995, a team of 25 from Tea Tree Gully Baptist Church, Westfield Shopping Town Tea Tree Plaza, Australia, pushed a bath tub and its passenger 318.96 miles (513.32 km).

MOST DISHES WASHED After a 8,265-lb. (4.13-ton) serving of pasta bolognese, a team of 150 people from Vester Hæsinge Idrætsforening, Brobyværk Idrætsforening, and Sandholt-Lyndelse Forsamlingshus (Denmark) cleaned 23,892 dishes using 0.26 gal. (1 liter) of dishwashing liquid at the Langelandsfestivalen in Rudkøbing, Denmark, on July 28, 2004.

MOST PEOPLE TO WEAR A GROUCHO MARX DISGUISE AT SAME TIME
The greatest number of people to wear Groucho Marx–style glasses, nose, and mustache simultaneously at one location is 937 students and staff from East Lansing High School, Michigan, U.S.A., on May 23, 2003.

★**Greatest distance traveled on a water slide in 24 hours (team)**
A team of 10 lifeguards covered a total distance of 432.97 miles (696.81 km) on a water slide at the Pfaffenhofen public swimming pool, Germany, on July 12, 2003.

Greatest coal-carrying distance A team of eight men carried a hundredweight (112-lb.; 51-kg) bag of coal for 80 miles (128.7 km) in 11 hr. 28 min. 33 sec., in West Yorkshire, UK, on May 20, 2000.

☆**Longest paper-clip chain (team)** On March 26–27, 2004, students from Eisenhower Junior High School, Taylorsville, Utah, U.S.A., made a 22.14-mile (35.63-km-long) paper-clip chain.

Longest wheelchair push in 24 hours A team of 75 volunteers pushed a wheelchair for 240 miles (386 km) in 24 hours, in Cumbria, UK, on September 8–9, 2000.

ODD TALENTS

LOUDEST...

★**Finger snap** Bob Hatch (U.S.A.) snapped his fingers with a decibel meter reading of 108 dBA on May 17, 2000. This is equivalent to the volume of a lawn mower heard from 3 ft. (1 m) away.

Scream Classroom assistant Jill Drake (UK) had a scream that reached 129 dBA when measured at the Halloween festivities held in the Millennium Dome, London, UK, in October 2000. Jill believes she developed her vocal skills from working in a classroom!

Shout On April 16, 1994, Annalisa Wray (UK) shouted at 121.7 dBA at the Citybus Challenge in Belfast, Antrim, UK. The word shouted was "quiet."

★**Tongue click** Kunal Jain (Canada) generated a decibel reading of 114.2 by clicking his tongue at Richmond Hill, Ontario, Canada, on August 6, 2003.

☆**MOST STRAWS STUFFED IN THE MOUTH** Marco Hort (Switzerland) stuffed 258 drinking straws in his mouth and held them there for 10 seconds in Belp, Bern, Switzerland, on April 22, 2005.

★Whistle Marco Ferrera (U.S.A.) achieved a whistle measuring 125 dBA from 8 ft. 2 in. (2.5 m) away at Schtung Music Studios, Santa Monica, California, U.S.A., on March 5, 2004.

Snore Although snoring is technically not a talent, Kåre Walkert (Sweden), who suffers from the breathing disorder apnea, recorded peak snoring levels of 93 dBA on May 24, 1993.

★Clap Standing 8 ft. 2 in. (2.5 m) from a noise level meter, Martha Gibson (UK) produced a 73-dBA hand clap at Harrogate, North Yorkshire, UK, on March 9, 2005.

MOST . . .

☆**Clothespins clipped on a face** Garry Turner (UK) clipped 159 ordinary wooden clothespins on his face during the *Guinness World Records 2005 Roadshow,* held in Manchester, UK, on November 27, 2004.

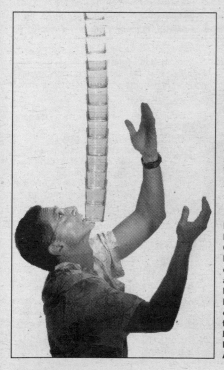

★Bras unhooked in a minute Chris Nicholson (UK) unhooked 20 bras in one minute using one hand on the set of *Guinness World Records: A Few Records More* (UK) in London, UK, on September 11, 2004.

☆**Beer mats flipped** Mat Hand (UK) flipped and caught a pile of 112 beer mats on May 9, 2001, at the Waterstone's

MOST GLASSES BALANCED ON THE CHIN After breaking hundreds of glasses during his practice attempts, Ashrita Furman (U.S.A.) finally balanced 75 UK pint (20-oz.) glasses on his chin for 10.6 seconds in his backyard in Jamaica, New York, U.S.A., on April 26, 2001.

bookstore in Nottingham, UK. It took him over four hours and 129 attempts to break the record.

★**Bullwhip cracks** Robert Dante (U.S.A.) cracked a bullwhip 214 times in a minute at the Third Annual Spirit of the West Festival in Sioux Falls, South Dakota, on September 19, 2004.

LONGEST . . .

★**Beer bottle cap throw** Paul van der Merwe (South Africa) threw a beer bottle cap a distance of 229 ft. 3 in. (69.9 m) at the Lime Acres Airfield, Northern Cape, South Africa, on May 15, 1999.

★**Thrown rifle exchange** Constantine Wilson and Clarence Robbins (both U.S.A.) exchanged their rifles at a distance of 18 ft. (5.48 m) apart—with both rifles completing 1.5 revolutions in the air before being caught—at George Mason University, Fairfax, Virginia, U.S.A., on April 23, 2004.

★**Coin spinning duration** Scott Day (UK) spun a coin that took a total of 19.37 seconds to come to a complete rest. The attempt was made at Earl's Court in London, UK, on July 9, 2003, as part of the BBC's *Tomorrow's World Roadshow.*

☆ **LONGEST GUM-WRAPPER CHAIN** March 2005 marked the 40th anniversary of the beginning of Gary Duschl's (U.S.A.) record-breaking gum-wrapper chain. Since March 11, 1965, Gary has been linking together chewing-gum wrappers to create a chain that currently measures 46,053 ft. (14,037 m)—longer than 125 football fields. Gary has the chain professionally measured each year, and at the last count it consisted of 1,076,656 wrappers and weighed 633 lb. (286 kg), representing $53,833 of gum!

☆ **LOUDEST BURP** Paul Hunn (UK) produced a burp with a decibel meter reading of 104.9 dBA at the offices of Guinness World Records, London, UK, on July 20, 2004—louder than a pile driver heard from a distance of 100 ft. (30 m). The burp was measured from a distance of 8 ft. 2 in. (2.5 m) and 3 ft. 3 in. (1 m) high, on a certified and calibrated class 1 precision measuring noise level meter.

FASTEST...

★ **Time to thread 20 needles on a single thread in the mouth** Meng Xu (China) threaded 20 needles onto a thread in the mouth using just his tongue in 6 min. 45 sec. at the China Millennium Monument, Beijing, China, on December 10, 2003.

☆ **Window cleaners** Terry "Turbo" Burrows (UK) cleaned three standard 45 × 45-in. (1,143 × 1,143-mm) office windows set in a frame with an 11.75-in.-long (300-mm) squeegee and 2.4 gal. (9 liters) of water in 9.24 sec. at the National Exhibition Centre, Birmingham, UK, on March 2, 2005.

The ★ **fastest female window cleaner** is Janet Palfreyman (UK), who cleaned the same standard office windows, with the same regulation equipment, in 25.99 seconds in Hinkley, Leicestershire, UK, on April 24, 2004.

Despite being deaf and blind, Graham "G-Force" Hicks (UK) holds the outright quadbike speed record and has also set aquabike (Personal Water Craft) speed records. He achieves his records with the help of "pillion" riders who ride behind him and tell him where to steer using a touch system.

What caused your deafblindness? My optic nerves were severely damaged at birth leaving me with only a very small amount of residual vision. My deafness was progressive from age seven and is believed to have been caused by a childhood illness—probably measles.

Why did you settle on motorized challenges as a way of setting records? I have always had a great interest and fascination in motorcycles and the sea. I fixed and rode battered old motorbikes in my late teens. Quadbiking and jetskiing are my top two passions!

What inspires you to attempt these records? I'm very committed to proving that, with the right attitude and support, deafblindness is no barrier to extreme sports. All my challenges are under the auspices of the charity Deafblind UK.

What do your family and friends think about your rather risky pastime? I think most have got used to the fact I'm a bit mad. My niece once said to me, "It's better to die on your feet than live on your knees."

What other challenges do you face? My greatest challenge has nothing to do with my disability directly—it's all about prejudice from others and the barriers that result.

What do you do in your free time? DIY (do-it-yourself), such as carpentry and plumbing. I also enjoy socializing and reading.

Competition window cleaning is highly regulated, and strict rules mean that time penalties are added for any water marks left on the glass.

Talker Sean Shannon (Canada) recited Hamlet's soliloquy "To be or not to be" (260 words) in a time of 23.8 seconds (655 words/minute) in Edinburgh, UK, on August 30, 1995.

★Balloon dog—made behind the back With his arms behind his back, Craig "Blink" Keith (UK) made a balloon poodle in just 9.26 seconds on May 25, 2004.

ECCENTRIC BEHAVIOR

Fastest time to type from one to one million Les Stewart (Australia) typed the numbers one to one million in words, manually, from 1982 to December 1998. His aim to become a "millionaire" cost him seven typewriters, 1,000 ink ribbons, and 19,900 sheets of paper. Les, left partially paralyzed after a tour of duty in Vietnam, typed with just one finger.

FASTEST FURNITURE Edd China (pictured) and David Davenport (both UK) design and build the world's fastest furniture, including bathroom suites and four-poster beds. The fastest to date is the "Casual Lofa," a motorized sofa with a top speed of 87 mph (140 km/h). Powered by a Mini 1300-cc (79.3-cu.-in.) engine, it is licensed for use on UK roads and has covered 6,219 miles (10,008.5 km) since it was built.

SHARING A BATHTUB WITH THE MOST RATTLESNAKES Jackie Bibby (pictured) and Rosie Reynolds-McCasland (both U.S.A.) jointly hold the record of having sat in two separate tubs each with 75 live Western Diamondback rattlesnakes on the set of *Guinness World Records: Primetime* on September 24, 1999, in Los Angeles, U.S.A.

Greatest distance walked backwards The greatest ever exponent of reverse pedestrianism was Plennie L. Wingo (U.S.A.), who completed his 8,000-mile (12,875-km) transcontinental walk from Santa Monica, California, U.S.A., to Istanbul, Turkey, from April 15, 1931, to October 24, 1932.

Longest duration to stand motionless Om Prakash Singh (India) stood motionless for 20 hr. 10 min. 6 sec. at Allahabad, India, on August 13–14, 1997.

Longest duration balancing on one foot Arulanantham Suresh Joachim (Sri Lanka) balanced on one foot for 76 hr. 40 min. from May 22 to 25, 1997. Under the rules, the disengaged foot cannot be rested on the standing foot and no object can be used for support or balance.

Longest distance walking on hands In 1900, Johann Hurlinger (Austria) walked on his hands for 870 miles (1,400 km). He walked from Vienna, Austria, to Paris, France, in 55 daily 10-hour stints at an average speed of 1.58 mph (2.54 km/h).

Heaviest vehicle pulled by hair On May 1, 1999, at Bruntingthorpe Proving Ground, Leicestershire, UK, Letchemanah Ramasamy (Malaysia) pulled a Routemaster double-deck bus weighing 17,359 lb. (7,874 kg) for a total distance of 98 ft. (30 m) using only his hair.

Longest banzai skydive Yasuhiro Kubo (Japan) jumped from a plane at an altitude of 9,842 ft. (3,000 m) without a parachute and in 50 seconds hooked on to a parachute that was thrown out prior to his jump on September 2, 2000, in Davis, California, U.S.A.

Longest lawn mower ride Gary Hatter (U.S.A.) drove 14,594.5 miles (23,487.5 km) in 260 consecutive days on a lawn mower. Hatter started his drive in Portland, Maine, U.S.A., on May 31, 2000, and passed through all 48 contiguous U.S. states, as well as Canada and Mexico, before arriving in Daytona Beach, Florida, on February 14, 2001.

★Most countries visited before returning to country of departure Mariea Crasmaru left her home in Bucharest, Romania, on March 18, 1997, and visited 102 countries and seven continents, creating a passport of 154 pages. Traveling 186,411 miles (300,000 km), she reached as far north as Murmansk in Russia (69°N), and as far south as the Marambio Research Base in Antarctica (64°S), but had to sell her home halfway through her trip

STRANGEST DIET Michel Lotito (France) is known as Monsieur Mangetout ("Mr. Eat Everything") because he has been eating metal and glass since 1959 (see interview, p. 68). Since 1966, he has consumed 18 bicycles, 15 shopping carts, 7 TV sets, 6 chandeliers, 2 beds, a pair of skis, a computer, and a Cessna light aircraft. He is also said to have provided the only example in history of a coffin ending up *inside* a man.

By October 1997, Monsieur Mangetout had eaten nearly 19,840 lb. (9 tons) of metal. Despite this "iron" constitution, he claims that bananas and hard-boiled eggs make him sick.

MONSIEUR MANGETOUT

Michel Lotito of Grenoble, France, known as Monsieur Mangetout, has been eating metal and glass since 1959.

Why did you start? I started to practice sophrology [literally "the science or study of the tranquil mind," a combination of self-hypnosis and other relaxation techniques that can assist pain control] when I was eight. Then, at the age of 16, I accidentally broke a glass while drinking, and I had a piece in my mouth. I knew other people had eaten glass in the past and decided that I could do it as well. Then I moved on to razor blades, plates, and small pieces of metal such as nuts and bolts.

Did you eat bigger things too? Yes, people started to ask me if I wanted to eat something bigger and so I said, "OK, I think I can eat a bicycle." It was a great success—they called me for TV shows in South America and Canada.

Does this mean you can actually digest metal? My teeth are incredibly strong—their strength has been measured at 56 tons per in.^{2}. But I also secrete strong juices that cause razor blades to begin to melt in my mouth; my gastric juices are so powerful that, during an endoscopy, doctors observed juices attacking objects with a corrosive foam that ate the metal.

Did you receive medical guidance during attempts? Yes, I would always ask for a doctor's assistance. They would give me all sorts of advice, such as to eat artichokes or paraffin oils together with metal to make things easier, but I soon realized that I was better off simply drinking several liters of water.

for funding. Along the way, she learned six languages and received eight marriage proposals!

Most scorpions eaten Rene Alvarenga (El Salvador) has eaten an estimated 35,000 live scorpions. He catches them with his bare hands and eats them at a rate of 20–30 a day.

Longest time pole-sitting The monk St. Simeon the Stylite (ca. A.D. 386–459) spent about 39 years on a stone pillar on the Hill of Wonders, near Aleppo, Syria. His motivation was self-persecution for people's sins and to be closer to God. He came down on only one occasion—so that the pole could be extended from 39 to 59 ft. (12 to 18 m).

★ Longest time spent in an attic Stephan Kovaltchuk spent 57 years in his attic in Montchintsi, Ukraine, before emerging at the age of 75 in 1999 because his sister, who had looked after him, had died. He originally went into hiding from Nazis who had occupied Ukraine in 1942, but remained in isolation to avoid the draft by the Red Army after Russia's victory over Germany.

Longest French knitting Edward Peter Hannaford (UK) has produced a piece of French knitting 11.62 miles (18.7 km) long since he began working on it in April 1989.

Most splits to a single human hair The greatest reported achievement in hair splitting has been that of Alfred West (UK), who succeeded in splitting a human hair 17 times, into 18 parts, on eight occasions.

Alfred learned how to set a razor during World War I when he worked on wooden component parts for aircraft. Later, he took his talents to unprecedented heights, creating elaborate works of art—including models of a boa constrictor, a monarch's crown, and the UK's Epping Forest—out of split hairs.

GAMES & PASTIMES

★ Casinos: most played in 24 hours On March 29–30, 2004, brothers Martin and David Lawrance Hallgarth (both UK) visited 55 casinos in 24 hours in Las Vegas, Nevada, U.S.A.

Chess: longest correspondence Dr. Reinhart Straszacker and Dr. Hendrik Roelof van Huyssteen (both South Africa) played their first game of correspondence chess in 1946. After 112 games—and with both men

CHESS: MOST MOVES IN A GAME Chess masters Goran Arsovic and Ivan Nikolic (both Yugoslavia, now Serbia and Montenegro) played a game with 269 moves on February 17, 1989. The drawn game was played in Belgrade, Yugoslavia (now Serbia and Montenegro), and took 20 hr. 15 min.

having won half each—their record play of over 53 years ended with the death of Straszacker on October 13, 1999.

Chess: most games simultaneously International chess master Andrew Martin (UK) played against 321 different opponents at Wellington College, Berkshire, UK, on February 21, 2004. Martin won 294 games, drew 26, and lost only one. The attempt took 16 hr. 51 min.

Chess: highest ratings The highest rating in chess by a male player is 2,851, achieved by Garry Kasparov (Russia) in January 2000. The **highest rating for a woman** is 2,675, achieved by Judit Polgar (Hungary) in 1996.

★**Conkers: most simultaneous matches** On October 14, 2004, 143 conkers matches (286 players) were played simultaneously at the inaugural competition for the Croft City Conker Cup in London, UK.

☆**Cup stacking: fastest cycle formation** Emily Fox (U.S.A.) was able to stack plastic cups in the cycle formation (a sequence of stacks combining a 3–6–3 stack, a 6–6 stack, and a 1–10–1 stack, concluding with cups in a 3–6–3 tower) in a time of 7.43 seconds at the Rocky Mountain Cup Stacking Championships, Colorado, U.S.A., on April 6, 2002.

Dominoes: most stacked on a single domino Matthias Aisch (Germany) stacked 726 dominoes on a single, vertically standing supporting domino on December 28, 2003. The stack remained standing for an hour.

Dominoes: most toppled single-handedly Ma Li Hua (China) single-handedly set up and toppled 303,621 dominoes at Singapore Expo Hall, Singapore, on August 18, 2003. Ma Li Hua spent an average of 10 hours daily from July 7 to August 17 setting up the dominoes. The event was organized by LG Electronics, Inc.

☆**Egg-and-spoon race: largest (multiple sites)** The largest simultaneous egg-and-spoon race involved 1,277 participants racing at various sites around Herefordshire, UK, in an event organized by Ready Steady Win (UK) on March 30, 2004.

Go: most games simultaneously In total, 1,000 players played 500 games of Go simultaneously at Take-machi-dohri and Chuo-cho Shopping Streets, Oita, Japan, on June 6, 1999.

DOMINOES: MOST TOPPLED BY A GROUP The greatest number of dominoes set up and toppled by a team is 3,992,397 during Domino Day 2004 in Leeuwarden, the Netherlands, on November 12, 2004. A team of 81 from the Netherlands, Germany, France, Spain, Poland, Estonia, Lithuania, Hungary, Czech Republic, Sweden, Austria, and Slovakia created 46 themed but connected projects covering an area of 278 × 295 ft. (85 × 90 m).

Hot Wheels: longest track The longest Hot Wheels track measured 1,650 ft. (502.92 m) and consisted of 2,100 pieces of track. The attempt, organized by Mattel Canada, Inc., for Big Brothers Big Sisters of Canada, was completed on July 7, 2002, at Thunder Alley, Toronto, Ontario, Canada.

☆**Hula hoop: fastest mile** Ashrita Furman (U.S.A.) walked a mile while continuously hula hooping in 14 min. 25 sec. at Moskvoretskaya, Naberezhnaya, Moscow, Russia, on May 31, 2004.

☆**Hula hoop: largest spun** On January 1, 2004, Nozomi Tsuji and Ai Kago (both Japan) hula hooped with a 13-ft. 4.6-in.-wide (4.08-m) hoop for 30 seconds each at the Nippon Television Network studios in Tokyo, Japan.

Jenga: fastest 30 levels The fastest time to build a stable tower of Jenga bricks 30 levels high—and within the official rules of the game—is 11 min. 55 sec. by Sabrina Ibrahim, John Chua, and Alex Agboola (all UK) on the *Big Toe Radio Show,* London, UK, on January 28, 2003.

Jigsaw puzzle: most pieces A puzzle with 212,323 pieces, measuring 35 ft. 5 in. × 38 ft. 3 in. (10.8 m × 11.68 m), was completed by the Yew Tee CC Youth Executive Committee, Singapore History Museum and members

HULA HOOPS: MOST HOOPED SIMULTANEOUSLY Alesya Goulevich (Belarus) was able to hula hoop with 99 hoops at the Big Apple Circus Big Top, Bayside Expo Center, Boston, Massachusetts, U.S.A., on April 26, 2004. As per the guidelines, Goulevich sustained three full revolutions of the standard hula hoops between her shoulders and her hips.

of the public during an event for the Youth Discovery Challenge 2002 in Singapore on June 29, 2002.

LEGO: largest flag A LEGO flag measuring 25 ft. 4 in. × 34 ft. 1.5 in. (7.72 m × 10.4 m) was made at the Franklin Institute Science Museum on August 22, 2001, to celebrate the hosting of the X Games in Philadelphia, Pennsylvania, U.S.A.

LEGO: longest structure Over 20,000 children built a LEGO structure in the shape of a millipede measuring 4,586.6 ft. (1,398 m) in Montréal, Quebec, Canada, on August 15, 2004, in an event organized by LEGO Canada.

★ FOOTBAG WORLD RECORDS ★

A footbag (or hackey sack) is a small bag filled with plastic pellets that is kept aloft for as long as possible using the feet.

Consecutive kicks (men's singles)	63,326	Ted Martin (U.S.A.) 8 hr. 50 min. 42 sec.	June 14, 1997
Consecutive kicks (women's singles)	24,713	Constance Constable (U.S.A.) 4 hr. 9 min. 27 sec.	April 18, 1998
Consecutive kicks (doubles)	132,011	Gary Lautt, Tricia George (U.S.A.)	March 21, 1998
Most kicks in 5 minutes	1,019	Andy Linder (U.S.A.)	June 7, 1996
Consecutive kicks with two footbags	68	Juha-Matti Rytilahti (Finland)	September 30, 2001
Most participants	964	Cornerstone Festival, Illinois, U.S.A.	July 6, 2001

JIGSAW PUZZLE: LARGEST (NONCOMMERCIAL) The world's largest jigsaw puzzle measured 58,435.1 ft.² (5,428.8 m²) and consisted of 21,600 pieces. Devised by Great East Asia Surveyors & Consultants Co. Ltd., it was assembled by 777 people at the former Kai Tak airport, Hong Kong, China, on November 3, 2002.

☆**LEGO: tallest structure** A LEGO tower constructed at Legoland in Carlsbad, California, U.S.A., reached a height of 92 ft. 6 in. (28.19 m) on February 21, 2005.

★**Miniature golf: most holes in 24 hours** Matt Majikas (U.S.A.) played 3,035 holes of miniature golf in 24 hours at Mulligan's Miniature Golf, Sterling, Massachusetts, U.S.A., on May 26–27, 2004. The 18-hole course was 1,097 ft. (334 m) long, and Matt played the whole course nearly 169 times in 24 hours—a total distance of more than 33 miles (54 km).

Monopoly: largest permanent game A granite Monopoly board measuring 31 × 31 ft. (9.44 × 9.44 m) was opened to the public on July 26, 2002, in San Jose, California, U.S.A. The pieces, dice, houses, and hotels are all in proportion.

Piggyback race: fastest 100 m The fastest piggyback race over 100 m (328 ft.) lasted 19.6 seconds, achieved by Andrew Gadd carrying Lance Owide (both UK) at Kings Langley, Hertfordshire, UK, on August 31, 2003.

☆**PARACHUTE: MOST GAMES SIMULTANEOUSLY** On January 17, 2004, the Chinese YMCA at Wu Kwai Shai Youth Village, Hong Kong, China, organized a record 21 simultaneous games of parachute with 510 participants. Players had to complete four different disciplines with their parachute, including raising it from the ground and lowering it until taut four consecutive times, and controlling a ball around the parachute in both a clockwise and counterclockwise circle.

☆**LOTTERY: LARGEST INDIVIDUAL WIN** Andrew "Jack" Whittaker Jr. (U.S.A.) won $314.9 million in the Powerball jackpot on December 24, 2002. He decided to take just over half the prize as a lump sum—$170 million before taxes—instead of the full prize in 30 annual installments.

Playing cards: house of cards with most stories On November 6, 1999, Bryan Berg (U.S.A.) built a freestanding house of playing cards that stood 131 stories high and 25 ft. 3.6 in. (7.71 m) tall. Made from 91,800 standard cards, it was built in the lobby of the casino at Potsdamer Platz, Berlin, Germany, and filmed for the *Guinness—die Show der Rekorde* TV show.

★**Pogo stick: most rope jumps in one minute** Ashrita Furman (U.S.A.) made 156 jumps over a jump rope on a pogo stick in one minute at Yellowstone National Park, Wyoming, U.S.A., on September 25, 2004. He also holds the record for the **fastest mile on a pogo stick:** he took 12 min. 16 sec. to travel a mile at Iffley Field, Oxford, UK, on July 24, 2001.

☆**Rubik's cube: fastest solve** Shotaro Makisumi (Japan) solved a Rubik's cube puzzle in 12.11 seconds at the Caltech Fall Tournament, Pasadena, California, U.S.A., on October 16, 2004.

At the same event, Shotaro also set the record for the ★**fastest average**

time to solve a Rubik's cube in competition, which he achieved in a time of 14.52 seconds.

Finally, Shotaro is also the holder of the record for the ☆fastest time to solve a Rubik's cube blindfolded. He achieved this feat in a time of 3 min. 10.54 sec. at the same event in Pasadena, California, U.S.A., on October 16, 2004.

Shotaro currently holds all the Guinness World Records for manipulation of a Rubik's cube.

Sack race: most competitors A total of 2,095 competitors took part in a sack race involving students from Agnieton College and elementary

RUSSIAN NESTING DOLLS: LARGEST SET Youlia Bereznitskaia (Russia) has hand-painted a 51-piece set of nesting dolls (matrioshkas). The largest is 1 ft. 9.25 in. (54 cm) high and the smallest is 0.12 in. (0.31 cm) high. The set was completed on April 25, 2003.

☆**PLAYING CARDS: FASTEST DECK REARRANGEMENT** Kunihiko Terada (Japan) arranged a shuffled deck of cards in order (ace through 10, jack, queen, king for diamonds, clubs, hearts, and spades) in his hands in 40.36 seconds at the Hard Rock Café, Tokyo, Japan, on January 25, 2004.

school pupils from Zwolle, Wezep, and Hattem on October 11, 2002, in Zwolle, the Netherlands.

★**Jump rope: most in one minute** S. Namasivayam (India) achieved 234 jumps at Indira Gandhi Stadium, Pondicherry, India, on July 3, 2004.

Tiddlywinks: fastest potting of 10,000 Allen R. Astles (UK) potted 10,000 winks in 3 hr. 51 min. 46 sec. at Aberystwyth, Ceredigion, UK, in February 1966.

Tiddlywinks is a child's game (but often played by adults in competition) that involves flipping a wink—a small plastic counter—into a pot by pressing down onto its edge with a larger counter known as a squidger.

Tiddlywinks: fastest mile Edward Wynn and James Cullingham (both UK) achieved the fastest tiddlywink mile—i.e., they covered the whole distance by means of flipping wink shots—in 52 min. 10 sec. in Stradbroke, Suffolk, UK, on August 31, 2002.

Tiddlywinks: farthest distance traveled in 24 hours Advancing only by means of flipping wink shots, Sean Booth and Barry Green (both UK) traveled from Bacup to Rawtenstall, Lancashire, UK, on November 22, 2003—a distance of 2.4 miles (3.9 km).

Tunnel ball: most players A total of 60 students from St. Columba's School, Wilston, Queensland, Australia, took part in a single game of tunnel ball on November 27, 2002.

Twister: largest board In February 1998, a single Twister sheet measuring 60 × 20 ft. (18.28 × 6 m) was manufactured by Vision International of Salt Lake City, Utah, U.S.A.

Wheelbarrow race: fastest 100 m On August 31, 2003, Andrew Gadd (pushing the wheelbarrow) and Freddie Gadd (riding) covered 100 m (328 ft.) in 18.1 seconds, at Framptons, Kings Langley, UK.

Yo-yo: largest A yo-yo measuring 10 ft. 4 in. (3.17 m) in diameter and and weighing 897 lb. (407 kg) was devised by J. N. Nichols (Vimto) Ltd. and made by engineering students at Stockport College, UK. On August 1, 1993, in Manchester, UK, it was launched by crane from a height of 188 ft. 7 in. (57.5 m) and yo-yo-ed about four times.

☆**Yo-yo: most tricks in one minute** Hans Van Dan Helzen (U.S.A.) completed 51 yo-yo tricks in one minute on the set of children's TV show *Blue Peter,* London, UK, on May 17, 2004.

FANTASTIC FOODS

LARGEST...

☆**Black forest gateau** Spanhacke's (Germany) created a 23-ft.-wide (7-m) giant gateau weighing 5,511 lb. (2.75 tons) and displayed it at the Vielstedter Bauernhaus restaurant in Hude, Germany, on August 17, 2003.

Candy A butterscotch candy made by Nidar (Norway) in August 1997 weighed 3,527 lb. (1.76 tons).
   The ★**longest candy** is a 2,204-lb. (1.76-ton) strawberry-sour belt made by Candy Castle (Netherlands) that stretched 6,574 ft. (2,004 m) when un-rolled in 's-Heerenberg, the Netherlands, on August 28, 2004.

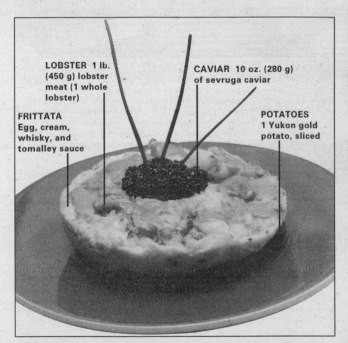

LOBSTER 1 lb. (450 g) lobster meat (1 whole lobster)

CAVIAR 10 oz. (280 g) of sevruga caviar

FRITTATA Egg, cream, whisky, and tomalley sauce

POTATOES 1 Yukon gold potato, sliced

★ **MOST EXPENSIVE OMELETTE** The most expensive omelette commercially available is the Zillion Dollar Lobster Frittata, which costs $1,000 and is featured on the menu at Norma's restaurant, Le Parker Meridien Hotel, New York City, U.S.A.

MOST EXPENSIVE COFFEE Only 500 lb. (227 kg) of Kopi Luwak coffee is available every year, and it sells for $300 per pound (0.45 kg). The price reflects the manner in which it is processed: the beans are collected from the excrement of the Sumatran civet cat (*Paradoxurus*), which lives in the mountain ranges of Irian Jaya, Indonesia. The civet climbs into the coffee trees and eats the ripest coffee cherries it can find. Eventually these are digested and reappear in the animal's excrement, after which they are gathered by locals and sold as coffee.

☆**Chocolate** In February 2004, The Hard Rock Café in Madrid, Spain, exhibited a single heart-shaped chocolate weighing 15,026 lb. (7.5 tons). It measured 16 ft. (5 m) wide and 13 ft. (4 m) high, and was created by www.match.com with Marco de Comunicación (Spain).

☆**Mug of coffee** A mug containing 793.04 gal. (3,002 liters) of latte was created by Nestlé and unveiled in New York City, U.S.A., on May 13, 2004. The mug was 5 ft. 7 in. (1.69 m) tall, had a diameter of 4 ft. 8 in. (1.41 m), and required 45 lb. (20 kg) of coffee.

☆**Fudge** NorthwestFudgeFactory.com (Canada) made a 3,010-lb. (1.5-ton) slab of maple and chocolate fudge for the FedNor Pavilion Royal Winter Fair, Toronto, Canada, on November 5, 2004. The fudge measured 16 × 8 ft. (4.87 × 2.43 m) and was 4 in. (10.16 cm) high.

☆**Hot cross bun** Manna European Bakery & Deli (Canada) baked a hot cross bun weighing 114 lb. 13.5 oz. (52.08 kg) on April 16, 2004, in aid of the Canadian Cancer Society.

☆**Ice cream cake** Carvel (U.S.A.) made a giant ice cream cake weighing 12,096 lb. (6.04 ton) and displayed it on May 25, 2004, at Union Square Park, New York City, U.S.A., to celebrate the company's 70th birthday.

★**Jawbreaker** Nick Calderaro (Canada), an employee of Oak Leaf Confection (Canada), made a jawbreaker with a circumference of 37.25 in. (94.6 cm). It weighed 27.8 lb. (12.6 kg) and took 476 hours to make from January 7 to May 29, 2003.

☆**Pasta** A bowl holding 7,355 lb. (3,336 kg) of pasta was made for *The Keeler Show* (U.S.A.) in conjunction with Tony's Pizzeria at the Sangerton Square Mall, Hartford, New York, U.S.A., on February 14, 2004. The TV show sponsored a contest in which one "lucky couple" was married inside the giant bowl of macaroni.

☆**Potato chips (bag)** On March 11, 2004, Seabrook Potato Crisps of Bradford, West Yorkshire, UK, unveiled a giant bag containing 113 lb. 3 oz. (51.35 kg) of salted crinkle-cut potato chips. The bag was 5.87 ft. (1.79 m) high, 3.96 ft. (1.21 m) wide, and 2.03 ft. (0.62 m) deep—and held over 275,000 calories-worth of potato chips!

☆**Pretzel** A 599-lb. (272-kg) pretzel was made by Die Wethje GmbH Kunstostofftechnik (Germany) on January 30, 2004, and exhibited in Hengersberg, Germany.

☆**LONGEST HOT DOG** Students from the University of Pretoria, South Africa, made a hot dog measuring 34 ft. 5.25 in. (10.5 m), smashing the previous record of 22 ft. 8 in. (6.9 m) set in August 2002. The single, unbroken sausage—nearly 60 times the length of a regular hot dog—was displayed at the Sonop Hostel in Pretoria, South Africa, on October 18, 2003. To cook their record-breaking wiener, the students had to design and build their own charcoal oven and *braai* (barbecue).

GILDED FLOWERS
Candied flowers covered in edible gold leaf

CAVIAR Grande Passion caviar with Armagnac and the juice of blood oranges and passion fruit

ICE CREAM Five scoops of Tahitian vanilla-bean ice cream covered in 23-karat edible gold leaf

EXOTIC CANDIED FRUITS Pineapple, figs, star fruit, and prickly pear

CHOCOLATE "Amedei Porcelana" and "Chuao" chocolate, chunked, flaked, and melted

GOLD DRAGÉES 12 almonds with gold leaf

CRYSTAL Served in a Baccarat Harcourt crystal goblet

GOLD SPOON Eat with a spoon of 18-karat gold and mother-of-pearl inlay

★**MOST EXPENSIVE ICE CREAM SUNDAE** The Serendipity Golden Opulence Sundae—introduced to the menu of the Serendipity 3 restaurant, New York City, U.S.A., in September 2004 to celebrate the restaurant's 50th anniversary—cost $1,000.

☆ **Sandwich** A ham, cheese, and mayonnaise sandwich weighing 5,297 lb. (2.64 tons) was made by Grupo Bimbo (Mexico) in conjunction with McCormick, Fud, Chalet, and Pétalo Jumbo in the Zócalo, Mexico City, Mexico, on April 24, 2004. The filling included 981 lb. (445 kg) of ham, 809 lb. (367 kg) of cheese, 147 lb. (67 kg) of mayo, and 81 lb. (37 kg) of lettuce.

☆ **Stir-fry** TV chef Nancy Lam (Singapore) stir-fried a 1,543-lb. (700-kg) dish of cabbage, carrots, baby corn, bok choy, and bean sprouts on January 23, 2004, in Leicester Square, London, UK, in aid of the National Children's Home charity.

★ MOST EXPENSIVE FOOD & DRINKS ★

If money is no object, why not indulge yourself with the world's most costly food and drinks?

☆ **Hamburger***	Bistro Moderne, New York City, U.S.A.	$120
	db Double Truffle	
*Cocktail***	Hemingway Bar, Paris Ritz, France	£400
	Ritz Side Car	($528)
Fruit	Helpston Garden Centre, Cambridge, UK	£700
	A single grape	($1,040)
Wine (bottle)*	*Chateau d'Yquem Sauternes, 1787*	$60,000
Wine (bottle)	Christie's, London, UK	£105,000
	Château Lafite claret, 1787	($156,030)
Wine (glass)	Pickwick's Pub, Beaune, France	FF8,600
	Beaujolais Nouveau, 1993	($1,601)
Liquor (bottle)	Fortnum & Mason, London, UK	£11,000
	60-year-old Macallan whisky	($15,662)
Chocolate bar	Christie's, London, UK	£470
	A bar of Cadbury's chocolate from	
	Captain Robert Scott's (UK) 1901	
	Antarctic expedition	($687)
☆ **Truffle**	Alba, Italy	$41,000
	1.08-kg (2.4-lb.) white truffle, 2004	
Wedding cake	Sotheby's, New York City, U.S.A.	$29,900
(piece)	*The Duke & Duchess of Windsor's (UK)*	
	wedding cake, 1937	

*Commercially available

BODY MODIFICATION

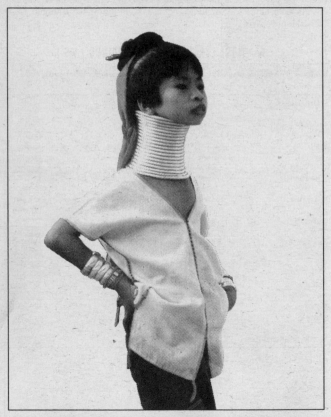

LONGEST NECKS The maximum known extension of a human neck is 15.75 in. (40 cm) and was created by the successive fitting of copper coils, as practiced by the women of the Padaung or Kareni tribe of Myanmar as a sign of beauty. Their necks eventually become so long and weak that they cannot support their heads without the coils. In some tribes the coils are removed to punish women who have committed adultery.

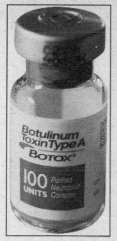

★ MOST POPULAR COSMETIC OPERATIONS
According to a survey of 46 countries, the
★ most popular *nonsurgical* aesthetic
procedure performed in 2003 was Botox
injections, representing 14.73% of all aesthetic
plastic surgeries performed.

The ★ most popular *surgical* aesthetic
procedure was blepharoplasty (eyelid
reshaping), at 10.89%.

★ MOST PLASTIC SURGERY Cindy Jackson (U.S.A.) has spent $99,600
on 47 cosmetic operations since 1988. These include three full face-lifts;
two eye lifts; liposuction; two nose operations; thigh, knee, waist,
abdomen and jaw-line surgery; lip and cheek implants; chemical peels;
chinbone reduction; and semipermanent make-up.

MOST PIERCED WOMAN Since having her first piercing in January 1997, Elaine Davidson (UK) has had 2,520 piercings over and inside her body, as of October 13, 2004. During her last examination, she was found to have 192 piercings on her facial area alone, including her ears, forehead, eyebrows, chin, nose, and tongue. She also has piercings on her stomach, breasts, and hands, among other areas.

MOST BODY PIERCINGS IN ONE SESSION Kam Ma (UK) received a total of 600 new piercings to his body without the aid of an anesthetic. All piercings were executed by Charlie Wilson (UK) in one continuous session from 9:15 a.m. to 5:47 p.m. at Sunderland Body Art, Tyne and Wear, UK, on May 26, 2002.

☆ **MOST PIERCED MAN** Luis Antonio Agüero from Havana, Cuba, sports 230 piercings on his body and head. His face alone carries over 175 rings.

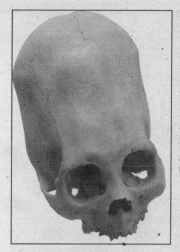

★**LARGEST SKULL** The largest skull documented in medical literature belonged to a retarded man who had a cranial capacity of 120 in.³ (1,980 cm³)—normal capacity is between 57.9 and 109 in.³ (950–1,800 cm³). The shape of this skull was normal, if enlarged. However, elongated skulls discovered in Mexico and South America (left) were found with a cranial capacity of up to 152 in.³ (2,500 cm³). These modified skulls are believed to have resulted from binding the head at birth.

LARGEST LIP PLATES Although lip plates are normally worn for decoration, for the Surma people of Ethiopia they also have a financial significance. The process of inserting these plates (made by the women themselves, from local clay which is then colored with ochre and charcoal and fire-baked) begins approximately a year before marriage. The final size indicates the number of cattle required by the girl's family from her future husband for her hand. The plates can reach up to 6 in. (15 cm) in diameter, which would require a payment of 50 cattle.

MOST TATTOOED MAN Tom Leppard (UK, pictured) and Lucky Rich (Australia) have both had 99.9% of their bodies covered with tattoos. Tom has a leopard skin design, with all the skin between the dark spots tattooed saffron yellow. Lucky Rich has had his existing tattoos blacked over with a white design tattooed on top.

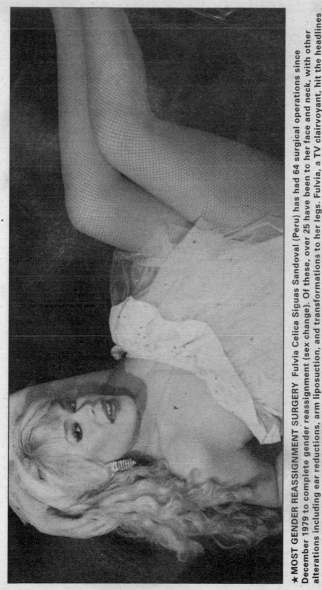

★ MOST GENDER REASSIGNMENT SURGERY Fulvia Celica Siguas Sandoval (Peru) has had 64 surgical operations since December 1979 to complete gender reassignment (sex change). Of these, over 25 have been to her face and neck, with other alterations including ear reductions, arm liposuction, and transformations to her legs. Fulvia, a TV clairvoyant, hit the headlines in 1998 when she registered as a candidate in the mayoral elections in Lima, Peru.

★**LONGEST EARLOBES** The practice of ear elongation, thought to have been used since the Neolithic period (about 8000–6000 B.C.), can still be found today carried out by tribes of south and southeast Asia. Traditionally associated with either a long life, beauty, or cultural identity, stretched lobes are attained by inserting earplugs or heavy rings into the lower ear—in some cases reaching a weight of 1 lb. (0.5 kg) per ear. Commonly seen on Hindu and Buddhist statues, elongated earlobes are said to represent extraordinary wisdom and spiritual advancement.

BUGS, SLUGS, & CREEPY CRAWLIES

MOST DANGEROUS

Ant The most dangerous ant is the bulldog ant (*Myrmecia pyriformis,* below) of Australia. It is so named because of its ferocity during an attack. The ant stings its prey a number of times, injecting more venom each time. It holds on to its victim with long-toothed mandibles, curls its body underneath, and thrusts its long, barbless sting into the skin. The sting has been known to kill an adult human within 15 minutes.

Bee The Africanized honeybee (*Apis mellifera scutellata*) is descended from the African subspecies. It is very aggressive when provoked and fiercely protective of territories up to a radius of 0.5 mile (0.8 km). Its venom is no more potent than that of other bees, but it attacks in swarms, which can inflict a potentially fatal number of stings.

LARGEST SPIDER The world's largest known spider is a male goliath bird-eating spider (*Theraphosa blondi*) collected by members of the Pablo San Martin Expedition at Rio Cavro, Venezuela, in April 1965. It had a record legspan of 11 in. (28 cm)—sufficient to cover a dinner plate. This species is found in the coastal rainforests of Suriname, Guyana, and French Guiana, but isolated specimens have also been reported from Venezuela and Brazil.

HEAVIEST INSECTS The heaviest insects are the goliath beetles (family Scarabaeidae) of equatorial Africa. The largest are *Goliathus regius, G. meleagris, G. goliathus* (*G. giganteus*), and *G. druryi,* and in measurements of one series of males (females are smaller) the lengths from the tips of the small frontal horns to the end of the abdomen were up to 4.33 in. (11 cm), with weights of 2.5–3.5 oz. (70–100 g).

GREEDIEST ANIMAL The làrva of the polyphemus moth (*Antheraea polyphemus*) of North America eats an amount equal to 86,000 times its own birth weight in its first 56 days. In human terms, this would be the same as a 7-lb. (3.2-kg) baby taking on a staggering 602,000 lb. (273 tons) of nourishment!

LARGEST MOTH The world's largest moth, in terms of overall size, is the atlas moth (*Attacus atlas*), which is native to southeast Asia. Its wingspan alone is 12 in. (30 cm), and it is often mistaken for a bird. Atlas moths have no mouth, and consequently live only for about four days, relying on their fatty deposits.

LARGEST SNAIL The largest known land gastropod is the African giant snail (*Achatina achatina*). The largest recorded specimen, examined in December 1978, measured 15.5 in (39.3 cm) from snout to tail when fully extended, with a shell length of 10.75 in (27.3 cm). It weighed exactly 2 lb. (900 g). Named Gee Geronimo, this snail was owned by Christopher Hudson (UK) and was collected in Sierra Leone in June 1976.

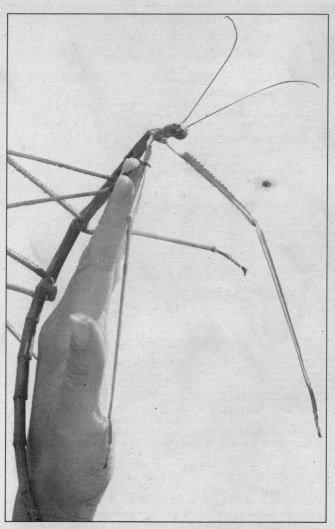

LONGEST INSECT The stick insects from the rainforests of Borneo are the longest in the world. The longest known specimen is in the Natural History Museum in London, UK. It has a body length of 12.9 in. (328 mm) and a total length, including the legs, of 21.5 in. (54.6 cm). In the wild, this species is often found with some legs missing because they are so long and easily trapped when the insect sheds its skin.

LARGEST COCKROACH The world's largest winged cockroach is *Megaloblatta longipennis,* found in Peru, Ecuador, and Panama. A preserved female in the collection of Akira Yokokura of Yamagata, Japan, measures 3.8 in. (97 mm) in length and 1.75 in. (45 mm) across. The average cockroach ranges from 0.25 to 3 in. (0.6 to 7.6 cm) in length.

MOST EXPENSIVE INSECT A giant 3.1-in. (7.8 cm) stag beetle (*Dorcus hopei*) is reported to have been sold for ¥10,035,000 (then $90,000) in Tokyo on August 19, 1999. A 36-year-old company president bought it for his collection, but he remains unidentified for fear of being targeted by thieves.

The word "insect"—which comes from this Greek for "to cut up"—was originally used to describe small animals that appeared to be divided or cut up into two or three parts. Members of this family usually have six legs and three body parts, and include flies, butterflies, and bees. Of course, slugs and snails aren't insects, they're molluscs, and spiders are arachnids.

STRONGEST SPIDER The California trap-door spider (*Bothriocyrtum californicum*) can resist a force 38 times its own weight. This display of strength is equivalent to a man trying to keep a door closed while it is being pulled from the other side by the weight of a small jet aircraft.

PETS

☆ **SMALLEST DOG (HEIGHT)** A long-haired chihuahua called Danka Kordak Slovakia—owned by Ing. Igor Kvetko (Slovakia)—measured 5.4 in. (13.8 cm) tall and 7.4 in. (18.8 cm) long when examined on May 30, 2004.

☆ LONGEST CAT WHISKERS On July 30, 2004, a whisker belonging to Mingo, a Maine coon cat, was measured at 6.8 in. (17.4 cm). Mingo lives with her owner, Marina Merne, in Turku, Finland.

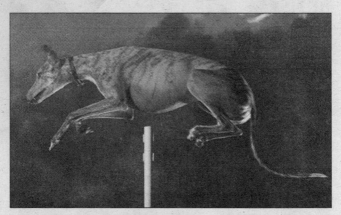

HIGHEST JUMP BY A DOG The world record for the highest jump cleared by a dog is 66 in. (167.6 cm), achieved by Cinderella May A. Holly Grey, a greyhound trained by Lourdes Edlin and Sally Roth and owned by Kathleen Conroy and Kate Long (all U.S.A.). The record-breaking leap was made at a dog show in Gray Summit, Missouri, U.S.A., on October 3, 2003.

☆ **SMALLEST DOG (LENGTH)** Heaven Sent Brandy, a female chihuahua belonging to Paulette Keller (U.S.A.), measured 6 in. (15.2 cm) from the nose to the tip of the tail on January 31, 2005.

☆ **LARGEST LITTER OF PUPPIES** On November 29, 2004, 24 puppies were born to Tia, a Neopolitan mastiff owned by Damian Ward (UK) and Anne Kellegher (Ireland) of Manea, Cambridgeshire, UK.

PLEASE NOTE: WE DO **NOT** ACCEPT CLAIMS FOR "HEAVIEST PET," SO PLEASE DON'T OVERFEED ANY ANIMAL IN ORDER TO CLAIM A GUINNESS WORLD RECORD.

★ **HIGHEST JUMP BY A PIG** The world record for the highest jump by a pig is 27.5 in. (70 cm), achieved by Kotetsu, a pot-bellied pig, on August 22, 2004, at the Mokumoku Tedsukuri Farm in Mie, Japan.

★ PET LONGEVITY ★

ANIMAL	NAME	RECORD AGE
Cat	Creme Puff	37 years 6 months
Chinchilla	Bouncer	27 years
Dog	Bluey	29 years 5 months
Goldfish	Tish	43 years
Guinea pig	Snowball	14 years 10.5 months
Hamster	*Unnamed*	4 years 6 months
Horse	Old Billy	62 years
Mouse	Fritzy	7 years 7 months
Pony	Sancho	54 years
Rabbit	Flopsy	18 years 10.75 months
Rat	Rodney	7 years 4 months

★LONGEST DOG TUNNEL The record for the longest human tunnel through which a dog has run involved 222 people and four dogs in an event organized by the North Northumberland Dog Training Club at The Alnwick Castle Tournament in Northumberland, UK, on July 25, 2004.

VE. AGE	OWNER	DIED
–15 years	J. Perry (U.S.A.)	*alive*
–14 years	J. Bowen (UK)	*alive*
–15 years	L. Hall (Australia)	1939
+ years	H. & G. Hand (UK)	1999
8 years	M. A. Wall (UK)	1979
2.5 years	K. Smeaton (UK)	*unknown*
–30 years	E. Robinson (UK)	1822
5–2 years	B. Beard (UK)	1985
years	E. Saunders (UK)	2003
10 years	L. B. Walker (Australia)	1982
2.5 years	R. Mitchell (U.S.A.)	1990

Pets

☆ SMALLEST LIVING CAT This year, we received two claims for the world's smallest cat. The first came from the owners of Mr. Peebles (pictured), who measures 6.1 in. (15.5 cm) high and 19.2 in. (49 cm) long. But then we heard about Itse Bitse who belongs to Mayo and Dea Whitton (both U.S.A.)—even smaller at 3.75 in. (9.52 cm) high and 15 in. (38.1 cm) long from nose tip to tail tip.

MOST TENNIS BALLS HELD IN THE MOUTH BY A DOG Augie, a golden retriever owned by the Miller family of Dallas, Texas, U.S.A., successfully gathered and held a record five regulation-sized tennis balls in his mouth on July 6, 2003.

TALLEST HORSE Radar, a Belgian draft horse, measured 19 hands 3.5 in. (79.5 in.; 202 cm), without shoes, on July 27, 2004, at the North American Belgian Championship in London, Ontario, Canada. Radar is owned by Priefert Manufacturing, Inc., of Mount Pleasant, Texas, U.S.A.

MOST VALENTINE CARDS SENT TO A GUINEA PIG Sooty, a three-year-old guinea pig from South Wales in the UK, became globally infamous in 2001 for "romancing" 24 partners in a single evening and fathering 43 guinea piglets. On Valentine's Day that year, Sooty proved that his romantic reputation was still intact when he received over 206 cards from as far away as New Zealand.

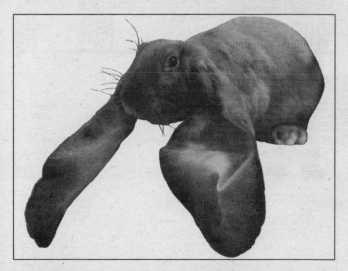

☆ **LONGEST EARS ON A RABBIT** The longest rabbit ears measured 31.125 in. (79 cm) in a complete span on November 1, 2003, at the U.S. Rabbit Breeders Association National Show in Wichita, Kansas, U.S.A. The ears belong to an English lop called Nipper's Geronimo, owned by Waymon and Margaret Nipper (both U.S.A.).

7.9 in.	2.8 in.
(20 cm)	(7.11 cm)
Highest jump by a guinea pig	Smallest dog ever
6.8 in.	**2.7 in.**
(17.4 cm)	(7 cm)
Longest cat whiskers	Smallest cat ever
5.4 in.	**1.5–2 in.**
(13.8 cm)	(4–5 cm)
Smallest living dog	Smallest breed of domestic hamster
4.6 in.	
(11.7 cm)	
Longest eyelashes on a dog	
3.7 in.	
(9.52 cm)	
Smallest living cat	

FOOD FEATS

PLAYING WITH YOUR FOOD . . .

☆ **Fastest jelly bean sorting by straw** The fastest time in which 30 Jelly Belly jelly beans have been sorted into five flavors using a drinking straw is 27.78 seconds by Richard Parry (UK) as part of the *Guinness World Records* 2005 Roadshow at the Trafford Centre, Manchester, Lancashire, UK, on November 27, 2004.

☆ **Farthest distance to squirt milk** Ilker Yilmaz (Turkey) squirted milk from his eye across a distance of 9 ft. 2 in. (2.795 m) at the Armada Hotel, Istanbul, Turkey, on September 1, 2004.

☆ **Fastest time to eat a raw onion** Brian Duffield (UK) ate a raw onion in 1 min. 32 sec. on the set of *The Paul O'Grady Show* at the London Television Centre, UK, on November 17, 2004. The onion weighed 7.47 oz. (212 g) after preparation. The minimum weight requirement is 210 g (7.4 oz.).

☆ **Most bananas snapped in one minute** Thomas Schuster (Germany) snapped 72 bananas in a minute at the Ravensburg town fair, Germany, on September 6, 2003.

☆ **MOST BIG MACS CONSUMED** Donald Gorske (U.S.A.) consumed his 20,500th McDonald's Big Mac on March 27, 2005, in his 33rd year of eating Big Macs on a daily basis. Donald is proud to declare that he has eaten Big Macs from all 50 states of the U.S.A., at all 32 National Football League stadiums, all 30 Major League Baseball stadiums, and over 30 NASCAR/Busch racetracks.

☆ **Most watermelons crushed with the head** Leonardo D'Andrea (Italy) smashed 22 watermelons with his head in one minute on the set of *Guinness World Records: 50 Years, 50 Records,* at London Television Studios, UK, on September 11, 2004.

Most eggs crushed with the toes in 30 seconds Alan "Nasty" Nash (UK) crushed 23 eggs with his toes on the set of *Guinness World Records: A Few Records More* in London, UK, on September 11, 2004.

☆ **Most ice cream cones prepared in one minute** Mitch Cohen (U.S.A.) prepared 18 ice cream cones in one minute at Times Square, New York, U.S.A., as part of ABC's *Good Morning America* TV show on July 22, 2004.

☆ **Largest custard pie fight** On April 11, 2000, 3,312 custard pies were thrown in 3 minutes by 20 people at the Millennium Dome in London, UK.

☆**FASTEST TIME TO PUSH AN ORANGE 1 MILE WITH THE NOSE** Using only his nose, multiple record-holder Ashrita Furman (U.S.A.) pushed an orange 1 mile (1.6 km) in a time of 24 min. 36 sec. at Terminal 4 of JFK Airport, New York, U.S.A., on August 12, 2004. The secret of Ashrita's success was partly owing to his choice of an unripe (green) orange.

In total, 1,100 lb. (0.5 ton) of custard powder was mixed in with 264 gal. (1,000 litres) of water in six cement mixers to make the pies.

★**Fastest time to eat a 12-inch pizza** Zaphod Xerxes Leigh (UK) ate a regulation-sized 12-inch pizza in 4 min. 56 sec. at Caffé Mamma Restaurant, Richmond, Surrey, UK, on November 16, 2003. The pizza weighed 0.76 lb. (0.34 kg).

☆**Longest pizza delivery** On November 17, 2004, Domino's Pizza UK, in conjunction with Make-A-Wish Foundation UK, hand-delivered a pizza to the set of Australian TV show *Neighbours* in Melbourne, Victoria, Australia, from the Domino's Pizza franchise in Feltham, London, UK, a distance of 10,532 miles (16,659 km) as the crow flies.

☆**Fastest time to eat three soda crackers** Ambrose Mendy (UK) ate three crackers in 37.44 seconds at the MTV Studios in Leicester Square, London, UK, on November 16, 2004.

Fastest turkey plucker Vincent Pilkington (Ireland) plucked a turkey in 1 min. 30 sec. on RTE television in Dublin, Ireland, on November 17, 1980.

★ WORLD'S FASTEST EATERS ★

FOOD	MOST EATEN IN 30 SEC.	HOLDER
Ice cream	9.3 oz. (264 g)	Diego Siu (U.S.A.)
☆ Worms	200	C. Manoharan "Snake" Manu (India)

IN 1 MIN.

FOOD	MOST EATEN	HOLDER
Brussels sprouts	43	Dave Mynard (UK)
Jalapeño chillies	8	Anita Crafford (South Africa)
Sausages (eaten)	8	Stefan Paladin (New Zealand)
☆ Sausages (swallowed whole)	8	Cecil Walker (U.S.A.)
☆ M&Ms (with chopsticks)	170	Kathryn Ratcliffe (UK)
Meatballs (with cocktail stick)	27	Nick Marshall (UK)
Cockroaches	36	Ken Edwards (UK)

IN 3 MIN.

FOOD	MOST EATEN	HOLDER
Grapes (with teaspoon)	133	Mat Hand (UK)
Hot dogs (inc. bun)	4	Peter Dowdeswell (UK)
Doughnuts (jam)	6	Steve McHugh (UK)
Doughnuts (powdered)	4	Simon Krischer, Jay Weisberger, Adam Fenton, Anthony Albelo (all U.S.A.)
☆ Oysters	187	Rune Naeri (Norway)
Shrimp	9.6 oz. (272.1 g)	William E. Silver (U.S.A.)
Sweet-corn kernels (with cocktail stick)	236	Ian Richard Purvis (UK)
Grains of rice (with chopsticks)	64	Tae Wah Gooding (South Africa)
Canned peas (with cocktail stick)	211	Mat Hand (UK)

. . . AND DRINK

★**Fastest milkshake drinker** Dan Orchard (Canada) drank 5 fl. oz. (500 ml) of milkshake through a straw in 10 seconds as part of Nestlé's "Grab, Gulp, and Go" event at Yonge-Dundas Square, Toronto, Canada, on September 18, 2003.

☆**Largest shot "slam"** A total of 1,044 students from Macquarie University, North Ryde, New South Wales, Australia, slammed shots of liquor on September 26, 2003, to honor the founding of the university.

☆**DINING OUT AT THE HIGHEST ALTITUDE** Henry Shelford, Thomas Shelford, Nakul Misra Pathak, Robert Aitken, Robert Sully (all UK), Caio Buzzolini (Australia), and appointed butler Joshua Heming (UK) enjoyed a formal meal at 22,326 ft. (6,805 m) on Lhakpa Ri, Tibet, on May 3, 2004. The team carried the tables, chairs, and silver cutlery as part of their expedition to celebrate Henry Shelford's 30th birthday.

Fastest time to drink two pints of milk Peter Dowdeswell (UK) drank 2 pints (1.13 litres) of milk in 3.2 seconds at Dudley Top Rank Club, West Midlands, UK, on May 31, 1975.

Fastest ketchup drinker Dustin Phillips (U.S.A.) consumed 91% of a standard 14-oz. (396-g) glass bottle of Heinz Tomato Ketchup though a 0.25-in.-wide (0.63-cm) drinking straw in just 33 seconds at the studios of *Guinness World Records: Primetime* in Los Angeles, California, U.S.A., on September 23, 1999.

COLLECTIONS

☆**Airplane sick bags** Niek Vermeulen (Netherlands) has collected 3,728 airline sickness bags from 802 different airlines since the 1970s. "Somebody has to do it," says Niek, who began collecting airsickness bags when he and a friend made a bet to see who could accumulate the most of any one item and make it into the *Guinness World Records* book.

☆ **TALLEST SUGAR CUBE TOWER** Anita Cash (UK) erected a circular tower of sugar cubes measuring 55.3 in. (140.5 cm) high at the offices of *K-Zone Magazine* in Shrewsbury, Shropshire, UK, on September 30, 2003.

☆**Airline tags** Raghav Somani (India) has a collection of 637 airline tags from 174 airlines around the world. Raghav started his collection in 1994.

☆**Badges** Daniel Hedges (UK) began collecting badges as a Boy Scout in 1994, and has since amassed a total of 13,516 different items, including badges donated personally by pop stars Madonna and Janet Jackson.

★**Bar towels** Terry Sanderson (UK) has 1,815 bar towels that he has been collecting from around the world since 1997. Terry estimates that if laid out they would cover an area of 2,040.8 ft.^{2} (189.6 m^2)—enough to cover at least two badminton courts!

☆**Beer bottles** Ron Werner (U.S.A.) has amassed a collection of 16,321 beer bottles since 1982. This includes 10,755 bottles that are still unopened.

★**Chewing gum packs** Former art and design teacher Steve Fletcher (UK) began collecting chewing gum and bubble gum packs in 1980, following an art assignment with his pupils. Today, his collection numbers a record 5,100 different packs.

Colored vinyl records Alessandro Benedetti (Italy) has collected 1,180 music records made of colored vinyl. His collection includes 866 LPs (792 colored, 74 with pictures), 291 singles (277 colored, 14 with pictures), and 23 in unusual shapes.

★**Potato chip bags** Bernd Sikora (Germany) owns 1,482 potato chip bags from 43 countries. He has been collecting since 1993.

DO YOU HAVE A RECORD-BREAKING COLLECTION?

1. A record-breaking collection is based on the number of items of a particular kind that are distinguishable in some way (i.e., no two items should be the same).

2. All items should have been accumulated by an individual over a significant period of time.

3. An inventory of all items should be compiled in the presence of two witnesses. The final total should be included in the form of two independent witness statements.

4. Owing to the infinite number of items it is possible to collect, priority will be given to those that reflect proven widespread interest.

For the full details on how to register your record claim, visit www.guinnessworldrecords.com or see p. xix.

CREDIT CARDS Walter Cavanagh (U.S.A.) has collected 1,497 individual valid credit cards. The cost of acquisition to "Mr. Plastic Fantastic" was nothing, but they are worth more than $1.7 million in credit.

★**Crosses** Since 1938, Ernie Reda (U.S.A.) of San Jose, California, has collected 13,014 individual religious crosses. Reda's home and garage also house a collection of more than 4,000 different religious artifacts and books.

★**Dice** Kevin Cook (U.S.A.) has a collection of 11,097 dice that he has amassed since 1977. A member of the Dice Maniacs Club (a.k.a. the Random Fandom), Kevin began collecting dice from gaming shops after taking up Dungeons & Dragons. Since 1998, about 80% of his dice have been acquired from eBay, the online auction company.

☆**Pacifiers** Since 1995, Dr. Muhammad Mustansar (Pakistan) of the Children's Hospital and Institute of

Child Health in Lahore, Pakistan, has been collecting pacifiers as part of an educational movement to warn of the possible hazards of their use. The current collection includes 1,994 pacifiers of different colors and shapes, each of which has been obtained from individual mothers.

★**Erasers** Leanna Allison (U.S.A.) has accumulated 6,003 non-duplicate erasers since 1998.

★**Golf clubs** Robert Lantsoght (Spain) has a collection of 4,393 individual golf clubs that he has been collecting since 1992.

Hotel baggage labels Robert Henin (U.S.A.) has collected 2,016 hotel baggage labels from different countries worldwide over the past 40 years.

★**Model cars** Michael Zarnock (U.S.A.) has a collection of 3,711 Hot Wheels model cars that he has amassed since 1968, when he was a child. Michael's favorites are the replicas of cars dating from his childhood including the '56 Ford Panel, the '65 Mustang, and the '70 RoadRunner.

★**Passports** Guy Van Keer (Belgium) owns 8,110 used passports and travel documents presented in lieu of passports. They represent 130 countries and passport-issuing authorities, including many countries that no longer exist. The oldest dates back to 1615.

TRAFFIC CONES David Morgan (UK) has put together a collection of 137 traffic cones, each of them different. David—the proprietor of a plastics factory that produces more than 1 million cones each year—owns a cone from approximately two-thirds of all cone types ever made.

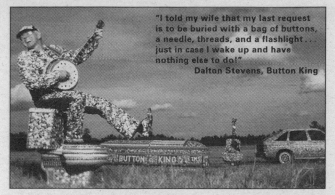

> "I told my wife that my last request is to be buried with a bag of buttons, a needle, threads, and a flashlight . . . just in case I wake up and have nothing else to do!"
> **Dalton Stevens, Button King**

BUTTONS Dalton Stevens (U.S.A.) has collected 439,900 buttons with no duplicates. The "Button King of Bishopville" suffers from chronic insomnia. To relieve the boredom of many a sleepless night, he has resorted to decorating various objects with buttons, including a car, an outhouse, a coffin, a hearse, and a guitar.

★**Rubber ducks** Charlotte Lee (U.S.A.) has 1,439 different rubber ducks, which she has collected since 1996.

★ TOP 20 COLLECTIONS ★

The following list reveals the 20 largest collections from the Guinness World Records archives.

1. Matchbook covers	Ed Brassard (U.S.A.)	3,159,119
2. Human teeth	Giovanni Battista Orsenigo (Italy)	2,000,744
3. Books (private)	John Q. Benham (U.S.A.)	1,500,000
4. Matchbox labels	Teiichi Yoshizawa (Japan)	743,512
5. Buttons	Dalton Stevens (U.S.A.)	439,900
6. Beer labels	Jan Solberg (Norway)	424,868
7. Scratch cards	Darren Haake (Australia)	319,011
8. Ballpoint pens	Angelika Unverhau (Germany)	285,150
9. Cigar bands	Alfred Manthe (Germany)	211,104
10. Train tickets	Frank Helker (Germany)	163,235
11. Beer mats	Leo Pisker (Austria)	152,860
12. Paper and plastic bags	Heinz Schmidt-Bachem (Germany)	150,000
13. Cigarette packets	Claudio Rebecchi (Italy)	143,027
14. Bottle caps	Poul Høegh Paulsen (Denmark)	101,733
15. Beer cans	William B. Christensen (U.S.A.)	75,000
16. Golf balls	Ted Hoz (U.S.A.)	74,849
17. Four-leaf clovers	George J. Kaminski (U.S.A.)	72,928
18. Cigarette lighters	Francis Van Herle (Belgium)	58,529
19. Refrigerator magnets	Louise J. Greenfarb (U.S.A.)	35,000
20. Fruit stickers	Antoine Secco (France)	34,500

NATURAL WORLD

CONTENTS

EARTH

METEORITES & IMPACT CRATERS

Largest impact crater The Vredefort crater near Johannesburg, South Africa, has an estimated diameter of 186 miles (300 km) and is the largest of about 150 known impact craters. Formed 2 billion years ago when an asteroid or comet struck Earth, it is large enough to accommodate more than 270,000 tennis courts!

Greatest impact Most astronomers believe that a planet the size of Mars collided with the Earth 4.5 billion years ago. Some of the debris from this cataclysm went into orbit around the Earth and collected together under its own gravity to form the Moon. The effect of this impact would have been devastating to the Earth. The planet's crust would probably have been blasted off into space, leaving behind an Earth whose entire surface was an ocean of molten magma.

Oldest confirmed impact On August 23, 2002, a team of U.S. scientists led by Gary Byerly (Louisiana State University) and Donald Lowe (Stanford University) announced their discovery of the impact of an asteroid on Earth 3.47 billion years ago. Geological evidence suggests that the asteroid had a diameter of about 12 miles (20 km), but no crater has been found as Earth's geological processes have had plenty of time to erase it.

Largest meteorite A meteorite measuring 9 ft. (2.7 m) long by 8 ft. (2.4 m) wide, and weighing an estimated 130,000 lb. (59 tons), was found in 1920 at Hoba West, Namibia.

DEFINITIONS

Meteoroid: A tiny speck of dust, often no larger than the period at the end of this sentence, in orbit around the Sun.

Meteor: The shooting star caused by a meteoroid vaporizing as it enters Earth's atmosphere at speeds of about 31 miles (50 km) a second.

Meteorite: Often seen entering Earth's atmosphere as a fireball, these are larger iron or rocky chunks from space that survive to hit the ground.

Tektite: Glassy piece of rock formed during the impact of large meteorites and asteroids with the Earth's surface.

GREATEST MASS EXTINCTION About 248 million years ago, at the end of the Permian geological period, a mass extinction wiped out approximately 90% of all marine species and 70% of all higher land animals. Factors that could have contributed to it include: comet or asteroid impact (illustrated), environmental change owing to Earth's shifting continents, and changes in the composition of the oceans.

★**Largest lunar meteorite** About 30 of the meteorites on Earth originated from the Moon. The largest is Dar al Gani 400, with a mass of 3 lb. 2.24 oz. (1.425 kg). It was discovered in Libya in 1998.

★**Largest Martian meteorite** At 40 lb. (18 kg), the Zagami meteorite, which struck Earth on October 3, 1962, in a field near Zagami, Nigeria, is the largest of at least 30 meteorites known to have originated from Mars.

★**Largest tektite** A tektite weighing 7 lb. (3.2 kg) was discovered in 1932 at Muong Non, Laos. It is now on display at the Paris Museum, France.

WHERE'S THE DEADLIEST LAKE ON EARTH? FIND OUT ON P. 126

MOUNTAINS

Highest mountain Mount Everest, in the Himalayas, is 29,028 ft. (8,848 m) high, and its peak is the highest point in the world. It was first conquered in 1953 by Sherpa Tenzing Norgay (Nepal) and Sir Edmund Hillary (New Zealand).

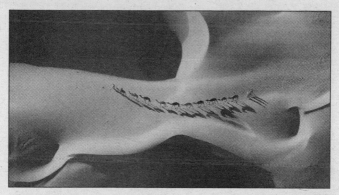

LARGEST DESERT Nearly an eighth of the world's land surface is arid, with a rainfall of less than 10 in. (25 cm) a year. The Sahara in north Africa is the largest hot desert in the world. At its greatest length it is 3,200 miles (5,150 km) from east to west, and from north to south it is between 800 and 1,400 miles (1,280 and 2,250 km) long. The area covered by the desert is about 3,579,000 miles² (9,269,000 km²).

LONGEST MOUNTAIN RANGE ON LAND The Andes in South America stretches for 4,700 miles (7,600 km) across seven countries and includes more than 50 peaks of over 20,000 ft. (6,000 m) high. For most of its extent, it is about 200 miles (300 km) wide.

Tallest mountain Mauna Kea (White Mountain) on the island of Hawaii, U.S.A., is the world's tallest mountain. From its submarine base in the Hawaiian Trough to its peak, it has a combined height of 33,480 ft. (10,205 m), of which 13,796 ft. (4,205 m) is above sea level.

☆**Longest lines of sight** In Alaska, U.S.A., Mount McKinley (20,320 ft.; 6,194 m) can be seen from Mount Sanford (16,237 ft.; 4,949 m)—a direct distance of 230 miles (370 km).

Owing to the light-bending effects of atmospheric refraction, Vatnajökull (6,952 ft.; 2,119 m) in Iceland can sometimes be seen from the Faroe Islands, some 340 miles (550 km) away.

DEEP EARTH

☆**Deepest cave** The world's deepest cave is Krubera (or Voronja) beneath the Arabika Massif in Georgia. In 2004, an expedition of the Ukrainian Speleological Association explored it to a depth of 6,824 ft. (2,080 m).

Largest cave The Sarawak Chamber, Lubang Nasib Bagus, in the Gunung Mulu National Park, Sarawak, Malaysia, is 2,300 ft. (700 m) long and at least 230 ft. (70 m) high. Ten 747 jumbo jets, parked end to end, could be accommodated within the cave.

Deepest valley The Yarlung Zangbo valley, Tibet, has an average depth of 16,400 ft. (5,000 m), but in 1994 explorers discovered that its deepest

LONGEST NATURAL ARCH Landscape Arch (above) in Arches National Park, and Kolob Arch in Zion National Park—both in Utah, U.S.A.—stand over openings 310 ft. (94.5 m) wide. Landscape Arch is the more dramatic, as it spans an open gully and narrows to only 16 ft. (5 m) thick.

The highest natural arch—Rainbow Bridge in Lake Powell National Monument, Utah—is just 270 ft. (82.3 m) long but rises to a height of 290 ft. (88 m)—nearly twice the height of the Statue of Liberty.

★LARGEST SWAMP The Pantanal in the states of Mato Grosso and Mato Grosso do Sul in Brazil is the world's largest tract of swamp, covering an area of 42,000 miles² (109,000 km²). The diverse areas of the swamp include rivers and lakes, seasonally flooded grasslands, forests, and wetlands. During the wet season, heavy tropical rains cause the Pantanal waters to overflow, flooding an area roughly the size of Cuba. During the region's dry season, the floodwaters recede and leave behind a rich landscape of lakes, forests, and lagoons.

point was 17,657 ft. (5,382 m)—three times deeper than the Grand Canyon and sufficient to house a stack of almost 10 CN Towers, the world's tallest tower.

Deepest natural shaft Vrtiglavica (meaning "vertigo") in Monte Kanin, Slovenia, is an unbroken vertical shaft 2,110 ft. (643 m) deep—enough to accommodate two Eiffel Towers.

Largest single crystal Earth's inner core is a sphere of about 1,516 miles (2,442 km) in diameter, with a temperature of 9,000–11,000°F (5,000–6,000°C), and is composed mostly of iron. Many geologists believe that this gigantic ball is a single crystal with a mass of about one hundred million million million tons. This assumption is based on differences in the behavior of seismic waves passing through the core in different directions.

Largest liquid body Earth's liquid outer core has a width of about 758 miles (1,221 km) and a volume of about 60.7×10^{20} ft.³ (1.7×10^{20} m³). This represents about 29.3% of Earth's mass and 16% of its volume.

Earliest evidence for plate tectonics On July 8, 2002, a team of Chinese and U.S. scientists announced their discovery of rocks indicating that plate tectonics were active on Earth some 2.5 billion years ago.

This is approximately 500 million years earlier than previously thought.

ICE & GLACIERS

★ **Largest area of sea ice** The Southern Ocean around Antarctica is covered in an area of ice larger than Russia. Between 6.5 and 7.7 million miles² (17 and 20 million km²) of ocean is covered by ice during winter, decreasing to 1.1–1.5 million miles² (3–4 million km²) in summer. By comparison, the Arctic Ocean is covered by 6 million miles² (16 million km²) of ice in winter and 2.7–3.5 million miles² (7–9 million km²) in summer.

Fastest glacier The Columbia Glacier, between Anchorage and Valdez in Alaska, U.S.A., was measured in 1999 to be flowing at an average rate of 115 ft. (35 m) per day.

Longest glacier The Lambert Glacier, discovered by an Australian aircraft crew in Australian Antarctic Territory in 1956–57, is up to 40 miles (64 km) wide. Including its seaward extension (the Amery Ice Shelf), it measures at least 440 miles (700 km) in length—longer than the entire state of Florida. It drains about a fifth of the East Antarctic ice sheet.

Largest subglacial lake Lake Vostok in Antarctica was discovered in 1994 by analyzing radar imagery of the icy continent. Buried under 2.5 miles (4 km) of ice, it is one of the oldest and most pristine lakes on Earth, having been isolated from the rest of the world for at least 500,000 years. Covering about 5,400 miles² (14,000 km²), it is the 18th largest lake in the world and has a depth of at least 330 ft. (100 m).

★ **Longest ice core** In 1998, an ice core measuring 11,886 ft. (3,623 m) in length was drilled from the ice above Lake Vostok. The drilling stopped about 492 ft. (150 m) above the surface in order to avoid possible contamination of the lake's pristine environment.

Largest pingo Pingos—conical mounds that have a core of ice—form when lakes in permafrost regions drain. As residual water in the ground under the lake freezes, it expands, pushing up a mound of land. Ibyuk Pingo, on the western Arctic coast of Canada, is the largest in the world. It measures about 160 ft. (50 m) high and has a 990-ft. (300-m) circumference.

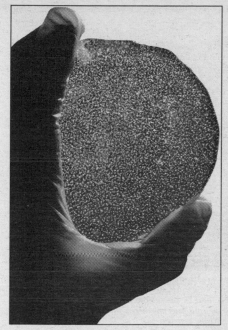

★ **OLDEST CONTINUOUS ICE CORE** An "ice core" is a long cylinder of ice extracted from an ice sheet. The farther down the core the older the ice, so scientists can investigate the history of global climate change by slicing into the core and studying ancient bubbles of air trapped in the ice. The oldest continuous ice core covers 740,000 years of climate history. It measures 10,298 ft. (3,139 m) in length and is 4 in. (10 cm) in diameter. It was drilled at Dome C, Antarctica, by the European Project for Ice Coring in Antarctica (EPICA) and announced on June 9, 2004.

LAKES

Largest lake The Caspian Sea (in Azerbaijan, Turkmenistan, Iran, Russia, and Kazakhstan) is 760 miles (1,225 km) long, with an area of 143,550 miles^2 (371,800 km^2)—large enough to accommodate the UK and the island of Cuba. Its maximum depth is 3,360 ft. (1,025 m), and the surface is 93 ft. (28.5 m) below sea level.

Deepest lake Lake Baikal in the southern part of eastern Siberia, Russia, was measured in 1974 by the Soviet Pacific Navy's Hydrographic Service and found to be 5,371 ft. (1,637 m) deep, of which 3,875 ft. (1,181 m) is below sea level.

Largest lake within a lake The largest lake within a lake is Manitou Lake, with an area of 41 miles^2 (106 km^2). It is situated on the world's **largest lake island** Manitoulin Island (1,068 miles^2; 2,766 km^2), in the Canadian part of Lake Huron. The lake itself contains a number of islands.

Largest freshwater lake by surface area Lake Superior on the U.S.A.–Canada border has the greatest area of any freshwater lake. Covering 31,700

DEADLIEST LAKE The lake responsible for the most deaths without drowning is Lake Nyos in Cameroon, west Africa, where toxic gases have claimed nearly 2,000 lives in recent decades. On one night in August 1986, up to 1,800 people and countless animals were killed by a large natural release of carbon dioxide gas.

Scientists disagree on the source of Nyos's deadly gas. The lake lies in the crater of an old volcano, suggesting that the gas is volcanic in origin. But the decomposition of organic matter, plus changes in surface temperature, may also be responsible.

miles^2 (82,100 km^2), more than 500,000 people live along its 2,726-mile (4,385-km) shoreline.

Largest freshwater lake by volume Lake Baikal in Siberia, Russia, boasts an estimated volume of 5,500 miles^3 (23,000 km^3)—one-fifth of the planet's fresh surface water. It is also the **oldest freshwater lake,** having formed 20–25 million years ago.

Largest underground lake In 1986, a lake some 217 ft. (66 m) underground was discovered in the Drachenhauchloch (Dragon's Breath) cave near Grootfontein, Namibia. It has a surface area of 280,900 ft.^{2} (26,100 m^2) and is 276 ft. (84 m) deep.

Saltiest lake Don Juan Pond in Wright Valley, Antarctica, contains 671 parts per thousand salt (compared with 35 parts per thousand for the ocean). It is so salty that it remains liquid at temperatures as low as -63.4°F (-53°C).

ISLANDS

Highest islands Lake Orba in Tibet stands 17,090 ft. (5,209 m) above sea level. It has a surface area of 38 miles² (100 km²) and houses several small islands.

Largest island within an island Samosir in Lake Toba, Sumatra, Indonesia, has an area of 245 m² (630 km²).

★ WORLD'S GREATEST RIVERS ★

RIVER	SOURCE	LENGTH
Nile	Burundi	4,145 miles (6,670 km)
Amazon	Lago Villafro, Peru	4,007 miles (6,448 km)
Yangtze	Kunlun Shan, China	3,915 miles (6,300 km)
Mississippi-Missouri	Montana, U.S.A.	3,741 miles (6,020 km)
Yenisey-Angara	Mongolia	3,442 miles (5540 km)
Hwang He (Yellow River)	Qinghai Province, China	3,395 miles (5,464 km)

LONGEST RIVER
The Nile's main source is Lake Victoria in east-central Africa, and from its farthest stream in Burundi, it extends 4,145 miles (6,670 km) in length—nearly twice the length of the Great Wall of China. The picture left shows the Nile in Egypt.

VOLCANOES

ERUPTIONS

Greatest eruption volume The volume of matter discharged in the eruption of Tambora, a volcano on the Indonesian island of Sumbawa, in April 1815, was 36–43 miles³ (150–180 km³)—a volume equivalent to that of 72,000 Great Pyramids. This compares with about 16 miles³ (65 km³) of matter ejected by Santorini (Greece) and 5 miles³ (20 km³) by Krakatau. Tambora also holds the record for the **highest death toll from a volcano:** an estimated 92,000 people were killed following the 1815 eruption.

★**Largest flood basalt eruption** The Siberian Traps eruption began 248.3 million years ago and lasted 1 million years. The volume of lava that erupted in this event is estimated at several million miles³—enough to cover the Earth's surface to a depth of a few yards.

★**HIGHEST DEATH TOLL FROM A PYROCLASTIC FLOW** On May 8, 1902, Mont Pelee on the island of Martinique in the West Indies erupted, releasing a pyroclastic flow—or *nuée ardente* ("glowing cloud")—of incandescent rock and gas that traveled down the volcano's flank at speeds of up to 100 mph (160 km/h). The pyroclastic flow enveloped the city of St. Pierre, killing some 30,000 inhabitants.

LARGERST ACTIVE VOLCANO Mauna Loa in Hawaii has the shape of a broad, gentle dome 75 miles (120 km) long and 31 miles (50 km) wide above sea level. It rises 13,680 ft. (4,170 m) and has a total volume of 10,200 miles³ (42,500 km³), of which 84.2% is below sea level. Its caldera (volcano crater), Mokuaweoweo, measures 4 miles² (10.5 km²) and is 500–600 ft. (150–180 m) deep. The volcano's last major eruption was in 1984.

Farthest distance from which a volcanic eruption has been heard

The 1883 eruption of Krakatau (Indonesia) was heard 2,908 miles (4,653 km) away by people on Rodriguez Island. This makes it the **loudest noise heard by humans** in recorded history.

Krakatau erupted with a force nearly 10,000 times that of the Hiroshima atomic bomb. It caused a wave 40 m (131 ft.) high, which carried a steamship a distance of 1.5 miles (2.5 km).

★Northernmost volcano

Mount Beerenberg is 7,470 ft. (2,276 m) high and is found on the island of Jan Mayen (71°05′N) in the Greenland Sea. It erupted on September 20, 1970, and the island's 39 inhabitants (all men who were working on whaling stations) had to be evacuated.

★Southernmost volcano

Mount Erebus, an active volcano standing 12,447 ft. (3,794 m) high, is located on Ross Island (77°35′S) in the Southern Ocean.

★Highest volcano Cerro Aconcagua, a snow-clad peak 22,834 ft. (6,960 m) high in the Andes of Argentina, is the world's highest volcano, although it is no longer active. The **highest active volcano** is Ojos del Salado (22,595 ft.; 6,887 m) on the border between Chile and Argentina.

★Youngest volcano Paricutin, 200 miles (320 km) west of Mexico City, Mexico, is a volcanic cone that erupted from a cornfield on February 20, 1943, and was active until 1953. Most of the activity occurred in the first year, when the volcanic cone grew to a height of 1,100 ft. (336 m), offering geologists a rare opportunity to witness the birth, evolution, and death of a volcano.

Largest steam rings Mount Etna, in Sicily, is the **tallest and most active volcano in Europe.** A complex physical process is causing it to emit huge steam rings, similar to smoke rings. The steam rings of Mount Etna are approximately 650 ft. (200 m) across and can last up to about 10 minutes as they slowly drift upward to a height of 3,300 ft. (1,000 m) above the volcanic vent.

The rings are thought to be due to unusual geometric conditions in the shape of the volcanic vent that produces them.

WHERE IS THE LONGEST SUBMARINE MOUNTAIN RANGE? FIND OUT ON P. 139

LAVA

★Fastest lava flow Nyiragongo, in the Democratic Republic of the Congo (formerly Zaire), erupted on January 10, 1977. Lava burst through the volcano's flank at up to 40 mph (60 km/h); around 2,000 people died when it hit the city of Goma.

Greatest modern-day landslide The landslide on Mount St. Helens on May 18, 1980, was the largest witnessed by a survivor. About 96,000 million ft.^{3} (2,800 million m^3) of rock slipped off the mountain prior to the eruption—equivalent to a block of earth nearly 0.8 miles (1.5 km) high, wide, and long.

★Longest lava cave The longest and **deepest lava cave** (an open tube down the inside of a lava flow) is Kazumura Cave on Hawaii, U.S.A. The 36.9-mile-long (59.3-km) cave descends 3,604 ft. (1,099 m) down the eastern flank of the Kilauea volcano.

Coldest erupting lava Common basaltic lavas erupt at 2,012–2,192°F (1,100–1,200°C), but the natrocarbonatite lava of Ol Doinyo Lengai, Tanzania, erupts at just 932–1,112°F (500–600°C).

MOST ACTIVE VOLCANO The world's most active volcano is Kilauea in Hawaii, U.S.A., which has erupted continually since 1983. Lava is being discharged from the volcano at a rate of 176.5 ft.³ (5 m³) per second, hence the Hawaiian name "Kilauea," which means "spewing," or "much spreading."

Greatest lava flow diversion In 1973, the Eldfell volcano on the Icelandic island of Heimaey erupted and vast quantities of molten lava flowed toward the town of Vestmannaeyjar.

One third of the town was destroyed before islanders could defend the remaining area by spraying vast quantities of water onto the approaching lava, forcing it to cool and solidify to form a series of rock dams.

VOLCANO	DATE	EFFECT
Mount St. Helens (Washington, U.S.A.)	1980	Avalanche traveled at a record 250 mph (402.3 km/h); smoke and ash rose 20,000 ft. (6,000 m); ash deposited 440 miles (800 km) away
Krakatau (Krakatau, Indonesia)	1883	10,000 times more powerful than Hiroshima bomb; rocks hurled 34 miles (55 km) into air; dust still falling 3,313 miles (5,330 km) away 10 days later
Etna (Sicily, Italy)	1669	Eruption continued for over one month; lava overran western part of city of Catania, 17 miles (28 km) from summit; up to 20,000 people killed
Vesuvius (Bay of Naples, Italy)	A.D. 79	Towns of Pompeii, Stabiae, and Herculaneum buried under cinders and ash, preserving sites until 1748; 35,000 deaths estimated
Santorini (Cyclades, Greece)	1550 B.C.	Huge explosion—estimated to be four times more powerful than 1883 eruption of Krakatau—almost completely destroyed the island

WEATHER

CLOUDS

Highest clouds The highest clouds are noctilucent clouds, which are best seen in the lower and higher latitudes. These beautiful, tenuous phenomena form at altitudes of about 50 miles (80 km), above 99.9% of the atmosphere. They can be seen after the Sun has set when, owing to their altitude, they are still lit by the Sun's rays. They are believed to be formed from a mixture of ice crystals and dust from meteors.

Highest cloud extreme The highest standard cloud form is cirrus, averaging 29,500 ft. (9,000 m), but the rare nacreous or mother-of-pearl formation may reach 80,000 ft. (24,500 m). The **lowest standard cloud form** is stratus, which lies below 1,500 ft. (460 m).

Clouds with the greatest vertical range Cumulonimbus has been observed to reach a height of nearly 65,600 ft. (20,000 m) from a base of about ground level—nearly three times the height of Mount Everest—in the tropics.

136°F (58°C) Highest recorded temperature
Al'Aziziyah, Sahara Desert, Libya, September 13, 1922

**88.5°F (31.4°C) to 67.3°F (19.6°C) Most equable
temperature** From 1927 to 1935, Garapan, on Saipan
Island in the Pacific Ocean, experienced a temperature
range of just 21.2°F (11.8°C)

58.2°F (14.6°C) Average global temperature (2004)

Most freakish temperature rise The temperature rose
from -4°F (-20°C) to 44°F (7°C) In 2 min. at Spearfish,
South Dakota, U.S.A., on January 22, 1943

Greatest temperature variation (1 day) The
temperature dropped 100°F (56°C) from 44°F (7°C) to
-56°F (-49°C) at Browning, Montana, U.S.A., on January
23–24, 1916

-90°F (-68°C) Coldest inhabited place Oymyakon,
Siberia, Russia

-128.6°F (-89.2°C) Lowest recorded temperature
Vostok, Antarctica, July 21, 1983

GREATEST PRESSURE DROP MEASURED IN A TORNADO On June 24, 2003, severe storms researcher Tim Samaras (U.S.A.) placed an instrument probe into the path of an F4 tornado near Manchester, South Dakota, U.S.A., and measured a pressure drop of 100 millibars. The tornado destroyed a 25-mile-long (40-km) stretch of the community of Manchester. The work was co-funded by National Geographic.

The F rating refers to the Fujita tornado intensity scale—an F4 being a tornado clocked at 207–260 mph (93–116 m/sec.).

RAINFALL

Greatest rainfall in 24 hours A record 73 in. (1,870 mm) of rain fell in 24 hours at Cilaos, Reunion, Indian Ocean, on March 15–16, 1952. This equals 16,653,700 lb. (6,852.9 tons) of rain per acre.

Most rainy days Mount Wai-'ale-'ale (5,148 ft.; 1,569 m) in Hawaii has up to 350 rainy days a year—an average rainfall of over 33 ft. (10 m).

Oldest fossilized raindrops On December 15, 2001, Indian geologist Chirananda De announced his discovery of the fossilized imprints of raindrops in ancient rocks in the lower Vindhyan range, Madhya Pradesh, India. These rocks prove that rain fell on Earth at least 1.6 billion years ago.

★Largest raindrops Raindrops measuring a minimum of 0.3 in. (8.6 mm) across have been detected on two occasions: in September 1995 (in Brazil) and July 1999 (in the Marshall Islands). The raindrops were measured while falling by a laser instrument on board a research aircraft in stud-

HEAVIEST RAINFALL By average annual rainfall, the wettest place is Mawsynram in Meghalaya, India, with 467 in. (11,873 mm) of rain a year. Most of the rain in Meghalaya—which means "land of the clouds"—occurs during the monsoon season, from June to September. The highest rainfall in a calendar month is 366 in. (9,300 mm) and occurred at Cherrapunji, also in Meghalaya, in July 1861.

ies by Peter V. Hobbs and Arthur Rango (both U.S.A.) of the University of Washington (U.S.A.).

SNOW & HAIL

Greatest snowfall Between 1971 and 1972, a total of 1,224 in. (31,102 mm) of snow fell at Paradise, Mount Rainier, Washington, U.S.A. The **greatest recorded depth of snow** was 37 ft. 7 in. (11.46 m) at Tamarac, California, U.S.A., in March 1911.

Worst damage toll from a snowstorm A total of 500 people died in a snowstorm that crossed the entire east coast of the U.S.A. on March 12–13, 1993. The storm, described by one meteorologist as "a storm with the heart of a blizzard and the soul of a hurricane," caused $1.2 billion worth of damage.

Heaviest hailstones Hailstones weighing up to 2.2 lb. (1 kg) were reported to have killed 92 people in the Gopalganj district of Bangladesh on April 14, 1986. The **highest death toll in a hailstorm,** however, occurred on April 20, 1888, when a total of 246 people died during a storm at Moradabad, Uttar Pradesh, India.

Largest piece of fallen ice On August 13, 1849, a piece of ice 20 ft. (6 m) long was reported to have fallen from the sky in Ross-shire, UK. The ice was clear but appeared to be composed of smaller pieces. One explanation is that hailstones were fused together by a bolt of lightning.

☆ **FASTEST JET STREAM** Jet streams are narrow, fast-flowing currents of air in the upper atmosphere. They average speeds of 250 mph (400 km/h), although the fastest measured to date is 408 mph (656 km/h) above South Uist, Western Isles, UK, at a height of 154,200 ft. (47,000 m) on December 13, 1967. Pictured here are clouds being carried by a jet stream at more than 100 mph (160 km/h) over Egypt and the Red Sea.

LIGHTNING

Most strokes in a lightning flash The majority of lightning flashes consist of several "strokes"—major pulses of current. It is these pulses that can cause some flashes to appear to flicker. The most detected in a single flash is 26, in a cloud-to-ground flash in New Mexico in 1962, recorded by Marx Brook (U.S.A.).

Longest lightning flash At any one time, about 100 lightning bolts a second hit the Earth. Typically, the actual length of these bolts can be around 5.5 miles (9 km). In 1956, meteorologist Myron Ligda (U.S.A.) observed and recorded a lightning flash, using radar, that covered a horizontal distance of 93 miles (149 km) inside clouds.

Highest death toll from a lightning strike A total of 81 people on board a Boeing 707 jet airliner died when the plane was struck by lightning near Elkton, Maryland, U.S.A., on December 8, 1963.

Most lightning strikes survived Roy C. Sullivan (U.S.A.) remains the only man in the world to survive being struck by lightning seven times. The

DRIEST PLACE For the period 1964 to 2001, the average annual rainfall for the meterological station in Quillagua in the Atacama Desert, Chile, was just 0.01 in. (0.5 mm). This discovery was made during the making of the documentary series *Going to Extremes* by Keo Films in 2001. The oddly shaped salt deposits seen above are located in a former lake bed in the desert.

"human lightning conductor" was first struck in 1942 (losing his big toenail), then again in 1969 (lost eyebrows), 1970 (left shoulder seared), 1972 (hair set on fire), 1973 (regrown hair singed and legs seared), 1976 (ankle hurt), and 1977 (stomach and chest burns). In 1983, he died by his own hand, reportedly rejected in love.

OCEANS

★**Clearest sea** The Weddell Sea, off Antarctica, has the clearest water of any sea or ocean. On October 13, 1986, scientists from the Alfred Wegener Institute in Bremerhaven, Germany, measured its clarity using a Secchi disc—a piece of black-and-white PVC measuring 1 ft. (30 cm) wide. The disc is dropped into the water and monitored until it is no longer visible. In the Weddell Sea, the Secchi disc was visible until it reached a depth of 262 ft. (80 m)—clarity similar to that of distilled water.

★**Strongest natural whirlpool** There are several permanent whirlpools in the world, caused by tides, narrow straits, and fast-flowing water.

LARGEST OCEAN The Pacific is the world's largest ocean. Excluding adjacent seas, it represents 45.9% of the world's oceans and covers 60,060,900 miles² (155,557,000 km²) in area. Its average depth is 12,925 ft. (3,940 m).

The most powerful are Moskenstraumen, near Lofoten Islands, Norway, and Old Sow, off the coast of Maine, U.S.A. Both have experienced currents measuring 17 mph (28 km/h).

Highest temperature The highest temperature recorded in the ocean is 759°F (404°C) for a hydrothermal vent, measured by a U.S. research submarine 300 miles (480 km) off the American west coast in 1985.

Strongest global current The Antarctic Circumpolar Current, or West Wind Drift, is the greatest current in the oceans. It moves at about 4.59 billion ft.³ (130 million m³) of water per second—six to seven times the flow rate of the Gulf Stream.

★ WORLD OCEANS ★

Pacific Ocean	60,060,900 miles²	(155,557,000 km²)
Atlantic Ocean	29,638,000 miles²	(76,762,000 km²)
Indian Ocean	26,469,600 miles²	(68,556,000 km²)
Southern Ocean	7,848,300 miles²	(20,327,000 km²)
Arctic Ocean	5,427,050 miles²	(14,056,000 km²)

Fastest current During the monsoon, the Somali current flows at 9 mph (12.8 km/h) in the northern Indian Ocean.

UNDERWATER

Tallest mountain Monte Pico in the Azores islands (Portugal) has an altitude of 7,711 ft. (2,351 m) above sea level and extends a record 20,000 ft. (6,098 m) from the surface to the sea floor—in total 1,317 ft. (399 m) shorter than Mt. Everest.

Longest submarine mountain range The Mid-Ocean Ridge extends 40,000 miles (65,000 km) from the Arctic Ocean to the Atlantic Ocean, around Africa, Asia, and Australia, and under the Pacific Ocean to the west coast of North America. It has a maximum height of 13,800 ft. (4,200 m) above its base on the ocean floor.

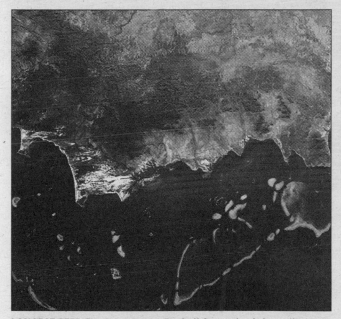

LONGEST REEF The Great Barrier Reef off Queensland, Australia, is about 1,260 miles (2,027 km) in length. It is not actually a single reef but consists of thousands of separate reefs. It is also the largest marine structure built by living creatures, as it consists of countless billions of dead and living stony corals (order Madreporaria and Scleractinia).

★**Widest continental shelf** Continental shelves are extensions of coastal plains and are characterized by broadly sloping submerged plains. About 7.4% of the world's ocean surface sits above continental shelves, which have a global average width of 48 miles (78 km). The widest shelf extends 750 miles (1,210 km) off the coast of Siberia, Russia, into the Arctic Ocean.

LARGEST . . .

Gulf The Gulf of Mexico stretches from Cape Sable in Florida, U.S.A., to Cabo Catoche in Mexico. It has a total area of 596,000 miles^2 (1,544,000 km^2) and a shoreline of 3,100 miles (5,000 km).

Bay The world's largest bay—in terms of shoreline length—is Hudson Bay, Canada, with a shoreline of 7,623 miles (12,268 km)—similar to the length of the UK coastline—and an area of 476,000 miles^2 (1,233,000 km^2). Measured by area, the Bay of Bengal in the Indian Ocean is larger, at 839,000 miles^2 (2,172,000 km^2).

Atoll Kwajalein, part of the Marshall Islands in the Pacific Ocean, is the world's largest atoll. Its coral reef, 176 miles (283 km) long, encloses a 1,100-mile^2 (2,850-km^2) lagoon.

Polynya A polynya is an area of open sea surrounded by sea ice. During the winter months of 1974, 1975, and 1976, a polynya about 620 × 220 miles (1,000 × 350 km) occurred in the Weddell Sea, Antarctica.

★**Area of still water** The still waters of the Sargasso Sea in the north Atlantic Ocean cover about 2.4 million miles^2 (6.2 million km^2). The sea is so calm that sargassum seaweed has been able to grow on it and now covers most of the surface.

LARGEST ARCHIPELAGO The world's largest archipelago is the East Indian or Malay Archipelago crescent that forms Indonesia. It is 3,500 miles (5,600 km) long and contains more than 17,000 islands—including Sipadan Island, pictured—with a combined coastline length of over 50,000 miles (80,000 km).

LARGEST DELTA The world's largest delta—a triangular area of clay, silt, and sand deposits at the mouth of a river—is the Bengal Delta created by the rivers Brahmaputra and Ganges in Bangladesh and West Bengal, India. It covers a total area of 30,000 miles² (75,000 km²)—nearly twice the size of Switzerland.

TIDES & WAVES

Highest wave The highest officially recorded sea wave—dependent on weather or climate—was calculated as 112 ft. (34 m) from trough to crest. It was measured by Lt. Frederic Margraff, of the U.S. Navy, from the USS *Ramapo* proceeding from Manila, Philippines, to San Diego, California, U.S.A., on the night of February 6–7, 1933, during a 78-mph (126-km/h) hurricane.

★Largest wave wavelength The longest wavelength (the distance between successive peaks or troughs) of any ocean wave is about 7,500 miles (12,000 km) for the tides caused by the Sun and Moon.

By way of comparison, normal wind-driven ocean waves have a wavelength of around 165–330 ft. (50–100 m).

Highest average tide The greatest tides occur in the Bay of Fundy, which divides the peninsula of Nova Scotia, Canada, from the U.S. state of Maine and the Canadian province of New Brunswick. Burncoat Head in the Minas Basin, Nova Scotia, has the greatest mean spring range, with 47 ft. 6 in. (14.5 m).

HIGHEST TSUNAMI WASH The highest known tsunami (meaning "harbor wave") was 1,719 ft. (524 m) high and occurred along the fjord-like Lituya Bay in Alaska, U.S.A., on July 9, 1958. The wave was caused by a giant landslip and moved at 100 mph (160 km/h). It would have swamped New York's Empire State Building, which, at 1,472 ft. (449 m), was the world's tallest building at the time.

Highest tide ever A tide range of 54 ft. 6 in. (16.6 m) was recorded at springs in Leaf Basin, Quebec, Canada, in 1953.

Largest continuous current system The Thermohaline Conveyor is a global system of ocean circulation, driven by differences in seawater density and salinity. It moves cold, salty water from the north Atlantic down to the Southern Ocean, where it travels east and north to the Indian and Pacific Oceans. Here it rises and becomes warm, travelling back westward where it sinks again in the north Atlantic. The entire cycle can last for 1,000 years.

★ **LARGEST UNITED NATIONS EMERGENCY APPEAL** On December 26, 2004, a tsunami wave inundated the coastlines of at least 12 countries around the Indian Ocean, resulting in the ☆ **highest death toll from a tsunami**, with up to 285,000 confirmed dead. The subsequent emergency appeal launched by the United Nations was the largest ever for a natural disaster—providing $977 million to five million people in Southeast Asia, the Seychelles, Sri Lanka, and Somalia.

THE DEEP

SALVAGE & RECOVERY

★ **Deepest aircraft recovery** A helicopter that crashed into the Pacific Ocean in August 1991 was successfully recovered by the crew of the USS *Salvoron* on February 27, 1992, from a depth of 17,251 ft. (5,258 m), allowing the cause of the crash to be studied.

★ **Deepest commercial recovery** On July 20, 1999, the U.S. spacecraft *Liberty Bell 7* was recovered from the bottom of the Atlantic Ocean, where it had sat since splashdown on July 21, 1961. The spacecraft was in over 15,000 ft. (4,500 m) of water before being raised by the ship *Ocean Project,* in a project financed by the Discovery Channel.

★**Deepest underwater salvage with divers** The UK cruiser *Edinburgh,* sunk on May 2, 1942, in the Barents Sea off northern Norway, is in 803 ft. (245 m) of water. From September 7 to October 7, 1981, 12 divers worked on the wreck in pairs, recovering 460 gold ingots.

663 ft. (202 m)
Deepest sea cave: Dean's Blue Hole, Bahamas

690 ft. (210 m)
Deepest dive by a flying bird: Thick-billed murre (*Uria lomvia*)

927.1 ft. (282.6 m)
Deepest freshwater cave dive: Nuno Gomes (South Africa), Boesmansgat Cave, South Africa

1,010 ft. (307.8 m)
Deepest seawater scuba dive: John Bennett (UK), Escarcia Point, Puerto Galera, Philippines

1,751 ft. (534 m)
Deepest dive by a bird: Emperor penguin (*Aptenodytes forsteri*)

3,937 ft. (1,200 m)
Deepest dive by a chelonian: leatherback turtle (*Dermochelys coriacea*)

5,017 ft. (1,529 m)
Deepest pinniped dive: northern elephant seal (*Mirounga angustirostris*), California, U.S.A.

6,500 ft. (2,000 m)
Deepest dive by a mammal: sperm whale (*Physeter macrocephalus*)

1.5 miles (2,400 m)
Deepest live TV broadcast: *Abyss Live* (BBC, UK), mid-Atlantic Ridge

15,000 ft. (4,500 m)
Deepest commercial recovery: U.S. spacecraft *Liberty Bell 7,* Atlantic Ocean

18,500 ft. (5,650 m)
Deepest sponges

21,414 ft. (6,526 m)
Deepest diving submersible: *Shinkai 6500* (Japan)

24,881 ft. (7,584 m)
Deepest starfish: *Porcellanaster ivanovl*

27,460 ft. (8,370 m)
Deepest fish: cuskeel (*Abyssobrotula galatheae*)

35,797 ft. (10,911 m)
Deepest point in the ocean: Challenger Deep

MOST HEAT-TOLERANT ORGANISM Strain 121 is a microbe belonging to the ancient group of bacteria-like organisms called archae. Strain 121 was discovered in superheated water from hydrothermal vents at the bottom of the Pacific Ocean, and can survive temperatures of 250°F (121°C).

★**LARGEST EYE-TO-BODY RATIO** *Vampyroteuthis infernalis*—literally, the "vampire squid from hell"—resides in tropical waters at depths of over 1,970 ft. (600 m). It has a maximum body length of 11 in. (28 cm) and eyes with a diameter of 0.9 in. (2.5 cm)—a ratio of 1:11, the greatest in the animal kingdom. The human equivalent would be eyes the size of table-tennis paddles!

Deepest shipwreck On November 28, 1996, Blue Water Recoveries Ltd (UK) discovered the wreck of the SS *Rio Grande,* using side-scanning sonar at the bottom of the South Atlantic Ocean. The find was confirmed by Blue Water on November 30, 1996, using a remotely operated vehicle. The wreck, a World War II German-blockade runner, lies at a depth of 18,904 ft. (5,762 m).

Greatest treasure recovered from a shipwreck An estimated $2 billion in gold and platinum was retrieved in August 1984 from the Czarist battleship *Admiral Nakhimov* lying 200 ft. (60 m) down off the Japanese island of Tsushima.

Also, the *Nuestra Señora de Atocha,* which sank off the Florida coast in 1622, was salvaged on July 20, 1985. The ship carried 88,000 lb. (44 tons) of gold and silver and some 70 lb. (31.75 kg) of emeralds.

DEEPEST . . .

Manned descent Jacques Piccard (Switzerland) and Donald Walsh (U.S.A.) piloted the Swiss-built U.S. Navy bathyscaphe *Trieste* to a depth of 35,797 ft. (10,911 m) in the "Challenger Deep" section of the Mariana

DEEPEST DIVING SUBMERSIBLE IN SERVICE Of the submersibles now in service, the Japanese research submarine *Shinkai 6500* is capable of diving the deepest. On August 11, 1989, it reached a depth of 21,414 ft. (6,526 m) in the Japan Trench off Sanriku, Japan. The three-person craft is 31 ft. 2 in. (9.5 m) long, 8 ft. 10 in. (2.7 m) wide, and 10 ft. 6 in. (3.2 m) high and continues to explore the seabed.

Trench on January 23, 1960. Challenger Deep is thought to be the **deepest point on Earth** and is situated 250 miles (400 km) southwest of Guam in the Pacific Ocean.

Seawater scuba dive John Bennett (UK) scuba-dived to a depth of 1,010 ft. (307.8 m) on November 6, 2001, off Escarcia Point in the Philippines. It took just over 12 minutes to descend, while the ascent took 9 hr. 36 min. to allow for decompression. Bennett used 60 air tanks.

WILDLIFE

Deepest plant The greatest depth at which plant life has been found is 882 ft. (269 m) for algae found in October 1984 by Mark and Diane Littler (both U.S.A.) off San Salvador Island in the Bahamas. These maroon-colored plants survived, even though 99.9995% of sunlight was filtered out.

LARGEST TEETH RELATIVE TO HEAD SIZE (FISH) The viperfish (*Chauliodus sloani*) has teeth so large it must open its mouth to make its jaws vertical before it can swallow prey. Its body is approximately 11 in. (28 cm) long, its head about 0.8 in. (2 cm), and its teeth are just over half this length. The teeth overlap the jaws when the mouth is closed.

The viperfish eats large prey by lowering the internal skeleton of the gills, allowing the prey to pass into the throat without interference. It can impale prey on the teeth by swimming at them, with the first vertebra behind the head acting as a shock absorber.

Deepest fish A cuskeel (family Ophidiidae) called *Abyssobrotula galatheae* has been collected from the Puerto Rico Trench at a depth of 27,460 ft. (8,370 m).

Deepest dive by a mammal The deepest dive by a mammal was made by a bull sperm whale (*Physeter macrocephalus*) in 1991 off the coast of Dominica in the Caribbean. Scientists from the Woods Hole Oceanographic Institute (U.S.A.) recorded the dive to be 6,500 ft. (2,000 m) deep, and it lasted a total of 1 hr. 13 min.

★Deepest dive by a pinniped In May 1989, scientists testing the diving abilities of northern elephant seals (*Mirounga angustirostris*) off the coast of San Miguel Island, California, U.S.A., documented an adult male that reached a maximum depth of 5,017 ft. (1,529 m).

★Largest creature never observed in its habitat Scientists do not know exactly where in the sea the *Architeuthis dux* ("king of the giant squids") lives, and so have never been able to study it, but specimens have been measured at up to 59 ft. (18 m) in length and 1,980 lb. (900 kg) in weight.

Longest animal The siphonophore *Praya dubia* (a variety of jellyfish) is considered to be the longest organism in the world, measuring up to 160 ft. (50 m)—the length of an Olympic swimming pool. This blue bioluminescent recluse lives in the mid-water zone that extends down from 1,000 ft. (300 m) below the surface. It has large, paired swimming bells at the head, and trailing behind is a long stem of reproductive units called cormidia, and thin tentacles that can deliver a powerful sting.

WATER LIFE

CRUSTACEANS

Heaviest marine crustacean An American or North Atlantic lobster (*Homarus americanus*) caught off Nova Scotia, Canada, on February 11, 1977, measured 3 ft. 6 in. (1.06 m) from the end of the tail-fan to the tip of the largest claw and weighed 44 lb. 6 oz. (20.14 kg). It was later sold to a restaurant owner in New York City, U.S.A.

Largest marine crustacean The largest of all marine crustaceans, as opposed to the heaviest, is the taka-ashigani or giant spider crab (*Macrocheira kaempferi*). One known specimen had a clawspan of 12 ft. 18 in. (3.7 m) and weighed 41 lb. (18.6 kg).

Largest land crab The robber or coconut crab (*Birgus latro*), which lives on islands and atolls in the Indo-Pacific region, weighs up to 9 lb. (4.1 kg) and has a legspan of up to 39 in. (1 m). It is almost entirely terrestrial and will drown if submerged.

Most abundant animal Copepods are crustaceans and are found almost everywhere that water is available. They include more than 12,000 species and, with krill, form the most important members of zooplankton. Copepods form groups that can reach a trillion individuals. Most are very small—less than 0.04 in. (1 mm) long—but some rare oceanic species are over 0.4 in. (1 cm) in length. They are also the **only known animal with just one eye.**

HIGHEST CRAB DENSITY An estimated 120 million red crabs (*Gecarcoidea natalis*) live exclusively on the 52-mile² (135-km²) Christmas Island in the Indian Ocean—a density of approximately one crab per square meter for the whole island. Every year (from about November until Christmas, appropriately enough), millions of the crabs swarm out of their forest burrows to mate and spawn at the coast.

★**Oldest fossil crustacean** The discovery of a complete fossilized crustacean measuring less than 0.019 in. (0.5 mm) long was announced in July 2001 by geologists Mark Williams, David Siveter (both UK), and Dieter Waloszek (Germany). At 511 million years old, this tiny life-form—found in Shropshire, UK—is the oldest crustacean ever discovered.

WHAT'S THE GREEDIEST ANIMAL IN THE WORLD?
FIND OUT ON P. 93

FISH

Fastest fish In a series of speed trials carried out at Long Key Fishing Camp, Florida, U.S.A., a cosmopolitan sailfish (*Istiophorus platypterus*) took out 300 ft. (91 m) of line in 3 seconds—equivalent to a velocity of 68 mph (109 km/h).

In comparison, the cheetah—the **fastest mammal on land over short distances**—reaches speeds of 62 mph (100 km/h).

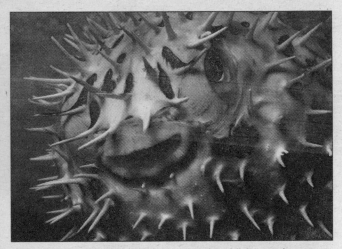

MOST POISONOUS EDIBLE FISH Many species of fish are poisonous to eat, but the most poisonous are the puffer fish (*Tetraodon*) of the Red Sea and Indo-Pacific region, which deliver a fatal poison called tetrodotoxin, one of the most powerful nonproteinous poisons. The fish's ovaries, eggs, blood, skin, liver, and intestines contain the poison, and less than 0.004 oz. (0.1 g) is enough to kill a human in as little as 20 minutes.

Largest fish The rare plankton-feeding whale shark (*Rhincodon typus*) is found in the warmer areas of the Atlantic, Pacific, and Indian oceans. The largest scientifically recorded specimen was 41 ft. 6 in. (12.65 m) long, measured 23 ft. (7 m) around the thickest part of the body and weighed an estimated 33,000–46,200 lb. (16–23 tons).

Lightest fish The Indo-Pacific dwarf goby (*Schindleria praematurus*) is just 0.47–0.74 in. (12–19 mm) long, and in terms of weight is equivalent to 14,184 fish to an ounce.

Largest predatory fish The largest predatory fish is the great white shark (*Carcharodon carcharias*). Adult specimens average 14–15 ft. (4.3–4.6 m) in length, and generally weigh 1,150–1,700 lb. (520–770 kg). Circumstantial evidence suggests that some terrifying great whites grow longer than 20 ft. (6 m).

Longest fin The largest and most common species of thresher shark (*Alopias vulpinus*) has a huge scythe-shaped caudal (tail) fin that is roughly as long as the body itself. Found worldwide in temperate and tropical seas, the shark can grow to a length of 20 ft. (6 m), of which almost 10 ft. (3 m) consists of the greatly elongated upper tail fin.

AMPHIBIANS

Largest amphibian One specimen of Chinese giant salamander (*Andrias davidianus*)—the largest of all amphibians—collected in Hunan Province, China, measured 5 ft. 11 in. (1.8 m) long and weighed 143 lb. (65 kg). Giant salamanders are also the **longest-living amphibians** and have been known to survive for 55 years.

Farthest jump by a frog A South African sharp-nosed frog (*Ptychadena oxyrhynchus*) named Santjie achieved a "triple jump" of 33 ft. 5.5 in. (10.3 m)—about half the length of a basketball court—at a frog derby held at Petersburg, KwaZulu-Natal, South Africa, on May 21, 1977. Competition jumps are the aggregate length of three consecutive leaps.

Most cold-resistant animal The wood frog (*Rana sylvatica*) is the only animal that is able to survive after it has been frozen. These frogs live north of the Arctic Circle and survive for weeks in a frozen state. Glucose in their blood acts as a kind of antifreeze that concentrates in the frogs' vital organs, thereby protecting them from damage while the rest of the body freezes solid.

★ **SMALLEST AMPHIBIAN** *Eleutherodactylus limbatus* of Cuba is 0.33–0.47 in. (8.5–12 mm) long from snout to vent when fully grown. The **largest frog** is the goliath (*Conraua goliath*), which measures up to 14.5 in. (36.8 cm) from snout to vent.

LARGEST TOAD The cane or marine toad (*Bufo marinus*) of tropical South America and Queensland, Australia (introduced, not native), averages 1 lb. (450 g) in weight. The largest-known specimen was a male owned by Håkan Forsberg (Sweden). In March 1991, it weighed 5 lb. 13.5 oz. (2.65 kg) and measured 15 in. (38 cm) from snout to vent. By comparison, the **smallest toad** is Africa's *B. taitanus beiranus,* which is just 0.9 in. (24 mm) long.

MOLLUSCS

Largest mollusc The body of a giant squid (*Architeuthis dux*) that washed ashore in Thimble Tickle Bay, Newfoundland, Canada, on November 2, 1878 was 20 ft. (6 m) long. One of its tentacles measured 35 ft. (10.7 m).

Largest oyster In 1999, a common oyster (*Ostrea edulis*) from Chesapeake Bay, Virginia, U.S.A., measured 12 in. (30.5 cm) long, 5.5 in. (14 cm) wide and weighed 8.1 lb. (3.7 kg).

ZOO & FARM ANIMALS

FARMS & MARKETS

★**Largest cattle market** Every day, an estimated 12,000–18,000 head of cattle reach Liniers Market in Buenos Aires, Argentina, to be bought or sold. The cattle market covers a total area of 84 acres (34 hectares), has 450 entry/exit pens for the cattle, 2,000 corrals for selling, and 40 weighing scales and employs approximately 4,000 people.

Largest farm ever The pioneer farm owned by Laucidio Coelho (Brazil) near Campo Grande, Mato Grosso, Brazil, covered 3,360 miles² (8,700 km²) and supported 250,000 head of cattle at the time of the owner's death in 1975. The smallest U.S. state, Rhode Island, would fit into this area three times.

Largest cattle breed Chianini cattle were brought to the Chiana Valley, Italy, from the Middle East in pre-Roman times. Four types exist, the largest of which is the Val di Chianini, found on the plains and low hills of Arezzo and Siena. Bulls average 5 ft. 8 in. (1.73 m) at the shoulder and weigh 2,865 lb. (1,300 kg), but Chianini oxen have been known to attain heights of 6 ft. 2.75 in. (1.9 m).

LARGEST HORNS (STEER) Lurch, an African watusi steer owned by Janice Wolf (U.S.A.), has horns with a circumference that measured 37.5 in. (95.25 cm) on May 6, 2003.

The ★**largest horn circumference on a bull** measured 40.75 in. (103.5 cm) on September 20, 2004, and belong to C. T. Woodie, an Ankole watusi bull owned by Duane and Kolene Gilbert (both U.S.A.).

☆ **LARGEST BEAR LITTER** A litter of five brown bears (*Ursus arctos*) were born in captivity at Zoo Kosice, Kosice-Kavecany, Slovakia, on January 6, 2002. There were three males and two females, named Miso, Tapik, Dazzle, Bubu, and Cindy. Pictured are three of the cubs being bottle-fed by their caregivers.

★ **Smallest cattle breed** The average height of the Vechur cattle breed, from the ground to the hump, is 31–35 in. (81–91 cm) for the cow and 32–41 in. (83–105 cm) for the bull. The cattle are native to Kerala, India.

Largest horn spread for domestic cattle A pair of horns from a Texas longhorn measured a total length of 98 in. (251 cm) in July 2002. The horns are owned by Jim Williams (U.S.A.) of Midland, Texas, U.S.A. Measured vertically in a straight line from the ground to the base of the horn, one was 50.5 in. (128.2 cm) and the other 48.3 in. (122.8 cm).

SHELTERS

★ **Largest dog shelter** Ute Langenkamp: lubiti Maidanezii, a dog rescue shelter near Pitesti, Romania, can comfortably house up to 3,000 dogs over an area of 490,220 ft.² (45,543 m²). The German-Romanian project has been involved in the sheltering, treating, and rehousing of dogs since May 2001.

★ **Oldest koala ever** A koala named Sarah died in 2001 aged 23 years old. Sarah was born in 1978 and lived at the Lone Pine Koala Sanctuary, Queensland, Australia. The average age for a koala is 12 years in the wild and 16 years in captivity.

★Oldest koala sanctuary The Lone Pine Koala Sanctuary, Brisbane, Queensland, Australia, was established in 1927 by Claude Reid (Australia) and still operates today. As of December 9, 2004, the sanctuary housed 137 koalas—the largest number in captivity.

ZOOS

First zoo The earliest known collection of animals was established at modern-day Puzurish, Iraq, by Shulgi, a third-dynasty ruler of Ur from 2097 to 2094 B.C.

☆Oldest elephant Lin Wang, an Asian elephant (*Elephas maximus*), died at the age of 86 on February 26, 2003, at Taipei Zoo, Taiwan. Grandpa Lin, as Lin Wang became known, carried supplies through the jungles of Myanmar for the Japanese army during World War II. He was even taken prisoner by the Chinese in 1943.

Largest lion ever Simba, a black-maned lion, had a shoulder height of 44 in. (1.11 m) in July 1970. He lived at Colchester Zoo, Essex, UK (afterward Knaresborough Zoo, North Yorkshire, UK) until his death on January 16, 1973, aged 14. He weighed 826 lb. (375 kg).

★LONGEST GIANT PANDA PREGNANCY Shu Lan, a giant panda (*Ailuropoda melanoleuca*), endured a pregnancy that lasted 200 days before giving birth to a healthy male cub on October 21, 2004, at Chengdu Research Base for Giant Pandas, Sichuan Province, China. The average pregnancy for a panda is 95–160 days.

★**LARGEST CAT HYBRID** The largest hybrid of the cat family (Felidae) is the liger (no scientific name), which is the offspring of a male lion and a tigress. Ligers typically grow larger than either parent, reaching lengths of 10–12 ft. (3–3.6 m). The size and appearance of the liger can vary, depending upon which subspecies of lion or tiger is involved. Although these hybrids could occur in the wild (where lions and tigers inhabit the same territory), such cross-breeding usually happens in zoos or private menageries.

★Largest litter of tigers born in captivity On November 18, 2003, six tigers were born to parents Bety and Conde at Buenos Aires Zoo, Argentina. The three male and three female cubs are Bengal white tigers (*Panthera tigris tigris*).

Longest tusk Excluding prehistoric examples, the longest tusks are a pair from an African elephant, *Loxodonta africana,* obtained in the Democratic Republic of the Congo and kept in the New York Zoological Society in Bronx Park, New York City, U.S.A. The right tusk measures 11 ft. 5 in. (3.49 m) along the outside curve and the left is 10 ft. 11 in. (3.35 m).

★ ANIMAL HYBRIDS ★

PARENTS	OFFSPRING
Lion + tiger	Liger; tiglon; tigon; tigron; tion
Horse + zebra	Zebrinny; zebroid; zinny; zors
Bison + cow	Beefalo; cattalo
Horse + donkey	Mule; hinny
Lion + leopard	Leopon
Camel + llama	Cama
Cow or bull + yak	Dzo
Dog + wolf	Wolfdog
Whale + dolphin	Wolphin

MAMMALS

CARNIVORES

Largest land carnivore Adult male polar bears (*Ursus maritimus*) weigh up to 1,320 lb. (600 kg) and have a nose-to-tail length of 7 ft. 10 in.–8 ft. 6 in. (2.4–2.6 m). In 1960, a bear estimated at about 1,980 lb. (900 kg) was shot on an ice pack in the Chukchi Sea off Alaska, U.S.A. It measured 11 ft. 5 in. (3.5 m) from nose to tail over the contours of the body and 4 ft. 11 in. (1.5 m) around the body.

★Largest home range for a land mammal The polar bear has the largest home range of any land mammal. Typically, it will tramp over areas of 11,500 miles² (30,000 km²)—the size of Italy—in a single year.

★Most sensitive nose for a land mammal Polar bears can detect prey, such as seals, over 18 miles (30 km) away and often under thick ice. One bear was recorded walking in a direct line for 20 miles (32 km) to reach food.

★LARGEST MARSUPIAL CARNIVORE Adult male Tasmanian devils (*Sarcophilus harrisii*) typically measure 12 in. (30 cm) to the shoulder, 30 in. (78 cm) in length, and weigh 26 lb. (12 kg). Found naturally only in Tasmania, Australia, they use their powerful jaws and long teeth to feed on mammals, birds, reptiles, and insects, eating everything—even the bones and fur.

Australia is also home to the **smallest marsupial carnivores**. The long-tailed planigale (*Planigale ingrami*) weighs up to 0.15 oz. (4.5 g) and has a body length of 2.1–2.4 in. (5.5–6.3 cm); the Pilbara ningaui (*Ninguai timealeyi*) measures 1.8–2.2 in. (4.6–5.7 cm) and weighs up to 0.33 oz. (9.4 g).

★**Largest prey** An adult male polar bear has a stomach capacity of about 150 lb. (68 kg) and is known to kill prey as large as walruses weighing 1,100 lb. (500 kg) and beluga whales at 1,320 lb. (600 kg). Its digestive system is also more adapted for processing meat than plant material, making the polar bear one of the most carnivorous bear species.

WHICH MAMMAL HAS THE LARGEST BRAIN? FIND OUT ON P. 165

Largest feline carnivore The male Siberian tiger (*Panthera tigris altaica*) averages 10 ft. 4 in. (3.15 m) in length from the nose to the tip of the tail, stands 39–42 in. (99–107 cm) at the shoulder, and weighs about 580 lb. (265 kg). Because it can go for days without eating, a Siberian tiger can eat about 100 lb. (45 kg) of meat at one sitting.

Smallest feline carnivore The rusty-spotted cat (*Prionailurus rubiginosus*) of southern India and Sri Lanka has a head-to-body length of 13.7–18.8 in. (350–480 mm), a tail of 5.9–9.8 in. (150–250 mm), and a weight of 2 lb. 3 oz. (1 kg) for the female and 3 lb. 5 oz. (1.5 kg) for the male.

★FASTEST EATER According to research published in February 2005 by Dr. Kenneth Catania at Vanderbilt University, Tennessee, U.S.A., the star-nosed mole (*Condylura cristata*) has an average food "handling time"—identifying food as edible, capturing it, eating it, and moving on to the next piece—of 230 milliseconds, with the fastest time being 120 milliseconds. The semiaquatic star-nosed mole gets its name from its 22-probed nose, which is the **most sensitive mammal touch organ**, five times as sensitive as the human hand.

RODENTS

Largest mammal group Living in every continent except Antarctica, rodents account for almost 40% of all mammal species on Earth. Out of about 4,000 mammal species, rodents make up 1,500, followed by bats, with 1,000 species.

Largest mammal colony The black-tailed prairie dog (*Cynomys ludovicianus*), a rodent of the family Sciuridae found in the western U.S.A. and northern Mexico, builds huge colonies. One single "town" discovered in 1901 contained 400 million individuals and was estimated to cover 23,700 miles² (61,400 km²), almost the size of Ireland.

★Largest rodent The capybara or carpincho (*Hydrochoerus hydrochaeris*) of South America has a head and body length of 3 ft. 3 in.–4 ft. 3 in. (1–1.3 m) and can weigh up to 174 lb. (79 kg), although one cage-fat specimen attained a record weight of 249 lb. (113 kg).

Smallest rodent At least two species vie for this record title. The northern pygmy mouse (*Baiomys taylori*) of Mexico and the U.S.A., and the Baluchistan pygmy jerboa (*Salpingotus michaelis*) of Pakistan both have a head–body length of as little as 1.4 in. (3.6 cm) and a tail length of 2.8 in. (7.2 cm).

PRIMATES

Largest primate The male eastern lowland gorilla (*Gorilla gorilla graueri*) found in the eastern Congo has a bipedal (two-footed) standing height of up to 5 ft. 9 in. (1.75 m) and weighs up to 360 lb. (163 kg).

Smallest primate Excluding tree shrews, which are normally classified separately, the smallest true primate is the pygmy mouse lemur (*Microcebus myoxinus*), which was discovered in the deciduous forests of western Madagascar. It has a head–body length of about 2.4 in. (62 mm), a tail length of 5.4 in. (136 mm), and an average weight of 1.1 oz. (30.6 g).

★Largest tree-dwelling mammal The orangutan is the largest arboreal mammal. It lives in the canopy of tropical rainforests in Borneo and Sumatra, Malaysia. Sumatran orangutan (*Pongo abelii*) and Bornean orangutan (*P. pygmaeus*) males typically weigh 183 lb. (83 kg) and measure 5 ft. (1.5 m) tall. "Orangutan" is Malay for "man of the forest."

★Fastest primate The patas monkey (*Erythrocebus patas*) of western and eastern Africa can reach speeds of 34 mph (55 km/h) over the ground. With their long, slender limbs, patas monkeys are often called "primate cheetahs."

LARGEST MAMMAL ON LAND The adult male African elephant (*Loxodonta africana*) typically weighs 8,800–15,400 lb. (3.6–6.3 tons) and stands 9 ft. 10 in.–12 ft. 1 in. (3–3.7 m) at the shoulder. *See page 162 for the largest-ever specimen.*

BURROWERS & GLIDERS

★**Largest burrower** The wombat (*Vombatus ursinus*), an Australian bear-like marsupial, can grow up to 4 ft. (1.2 m) long and weigh up to 77 lb. (35 kg). Its large paws, strong claws, and backward-opening pouch help it dig burrows up to 65 ft. (20 m) long and 6 ft. (2 m) deep.

★**Smallest burrower** Savi's pygmy shrew (*Suncus etruscus*) has an average body length of 1.4–2 in. (36–53 mm) and a tail 0.9–1 in. (24–29 mm) long, enabling it to utilize tunnels and holes dug by large earthworms!

★**Largest claws** The anterior claws on the third digit of the giant armadillo (*Priodontes maximus*) typically measure 8 in. (20 cm) long. These burrowers, found throughout South America, use their claws—the largest in the animal kingdom—for digging and ripping apart termite mounds. The armadillo is also the ★**land mammal with the most teeth,** typically having up to 100 in its jaws.

★**Largest gliding mammal** The giant flying squirrels (genus *Petaurista*) of Asia are able to "fly" between trees using the skin-membranes on the sides of their bodies, which act as a parachute. Up to 3.6 ft. (1.1 m) long, including tail, these squirrels can glide for 1,310 ft. (400 m), although the farthest recorded distance covered by one—and the ★**farthest glide by any mammal**—is 1,475 ft. (450 m), or four lengths of a football field.

★**Smallest gliding mammal** The feathertail glider (*Acrobates pygmaeus*) of Australia can glide between trees up to 82 ft. (25 m) apart—slightly more than the length of a tennis court—despite its tiny body length of just 2.5–3.1 in. (65–80 mm).

Land mammal extremes

Largest: A bull African elephant shot in 1974 measured 13 ft. 7 in. (4.16 m) to the shoulder and weighed 26,984 lb. (11.1 tons)

Tallest: A Masal bull giraffe named George stood at 19 ft. (5.8 m) tall when measured in 1959 at Chester Zoo, UK

Smallest: A typical bumblebee bat/Kitti's hog-nosed bat has a body length of 1.14–1.29 in. (29–33 mm) and weighs 0.05–0.07 oz. (1.7–2 g)

★**Smallest (nonflying):** Savi's pygmy shrews measure just 1.4–2 in. (36–53 mm) and weigh 0.05–0.09 oz. (1.5–2.6 g)

Fastest: In 1965, a 77-lb. (35-kg) adult female cheetah was recorded running at 64.3 mph (104.4 km/h) over a measured distance of 660 ft. (201.2 m)

FASTEST MARINE MAMMAL On October 12, 1958, a bull killer whale (*Orcinus orca*) was timed at 34.5 mph (55.5 km/h) in the northeastern Pacific. Similar speeds have also been reported for a Dall's porpoise (*Phocoenoides dalli*) in short bursts.

PINNIPEDS

Largest pinniped The largest of the 34 known species of pinniped—the aquatic suborder that includes seals and walruses—is the southern elephant seal (*Mirounga leonina*) of the sub-Antarctic islands. Bulls average 16 ft. 6 in. (5 m) in length, from the inflated snout to the tips of the outstretched tail flippers, have a maximum girth of 12 ft. (3.7 m), and weigh about 4,400–7,720 lb. (2,000–3,500 kg).

The **largest accurately measured specimen** was a bull caught in 1913 that measured 21 ft. 4 in. (6.5 m) and weighed at least 8,810 lb. (3.6 tons).

Smallest pinniped The female Galapagos fur seal (*Arctocephalus galapagoensis*) averages 3 ft. 11 in. (1.2 m) in length and weighs about 60 lb. (27 kg). Males are usually considerably larger, averaging 4 ft. 11 in. (1.5 m) in length and weighing about 141 lb. (64 kg).

Oldest pinniped The greatest authenticated age for a pinniped was estimated by scientists at the Limnological Institute in Irkutsk, Russia, to be 56

MOST DANGEROUS PINNIPED The carnivorous leopard seal (*Hydrurga leptonyx*) is the only species with a reputation for apparently unprovoked attacks on humans. There are a number of documented cases of leopard seals suddenly lunging through cracks in the ice to snap at people's feet. Divers have also been attacked by these seals on at least one occasion and there are instances of several people being chased across the ice over distances of up to 330 ft. (100 m) by them. Scientists believe that the seals confuse the dark vertical shape of a person with that of an emperor penguin.

years for the female Baikal seal (*Phoca sibirica*) and 52 years for the male. This estimate was based on cementum layers in the canine teeth.

Largest gray seal colony The gray seal (*Halichoerus grypus*) colony on Sable Island off Nova Scotia, Canada, numbers around 100,000 individuals every winter during the breeding season. After 18 days, the newly born pups are left to fend for themselves.

CETACEANS

Largest mammal The blue whale (*Balaenoptera musculus*) is the largest mammal—and the **largest animal**—on Earth. The whale's average length is 80 ft. (24 m) and it can weigh up to 352,000 lb. (145.1 tons). A huge specimen caught in the Southern Ocean, Antarctica, on March 20, 1947, weighed 418,000 lb. (172.3 tons), making it the **heaviest mammal recorded.** The **longest known mammal** was a female blue whale measuring 110 ft. 28 in. (33.58 m) that landed in 1909 at Grytviken, South Georgia, in the South Atlantic.

By comparison, the blue whale is 80,000,000 times heavier than the **smallest mammal!** The bumblebee bat or Kitti's hog-nosed bat (*Craseonycteris thonglongyai*) has a head–body length of only 1.14–1.29 in. (29–33 mm) and a weight of 0.05–0.07 oz. (1.7–2 g). It can be found only in a few caves on the Kwae Noi river, Kanchanaburi Province, southwest Thailand.

Slowest heartbeat in a mammal

The blue whale is presumed to have the slowest heartbeat of any warm-blooded animal, with four to eight beats per minute (dependent upon whether the whale is diving or not). By comparison, the average adult human heart beats 70 times per minute.

Loudest animal sound

Fin whales (*B. physalus*) and blue whales utter low-frequency pulses when "singing" to each other. These whales reach an amazing 188 dB on the decibel scale, creating the **loudest sounds emitted by any living source.** Using specialist equipment, scientists have detected the whale sounds 530 miles (850 km) away.

Largest mammal jaw

A jaw belonging to a sperm whale or cachelot (*Physeter macrocephalus*) and measuring 16 ft. 5 in. (5 m) long was exhibited in the Natural History Museum in London, UK. The massive lower jaw belonged to a male whale nearly 84 ft. (25.6 m) in length. Sperm whales are also the **largest-toothed whales.**

Smallest whale

There are two contenders for the smallest cetacean: Hector's dolphin (*Cephalorhynchus hectori*) and vaquita (*Phocoena sinus*), both of which can be as small as 3 ft. 11 in. (1.2 m) long.

LARGEST ANIMAL BRAIN The largest brain of any animal belongs to the sperm whale (*Physeter macrocephalus*) and weighs approximately 19 lb. 13 oz. (9 kg). In comparison, the weight of a bull African elephant's (*Loxodonta africana*) brain can reach 11 lb. 14 oz. (5.4 kg) and a human brain is, on average, 3 lb. (1.4 kg).

DENSEST FUR The sea otter (*Enhydra lutris*)—found mostly off the coast of Alaska, U.S.A.—has the densest fur of any animal, with more than 650,000 hairs per in.^{2} (101,560 hairs per cm^2). By comparison, humans typically have just 1,000 hairs per in.^{2} (156 hairs per cm^2).

HOW MUCH DID THE HEAVIEST EVER HUMAN BRAIN WEIGH? FIND OUT ON P. 23

BIRDS

SIZE

Heaviest bird of prey The male Andean condor (*Vultur gryphus*) has an average weight of 20–27 lb. (9–12 kg) and a wingspan of 10 ft. (3 m). A weight of 31 lb. (14.1 kg) has been claimed for a male California condor (*Gymnogyps californianus*), now preserved in the California Academy of Sciences in Los Angeles, U.S.A., but this species is generally much smaller than the Andean condor and rarely exceeds 23 lb. (10.4 kg).

Smallest bird of prey This title is held jointly by the black-legged falconet (*Microhierax fringillarius*) of Southeast Asia and the white-fronted or Bornean falconet (*M. latifrons*) of northwestern Borneo. Both species have an average length of 5.5–6 in. (14–15 cm), including a 2-in. (5-cm) tail, and weigh about 1.25 oz. (35 g).

Heaviest flying bird Mute swans (*Cygnus olor*) can reach 40 lb. (18 kg), although there is a record from Poland of a cob (male) that weighed 49 lb. 10 oz. (22.5 kg). It had temporarily lost the power of flight.

Largest bird Male north African ostriches (*Struthio camelus camelus*) have been recorded up to 9 ft. (2.75 m) tall and weighing 345 lb. (156.5 kg). The north African ostrich is a ratite (flightless) subspecies.

Largest eagle The Stellar's sea eagle (*Haliaeetus albicilla*) weighs between 11 and 20 lb. (5 and 9 kg) with a wingspan of 7.2–8 ft. (2.2–2.45 m). It breeds mainly in Russia, but has also been located in Korea and Japan.

Smallest flightless bird The Inaccessible Island rail (*Atlantisia rogersi*) of Inaccessible Island, South Atlantic, weighs a mere 1.04 oz. (40 g).

Largest bird egg An ostrich egg weighing 5 lb. 2 oz. (2.35 kg) was laid in June 1997 at Datong Xinda ostrich farm, Datong, Shanxi, China.

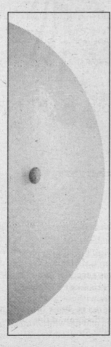

Largest avian reproductive organ The penis of the Argentinian lake drake (*Oxyura vittata*) has been measured everted (upside down) and unwound at 16.7 in. (42.5 cm).

The base of this retractable penis is covered with spines, yet the tip is soft and brush-like.

ON THE WING

Most airborne bird After leaving the nesting grounds as a youngster, the sooty tern (*Sterna fuscata*) remains aloft for three to ten years while maturing, settling on water from time to time before returning to land to breed as an adult.

Tallest flying bird Cranes, which are wading birds, belong to the family Gruidae. The largest can stand to a height of almost 6 ft. 6 in. (2 m).

SMALLEST BIRD EGG Jamaica's vervain hummingbird (*Mellisuga minima*) produces the smallest egg of any bird species (left, seen next to an ostrich egg, the largest bird egg). Two known specimens measure less than 0.39 in. (10 mm) in length and weigh 0.0128 oz. (365 mg) and 0.0132 oz. (375 mg).

Greatest distance flown A common tern (*Sterna hirundo*), banded as a juvenile on June 30, 1996, in central Finland was recaptured alive at Rotamah Island, Victoria, Australia, in January 1997, some 16,250 miles (26,000 km) away. To have reached this destination, it is believed that the bird had to travel 124 miles (200 km) a day.

Longest migration The Arctic tern (*Sterna paradisaea*) breeds north of the Arctic Circle, then flies south to the Antarctic during the northern winter and back again—a round-trip of about 21,750 miles (35,000 km), more than twice the Earth's diameter.

The terns spend a second summer in the southern hemisphere so they can use the long days to feed.

HIGHEST FLYING BIRDS The highest altitude recorded for a bird is 37,000 ft. (11,300 m) for a Ruppell's vulture (*Gyps rueppellii*), which collided with a commercial aircraft over Abidjan, Ivory Coast, on November 29, 1973. The impact damaged one of the aircraft's engines, causing it to shut down, but the plane landed safely without further incident. Sufficient remains of the bird were recovered to allow the U.S. Museum of Natural History to make a positive identification of this high-flier, which is rarely seen above 20,000 ft. (6,000 m).

ACTUAL SIZE

SMALLEST BIRD The smallest bird is the bee hummingbird (*Mellisuga helenae*) of Cuba and the Isle of Youth. Males measure 2.24 in. (57 mm) in length, half of which is taken up by the bill and tail, and weigh 0.056 oz. (1.6 g). Females are slightly larger. The bee hummingbird is believed to have the lowest weight limit of any warmblooded animal.

LONGEST . . .

Feathers A phoenix fowl (or Yokohama chicken)—a strain of red jungle fowl (*Gallus gallus*)—had a tail covert measuring 34 ft. 9.5 in. (10.6 m) in 1972. It was owned by Masasha Kubota (Japan).

Feathers on a wild bird When courting, the male crested Argus pheasant (*Rheinhartia ocellata*) displays feathers up to 5 ft. 8.4 in. (1.73 m) long.

Bills The bill of the Australian pelican (*Pelecanus conspicillatus*) is 13–18.5 in. (34–47 cm) long, but the longest beak in relation to overall body length is that of the sword-billed hummingbird (*Ensifera ensifera*). The beak measures 4 in. (10.2 cm)—longer than the bird's body if the length of the tail is excluded.

The **shortest bills** belong to the smaller swifts (the Apodidae family), and in particular the glossy swiftlet (*Collocalia esculenta*), whose bill is almost nonexistent.

SMALLEST BIRD NEST The nest (left) built by the vervain hummingbird (*Mellisuga minima*) is about half the size of a walnut shell, while the deeper but narrower one of the bee hummingbird (*M. helenae*) is thimble-sized.

LARGEST WINGSPAN OF ANY LIVING SPECIES OF BIRD A male wandering albatross (*Diomedea exulans*) of the southern oceans, caught by members of the Antarctic research ship USNS *Eltanin* in the Tasman Sea on September 18, 1965, had a wingspan of 11 ft. 11 in. (3.63 m)—the length of a Mini Cooper!

OLDEST . . .

Bird An unconfirmed age of 82 years was reported for a male Siberian white crane (*Grus leucogeranus*) named Wolf at the International Crane Foundation, Baraboo, Wisconsin, U.S.A. The **greatest irrefutable age** reported for any bird is over 80 years for a male sulphur-crested cockatoo (*Cacatua galerita*) named Cocky, who died at London Zoo in 1982.

Living pigeon Former racing pigeon Old Man, owned by George Seagroatt (UK), was born on February 16, 1980.

FASTEST BIRDS

Fastest dive: Peregrine falcon (*Falco peregrinus*) 186 mph (300 km/h)

Fastest in level flight: Ducks and geese (*Anatidae*) 56–62 mph (90–100 km/h)

Fastest on land: Ostrich (*Struthio camelus*) 45 mph (72 km/h)

Fastest swimming: Gentoo penguin (*Pygoscelis papua*) 17 mph (27 km/h)

Slowest in flight: American woodcock (*Scolopax minor*) and Eurasian woodcock (S. rusticola) 5 mph (8 km/h)

REPTILES

SNAKES

Fastest on land The black mamba (*Dendroaspis polylepis*) of tropical Africa can reach speeds of 10–12 mph (16–19 km/h) in short bursts over level ground.

Heaviest living A Burmese python (*Python molurus bivittatus*) called Baby weighed 403 lb. (182.76 kg) on November 20, 1998. She is 27 ft. (8.22 m) long with a girth of 28 in. (71.12 cm). It takes nine people to lift her and she eats four to five chickens every two weeks. Baby lives at the Serpent Safari Park in Gurnee, Illinois, U.S.A., and is owned by Lou Daddano (U.S.A.).

OLDEST LIVING CHELONIAN The term "chelonian" refers to members of the order Testudines (formerly Chelonia), including tortoises and turtles. A female giant Galapagos land tortoise (*Geochelone nigra porteri*) called Harriet, one of three collected by Charles Darwin from the Galapagos Islands in 1835, is, at 175 years, the world's oldest resident.

Born on November 15, 1830, she weighs about 180 lb. (81 kg) and currently resides at Australia Zoo, near Brisbane, Australia. (*Find out more about Harriet in the interview with Steve Irwin, on p. 172.*)

★ **Rarest** The Antiguan racer (*Alsophis antiguae*) is restricted to Great Bird Island, a 24.5-acre (9.9-hectare) area off the coast of Antigua in the Lesser Antilles. From 1996 to 2001, the number of species aged one year or more fluctuated between 51 and 114, and currently stands at about 80.

STEVE IRWIN

World-famous crocodile hunter Steve Irwin has been fascinated by reptiles since he was a boy. He runs a wildlife park in Queensland, Australia, with his wife Terri, and works at Australia Zoo, home to Harriet the giant Galapagos land tortoise.

Harriet holds the Guinness World Record for the oldest living chelonian, but is she also the oldest creature on Earth? She would definitely be the oldest living animal on Earth. She was hatched in 1830 on the island of Santa Cruz, which is in the Galapagos Islands. Harriet was collected by Sir Charles Darwin in 1835 when she was five years old, then came to Australia, after being in England, with John Wickham in 1842.

How is she? She's 175 years old and in perfect health!

Does anyone know how long Harriet will live? Nobody knows. I can't see why she shouldn't live till 200, though.

What's the worst injury an animal has given you? When we were filming our movie *The Crocodile Hunter* in 2000, a crocodile did a very severe thrash and I had all his weight on my knee—it pulled all the cartilage off both sides of the joint and snapped off pieces of bone inside my knee. I had to have an artificial knee put in.

How would somebody follow in your footsteps? If you want to become a zoologist you've got to do all the tertiary education, but don't lose your passion or enthusiasm despite the hard work and homework that you have to do. Just follow through. Passion and enthusiasm will get you everywhere you want to go in the world.

Read the full interview at www.guinnessworldrecords.com/steveirwin

MOST WIDELY DISTRIBUTED VENOMOUS SNAKE The saw-scaled or carpet viper (*Echis carinatus*), which ranges from west Africa to India, bites and kills more people in the world than any other species. The snake has an extremely toxic hemorrhagic poison and is very aggressive when provoked. A hemorrhagic poison is a toxin that causes uncontrollable bleeding.

SNAKE WITH THE LONGEST FANGS The longest fangs of any snake are those of the highly venomous gaboon viper (*Bitis gabonica*) of tropical Africa. In a specimen of 6 ft. (1.83 m) in length, they measured 2 in. (50 mm).

Heaviest venomous The eastern diamondback rattlesnake (*Crotalus adamanteus*) of the southeastern United States weighs about 12–15 lb. (5.5–6.8 kg) and is 5–6 ft. (1.52–1.83 m) in length. The heaviest diamondback rattlesnake on record weighed 34 lb. (15 kg) and was 7 ft. 9 in. (2.36 m) long.

Longest The reticulated python (*Python reticulatus*) of Southeast Asia, Indonesia, and the Philippines regularly exceeds 20 ft. 6 in. (6.25 m). The record length is 32 ft. 9.5 in. (10 m) for a specimen shot in Celebes, Indonesia, in 1912.

Oldest The greatest reliable age recorded for a snake is 40 years 3 months 14 days for a male common boa (*Boa constrictor*) named Popeye, who died at Philadelphia Zoo, Pennsylvania, U.S.A., on April 15, 1977.

CROCODILES

★**Most fatalities from an attack** On February 19, 1945, an imperial Japanese army unit guarding a stronghold on the Burmese island of Ramree was outflanked by a British naval force, and forced to cross 10 miles (16 km) of mangrove swamps to rejoin a larger force of Japanese infantry. The swamps were home to many 15-ft.-long (4.5-m) saltwater crocodiles

LARGEST CROCODILE EVER *Sarchosuchus imperator* was a prehistoric species of crocodile that lived around 110 million years ago. Recent fossilized remains found in the Sahara Desert suggest that this creature took about 50–60 years to grow to its full length of about 37–40 ft. (11–12 m) and its maximum weight of 17,600 lb. (7.25 tons).

(*Crocodylus porosus*). On the morning of February 20, of the 1,000 Japanese soldiers that entered the swamp, only 20 had survived.

Largest The estuarine or saltwater crocodile (*Crocodylus porosus*), which ranges throughout the tropical regions of Asia and the Pacific, is the world's largest crocodile. The Bhitarkanika Wildlife Sanctuary in India houses four protected estuarine crocodiles measuring more than 19 ft. 8 in. (6 m) in length, the largest being more than 23 ft. (7 m) long. There are several unauthenticated reports of specimens up to 33 ft. (10 m) in length.

TORTOISES

★**Fastest** A tortoise named Charlie covered an 18-ft. (5.48-m) course at the National Tortoise Championship at Tickhill, South Yorkshire, UK, in 43.7 seconds at a speed of 0.28 mph (0.45 km/h) on July 2, 1977.

Loneliest creature The Abingdon Island giant tortoise (*Geochelone elephantopus abingdoni*) is represented by a single living specimen, an aged male called Lonesome George. Attempts to mate him with his closest relatives on other islands have so far been unsuccessful, and so this particular subspecies of Galapagos giant tortoise is effectively extinct, though still alive.

LIZARDS

Fastest The highest burst of speed recorded for any reptile on land is 21.7 mph (34.9 km/h) by a *Ctenosaura,* a spiny-tailed iguana from Central America.

Largest The male Komodo dragon (*Varanus komodoensis*), otherwise known as the Komodo monitor or ora, averages 7 ft. 5 in. (2.25 m) in length and weighs about 130 lb. (59 kg). It is found on the Indonesian islands of Komodo, Rintja, Padar, and Flores.

PREHISTORIC LIFE

SIZE

★**Tallest mounted dinosaur skeleton** A *Brachiosaurus brancai* skeleton from Tanzania was constructed from the remains of several individuals. It measures 72 ft. 10 in. (22.2 m) long and has a raised head height of 46 ft. (14 m).

SMALLEST DINOSAUR The chicken-sized *Compsognathus* of southern Germany and southeast France measured 2 ft. (60 cm) from the snout to the tip of the tail and weighed about 6 lb. 8 oz. (3 kg).

★**Thickest dinosaur skull** *Pachycephalosaurus,* a dome-headed herbivore that lived during the Late Cretaceous period about 76 to 65 million years ago, had a skull 2 ft. (60 cm) long with a bone dome 8 in. (20 cm) thick.

Longest dinosaur A diplodocid excavated in 1980 from New Mexico, U.S.A., and reconstructed in 1999 at the Wyoming Dinosaur Center, U.S.A., was 134 ft. (41 m) long—equivalent to five buses.

★**Dinosaur with the longest neck** Fossils found in Oklahoma, U.S.A., in 1994, indicate that the sauropod *Sauroposeidon* was a herbivore with a neck that could stretch up to 55 ft. (17 m). Individual *Sauroposeidon* vertebrae have been found measuring up to 4 ft. (1.2 m) long. *Sauroposeidon* lived about 110 million years ago, during the Middle Cretaceous period.

Dinosaur with the longest tail The diplodocid *Diplodocus* was a long-necked sauropod dinosaur from the Late Jurassic period, 155 to 145 million years ago, with a tail 43–45 ft. (13–14 m) long.

★Largest carnivore coprolite In 1995, coprolite (fossilized excrement) from a *Tyrannosaurus rex* was discovered that measured 19.6 in. (50 cm) across and weighed about 15 lb. 6 oz. (7 kg).

OLDEST . . .

★Duck-billed dinosaur Fossils of the hadrosaur *Protohadros byrdi*, found near Flower Mound, Texas, U.S.A., in 1994 by Gary Byrd (U.S.A.), are thought to date back 95.5 million years.

★Tyrannosauroid *Dilong paradoxus*, the oldest known ancestor of *T. rex*, lived between 139 and 128 million years ago. It measured some 5 ft. (1.5 m) in length and stood on two legs. There is also evidence that this creature had hair-like protofeathers on its jaw and the tip of its tail.

DINOSAUR NAMES

Archaeopteryx—"ancient wing"

Brachiosaurus brancai—"arm lizard"

Compsognathus—"pretty jaw"

Dilong paradoxus—"dilong," from the Mandarin Chinese word for "emperor" and "dragon"; "paradoxus," referring to the creature's unusual features

Diplodocus—"double-beamed"

Dromornis stirtoni—"Stirton's thunder bird," after paleontologist Reuben Stirton

Pachycephalosaurus—"thick-headed lizard"

Pederpes finneyae—"Peder"—Norwegian for Peter (Peter Aspen, discoverer), "erpes" meaning "crawler," and "finneyae" after Sarah Finney, who prepared the fossil for study

Pikaia gracilens—After Mount Pika, British Columbia, and "gracilens," meaning "slender"

Protarchaeopteryx—"primitive, or first, ancient wing"

Protohadros byrdi—"Byrd's primitive hadrosaur" (duck-billed)—or "first hadrosaur"; discovered by Gary Byrd

Sauroposeidon—"earthquake god lizard"

Sinornithosaurus millenii—"millennium Chinese bird-lizard"

Titanis walleri—"terror bird"

Tyrannosaurus rex—"tyrant lizard king"

D. paradoxus was discovered in the famous fossil beds of Liaoning Province, China.

★**Known chordate** *Pikaia gracilens* is the oldest known chordate (a member of the phylum to which humans and all vertebrates belong). It lived during the Middle Cambrian age, over 500 million years ago. The first *P. gracilens* specimen was found in the Burgess Shale fossil site, British Columbia, Canada.

P. gracilens resembled a contemporary jawless marine invertebrate called the lancet.

BIRDS

Largest prehistoric bird The flightless *Dromornis stirtoni* was a huge emu-like creature that lived in central Australia between 15 million and 25,000 years ago. Fossilized leg bones found near Alice Springs in 1974 indicate that the bird must have stood about 10 ft. (3 m) tall and weighed about 1,100 lb. (500 kg).

★**Most complete feathered dinosaur fossil** In April 2001, a complete fossil of *Sinornithosaurus millenii,* a relative of the *Velociraptor,* was

discovered by farmers at the Yixian Formation fossil bed, Liaoning Province, China. It is approximately 2 ft. (60 cm) long, com-

★**FIRST NONFLYING BIRD** The earliest nonflying bird is the feathered dinosaur *Protarchaeopteryx.* A fossil was found in Liaoning Province, northeastern China, in 1997. The size of a turkey and similar in appearance to carnivorous therapod dinosaurs, this species had relatively short arms and symmetrical feathers—evidence that it could not fly.

The *Protarchaeopteryx* is believed to be an ancestor of the **first flying bird,** the *Archaeopteryx,* pictured left.

pletely covered in downy fluff and primitive feathers, and resembles a large duck with a long tail. This is the first time a complete feathered fossil has been found, and supports the theory that present-day birds evolved from dinosaurs.

Largest prehistoric carnivorous bird The *Titanis walleri* had a total body height of 8 ft. 2 in. (2.5 m) and its weight probably reached 440 lb. (200 kg). It is known to have lived until the Late Pleistocene (Ice Age).

FOOTPRINTS

Longest set of dinosaur footprints The Cal Orcko quarry near Sucre, Bolivia, contains more than 5,000 individual dinosaur footprints. More than 250 trackways have been identified among these prints, the longest of which measures some 1,150 ft. (350 m) in length and was made by a therapod dinosaur around 68 million years ago.

First animal to walk on land Remains of a tetrapod, *Pederpes finneyae*, discovered in 1971 north of Dumbarton, West Dunbartonshire, UK, are

★ SMALLEST DINOSAUR FOOTPRINT The smallest dinosaur footprint discovered to date measures just 0.7 in. (1.78 cm) from the heel to the tip of digit III. It was discovered on the Isle of Skye, Highland, UK, by Dr. Neil Clark (UK, pictured) of the Hunterian Museum of the University of Glasgow, UK, and announced in June 2004. The footprint was made during the Middle Jurassic period, about 165 million years ago.

LARGEST HERBIVORE DINOSAUR The largest ever land animals were sauropod dinosaurs, a group of long-necked, long-tailed, four-legged plant-eaters that lumbered around most of the world in the Jurassic and Cretaceous periods, 208–65 million years ago. The largest measured 131 ft. (40 m) and weighed up to 220,400 lb. (110 tons). The picture above shows a femur (thigh bone) from one of these creatures.

LARGEST DINOSAUR EGG COLLECTION The Heyuan Museum, Guangdong Province, China, held 10,008 individual dinosaur eggs as of November 2004. All come from the Late Cretaceous period (89–65 million years ago).

about 350 million years old. The legs and one complete foot were identified by Dr. Jenny Clack (UK) of the University Museum of Zoology, University of Cambridge, UK, and were announced on July 4, 2002.

☆ **Most dinosaur footprints discovered in one place** The Bolivian Cal Orcko quarry has a limestone wall 0.5 miles (800 m) long and 850 ft. (260 m) high that contains more than 5,000 individual dinosaur footprints. The variety of prints demonstrates that dinosaur species were diverse right up to the point of their extinction, 65 million years ago.

HOW BIG WAS THE LARGEST CROCODILE EVER? FIND OUT ON P. 174

MICROSCOPIC LIFE

★ DISEASES ★

Most common (noninfectious)	Periodontal disease (e.g. gingivitus)	Affects 60–90% of schoolchildren and the majority of adults
Most common (infectious)	Common cold (family of rhinoviruses)	At least 40 different airborne or direct-contact viruses, almost universal
Most virulent (reemerging)	Dengue (and dengue hemorrhagic fever)	275,000 cases in tropical Central and South America
Most virulent (viral)	Ebola hemorrhagic fever	Kills 90% of those who contract it; 1,200 deaths since first discovered in 1976
Oldest contagious	Leprosy	Described in ancient Egypt in 1350 B.C.
Rarest	Smallpox	Zero cases since 1978
Worst flesh-eating	Necrotizing fasciitis	Attacks layer of tissue below the skin and requires surgical removal of tissue

According to the World Health Organization, there are six contenders for the **deadliest disease** record: HIV, tuberculosis, malaria, measles, pneumonia, and diarrheal diseases caused 90% of all deaths from infectious diseases as of 1999. HIV is the ☆ **fastest growing disease.**

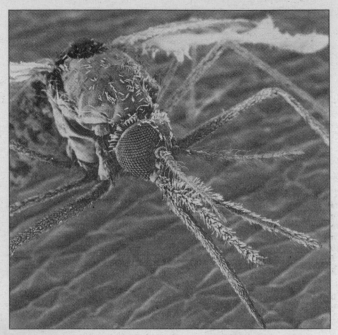

MOST DANGEROUS PARASITE The malarial parasites of the genus *Plasmodium,* carried by mosquitoes of the genus *Anopheles,* have, excluding wars and accidents, probably been responsible for half of all human deaths since the Stone Age. According to 1998 World Health Organization estimates, malaria causes more than 1 million deaths a year and is endemic in a total of 101 countries and territories.

BACTERIA

Deadliest natural toxin The anaerobic bacterium of spoiled food, which causes botulism (*Clostridium botulinum*) is so deadly (more so than strychnine, arsenic, or even snake venoms) that one pound (450 g) could, in theory, wipe out the human race.

Largest bacterium According to the journal *Science,* the bacterium *Thiomargarita namibiensis* (Sulfur Pearl of Namibia) is about 750 times larger than the typical bacterium—and visible to the naked eye.

☆**Pathogen with the highest mortality and morbidity rates** One third of the world's population is infected with *Mycobacterium tuberculosis,* the bacterium that causes tuberculosis (TB). About 8 million people con-

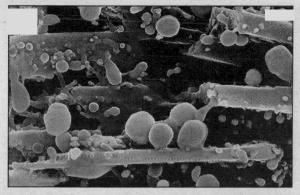

★ SMALLEST BACTERIA The smallest living bacteria, and the smallest organisms discovered to date, are "nanobes." Measuring just 20–150 nm (nanometers) across, they were found in sandstone samples 2–3 miles (3–5 km) beneath the ocean floor by Dr. Phillippa Uwins (Australia) and colleagues from the University of Queensland, Australia. These organisms are around 10 times smaller than the smallest conventional bacteria.

tract TB each year, and 1 million die from it. It is estimated that someone is infected by absorbing TB bacilli (germs) every second.

Oldest living bacteria In 2000, bacteria trapped in suspended animation inside salt crystals for 250 million years were revived and cultured by U.S. scientists. Designated *Bacillus 2–9–3,* this species is 10 times older than the previous oldest revived bacteria.

EXTREMOPHILES

Acid resistant The most acidic conditions in which microbial (or any) life has been discovered to survive is pH 0, equivalent to hydrochloric acid. Several organisms are known to thrive in these conditions—including *Cyanidium caldarium,* which lives in the vents of active volcanoes.

Alkaline resistant A bacteria discovered in 2003 near Chicago, Illinois, U.S.A., lives in groundwater contaminated by more than a century's worth of industrial iron slag dumping, where it survives pH levels of up to 12.8. By way of comparison, a pH of 12.8 is equivalent to sodium hydroxide or floor stripper.

Radiation resistant The bacterium *Deinococcus radiodurans* can withstand atomic radiation of 6.5 million roentgens, or 10,000 times more than the radiation levels that an average human could withstand.

LONGEST QUARANTINED ISLAND Gruinard Island off the west coast of Scotland, UK, was quarantined in 1942 following a release of anthrax to wipe out a flock of sheep. The test was ordered at a time when it was feared that Adolf Hitler might launch chemical or biological attacks on Britain. The quarantine was not lifted until April 24, 1990, a total of 48 years later.

The island was declared safe after a junior defense minister traveled to the 520-acre (210-ha) island to remove the red warning sign.

Longest survival in space From April 7, 1984, to January 11, 1990, *E. coli* bacteria cells survived unshielded on board NASA's Long Duration Exposure Facility satellite in Earth orbit.

In November 1969, hardware samples removed from the U.S. unmanned lunar probe *Surveyor 3* were returned to Earth by the crew of *Apollo 12*. Analysis of the hardware revealed bacterial organisms (*Streptococcus mitis*)—which had contaminated *Surveyor 3* before its launch on April 17, 1967—had survived over two-and-a-half years in space.

The **highest altitude** at which bacteria has been discovered is 25.5 miles (41.14 km).

WHERE WOULD YOU FIND THE MOST HEAT-TOLERANT ORGANISMS ON THE PLANET? FIND OUT ON P. 145

★**LONGEST FOSSIL RECORD** Stromatolites have the longest fossil record of any life-form on Earth. These cauliflower-shaped, rock-like structures are formed by the activity of cyanobacteria (blue-green algae), and appeared on Earth 3.5 billion years ago, during the Precambrian era. In 1954, a colony of living stromatolites was found in Shark Bay, Australia, with forms similar to these ancient ancestors.

VIRUSES

Largest virus The Mimivirus contains 900 genes and has a diameter of 0.0000157 in. (400 nm). It was discovered in 1992 in a sample from a water cooling tower in Bradford, UK. The virus was examined by researchers at the National Center for Scientific Research in Paris, France, who released their results on March 27, 2003, in the journal *Science*. Mimivirus has genetic similarities to the virus family that includes smallpox.

Most HIV sufferers In December 2003, South Africa had 5.3 million people infected with HIV (Human Immunodeficiency Virus)—around an eighth of the population. In December 2004, 39.4 million people worldwide had HIV, which can lead on to Acquired Immune Deficiency Syndrome (AIDS).

★**Only animal immune to rabies** The hyena is the only wild animal that is naturally immune to rabies. Researchers studied several hundred hyenas in the Serengeti, Africa, for up to 13 years and discovered that hyenas seem to be able to carry the virus without displaying any of the usual symptoms associated with it, i.e. hyperactivity, paralysis, and death.

WILD PLANTS

PLANTS

Largest single flower The mottled orange-brown and white parasite *Rafflesia arnoldii* has the largest of all flowers—up to 3 ft. (91 cm) wide and weighing around 24 lb. (11 kg). Their petals are 0.75 in. (1.9 cm) thick.

★**Largest bloom** An example of *Amorphophallus titanum* on display at the Botanical Gardens of Bonn University, Germany, was 10 ft. (3.06 m) tall on May 23, 2003. The species was discovered in Sumatra, Indonesia, in 1878, and has a very unpleasant smell. The **smelliest flower** is the "corpse flower." Its "rotting-flesh" odor can be detected 0.5 mile (0.8 km) away.

Smallest seed The seeds of epiphytic orchids (non-parasitic plants growing on others) number 28.13 billion per ounce (992.25 million seeds per gram)—similar in size to a speck of dust.

Largest seed The giant fan palm *Lodoicea maldivica*, commonly known as the "double coconut" or "coco de mer," is found wild only in the Seychelles. Its single-seeded fruit weighs up to 44 lb. (20 kg)—equivalent to the weight of approximately six newborn babies.

Most massive plant In December 1992, a network of quaking aspens (*Populus tremuloides*) growing from a single root system in the Wasatch

Mountains, Utah, U.S.A., was estimated to cover a total of 106 acres (43 hectares) and weigh 13,227,720 lb. (6,600 tons). The organism—nicknamed "Pando" (from the Latin for "I spread")—looks like a forest of trees, but is, in fact, what the scientists studying it call "suckers"—plants that have grown from the root system of a single tree.

Most poisonous plant Based on the amount it takes to kill a human, the most poisonous common plant in the world is the castor oil plant (*Ricinus communis*). According to the *Merck Index: An Encyclopedia of Chemicals, Drugs, and Biologicals* (1997), a dose of 2 millionths of an ounce (70 micrograms) of castor oil is enough to kill a person weighing 160 lb. (72 kg). The plant's poison is called ricin and is actually a protein found in the seeds of the castor bean. One gram of ricin is approximately 6,000 times more poisonous than cyanide and 12,000 more poisonous than rattlesnake venom.

Largest prey of any carnivorous plant Carnivorous plants belonging to the Nepenthaceae family (genus *Nepenthes*)—particularly *N. rajah* and *N. rafflesiana*—have been known to eat large frogs, birds, and even rats. They do so by using color, smell, and nectar to attract the prey, then trapping

LONGEST SEAWEED Pacific giant kelp (*Macrocystis pyrifera*) can reach 195 ft. (60 m) long. It grows at a rate of 18 in. (45 cm) in one day.

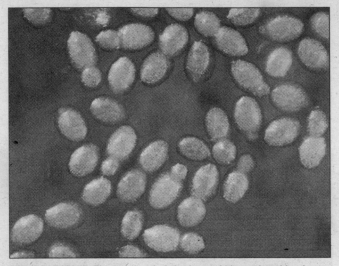

SMALLEST FRUIT The smallest fruit in the world is produced by the smallest flowering plant, the floating duckweed, which belongs to the genus *Wolffia*. The fruit of *W. augusta* is only 1/100th of an inch long (0.25 mm) and weighs about 1/400,000 of an ounce (70 micrograms)—smaller than a single grain of table salt.

and digesting them using enzymes. These species are commonly found in the rainforests of Asia, in particular Borneo, Indonesia, and Malaysia.

Most selective carnivorous plant *Nepenthes albomarginata* is the most selective of all carnivorous plants, attracting and feeding only on foraging termites called *Hospitalitermes bicolor.* Growing in the rainforests of Malaysia and Indonesia, *N. albomarginata* is also the only plant to offer its own tissue to secure a meal: it grows a ring of edible white hairs (called trichomes) that attracts the termites, which then slip down the "throat" of the plant to be digested.

Most dangerous stinger New Zealand's tree nettle (*Urtica ferox*) injects toxins into the skin powerful enough to kill dogs and horses. In one case, the plant is known to have killed a man within just five hours of his making contact with it.

Rarest plant Only 46 mandrinettes (*Hibiscus fragilis*) are left—at two locations on Mauritius in the Indian Ocean.

★**LARGEST FAMILY OF PLANTS** The largest family of plants is generally acknowledged to be the orchid family (Orchidaceae), with 25,000 species officially listed as of April 2004. The rate at which new orchids are confirmed, however, suggests that there are in excess of 30,000 species in total. Orchids occupy nearly all of the world's habitats except on the continent of Antarctica and underwater.

TREES . . .

★**Largest burl** Tree burls are abnormal swellings on branches or stems following a disturbance to wood cells in the cambial layer under the bark. The largest ever weighed 44,888 lb. (20,361 kg) and measured 61 ft. 4 in. (18.7 m) around its widest point when it was cut and moved in 1976. It was originally found growing at the base of a 351-year-old Sitka spruce (*Picea sitchensis*) tree in Port Mc-Neill, British Columbia, Canada.

★**Thickest bark** The bark of the giant sequoia (*Sequoiadendron giganteum*) growing in the Sierra Nevada mountains of California, U.S.A., varies in thickness between 10 and 48 in. (25 and 121 cm).

Highest ring count "Prometheus," a bristlecone pine (*Pinus longaeva*) felled in 1963 on Mount Wheeler, Nevada, U.S.A., had a record ring count of 4,867. The tree grew in a harsh environment and was possibly closer to 5,200 years old. This makes it the **oldest tree** ever recorded growing on Earth.

EX-TREE-MES

Tallest living: "Stratosphere Giant," a coast redwood (*Sequoia sempervirens*) in Humboldt Redwoods State Park, California, U.S.A., measures 370 ft. (112.7 m).

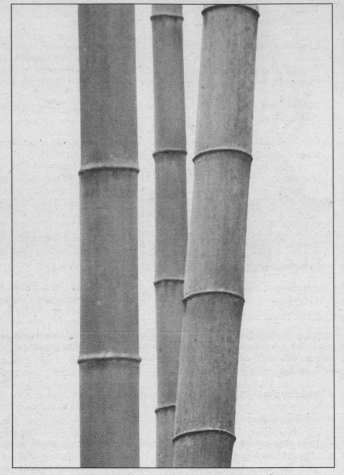

FASTEST GROWING PLANT Certain species of bamboo grow at up to 35 in. (91 cm) a day—a rate of 0.00002 mph (0.00003 km/h). At such a speed, the length of bamboo seen above would have taken just three hours to grow.

The **fastest growing flowering plant** is the *Hesperoyucca whipplei* of the Liliaceae family, one example of which grew 11 ft. 11 in. (3.65 m) in 14 days—a rate of about 10 in. (25.4 cm) a day. The **slowest flowering plant** is Bolivia's rare *Puya raimondii* (which is also the **largest herb**). The panicle (a cluster of flowers) emerges after about 80–150 years.

Tallest ever measured: A *Eucalyptus regnans* at Mount Baw Baw, Victoria, Australia, measured 470 ft. (143 m) in 1885.

Largest living: "General Sherman," a giant sequoia (*Sequoiadendron giganteum*) growing in Sequoia National Park, California, U.S.A., stands 271 ft. (82.6 m) tall, has a diameter of 27 ft. 2 in. (8.2 m), and a circumference of approximately 85 ft. (25.9 m)—enough wood to make over 5 billion matches.

Rarest: Just 43 adult Wollemi pines (*Wollemia nobilis*) exist—in Wollemi National Park, Australia.

Earliest species: The maidenhair (*Ginkgo biloba*) of China appeared about 160 million years ago.

Remotest: A Norwegian spruce (*Picea abies*) on Campbell Island, Antarctica, is more than 119.8 nautical miles (222 km) away from another tree.

CULTIVATED PLANTS

☆**Heaviest cantaloupe (muskmelon)** Scott and Mardie Robb (both U.S.A.) grew a cantaloupe that weighed 64 lb. 13 oz. (29.4 kg) at the Alaska State Fair, Palmer, U.S.A., on August 16, 2004.

Floral arrangement with most types of flowers A flower arrangement containing 1,010 different types of flowers was created on July 21, 2002, by 34 designers at the Floriade, Vijfhuizen, the Netherlands, in an event organized by The Flower Council of Holland. The arrangment measured 360 ft. (110 m) long, 3.2 ft. (1 m) high, and was built on a stand 9 ft. 9 in. (3 m) above the ground.

☆**Largest display of potato varieties** A total of 589 varieties of potato were shown on the Three Countries Potatoes display, sponsored by Thompson and Morgan, Furrows (Ford) Motors, and the Shropshire Horticultural Society, and held at the Shrewsbury Flower Show on August 13–14, 2004. The potato varieties on show included Adam's Apple, Russian Banana, and Voyager.

★**Largest flower auction** The world's largest flower auction and flower market is Bloemenveiling Aalsmeer (VBA) in Aalsmeer, the Netherlands. Every weekday, approximately 19 million flowers and 2 million plants of more than 12,000 varieties are sold, with a daily turnover of €6 million ($7.2 million).

The total area of the building covers 10 million ft.^{2} (999,000 m^2)—equal to 165 football fields.

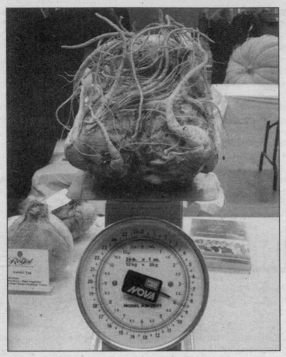

HEAVIEST PARSNIP The heaviest parsnip was grown by Norman Lee Craven (Canada) and weighed 8 lb. 6 oz. (3.8 kg) on November 4, 2003, at the Royal Agriculture Winter Fair, Ontario, Canada.

★**Most blooms in one night by the same plant** During the night of August 12–13, 2004, a night-blooming cereus (*Selenicereus grandiflorus*) produced 40 blooms. The plant is owned by Michie Taylor (U.S.A.). Also known as Queen of the Night, *S. grandiflorus* belongs to the cactus family. The buds bloom once per year, during midsummer, and generally wilt before dawn. The following evening, a further 23 bloomed.

☆**Largest carpet of flowers** The largest carpet of flowers measured 81,164 ft.² (7,540.4 m²) on July 13, 2004. The Union Jack design that formed the carpet was created by The Real Flower Petal Confetti Company using red, white, and blue delphiniums grown in Wick, Worcestershire, UK.

Tallest topiary Since 1983, Moirangthem Okendra Kumbi (India) has been shaping the shoots of a sky flower bush (*Duranta repens variegata*) in his "Hedge to Heaven" garden in Manipur, India, which has grown to a height of 61 ft. (18.59 m). Overall, with the help of a specially constructed ladder, he has cut 41 structural shapes repeating a design of a rounded umbrella followed by two discs.

★Oldest potted plant A prickly cycad (*Encephalartos altensteinii*), which was brought from South Africa to the UK and planted in 1775, is on display in the Palm House, Royal Botanical Gardens, Kew, Surrey, UK. These tree-fern-like cycads are often called "living fossils," as they are among the oldest surviving species of plants; scientists have established that they were growing more than 200 million years ago, during the Permian era.

Tallest homegrown cactus A homegrown cactus (*Cereus uruguayanus*) grown by Pandit S. Munji (India) in Dharwad, Karnataka, India, measured 70 ft. (21.3 m) on January 1, 2004. The "hedge cactus" was planted in January 1990 and typically grows to 19 ft. (6 m).

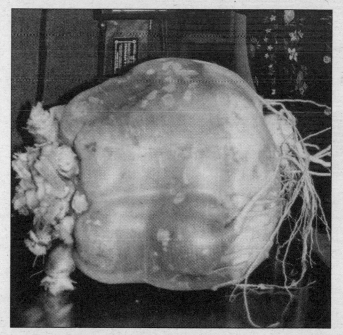

☆**HEAVIEST TURNIP** The heaviest turnip weighed 39 lb. 3 oz. (17.7 kg) and was grown by Scott and Mardie Robb (both U.S.A.), who presented it at the Alaska State Fair, U.S.A., on September 1, 2004.

☆**Largest vine** The Great Vine at Hampton Court Palace, Surrey, UK, has a circumference of 12 ft. 5 in. (3.8 m) and branches typically measuring up to 108 ft. (33 m) long. The longest branch measured 246 ft. (75 m) as of January 2005. It was planted by the famous gardener Lancelot "Capability" Brown (UK) in 1768 when he was head gardener to King George III.

★**Largest blossoming plant** The Chinese wisteria (*Wisteria sinensis*) at Sierra Madre, California, U.S.A., was planted in 1892 and by 1994 had branches measuring 500 ft. (152 m) long, covered a total area of 1 acre (0.4 ha), and weighed 48,500 lb. (22 tons).

An estimated 1.5 million blossoms were produced during the five-week blossoming period.

★**Tallest zinnia** The tallest zinnia (*Zinnia elegans*) measured 12 ft. 6 in. (3.81 m) on November 16, 2004, and was grown by Everett W. Wallace Jr., and Melody Wagner (both U.S.A.) in Riegelwood, North Carolina, U.S.A.

LARGEST PERMANENT HEDGE MAZE The Peace Maze at Castlewellan Forest Park, County Down, UK, is 2.771 acres (11, 215 m²) in area and has a total path length of 2.184 miles (3.515 km). It was designed by Beverley Lear (UK) and created by the Forest Service, Northern Ireland, and members of the public. It opened on September 12, 2001.

★ HEAVIEST FRUIT AND VEGETABLES ★

FRUIT/VEGETABLE	WEIGHT	NAME	DATE
Apple	3 lb. 11 oz. (1.67 kg)	Alan Smith (UK)	1997
Avocado	4 lb. 6 oz. (1.99 kg)	Anthony Llanos (Australia)	1992
Beet	51 lb. 9.4 oz. (23.4 kg)	Ian Neale (UK)	2001
Brussels sprout	18 lb. 3 oz. (8.3 kg)	Bernard Lavery (UK)	1992
Cabbage	124 lb. (56.24 kg)	Bernard Lavery (UK)	1989
Cabbage (Red)	42 lb. (19.05 kg)	R. Straw (UK)	1925
☆Cantaloupe	64 lb. 13 oz. (29.4 kg)	Scott & Mardie Robb (U.S.A.)	2004
Carrot	18 lb. 13 oz. (8.61 kg)	John Evans (U.S.A.)	1998
Cauliflower	54 lb. 3 oz. (24.6 kg)	Alan Hattersley (UK)	1999
Celery	63 lb. 4.8 oz. (28.7 kg)	Scott & Mardie Robb (U.S.A.)	2003
Cherry	0.76 oz. (21.69 g)	Gerardo Maggipinto (Italy)	2003
Courgette (Zucchini)	64 lb. 8 oz. (29.25 kg)	Bernard Lavery (UK)	1990
Cucumber	27 lb. 5.3 oz. (12.4 kg)	Alfred J. Cobb (UK)	2003
Garlic head	2 lb. 10 oz. (1.19 kg)	Robert Kirkpatrick (U.S.A.)	1985
Gooseberry	2.15 oz. (61.04 g)	K. Archer (UK)	1993
Gourd	94 lb. 5.7 oz. (42.8 kg)	Robert Weber (Australia)	2001
Grapefruit	6 lb. 12 oz. (3.065 kg)	Debbie Hazelton (Australia)	1995
★Jackfruit	76 lb. 4.4 oz. (34.6 kg)	George & Margaret Schattauer (U.S.A.)	2003
Kohlrabi	63 lb. 15 oz. (29 kg)	Dave Iles (U.S.A.)	2004
Leek	17 lb. 13 oz. (8.1 kg)	Fred Charlton (UK)	2002
Lemon	11 lb. 9.7 oz. (5.265 kg)	Aharon Shemoel (Israel)	2003
Mango	4 lb. 4 oz. (1.94 kg)	John Painter (U.S.A.)	1999
Vegetable marrow	135 lb. (61.23 kg)	John Handbury (UK)	1998
Onion	15 lb. 15.5 oz. (7.24 kg)	Mel Ednie (UK)	1994
Parsnip	8 lb. 6 oz. (3.8 kg)	Norman Lee Craven (Canada)	2003
Peach	25.6 oz. (725 g)	Paul Friday (U.S.A.)	2002
Pear	4 lb. 8 oz. (2.1 kg)	Warren Yeoman (Australia)	1999
Pineapple	17 lb. 12 oz. (8.06 kg)	E. Kamuk (Papua New Guinea)	1994
Potato	7 lb. 11 oz. (3.5 kg)	K. Sloane (UK)	1994
☆Potato (Sweet)	81 lb. 9 oz. (37 kg)	Manuel Pérez Pérez (Spain)	2004
☆Pumpkin	1,446 lb. (655.9 kg)	Allan Eaton (Canada)	2004
Quince	5 lb. 2 oz. (2.34 kg)	Edward Harold McKinney (U.S.A.)	2002
Radish	68 lb. 9 oz. (31.1 kg)	Manabu Ono (Japan)	2003
Rhubarb	5 lb. 14 oz. (2.67 kg)	E. Stone (UK)	1985
Rutabaga	75 lb. 12 oz. (34.35 kg)	Scott & Mardie Robb (U.S.A.)	1999
Squash	962 lb. (436 kg)	Steve Hoult (Canada)	1997
Strawberry	8.14 oz. (231 g)	G. Andersen (UK)	1983
Tomato	7 lb. 12 oz. (3.51 kg)	G. Graham (U.S.A.)	1986

★ TALLEST PLANTS ★

PLANT	HEIGHT	NAME	DATE
☆ Amaranthus	15 ft. 1.4 in. (4.61 m)	David Brenner (U.S.A.)	2004
Brussels sprout	9 ft. 3 in. (2.8 m)	Patrice and Steve Allison (U.S.A.)	2001
Cactus (homegrown)	70 ft. (21.3 m)	Pandit S. Munji (India)	2004
Celery	9 ft. (2.74 m)	Joan Priednieks (UK)	1998
Chrysanthemum	14 ft. 3 in. (4.34 m)	Bernard Lavery (UK)	1995
★ Coleus	8 ft. 4 in. (2.5 m)	Nancy Lee Spilove (U.S.A.)	2004
Collard	9 ft. 2 in. (2.79 m)	Reggie Kirkman (U.S.A.)	1999
Cosmos	12 ft. 3 in. (3.75 m)	Cosmos Executive Committee, Okayama, Japan	2003
Cotton	25 ft. 5 in. (7.74 m)	D. M. Williams (U.S.A.)	2004
Daffodil	5 ft. 1 in. (1.55 m)	M. Lowe (UK)	1979
Dandelion	39.3 in. (100 cm)	Ragnar Gille and Marcus Hamring (both Sweden)	2001
Fuchsia	21 ft. 7 in. (6.58 m)	The Growing Place, Lincolnshire, UK	2003
Herba cistanches	5 ft. 8 in. (1.75 m)	BOC Hong Kong Baptist University, Hong Kong, China	2003
Papaya tree	44 ft. (13.4 m)	Prasanta Mal (India)	2003
Parsley	55 in. (1.39 m)	Danielle, Gabrielle, Michelle Kassatly (all U.S.A.)	2003
Pepper	16 ft. (4.87 m)	Laura Liang (U.S.A.)	1999
Periwinkle	7 ft. 2 in. (2.19 m)	Arvind, Rekha, Ashish, and Rashmi Nema (all India)	2003
Petunia	19 ft. 1 in. (5.8 m)	Bernard Lavery (UK)	1994
Potato or brinjal	18 ft. 0.5 in. (5.5 m)	Abdul Masfoor (India)	1998
☆ Rosebush (self-supported)	12 ft. 8 in. (3.8 m)	Kathleen Mielke-Villalobos (U.S.A.)	2004
★ Rose (climbing)	91 ft. (27.7 m)	Anne & Charles Grant (both U.S.A.)	2004
Sunflower	25 ft. 5.5 in. (7.76 m)	M. Heijms (Netherlands)	1986
Sweet corn (maize)	31 ft. (9.4 m)	D. Radda (U.S.A.)	1946
Tomato	65 ft. (19.8 m)	Nutriculture Ltd., Lancashire, UK	2000
Umbrella	27 ft. (8.22 m)	Konstantinos Xytakis & Sara Guterbock (both U.S.A.)	2002

THE ENVIRONMENT

Acid rain: most acidic A pH reading of 2.83 was recorded over the Great Lakes, U.S.A./Canada, in 1982, and a reading of 1.87 was recorded at Inverpolly Forest, Highland, Scotland, UK, in 1983. These are the lowest pH levels ever recorded in acid precipitation, making it the most acidic acid rain.

Acid rain: most sulfates A sulfate reading of 5.52 mg/liter was recorded in Inverpolly Forest, Highland, Scotland, UK, in 1983. For the

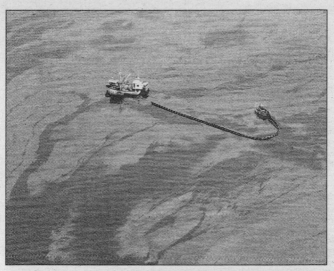

WORST COASTAL DAMAGE On March 24, 1989, the *Exxon Valdez* oil tanker ran aground in Prince William Sound, Alaska, U.S.A., spilling approximately 11 million gal. (41 million liters) of oil. In total, 1,500 miles (2,400 km) of coast was polluted, and the company was fined $5 billion on top of a cleanup bill of $3 billion.

most part, this high level of sulfate was the result of atmospheric fallout from industries in central Scotland.

Chemical pollution: most polluted town The Russian town of Dzerzhinsk (population 285,000 in 1995) is the world's most polluted industrial town. Life expectancy in the town—which is named after the founder of the Soviet secret police—is 42 for men and 47 for women. The town is home to dozens of factories that over the years have produced chlorine, pesticides, and chemical weapons.

Deforestation: greatest From 1990 to 2000, an average area of 8,596 miles² (22,264 km²) of forest was cleared in Brazil every year—a total area equivalent to the entire United Kingdom.

Radioactivity: most contaminated lake Lake Karachay in the Chelyabinsk province of Russia has accumulated 120 million curies of radioactivity and absorbed nearly 100 times more strontium-90 and cesium-137 than was released at Chernobyl. If you were to stand on the shore of the lake you would be contaminated at a radiation exposure rate of 600 roentgens an hour—strong enough to kill you within 60 minutes.

WORST NUCLEAR DISASTER A nuclear reactor disaster at Chernobyl No. 4 in the former USSR (now the Ukraine), on April 26, 1986, at 1:23 a.m. local time, resulted in an official death toll of 31 people. No systematic records were kept of subsequent deaths, but over 1.7 million people were exposed to radiation.

★LARGEST TREE TRANSPLANT On January 20, 2004, an oak tree (*Quercus lobata*) named "Old Glory," aged between 180 and 220 years, was moved 0.25 miles (0.4 km) by the Senna Tree Company (U.S.A.) to a new park in Los Angeles, California, U.S.A., where it was successfully replanted. The tree measured 58 ft. (17.6 m) tall, 104 ft. (31.6 m) wide (branch-span), weighed about 916,000 lb. (458 tons), and had a trunk girth of 16 ft. 2 in. (5 m).

Fire: worst destruction of natural environment Deliberately lit forest fires in 1997 made this the worst year in recorded history for the destruction of the environment. The largest and most numerous were in Brazil, where they raged on a 1,000-mile (1,600-km) front.

Toxic cloud: largest In September 1990, a fire at a factory handling beryllium in Ust Kamenogorsk, Kazakhstan (then USSR), released a toxic cloud that extended over an area of 186 miles (300 km) to the Chinese border and an unknown distance beyond.

Sulfur dioxide: greatest amount of pollution from a factory The Bulgarian Maritsa power complex releases 770 million lb. (385,000 tons) of sulfur dioxide into the Maritsa River every single year.

Sulfur dioxide is a pungent-smelling acidic gas, largely produced through volcanic eruptions but also by the burning of fossil fuels. When sulfur dioxide is released into the atmosphere it combines with water vapor in the clouds to form sulfuric acid. This is one of the major causes of acid rain in Europe and North America.

May 1973

August 1987

July 2000

GREATEST SHRINKAGE OF A LAKE The Aral Sea, on the border between Uzbekistan and Kazakhstan, has lost more than 60% of its area and approximately 80% of its volume since 1960. From 1960 to 1998, the lake decreased in area from 26,300 miles^2 (68,000 km^2) to 11,000 miles^2 (28,700 km^2) and in volume from approximately 250 miles^3 (1,040 km^3) to 43 miles^3 (180 km^3). The sea level has dropped about 60 ft. (18 m) in the same time period.

★ A SELECTION OF THE WORST ENVIRONMENTAL DISASTERS ★

TYPE/LOCATION	DATE	EFFECT
Chemical disaster Bhopal, India	December 3, 1984	Toxic cloud of methyl isocyanate (MIC) gas enveloped a settlement. Approximately 3,500 people killed; thousands more left with permanent disabilities.
Industrial explosion Scunthorpe, Flixborough, Lincolnshire, UK	June 1, 1974	Chemical plant explosion killed 55 people and injured 75, probably owing to a leak of about 110,000 lb. (55 tons) of cyclohexane gas. Explosion approximately equivalent to that of 35,000 lb. (17.63 tons) of TNT.
Land pollution Arctic Komi Republic, Russia	August–September 1994	30–400 million lb. (15,400–220,400 tons) of crude oil escaped across tundra. Contaminated area measured 8.1 miles^2 (21.1 km^2).
Marine pollution Minamata Bay, Kyushu, Japan	1953–1967	Fertilizer factory deposited mercury waste into the sea. Up to 20,000 people affected, 4,500 seriously—43 died from poison; another 800 deaths attributed to mercury poisoning by some sources; 111 others suffered permanent damage.
Nuclear waste accident Kyshtym, Russia	December 1957	Nuclear waste container explosion released radioactive compounds over an area of 8,900 miles^2 (23,000 km^2). A 1992 report suggested that 8,015 people died over a 32-year period as a result.
Oil spill Gulf of Campeche, Gulf of Mexico	Started June 3, 1979	Blowout beneath drilling rig *Ixtoc I* resulted in oil slick that had extended 400 miles (640 km) by August 5, 1979. Capped on March 24, 1980, after estimated loss of up to 168 million gal. (636 million liters; 550,000 tons) of oil.
River pollution Basel, Switzerland	November 1, 1986	Firemen fighting a blaze at Sandoz chemical works flushed 66,000 lb. (33 tons) of agricultural chemicals into the Rhine River. Resulted in death of half a million fish.
Sulfur dioxide fire Mosul, Iraq	Started June 24, 2003	Released average of 46.3 million lb. (23,000 tons) of sulfur dioxide gas a day for nearly a month. Resulted in about 1.3 billion lb. (660,000 tons) of pollution—greatest man-made release of SO$_2$ in history for a discrete event.

SCIENCE & TECHNOLOGY

CONTENTS

SOLAR SYSTEM

TECHNOLOGY

★ **MOST DISTANT LANDING** This is the first color image from the surface of Saturn's largest moon, Titan, taken by European Space Agency probe *Huygens,* which landed successfully on Titan on January 14, 2005. Saturn is an average of 890 million miles (1.433 billion km) from the Sun.

Farthest distance traveled on another world From January 16 to June 23, 1973, the unmanned Soviet *Lunokhod 2* rover traveled 23 miles (37 km) on the Moon's surface.

☆ **Farthest distance traveled on Mars in one Martian day (sol)** In February 2004 (corresponding to sol 362–363) NASA's Mars exploration rover *Opportunity* traveled 513 ft. 7 in. (156.55 m) across Meridiani Planum.
A sol is one Martian day, and is 24 hr. 39 min. 35 sec. long.

☆ **Heaviest spacecraft launched to the outer Solar System** On October 15, 1997, a *Titan IV* rocket with a Centaur upper stage launched the 12,467-lb. (5,655-kg) *Cassini-Huygens* spacecraft to explore Saturn and its moons. It entered the orbit of the ringed planet on July 1, 2004, to begin its four-year study of the Saturnian system.

★ **Longest flight to the Moon** The European Space Agency's (ESA) *SMART 1* spacecraft was launched on September 27, 2003, arriving in lunar orbit 13 months later on November 15, 2004.
Its engine, with a maximum thrust of 0.016 lb. (0.07 newtons), gradually pushed the spacecraft into larger and larger orbits of the Earth until it was captured by the Moon's gravity and pulled into a lunar orbit. *SMART 1* used an ion engine for propulsion.

Most distant image of Earth On February 4, 1990, NASA's *Voyager 1* spacecraft turned its camera back toward the Sun and the planets. After 12.5 years in space, traveling away from Earth, *Voyager 1*'s camera took a picture of our home planet from a distance of almost 4 billion miles (6.5 billion km).

★ **FIRST OBSERVED TRANSIT OF VENUS** The first person to observe, measure, and record the transit of the planet Venus across the Sun was Jeremiah Horrocks (UK), who monitored the event on November 24, 1639, from Lancashire, UK. The transit of June 8, 2004 (above), was witnessed by millions of people worldwide.

GREATEST RING SYSTEM The ring system of Saturn, seen here in an image taken by *Cassini* on March 8, 2004 (from a distance of 35 million miles, or 56.4 million km), has a combined mass of about 9×10^{19} lb. (4×10^{19} kg)—equivalent to 30 million Mount Everests. It consists of millions of tiny, independently orbiting particles of ice and dust. With a density of just 0.8 of that of water, Saturn is also the **least dense planet**—if there were an ocean large enough to accommodate the planet's mass, it would float in it!

HIGHEST RESOLUTION MARS CAMERA The image above was taken by the Pancam camera on the *Opportunity* rover (inset). The Pancam is the highest resolution camera ever used on the surface of another planet. It can see details as small as 0.03 in. (1 mm) per pixel in objects 10 ft. (3 m) from the rover. Although designed to last just a few months, the *Spirit* and *Opportunity* Mars rovers were still going strong in March 2005, and, hopefully, could pave the way for human exploration of the red planet.

Most planets visited by one spacecraft NASA's *Voyager 2* spacecraft, launched in 1977, visited all four of the outer gas giants—Jupiter, Saturn, Uranus, and Neptune—from 1979 to 1989.

Smallest planetary body ever landed on The *NEAR-Shoemaker* spacecraft touched down on asteroid Eros, which measures about 20 miles (33 km) across, on February 12, 2001. It transmitted 69 images of the surface of Eros.

NATURE

★**Shortest-period asteroid** Asteroid 2004 JG6 orbits the Sun in 184.46 days. It was discovered by Brian Skiff (U.S.A.) at the Lowell Observatory, Flagstaff, Arizona, U.S.A., and announced on May 13, 2004. The asteroid measures between 1,600 and 3,300 ft. (500 and 1,000 m) in diameter.

★**Tallest ridge in the Solar System** Observations of Saturn's moon Iapetus by *Cassini* on December 31, 2004, revealed an enormous ridge, at least 800 miles (1,300 km) long, which reaches an altitude of approximately 12 miles (20 km) above the surface. Iapetus is only 869 miles (1,400 km) across.

★**Most reflective body in the Solar System** Enceladus, a small moon of Saturn, reflects about 90% of the sunlight that illuminates it, making it more reflective than freshly fallen snow.

Hottest planet Venus has the hottest surface of any planet in the Solar System, with an average temperature of about 896°F (480°C).

If you were to step onto the surface of Venus, you would be simultaneously crushed by the pressure, incinerated by the heat, burnt by the sulfuric acid, and suffocated by the carbon dioxide atmosphere. Venus is also the **planet with the longest day,** with each one measuring 243.16 Earth days.

☆**Most volcanically active body in the Solar System** Images of Jupiter's moon Io taken by *Voyager 1* in 1979 revealed huge volcanic eruption plumes, some reaching several hundred miles into space. Io's activity is driven by tidal energy inside the moon, caused by gravitational interactions between Jupiter, Io, and Europa (another of Jupiter's moons). Rosaly Lopes (U.S.A.) has discovered 71 active volcanoes on Io, making her the **discoverer of more active volcanoes** on Io (or on Earth) than anyone else.

UNIVERSE

BRIGHTEST . . .

Nebula The Orion Nebula is the brightest nebula in the sky, with an apparent magnitude of 4. Located in the "sword" of the constellation of Orion, it is easily visible to the naked eye.

Supernova remnant The Crab Nebula (M1) in the constellation of Taurus has a magnitude of 8.4. It is a vast cloud of gas and debris, rapidly expanding at roughly 1,100 mps (1,800 km/s). The massive star that formed it was seen to explode in a supernova in 1054 A.D. by Chinese astronomers. The explosion was bright enough to be seen with the naked eye in broad daylight for 23 days.

Open star cluster Pleiades (M45), also known as the Seven Sisters, is located in the constellation of Taurus and contains about 500 individual stars in a region of space approximately 20 light-years across, and at an average

FARTHEST BLACK HOLE The most distant black hole discovered to date resides in the center of the quasar SDSS J1148+5251. This quasar has a redshift of 6.41, corresponding to a distance of about 13 billion light-years. The supermassive black hole has been measured to have a mass of about 3 billion times the mass of the Sun. The observations were made using the United Kingdom Infrared Telescope (UKIRT) in Hawaii, and the results were announced on March 20, 2003.

distance of about 380 light-years. Even from within a major light-polluted city, about six stars can be seen with the naked eye alone.

Globular cluster The brightest globular cluster in the sky is Omega Centauri in the southern constellation of Centaurus. It is easily visible to the naked eye, with an apparent magnitude of 3.6, and resembles a hazy star. Omega Centauri is a cluster of several million individual stars, located in a halo of about 140 such clusters that surrounds our galaxy (the Milky Way).

EXPLANATION OF TERMINOLOGY

For astronomical records, brightness and luminosity refer to different things. **Brightness** is a measure of how much light you see with your eyes, and is dependent upon distance as well as how much light an object is actually producing. **Luminosity** is a measure of how bright an object actually is, independent of distance from the Earth.

LARGEST SPACE TELESCOPE The $2.1 billion NASA Hubble Space Telescope weighs 24,250 lb. (12 tons) and is 43 ft. (13.1 m) long, with a 948-in. (240-cm) reflector. It was placed in orbit at an altitude of 381 miles (613 km) by the space shuttle *Discovery* on April 24, 1990. NASA has opted not to risk any more manned repair missions to Hubble, which will continue to operate until its instruments fail.

MOST LUMINOUS . . .

Star in the galaxy Observations of LBV 1806-20, 45,000 light-years from Earth, indicate it is between 5 and 40 million times more luminous than the Sun. It has a mass of at least 150 times that of the Sun and its diameter is at least 200 times that of the Sun.

Object Quasar APM08279+5255 was discovered in March 1998 by a team of astronomers using the 8-ft. (2.5-m) Isaac Newton Telescope (INT) at La Palma in the Canary Islands. It is between 4 and 5 million billion times brighter than the Sun and is estimated to be over 10 times brighter than any other known quasar. Most astronomers believe quasars to be a type of galaxy with an energetic supermassive black hole at its center.

LARGEST . . .

★ **Starquake** A starquake on the ultracompact stellar corpse SGR 1806-20 caused a flash of gamma rays equivalent to about 10,000 trillion trillion trillion watts in intensity. Known as a magnetar, it consists of a ball of neutrons some 12 miles (20 km) across, but with a mass similar to that of the Sun and spinning once every 7.5 seconds. It lies about 50,000 light-years away on the other side of our Milky Way galaxy. If this event had occurred

February 2004

December 2002

October 2002

September 2002

May 2002

★ GREATEST PLANETARY DESTRUCTION In a time-lapse series taken by the Hubble Space Telescope, the shells of dust surrounding the star V838 Monocerotis are illuminated by the light flash from the star when it flared up to 600,000 times its normal brightness in January 2002. Some astronomers believe that this unique outburst was a result of the energy released when three orbiting gas giant planets were engulfed and destroyed by the star—a cosmic event that has been predicted but never before witnessed.

FIRST SPIRAL GALAXY The Whirlpool galaxy (M51), seen here in one of the most famous images taken by the Hubble Space Telescope, was the first celestial object ever to be identified as being a spiral. Its spiral nature was discovered by William Parsons, Third Earl of Rosse (Ireland) in 1845. Parsons used his own telescope, *The Leviathan*—then the world's largest—at Birr Castle, County Offaly, Ireland.

within 10 light-years of Earth, it could have resulted in mass extinction. The flash was detected on December 27, 2004.

★**Diamond in the universe** The first direct evidence that white dwarf interiors crystallize into huge diamonds was announced in February 2004. Observations of BPM 37093 allowed astronomers from the Harvard-Smithsonian Center for Astrophysics, Massachusetts, U.S.A., to deduce that the carbon white dwarf had crystallized into a diamond some 2,500 miles (4,000 km) across.

☆**Structure in the universe** A team of astronomers led by Richard Gott III and Mario Juric (both U.S.A.) of Princeton University, New Jersey, U.S.A., has discovered a huge wall of galaxies some 1.37 billion light-years long. They used data from the Sloan Digital Sky Survey, which is mapping the locations of one million galaxies in the universe. Their discovery was announced in October 2003.

★**Alcohol nebula** Observations made in 1970 of the molecular nebula Sagittarius B2, close to the center of our galaxy, revealed vast quantities of gaseous alcohol. If it could be condensed into a liquid, a billion billion billion-liter container would be necessary to hold it. As the nebula is 150 light-years across, a volume of gas the size of the Earth would be required to make a glass of wine.

★**Nebula visible to the naked eye** The Tarantula Nebula in the constellation of Doradus in the southern sky is large and bright enough to be visible to the naked eye, despite being 170,000 light-years away. The huge cloud of glowing gas has a diameter of about 1,000 light-years and is the only nebula outside our galaxy that is visible to the naked eye.

PEOPLE IN SPACE

First manned spaceflight Cosmonaut Flight Major Yuri Alekseyevich Gagarin (USSR) flew on *Vostok 1* on April 12, 1961. The maximum altitude during the 25,394-mile (40,868.6-km) flight was recorded at 203 miles (327 km), with a top speed of 17,560 mph (28,260 km/h).

First men on the Moon Neil Armstrong (U.S.A.), commander of the *Apollo 11* mission, became the first man to set foot on the Moon when he stepped onto the Sea of Tranquility at 02:56:15 GMT on July 21, 1969 (or 22:56:15 EDT on July 20, 1969). He was followed out of the lunar module *Eagle* by Edwin "Buzz" Aldrin (U.S.A.), while the command module *Columbia,* piloted by Michael Collins (U.S.A.), orbited above.

First spacewalk Lt.-Col. (now Maj. Gen.) Alexei Arkhipovich Leonov (USSR) was the first person ever to engage in extravehicular activity (EVA), commonly known as a space walk, on March 18, 1965.

First woman in space Junior Lt. Valentina Vladimirovna Tereshkova (USSR) was launched in *Vostok 6* from the Baikonur Cosmodrome, Kazakhstan, at 9:30 a.m. GMT on June 16, 1963. She landed at 8:20 a.m. on June 19, after a flight of 2 days 22 hr. 50 min. and 48 orbits (1,225,000 miles; 1,971,000 km).

Greatest distance from Earth The crew of *Apollo 13* (Jack Swigert, Jim Lovell, and Fred Haise, all U.S.A.) were an unprecedented distance of 248,655 miles (400,171 km) from the Earth and 158 miles (254 km) from the Moon on April 15, 1970.

Most durable space station *Mir,* the central core module of the *Mir* Space Station (USSR/Russia), was launched into orbit on February 20, 1986. Over the following 10 years, five modules and a docking port for U.S. space shuttles were added to the complex. On March 23, 2001, the space

---

NB: in the text, the term USSR stands for Union of Soviet Socialist Republics, the collection of Communist states that existed from 1917 to 1991.

The term CIS stands for Commonwealth of Independent States, a collection of former Communist states that amalgamated on December 8, 1991, after the downfall of the USSR.

STS = Space Transportation System

★ **LONGEST MOON WALK** On their second excursion onto the surface of the Moon during the *Apollo 17* mission on December 12, 1972, U.S. astronauts Eugene Cernan (pictured) and Harrison Schmitt spent 7 hr. 37 min. outside their lunar excursion module, *Challenger.* During this time they traveled 12.6 miles (20.4 km) while taking geological samples of the region to the south and west of their landing site in the Taurus-Littrow valley.

station was de-orbited and destroyed in a controlled reentry over the Pacific Ocean. More than 100 people visited the space station in its 15-year operational history.

★ **Most heavily armed space station** *Salyut 3* (USSR, launched June 25, 1974) was the only armed space station. For defensive purposes it was equipped with a 23 mm Nudelmann aircraft cannon. Although never used in anger, it was test-fired once on January 24, 1975, and destroyed a target satellite.

Most people in space at the same time On March 14, 1995, there were seven Americans aboard the space shuttle STS-67 *Endeavour,* three CIS cosmonauts aboard the *Mir* Space Station, and two cosmonauts and a U.S. astronaut aboard *Soyuz TM21*—making a total of 13 people in space at the same time.

Longest manned spaceflight Valeriy Poliyakov (Russia) was launched to the *Mir* space station aboard *Soyuz TM18* on January 8, 1994, and landed in *Soyuz TM20* on March 22, 1995, after a spaceflight lasting 437 days 17 hr. 58 min. 16 sec.

Most reused spacecraft NASA's space shuttle *Discovery* was launched on August 10, 2001, at 4:10 p.m. Central Daylight Time (CDT). Its mission

(STS-105) was to deliver a new crew and the *Leonardo* cargo module to the *International Space Station*. This was the 30th mission for *Discovery*, which has operated since 1984.

★**Longest serving astronaut** John Young (U.S.A.) was selected as a NASA astronaut in September 1962. He has flown on two *Gemini* Earth-orbital missions, and two *Apollo* missions (10 and 16), and commanded STS-1, the first flight of the space shuttle in 1981. His sixth mission was as commander of STS-9—again on *Columbia*. He remained on active flight status until he retired in December 2004.

Most remote golf shot In February 1971, astronaut Alan Shepard (U.S.A.) struck two golf balls in the Fra Mauro region on the surface of the Moon. He used a club made from a sampling tool with a six-iron attached. One of the balls traveled a distance of about 50 ft. (15 m).

★**Largest room in space** The largest single habitable volume launched into space was the NASA space station *Skylab*, which was launched on May 14, 1973. This cylindrical space station had internal dimensions of 48.1 ft. (14.66 m) long by 22 ft. (6.7 m) in diameter, giving a habitable volume of 10,426 ft.^{3} (295.23 m^3).

★**Longest solo spaceflight** The longest duration spaceflight with a single person on board was the flight of *Vostok 5*, piloted by Soviet cosmonaut Valery Bykovsky. It was launched on June 14, 1963, and landed on June 19, 1963, with a total mission elapsed time of 4 days 23 hr. 7 min.

LARGEST SHUTTLE CREW Two shuttles have had a crew of eight: the STS-61A *Challenger*, which was launched on October 30, 1985, and STS-71 *Atlantis*, which docked with the *Mir* space station on July 7, 1995. Pictured are members of the *Atlantis* and *Mir* crews.

MOST TIME SPENT IN SPACE Russian cosmonaut Sergei Avdeyev (Russia, pictured above) logged a total of 747 days 14 hr. 22 min. on three spaceflights to the *Mir* space station from July 1992 to July 1999.

Avdeyev also experienced the **most time dilation by an individual**. As a direct consequence of the time he has spent in low Earth orbit, traveling at around 17,000 mph (27,000 km/h) relative to everyone else, he has essentially "time traveled" 1/50th of a second into the future—consistent with Albert Einstein's Theory of Relativity.

★**FIRST PRIVATELY FUNDED MANNED SPACE FLIGHT** On June 21, 2004, *SpaceShipOne*—a spacecraft designed, built, and operated by Scaled Composites of Mojave, California, U.S.A., and funded by Paul G. Allen (U.S.A.)—reached an altitude of 328,492 ft. (100,124 m). Piloted by Mike Melvill (U.S.A.), it took off from and landed at Mojave Airport.

COMMUNICATIONS

☆**Fastest text message** Kimberly Yeo Sue Fern (Singapore) typed a pre-agreed 160-character text on her cell phone in 43.2 seconds on June 27, 2004, at the Singtel SMS Shootout competition in Singapore. Attempts at this record must be made using text adapted from page 39 of the 1996 *Guinness Book of Records* (displayed on page 218).

First cell phone The concept of a portable telephone first appeared in 1947 at Lucent Technologies' Bell Labs in New Jersey, U.S.A., but the first portable telephone handset was invented by Martin Cooper (U.S.A.) of Motorola. He made the first call on April 3, 1973, to his rival, Joel Engel, head of research at Bell Labs. The first commercial cell phone network was launched in Japan in 1979.

☆**Most cell phone subscribers** Vodafone Group plc has the largest subscriber base, with 151.8 million subscribers globally as of December 31, 2004.

★**LARGEST CELL PHONE** The Maxi Handy (Maxi Mobile) measures 6.72 × 2.72 × 1.47 ft. (2.05 × 0.83 × 0.45 m) and was installed at the Rotmain Center, Bayreuth, Germany, on June 7, 2004, as part of the "einfach mobil" infotour. It is made from wood, polyester, and metal, and features a color Thin Film Transistor (TFT) screen. It is fully functional and can send and receive SMS and MMS messages.

★**Most durable cell phone number** David Contorno (U.S.A.) has owned and used the same cell phone number since August 2, 1985. His first cell phone was an Ameritech AC140, and his carrier has remained Ameritech Mobile Communications.

Largest telephone conference call On September 29, 2003, U.S. presidential Democratic candidate Howard Dean (U.S.A.) took part in a telephone conference call from Los Angeles, California, U.S.A., with some of his supporters. The total number of people simultaneously connected for at least 10 seconds was 3,466.

★**Oldest teletext service** Ceefax was launched in the UK by the BBC on September 28, 1974. It was developed by BBC engineers who were working on a way to provide subtitles for deaf people. They used the "spare lines" on top of an analog television signal to incorporate words and simple graphics.

First geostationary communications satellite *Syncom 3* was launched from Cape Canaveral, Florida, U.S.A., on August 19, 1964, and maneuvered to its orbit at an altitude of 22,238 miles (35,788 km) above Earth. At this altitude, the satellite took exactly 24 hours to orbit the planet and so appeared stationary from the ground. Today, more than 200 satellites operate in the geostationary or "Clarke" orbit, which is named after the science-fiction writer Arthur C. Clarke, who was the first person to lay down the principles of satellite communication.

★**Largest civil communications satellite** *Anik F2,* constructed by Boeing (U.S.A.), was launched in July 2004 to provide broadband Internet services to Canada and the U.S.A. It measures 157 ft. (47.9 m) across from the tips of its solar panels, and had a launch mass of 13,117 lb. (5,950 kg) and a mass in orbit of 8,390 lb. (3,805 kg). *Anik F2* will operate for 15 years.

Largest live digital satellite radio broadcast When Ana Ann (UK) performed her debut single "Ride" on February 13, 2002, at the offices of Worldspace, Soho Square, London, England, the song was uplinked to Worldspace's AfriStar satellite and then beamed down to Western Europe, the whole of Africa, and the Middle East.

★**LARGEST COMMUNICATIONS SURVEILLANCE NETWORK** Echelon, the electronic eavesdropping network run by the intelligence organizations of the U.S.A., UK, Australia, New Zealand, and Canada, was founded in 1947 by those nations to share intelligence data. Some analysts estimate that it can now intercept some 90% of all Internet traffic, as well as monitoring global telephone and satellite communications. Pictured are the radomes—giant golf ball–like satellite covers—used by Echelon at RAF Menwith Hill, near Narrowgate, North Yorkshire, UK.

STRONGEST RADIO SIGNAL BEAMED INTO SPACE On November 16, 1974, scientists at the Arecibo Radio Telescope, Puerto Rico, transmitted a binary radio signal to the M13 globular cluster in the constellation of Hercules, in an effort to communicate with extraterrestrial life. The message, which shows basic data about humanity, lasts for 169 seconds at 2,380 MHz. The message will arrive in about 25,000 years. If there is a reply, it will take another 25,000 years for us to receive it.

★**Longest communications baseline** The unmanned spacecraft *Voyager 1* (U.S.A.) was launched in 1977 on a tour of the outer solar system. As of February 2005, the craft was over 8.7 billion miles (14 billion km) from the Sun. At this distance, radio commands from Earth traveling at the speed of light take about 13 hours to reach the spacecraft.

★**Highest speed to transmit Morse code** On May 6, 2003, Andrei Bindasov (Belarus) successfully transmitted 216 Morse code marks of mixed text in one minute.

Largest fax machine WideCom Group, Inc. of Mississauga, Ontario, Canada, manufactures the WIDEfax 36—a facsimile machine able to print, copy, and transmit documents up to 36 in. (91 cm) wide.

The razor-toothed piranhas of the penera serrasalmus and pynocentrus are the most ferocious freshwater fish in the world. In reality they seldom attack a human.

Can you beat the world record time to type the above text? If you think you can, get in touch with Guinness World Records! Find out how on p. XIX

FIRST COMMUNICATIONS SATELLITE *Echo 1* (sometimes called *Echo 1A*) was launched on July 10, 1962, from Cape Canaveral, Florida, U.S.A. It was a 98-ft.-diameter (30-m) balloon with a reflective aluminum coating, allowing radio and television signals to be passively reflected back to Earth. It ceased operations on May 24, 1968.

INTERNET

★**Largest Internet trading site** Founded in 1995, eBay (U.S.A.) is a trade website allowing individuals around the world to buy and sell items. In 2004, 56.1 million users bought, sold, or bid for an item on the website. At the end of 2004, eBay had 135.5 million registered users around the world.

☆**Internet2 land speed record** On November 9, 2004, a team consisting of the University of Tokyo, Fujitsu Computer Technologies, and the WIDE Project (all Japan) successfully transmitted 541 gigabytes of data (equivalent to more than 100 DVD movies) across 12,828 miles (20,645 km) of network in 10 minutes. The resulting value of 148,850 terabit-meters per second was accomplished using IPv4.

Highest capacity intercontinental Internet route In 2003, the Internet routes between Europe and U.S.A./Canada had a bandwidth capacity of 386,221 Mbps (megabits per second). In second place was the combined

★ **LARGEST PANORAMIC DIGITAL PHOTO** Imaging experts from TNO (Netherlands) have created a huge online panoramic digital photograph of the city of Delft in the Netherlands. The image is 2.5 gigapixels in size and composed of 600 separate digital shots, taken from the same location and "stitched" together over three days in July 2004.

You can view the entire image by going to www.guinnessworld records.com/panorama.

routes between U.S.A./Canada and Asia & Pacific, with a bandwidth capacity of 103,282.3 Mbps. The lowest capacity was between U.S.A./Canada and Africa, with a bandwidth capacity of 1,351.5 Mbps.

★ **Largest online console community** Sony PlayStation 2 had more than 1.4 million registered users in August 2004. The Internet gaming service was launched in August 2002 and continues to grow by roughly 1,400 new users each day.

★ **Deepest live Internet broadcast** On July 24, 2001, live footage of HMS *Hood* was broadcast over the Internet from an ROV (remotely operated vehicle) at the bottom of the Denmark Strait (where she sank in 1941), at a depth of 9,200 ft. (2,800 m). This followed the discovery of the wreck by David Mearns (UK) of Bluewater Recoveries Ltd. (UK), in an expedition organized by ITN Factual for Channel 4 (UK).

★ **Largest independent Internet hub** The London Exchange (Linx) handles 76 gigabits of data every second at peak times, as of March 2005. It consists of eight high-capacity Internet routing sites around Docklands, London, UK.

☆ **Largest Internet search engine** Google, with over 8 billion pages, has the largest continually refreshed index of web pages of all search engines. Founded by Larry Page (U.S.A.) and Sergey Brin (Russia), their first office was a garage in Menlo Park, California, U.S.A., which opened in September 1998 with a staff of four people.

GARY THUERK

On May 3, 1978, Gary Thuerk (U.S.A.) sent the first "spam" (an un-solicited e-mail, usually advertising a product or service) via ARPAnet, a system seen as the predecessor to the Internet.

Why exactly did you send your first spam e-mail? I wanted to reach people in western U.S.A. to tell them about our mainframe-class server.

How many people were on your mailing list? Over 400, which was about 25% of everyone online in the world at that time. We took the names from a printed phone book and typed them in!

What do you think of spam today? I don't get a lot of spam because I don't leave my contact details on the Internet—chat rooms, etc. Also, when people forward jokes to friends, they leave the e-mail list in there and spammers can eventually get hold of it.

Does anybody ever blame you for the current volume of spam today? Oh yes—I get people who blame me but if I talk to them we normally end up smiling or laughing about it.

Do you feel guilty? No, of course not. If you take a plane flight and the airline loses your luggage, you don't blame the Wright brothers!

Why exactly are unsolicited e-mails called "spam"? It came from a Monty Python's Flying Circus sketch. Somebody who just watched it was going through his unsolicited e-mails and complained that he was being spammed—and every-one around him began singing the Monty Python spam song!

To receive a copy of the first spam and a message from Gary, send an e-mail—or spam him!—at: garythuerk@guinness worldrecords.com.

☆**Largest wireless Internet provider** NTT DoCoMo (Japan) is the world's largest wireless Internet provider, with more than 43.24 million sub-scribers to their i-mode service as of January 2005.

First e-mail Ray Tomlinson, an engineer at the computer company Bolt, Beranek, and Newman in Cambridge, Massachusetts, U.S.A., sent the first ever e-mail in 1971 in an experiment to see if he could get two computers to exchange a message. The message was: "QWERTYUIOP," and it was

★LONGEST GROUND-LEVEL WI-FI CONNECTION In July 2004, Ben Corrado, Andy Meng, and Justin Rigling (all U.S.A.) achieved Wi-Fi wireless contact between two PCs 55.1 miles (88.6 km) apart in the desert outside Las Vegas, U.S.A. They used homemade antennae (pictured) as well as the 802.1 lb. wireless protocol. This feat made them the 2004 winners of the Annual DefCon Wi-Fi Shootout.

Tomlinson who decided to use the "@" symbol to separate the recipient's name from their location.

Largest Internet joke vote Laughlab, an Internet experiment into humor, was conducted by psychologist Richard Wiseman (UK) of the University of Hertfordshire, UK, and the British Association for the Advancement of Science. Running from September 2001 to October 2002, over 40,000

FIRST JPEGS A set of four test images created in Copenhagen, Denmark, on June 18, 1987, and entitled "Boats," "Barbara" (both pictured), "Toys," and "Zelda" were the first to use the jpeg compression method. The jpeg was developed by the Joint Photographic Experts Group in order to standardize techniques for digital image compression, and is used on the Internet and on digital cameras.

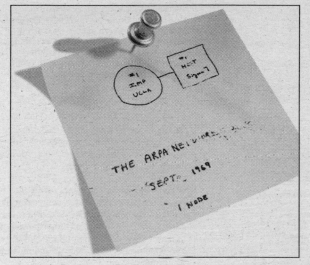

★**FIRST REMOTE COMPUTER CONNECTION** Pictured is the original sketch showing the plans to connect two computers remotely for the first time in a simple network; this would grow to become the Internet. At around 10:30 a.m. (PST) on 29 October 1969, computer scientists at the University of California, Los Angeles, U.S.A., tried to log in to a computer at the Stanford Research Institute. This first log-in failed, but a second attempt shortly thereafter succeeded.

jokes were submitted from the public worldwide, and about two million votes were cast on what was the funniest. Visit www.guinnessworld records.com/joke to see the winning joke for yourself.

POWER

LARGEST . . .

Natural gas field The Urengoy gas condensate field in Siberia, Russia, discovered in 1966, has estimated reserves of 280 trillion ft.³ (8 trillion m³). The gas field accounts for more than one third of the total annual Russian production of gas.

★**Electricity substation** Shin-noda at Chiba, Japan, has a maximum output of 7,860 MVA, starting commercial operation (at this capacity) on

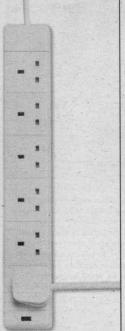

★ **LONGEST CHAIN OF ELECTRICAL CABLES** On June 14–15, 2003, a chain of electrical extension cables measuring 48,195 ft. (14,690 m) long was assembled from Thal to Stattegg, Austria. After completion, a current was passed along the cables, illuminating a light panel at the far end.

May 19, 1995. The substation, which is run by the Tokyo Electric Power Company, was established in 1961 and supplies the demands of eastern Tokyo and the northern area of the Chiba Prefecture.

★ **Hydroelectric power station** The Itaipu hydroelectric power station on the border between Paraguay and Brazil can generate 12,600 mW of electricity—enough to power the state of California, U.S.A. It began operation in 1985 and was upgraded to its current capacity in March 1991.

★ **Nuclear power station** Kashiwazaki Kariwa nuclear power station on the northern coast of Honshu Island, Japan, has a total output of 8,212 mW.

Producer of energy (country) The U.S.A. is the largest producer of commercial energy. In 2001, 75,295 PJ of commercial energy, including solid, liquid, and gaseous fuels, was produced, as well as primary electricity.

Wind generator The Mod-5B generator in Oahu, Hawaii, U.S.A., has two giant blades measuring 320 ft. (97.5 m) from tip to tip, making them as long as a 25-story building is high. First installed in August 1987, the turbine was built for the U.S. Department of Energy by the Boeing Company at a cost of $55 million, and produces 3,200 kW when the wind reaches 32 mph (51 km/h).

MOST POWERFUL . . .

★ **Tidal power station** The La Rance tidal barrage, in the mouth of the La Rance River estuary, France, has operated since 1966. It generates 240 mW of electricity from its 24 turbines, which are driven by the rising and falling tides.

★ **HIGHEST ENERGY OUTPUT ACHIEVED USING NUCLEAR FUSION** The highest energy output achieved using nuclear fusion is 16 mW by the Joint European Torus (JET) tokamak nuclear fusion reactor, Culham, Oxfordshire, UK, in 1997. Pictured is the doughnut-shaped reactor during firing (left) and beforehand (right).

★ **Battery** The Golden Valley Electric Association (U.S.A.) Battery Energy Storage System began operating in Alaska, U.S.A., in November 2003. On December 10, 2003, during a test of its maximum limit, it was discharged at a rate of 46 mW for 5 minutes. It is designed to prevent power loss to local residents during interruptions in the main electricity supply.

★ **Solar chimney** Enviromission's (Australia) prototype solar chimney power station in Manzanares, Spain, produced 50 kW of electricity from 1982 to 1989. It consisted of a large area of greenhouses in which air, heated by the Sun, expanded upward through a 656-ft.-tall (200-m) central tower, powering turbines as it escaped into the atmosphere.

MISCELLANEOUS

★ **Longest human electrical circuit** The longest human electrical circuit consisted of 250 people, who briefly carried sufficient electrical current (between 200 milliamps and 2 amps) to illuminate a light. The event occurred on November 21, 2004, at the Harrogate International Centre, Harrogate, North Yorkshire, UK, as part of the television show *Zapped,* by YAP Screenhouse Productions (UK).

★ **Longest continuous power plant operation** Stanwell Corporation's Unit 4 at the Stanwell Power Station in Queensland, Australia, operated

LARGEST WIND FARM At Altamont Pass, California, U.S.A., the Pacific Gas and Electric Company has built a wind farm covering 54 miles² (140 km²) with 7,300 wind turbines. The turbines have produced more than 6 billion kWh of electricity since 1981—enough to power 800,000 homes in California for approximately one year.

continuously from September 8, 1999 to August 16, 2002. This gives a total continuous operation time of 1,073 days and 1 hour.

★**Longest operating nuclear power station** The nuclear reactor in Obninsk, Russia, operated from June 27, 1954, until it was decommissioned on April 30, 2002. It was the world's first operating nuclear reactor.

★**MOST POWERFUL SOLAR TOWER POWER STATION** Solar II, in the Mojave Desert, California, U.S.A., uses an array of 1,800 curved heliostat mirrors that reflect sunlight onto a central heating element, generating a maximum output of 10 mW of electricity.

★**Smallest direct methanol fuel cell** In June 2004, Toshiba (Japan) announced its prototype direct methanol fuel cell designed for use in cellular technology, such as cellular telephones. Measuring just $0.87 \times 2.2 \times 0.18$ in. ($22 \times 56 \times 4.5$ mm), and weighing 0.29 oz. (8.5 g), it can power an MP3 player for about 20 hours on a single charge of 0.12 in.^{3} (2 cm^3) of highly concentrated methanol fuel.

CUTTING-EDGE SCIENCE

FASTEST . . .

Atomic clock A team of physicists led by Scott Diddams at the National Institute of Standards and Technology (U.S.A.) has built an atomic clock that "ticks" about a quadrillion (10^{15}) times a second. Eventually it is hoped that it will be accurate to 1 second in 100 million years, meaning that it would lose just a few minutes of accuracy for the whole of the age of the universe.

★**Matter in the universe** The fastest objects are blobs of superheated plasma ejected from black holes in the cores of extremely active galaxies known as blazars. These blobs, with as much mass as the planet Jupiter, have been observed moving at 99.99% of the speed of light.

LARGEST . . .

★**Centrifuge** The TsF-18 Centrifuge at the Yuri Gagarin Cosmonaut Training Center, Star City, Russia, has a rotating arm 59 ft. (18 m) long and can simulate up to 30 G with a payload mass of 770 lb. (350 kg).

Van de Graaf generator A Van de Graaf generator built in 1931 at the Massachussetts Institute of Technology, U.S.A., consists of two columns each with a 15-ft. (4.5-m-diameter) hollow aluminum sphere at the top.

★ **MOST SPHERICAL MAN-MADE OBJECT** The most perfect man-made spheres constructed to date are the fused solid quartz gyroscopic rotors built for NASA's Gravity Probe B spacecraft. There are four spheres on board, each measuring 1.5 in. (3.81 cm) across. Their average departure from mathematically perfect sphericity is 1.8×10^{-7} of the diameter. This means that if scaled up to the size of the Earth, the maximum height/depth of topographic features would be 4 ft. 6 in. (1.5 m).

SMALLEST . . .

★ **Atomic clock** In August 2004, the National Institute for Standards and Technology (NIST) in Boulder, Colorado, U.S.A., unveiled a prototype atomic clock the size of a grain of rice. With a volume of less than 0.000613 in.³ (10 mm³), and drawing just 75 milliwatts of power, the chip-scale cesium vapor atomic clock is accurate to one second in 300 years.

★ **Hominid** On October 28, 2004, Indonesian and Australian scientists announced in the magazine *Nature* that they had discovered the smallest known member of the hominid family. The remains were discovered in a cave at Liang Bua on the island of Flores, and the scientists named the species *Homo floresiensis*. Standing just 3 ft. (1 m) tall, the hominid inhabited Flores as recently as 13,000 years ago. This means that it existed at the same time as modern humans and probably interacted with them.

☆ **Test tube** A test tube made from a single-walled carbon nanotube measures just 2 micrometers long and 1.5 nanometers wide, giving an internal volume of only 3.5 zeptoliters (3.5×10^{-21} liters), or a billionth of a billionth of a milliliter. It was created by a team of scientists from the Department of Materials at Oxford University, Oxford, UK, and announced in December 2004.

★ HEAVIEST OBJECT WEIGHED
On January 23, 2004, the Revolving Service Structure (RSS) of launch pad 39B at NASA's Kennedy Space Center, Florida, U.S.A., was lifted up on 21 jacking points, which, between them, measured the mass of the RSS as 5,342,000 lb. (2,198 tons). The work was carried out by Industrial Steel, Inc. (U.S.A.) and Buffalo Hydraulic (U.S.A.).

★ Unit of time The smallest unit of time is known as Planck's time, 10^{-43} seconds. It is the amount of time it takes the **fastest thing**—light, traveling at 3×10^8 m/s—to cross the **smallest distance**—the Planck length, at 1.6×10^{-35} m.

WEIGHT

☆ Least dense solid Lawrence Livermore National Laboratory, California, U.S.A., has produced an aerogel with a density of just 0.25 grains/in.^{3} (1 mg/cm^3). This aerogel is lighter than air itself (0.3 grains/in.^{3}; 1.2 mg/cm^3) and is virtually invisible to the eye. Aerogel with this density was first created on April 10, 2003.

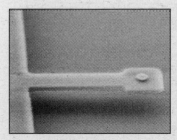

★ LIGHTEST OBJECT WEIGHED
Scientists at Cornell University (U.S.A.) have used a technique involving tiny oscillating cantilevers to physically detect a mass of just 6.3 attograms. (An attogram is a billionth of a billionth of a gram.) The work was carried out by Professor Harold Craighead and Rob Ilic (both U.S.A.) and published in April 2004.

LARGEST VACUUM CHAMBER The Space Power Facility, at NASA's Glenn Research Center, Plum Brook Station, Sandusky, Ohio, U.S.A., measures 100 ft. (30 m) in diameter and 122 ft. (37 m) in height. It can sustain a high vacuum of 10^{-6} torr and simulate solar radiation using a 4-megawatt quartz heat lamp array, as well as temperatures as low as -320°F (-195.5°C). It is used to test the performance of spacecraft and space hardware prior to launch.

MISCELLANEOUS

★**Longest pendulum** The longest pendulums were two lengths of number 24 steel piano wire, each 4,440 ft. (1,353.3 m) long. They were suspended down the number 4 shaft of the Tamarack Mines, Michigan, U.S.A., in September 1901 by students and staff of the Michigan College of Mining.

★**Highest temperature** At the very instant of the big bang, 13.7 billion years ago, the universe is thought to have had infinite temperature, as it existed as a single, infinitely small, and infinitely dense point. Just 10^{-43} seconds later—the Planck time—it had cooled to roughly 10^{32} K, and expanded to a size of about 10^{-33} cm across.

MOST ACCURATE KILOGRAM
The kilogram is the only base SI (Système International) unit of measurement whose definition is still based on a physical prototype—a cylinder of platinum and iridium, made in 1889, and maintained at the Bureau International des Poids et Mesures (BIPM) at Sevres near Paris, France. Scientists are currently attempting to change the definition of the kilogram by linking it to more and more precise measurements of Planck's constant.

CUTTING-EDGE TECHNOLOGY

COMPUTERS

Oldest computer mouse The computer mouse was invented by Douglas Engelbart (U.S.A.) in 1964. It was described in the patent as an "X-Y position indicator for a display system" and was nicknamed "mouse" because of the resemblance of the wire to a tail.

First microprocessor The 4004 chip, designed and built by Intel (U.S.A.), was completed in January 1971. The size of a thumbnail, this first single-processor CPU had the same power as ENIAC, the room-sized first electronic computer. The 4004 chip had 2,300 transistors and could perform around 100,000 instructions a second.

☆**Fastest computer** The Blue Gene/L prototype supercomputer, built by IBM (U.S.A.), is capable of 70.72 trillion calculations a second (70.72 teraflops). It was announced in November 2004.

SOUND & VISION

★**Most memory in a cell phone** The SPH-V5400, launched by Samsung (South Korea) in September 2004, is capable of holding 1.5 GB of data. It is the first ever cell phone to contain its own internal hard drive.

★**Highest resolution cell phone camera** The highest resolution digital camera integrated into a cell phone is the SCH-S250, which can take

★**STRONGEST HUMAN EXOSKELETON** The Berkeley Lower Extremity Exoskeleton (BLEEX) has been developed to provide enhanced strength and endurance. An onboard power source drives hydraulic muscles, allowing the "wearer" to carry a 70-lb. (32-kg) backpack, as well as the 100-lb. (45-kg) exoskeleton, while feeling the encumbrance of only 5 lb. (2.2 kg).

BLEEX was developed by the University of California, Berkeley, California, U.S.A., and funded by the Defense Advanced Research Project Agency (DARPA, U.S.A.). It was announced in March 2004.

5-megapixel images. It was launched in South Korea by Samsung (South Korea) in October 2004.

★**Largest LED screen** The world's largest light-emitting diode (LED) screen measures 187 × 206 ft. (57 × 63 m) high, with an area of 38,522 ft.² (3.591 m²). It is located on the side of the office building of Aurora Ltd., Shanghai, China, and was completed in September 2003.

☆**Largest television display** Panasonic SS Marketing Co. Ltd. has built a television display with a screen 196.53 × 36.53 ft. (59.90 × 11.13 m) in size, giving a total viewable area of 7,180.49 ft.² (667.09 m²). Its installation at the Suminoe Boat Race Stadium, Osaka, Japan, was completed on March 31, 2004.

SMALLEST PC (PERSONAL COMPUTER) OQO (U.S.A.) has developed a fully functioning personal computer with a 1 GHz processor, 10 GB or 20 GB hard drive, and 256 MB of RAM, capable of running a full version of Microsoft's Windows XP. Its dimensions are 4.1 × 2.9 × 0.9 in. (10.4 × 7.3 × 2.2 cm) and it weighs less than 9 oz. (225 g). It was unveiled on April 16, 2002, at the Microsoft Corp. Windows Hardware Engineering Conference 2002 (WinHEC 2002), New Orleans, Louisiana, U.S.A.

★**Most advanced planetarium projector** MEGASTAR-2 Cosmos can simultaneously project 5 million stars onto a planetarium dome. It was developed by Takayuki Ohira (Japan) and installed in the planetarium at the National Museum of Emerging Science and Innovation, Tokyo, Japan, in July 2004. Weighing 110 lb. (50 kg) and standing 23 in. (60 cm) tall, it can easily be carried in a car.

MISCELLANEOUS

Farthest distance between patient and surgeon On September 7, 2001, Madeleine Schaal (France) had her gallbladder removed by a robot in an operating room in Strasbourg, France, while her surgeons Jacques Marescaux and Michel Gagner remotely operated the ZEUS robotic surgical arms on a secured fiber-optic line from New York City, U.S.A. Patient and surgeon were a total distance of 3,866 miles (6,222 km) apart.

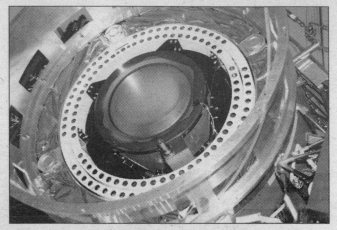

★ **MOST POWERFUL ION ENGINE USED IN SPACE** NASA's *Deep Space 1* spacecraft, launched on October 24, 1998, was propelled to its target, Comet Borrelly, by a revolutionary type of engine. A beam of ionized xenon atoms were expelled from the engine at 21 miles/s (35 km/s), providing a thrust of 0.02 lb. (0.09 newtons), equivalent to the force exerted by a sheet of paper resting on the palm of a hand. The ion engine was 10 times more efficient than a chemical rocket and was fired for 16,265 hours during the mission.

★**Largest criminal DNA database** As of March 31, 2004, the UK's National DNA Database contained 2,527,728 DNA profiles from 2,249,678 individuals. It was set up in April 1995 by the Forensic Science Service (UK) and was the world's first national intelligence DNA database.

★**Most patents held by an individual** Shunpei Yamazaki (Japan), president of Semiconductor Energy Laboratory Co. Ltd. (Japan), held a total of 3,245 patents as of May 31, 2004.

★**Longest space tether** The *SEDS-1* and *SEDS-2* satellites (U.S.A.), launched on March 29, 1993, and March 10, 1994, respectively, achieved a space tether 12.4 miles (20 km) long. Both tethers were eventually severed by orbital debris impact. They were also the first man-made objects in space visible from the ground as a line rather than a point.

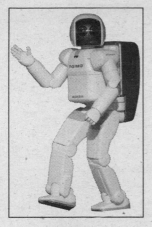

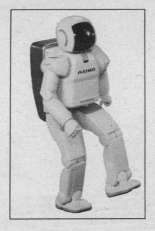

☆**FASTEST RUNNING HUMANOID ROBOT ASIMO**, which stands for Advanced Step in Innovative Mobility, has been developed and refined by Honda (Japan) since 2000 as the latest in its series of prototype humanoid robots designed to help people in the future. In December 2004, Honda announced that ASIMO had been improved in order to allow it to run at a speed of 1.8 mph (3 km/h).

MODERN SOCIETY

CONTENTS

BIRTHS, DEATHS, & MARRIAGES

BIRTH & DEATH

★**Largest population of children** In 2003, 50.8% of the population of Uganda was aged between 0 and 14 years old. Excluding the Vatican City, Italy has the ★**smallest population of children** with only 14% aged 0–14 years old in the same year.

Birth rates Latvia and Georgia both recorded the **lowest birth rates,** with just eight live births per 1,000 population in 2002. The world average for the same year was 21.

The countries with the **highest birth rates** are Somalia and Sierra Leone, both of which recorded 50 live births per 1,000 people in 2002.

☆**Natural population increases** The country with the ☆**highest natural population increase** (births minus deaths) is Somalia, with an estimated increase of 32 per 1,000 people in 2002. The world average was 12 per 1,000 for the same year.

Latvia and Ukraine both had the ☆**lowest natural population increase**

☆ **BRIDE WITH THE MOST BRIDESMAIDS** Bride Christa Rasanayagam (Canada) was accompanied by 79 bridesmaids, aged one to 79, when she married Arulanantham Suresh Joachim (Sri Lanka) at Christ the King Catholic Church, Mississauga, Ontario, Canada, on September 6, 2003.

☆ **GROOM WITH MOST USHERS/GROOMSMEN** Accompanied by 47 groomsmen, aged from two to 63, Arulanantham Suresh Joachim (Sri Lanka) married Christa Rasanayagam (Canada) on September 6, 2003, at Christ the King Catholic Church in Mississauga, Ontario, Canada.

(or fastest rate of decreasing population) over the same period with an increase of -6 per 1,000 people.

☆ **Infant mortality rates** Sweden has the ☆**lowest infant mortality rate** (that is, the fewest deaths of infants aged under one year), with 3.44 per 1,000 live births as of December 2003.

Angola has the ☆**highest infant mortality rate,** with 191.44 deaths per 1,000 live births in the same year.

☆ **Death rates** According to the most recent data available, both Sierra Leone and Malawi had the ☆**highest death rate,** with an estimated 25 deaths per 1,000 people for 2002. The world average for the same year was nine.

Kuwait and Oman both recorded the ☆**lowest death rate** of just three deaths per 1,000 people for 2002.

Leading cause of death In industrialized countries, diseases of the heart and of blood vessels (cardiovascular disease) account for more than 50% of deaths. The most common of these are heart attacks and strokes, generally due to atheroma (degeneration of the arterial walls) obstructing the flow of blood.

Most common cause of sudden death Coronary heart disease is the most common cause of sudden death. The main factors that put an individual at risk of the disease are smoking, high blood pressure, and high levels of cholesterol.

☆**Suicide rates** Lithuania had the world's ☆**highest suicide rate,** with 91.7 suicides per 100,000 people in 2000, according to the World Health Organization's latest figures. This breaks down to 75.6 male and 16.1 female suicides per 100,000 people.

According to the World Health Organization, the following countries all recorded the ☆**lowest suicide rates,** with no cases reported in the years shown: Antigua and Barbuda (1995), the Dominican Republic (1994), Saint Kitts and Nevis (1995), and Saint Vincent and the Grenadines (1986).

Longest will The will of Frederica Evelyn Stilwell Cook (U.S.A.)—proved at Somerset House in London, UK, on November 2, 1925—consisted of four bound volumes containing a total of 95,940 words and concerning $100,000 worth of property.

MARRIAGE

Longest marriage Sir Temulji Bhicaji Nariman and Lady Nariman were married for 86 years—from 1853 to 1940. The union took place when the two cousins were both five. Sir Temulji (b. September 3, 1848) died, aged 91 years 11 months, in August 1940 in Bombay, India.

Lazarus Rowe and Molly Webber, who were both born in 1725, were recorded as marrying in 1743. Molly died first, in June 1829 in Limington, Maine, U.S.A., at which time the couple had been married for 86 years.

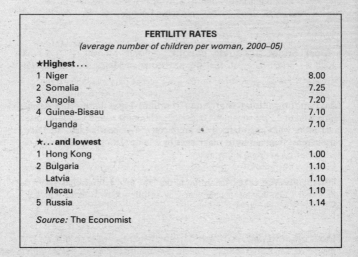

FERTILITY RATES
(average number of children per woman, 2000–05)

★Highest...

1	Niger	8.00
2	Somalia	7.25
3	Angola	7.20
4	Guinea-Bissau	7.10
	Uganda	7.10

★...and lowest

1	Hong Kong	1.00
2	Bulgaria	1.10
	Latvia	1.10
	Macau	1.10
5	Russia	1.14

Source: The Economist

☆**OLDEST LIVING MARRIED COUPLE** Tadao Watanabe (Japan, b. September 3, 1898) married Minoru Mita (Japan, b. May 14, 1907) on May 18, 1926. Aged 106 years 188 days and 97 years 298 days respectively, they have a record aggregate age of 203 years 285 days. Also, as of March 10, 2005, they had been married for 78 years 296 days, making theirs the ☆**longest marriage for a living couple.**

Most marriage vows renewed (same couple) Lauren Lubeck Blair and David E. Hough Blair (both U.S.A.) married each other for the 83rd time on August 16, 2004, at the Lighthouse Lounge at the Boardwalk Hotel & Casino, Las Vegas, Nevada, U.S.A.

☆**Most bridal bouquets caught** Stephanie Monyak (U.S.A.) has caught 11 bridal bouquets that were tossed at weddings she has attended since 1983.

Most monogamous marriages (female) Linda Essex (U.S.A.) has had a total of 23 monogamous marriages. Her most recent wedding was in June 1996, when she married Glynn "Scotty" Wolfe, who held the record for the **most monogamous marriages by a male** (29). He died 10 days before their first wedding anniversary.

Highest divorce rate According to the UN, the Maldives has 10.97 divorces per 1,000 inhabitants per year. This is followed by Belarus with 4.63, and the U.S.A. with 4.34.

★**Lowest marriage rate** In 1994, the latest year for which data is available, the Dominican Republic had just two marriages per 1,000 population.

★ BRIDEGROOM MARRIED AT THE HIGHEST ALTITUDE On August 10, 2003, Yuri Malenchenko (Ukraine) married Ekaterina Dmitriev (U.S.A.) from an altitude of 214.3 nautical miles (396 km). The ceremony was conducted over a videoconference link between the bride in Houston, Texas, U.S.A., and the groom who, at the time, was commander of the *Expedition 7* mission to the International Space Station. The closest the bride got to her husband on the day was standing next to his cardboard cutout.

Highest marriage rate Antigua and Barbuda had 22.1 marriages per 1,000 population in 1998. The U.S. figure from 2000, for comparison, was just 8.4 marriages per 1,000.

NATIONS

CITIES

Oldest capital city Damascus (Dimashq), Syria, has been continuously inhabited since *ca.* 2500 B.C.

Most remote city from the sea Urumqi, the capital of China's Xinjiang Uygur autonomous region, is 1,500 miles (2,500 km) from the nearest coastline.

★**City with the largest foreign-born population** In 2001, 59% of the population of Miami, Florida, U.S.A., was born outside the country.

COST OF LIVING

☆**Highest GNI per capita** According to available data from the World Bank Atlas' figures from September 2004, the country with the highest Gross National Income (GNI) per capita for 2003 was Luxembourg, with $43,940. GNI is the total value of goods and services produced by a country in one year, divided by its population. GNI per capita shows what part of a country's GNI each person would have if GNI was divided equally.

According to the same source, Ethiopia had the ☆**lowest GNI per capita** in 2003, with $90.

Most populous country
China (1,298,847,624)

Least populous country
Vatican City (921)

Largest country
Russia (143,782,338) 6,592,848 miles² or 17,075,400 km²

Smallest country
Vatican City 0.17 miles² or 0.44 km²

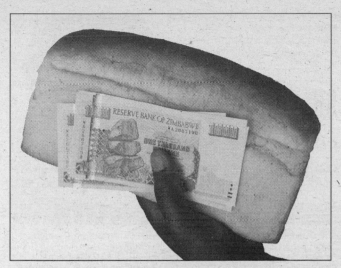

☆ **HIGHEST INFLATION** In 2003, Zimbabwe's annual rate of inflation stood at 385%. In 1998, for example, a loaf of bread cost Z$0.70 (less than $0.01), rising to Z$3,000 ($0.50) in 2003.

The country with the world's lowest annual inflation rate is Hong Kong, where consumer prices fell by 2.6% during 2003.

Highest rate of tax In Denmark, the highest rate of personal income tax is 62.9%, with the basic rate of income tax starting at 43.7% as of June 2003.

The sovereign countries with the **lowest rate of personal income tax** are Bahrain and Qatar, where the rate, regardless of income, is zero.

☆ **Highest military expenditure per capita** Israel spent $1,466.51 per capita on military expenditure, according to 2003 figures.

According to the CIA World Factbook, the country with the ☆**lowest military expenditure** is Iceland, with $0 spent as of December 2003.

GEOGRAPHY

★ **Fastest growing country through land reclamation (by percentage of original size)** In 1960, the total area of Singapore was 224.5 miles^2 (581.5 km^2); since then, it has added over 38.6 miles^2 (100 km^2) of land, which represents an increase of 17% of the original area.

★ **Most forested country** As of 2000, 95.7% of the Cook Islands in the South Pacific Ocean was covered in forest.

☆ **COUNTRY OF ORIGIN FOR MOST REFUGEES** The country with the most people seeking asylum elsewhere is Afghanistan. According to the provisional figures from the United Nations High Commission for Refugees (UNHCR) for the end of 2003, 2.1 million Afghans applied for political asylum in 74 countries. This represents 22% of the total global refugee population.

★**Largest area of land named after one person** The continents of North and South America, which total 16,407,701 miles^2 (42,495,751 km^2), were both named after the 15th-century Italian explorer Amerigo Vespucci.

POPULATIONS

★**Country that receives the most refugees** Pakistan receives more asylum seekers than any other country. According to the United Nations High Commission for Refugees (UNHCR), Pakistan received 1.1 million refugees in 2003.

★**Hardest working citizens (industrialized nations)** According to the Organization for Economic Co-operation and Development's (OECD) annual Employment Outlook Report 2004, the industrialized country with the hardest working citizens is South Korea, whose working population (excluding self-employed labor) clocked up a total of 2,390 hours per employee for 2003.

Largest shortage of men The country with the largest recorded shortage of males is Latvia, where 53.97% of the population was female and 46.03% was male in 2002.

The ☆**country with the largest recorded shortage of women** is the

☆ HIGHEST COST OF LIVING According to the latest Economist Intelligence Unit's Worldwide Cost of Living Survey—which compares the cost of a wide range of goods and services—the world's most expensive city is Tokyo, Japan. According to the same source, Tehran, the capital of Iran, offers the ★lowest cost of living.

United Arab Emirates, with the male population numbering 67.63% and female population at 32.37% in 2001.

MISCELLANEOUS

☆ **Highest unemployment** According to estimates of 2003, 85% of Liberia's labor force is not in paid employment.

According to available data, in 2002 Nauru and Andorra had the **lowest rate of unemployment** for any country in the world, with 0%.

☆ **Highest road fatality rate** Mauritius had 43.9 traffic fatalities per 100,000 people in 2000.

★ **Most corrupt country** As of October 2004, the most corrupt country is Bangladesh, according to Transparency International's Corruption Perceptions Index.

☆**LEAST CORRUPT COUNTRY** As of October 2004, the world's least corrupt country is Finland, according to Transparency International's Corruption Perceptions Index. This index compares the misuse of public office for private gain in 146 countries, as perceived by business and country analysts (resident and nonresident).

QUALITY OF LIFE

(based on various factors ranging from recreational options to political stability)

Highest...

1 Zurich, Switzerland
  Geneva, Switzerland
3 Vancouver, Canada
  Vienna, Austria
5 Auckland, New Zealand
  Bern, Switzerland
  Copenhagen, Denmark
  Frankfurt, Germany
  Sydney, Australia

...and lowest

1 Baghdad, Iraq
2 Bangui, Central African Republic
3 Brazzaville, Republic of the Congo
4 Pointe Noire, Republic of the Congo
  Khartoum, Sudan

Source: The Economist

TRAVEL & TOURISM

LAND

Densest road network The former Portuguese colony of Macau, today a Special Administrative Region of China, has 31.7 miles (50.9 km) of road per mile^2 (2.6 km^2) of land area. By comparison, the U.S.A., which has the world's **largest road network,** has a density of only 1.1 miles (1.8 km) per mile^2 because of its immense size. Of the world's fully sovereign countries, Malta has the densest network of roads, with 11.4 miles (18.4 km) per mile^2.

☆**Most crowded road network** Hong Kong, China, has 458.7 registered motor vehicles for every mile (1.6 km), in theory making its roads the most crowded in the world. The United Arab Emirates is second, with 370.5 vehicles per mile, while the U.S.A., because of its vast size and large road network, is in 42nd place, with 54.5 vehicles per mile.

Country with the busiest road network Indonesia's roads are the most heavily used in the world, with 8 million miles (12.8 million km) being driven for every mile (1.6 km) of the country's road network each year.

Longest bus route The "Liberator's Route" is 6,002 miles (9,660 km) long and is operated by Expreso Internacional Ormeño SA of Lima, Peru. It links Caracas, Venezuela, and Buenos Aires, Argentina, by bus, passing through the capitals of six South American countries. It takes 214 hours (8 days 22 hours) to complete, including breaks.

**TOP 10 POPULAR INTERNATIONAL TOURIST DESTINATIONS
(MOST VISITORS 2003)**

10. **Canada**—17.5 million

9. **Germany**—18.4 million

8. **Mexico**—18.7 million

7. **Austria**—19.1 million

6. **UK**—24.7 million

5. **China**—33 million

4. **Italy**—39.6 million

3. **USA**—41.2 million

2. **Spain**—51.8 million

LARGEST CRUISE SHIP LINE Carnival is the world's largest cruise company, with 12 distinct brands and over 77 ships and 128,000 berths. In 2003, Carnival Corporation merged with P&O Princess plc, and the company's brands now include Carnival Cruise Lines, Princess Cruises, P&O Cruises, and Windstar Cruises. Pictured is one of Carnival's ships, the *Carnival Valor,* passing Miami Beach en route to the Port of Miami.

SEA

☆ **Busiest port by cargo volume** In 2004, a total of 866 billion lb. (433 million tons) of cargo passed through the port of Singapore. Containerized cargo accounted for 492 billion lb. (245 million tons), with oil at 284 billion lb. (142 million tons) accounting for the second largest portion. The remainder consisted of "conventional" and non-oil bulk cargo.

First public hovercraft service From July to September 1962, a hovercraft service was run across the Dee estuary between Rhyl, Denbighshire, and Wallasey, Merseyside, UK.

Largest civilian hovercraft The SRN4 Mk III, a British-built civil hovercraft, weighs 683,400 lb. (340 tons) and can accommodate 418 passengers and 60 cars. It is 185 ft. (56.38 m) in length and has a top speed of 65 knots (75 mph). Service across the English Channel ceased in December 2000 when the hovercraft were replaced by slower but more economical Seacat catamarans.

AIR

★ **Most scheduled flight journeys within 30 days** Brother Michael Bartlett (UK) used a monthly Skypass issued by the Belgian national airline

Sabena to fly between London and Brussels 128 times between October 18 and November 17, 1993. He had the individual tickets stapled together to form an 83-ft.-long (25.3-m) ticket, and covered a total of 25,955 miles (41,771 km) during the month.

Most scheduled flights in a week Tae Oka (Japan) completed 70 flights in seven days on Thai Airways International from February 14 to 20, 2001. The flights were all internal between the Thai cities of Chiang Mai, Chiang Rai, and Mae Hong Son airports.

☆**Busiest airport by number of aircraft** A total of 928,691 takeoffs and landings were made during 2003 by aircraft at O'Hare International Airport, Chicago, Illinois, U.S.A., according to the Airports Council International (ACI), making it the world's busiest in terms of the number of aircraft using it.

★**Most airlines flown on in a year** John Bougen and James Irving (both New Zealand) flew on 104 different airlines from August 28, 2002, to February 12, 2003, as part of their All Nations Quest. Their journey started and finished in Auckland, New Zealand, passed through 191 countries, and so also set the record for the **most sovereign countries visited in six**

☆1. MOST POPULAR TOURIST DESTINATION In 2003, France attracted 75 million international visitors, according to the World Tourism Organization.

months (191 of the world's 193 sovereign countries in 167 days 15 hr. 39 min.).

During the same attempt, they took 242 flights on 54 aircraft types, and set a third record, that for ★most flights on a single journey. In accordance with the rules, the 191 airports visited excluded repeat visits to airports, and they did not return to New Zealand until the end of the trip.

Most supersonic passenger journeys By February 2003, Fred Finn (UK) had made 718 Atlantic crossings on Concorde. His first flight was

MAURIZIO GIULIANO

Maurizio Giuliano (Italy/UK, b. February 24, 1975) had visited all 193 of the world's sovereign countries by February 20, 2004, when he was 28 years 361 days old.

Did you set out to be the youngest person to travel to all sovereign countries? No, although the addiction to crossing borders is interesting...What causes me to travel so much is the passion to learn about different cultures and different mentalities, different peoples.

Is there a country that's been particularly hard to get into? Yes, North Korea was definitely the most difficult. I went in 2000 after trying for a long time to get a visa. I kept e-mailing and faxing embassies in various parts of the world for a whole year and finally in 2000 I was told that my visa had been approved.

How many passports do you have? I have a total of 42. Twelve of them are British and 30 are Italian.

Why so many? It's really helpful to have at least two valid passports because when you send your passport off for a visa, it can take quite a while to get it back. Also, I've been careful to have my visas and stamps in a way that is as aesthetic as possible, so I try not to get all my stamps jammed onto one page. I normally have three or four stamps on a page. I've been to many countries more than once, which means extra stamps.

☆BIGGEST TOURIST SPENDERS In 2003, German citizens spent $64.7 billion, excluding airfares, while on vacation abroad, according to the World Tourism Organization. Americans, the biggest spenders in 2002, were second with $56.5 billion, and British citizens were third with $48.5 billion.

May 26, 1976, for which he still has the special commemorative brief-case tag.

★Longest distance commercial scheduled flight A flight operated by Singapore Airlines between Singapore and New York City, U.S.A., covers a distance of some 10,300 miles (16,600 km). The 18-hour flight employs 181-seat Airbus A340–500 aircraft.

FEASTS & CELEBRATIONS

RELIGIOUS FESTIVALS

Largest gathering of religious leaders The Millennium World Peace Summit of Religious and Spiritual Leaders involved 1,000 delegates. It was held at the UN headquarters in New York, U.S.A., from August 28 to 31, 2000.

Largest gathering of Sikhs Over eight million Sikhs gathered at the Anandpur Sahib gurdwara (Sikh temple), Punjab, India, from April 13 to 17, 1999, to celebrate the 300th anniversary of the Sikh Khalsa, an order of the Sikh religion. More than 3.5 million people gathered there on April 13, the day of the Vaisakhi festival, to commemorate the day that the Sikh Khalsa was established.

★ LARGEST ELEPHANT BUFFET For the annual elephant parade held in 2003 in the Surin Province, Thailand, a record 269 Asian elephants gathered to eat over 110,000 lb. (55 tons) of fruit and vegetables that had been laid out for them on tables covered with silk cloth.

FOOD FESTIVALS:

February: **Crab festival,** San Francisco, U.S.A.

March: **Blood sausage festival,** Mortagne au Perche, France

April: **Maple syrup festival,** Saint-Georges, Canada

May: **Cheese rolling festival,** Stilton, UK

July: **Baby food festival,** Freemont, Michigan, U.S.A.

September: **Mooncake festival,** Singapore

October: **Truffle festival,** Alba, Italy, and **Date feast,** Erfoud, Morocco

November: **Cherry festival,** Ficksburg, South Africa

December: **Radish night,** Oaxaca, Mexico

Most Muslim pilgrims The annual hajj (pilgrimage) to Mecca, Saudi Arabia, attracts greater numbers than any other Islamic mission, an average of 2 million people a year from 140 countries.

Most Christian pilgrims The House of the Virgin Mary at Loretto, Italy, receives 3.5 million pilgrims (as opposed to tourists) a year—over three times the number visiting Lourdes, France.

Most Hindu pilgrims Every 12 years during the festival of Kumbha Mela, held at the confluence of the Ganges and Jumna (Yamuna) rivers in Uttar Pradesh state, India, worshipers gather to bathe in the waters. In 1995, an estimated 20 million pilgrims attended, the highest recorded total.

FOOD

Largest tamale festival The annual Indio International Tamale Festival held in Indio, California, U.S.A., to mark the Christmas holiday season, attracted over 154,000 people at its 11th event in December 2002. A tamale is a Mexican dish made up of assorted cheeses, chili powder, corn masa flour, lard, and chicken broth.

Largest silver service dinner On April 28, 2001, 11,483 people attended a silver service dinner party at Earl's Court, London, UK. The dinner

LARGEST FROGS' LEGS FESTIVAL The Fellsmere Frog Leg Festival held in Fellsmere, Florida, U.S.A., attracted 75,000 visitors from January 18 to 21, 2001. More than 6,600 lb. (3,000 kg) of golden batter-fried frogs' legs were served to 13,200 diners during the free, four-day festival.

LARGEST ANNUAL FOOD FIGHT On the last Wednesday in August, the town of Buñol, near Valencia, Spain, holds its annual tomato festival, *La Tomatina*. In 1999, about 25,000 people spent one hour at this giant food fight throwing about 275,500 lb. (125 tons) of tomatoes at each other. From the backs of trucks, attendants dump the red fruit onto the streets for people to scoop up and throw. By the time the food fight is over, the streets and everyone on them are saturated with gloppy tomato paste. Rivers of tomato juice, as much as 12 in. (30 cm) deep, run through the town until local fire trucks come in to hose down the streets and the people on them.

was sponsored by Vodafone Group plc. The event was developed and produced by Skybridge Group plc, and the caterers were Beeton Rumford Ltd.

☆ **Largest breakfast** A breakfast involving 23,291 diners took place at the Chung Shang Stadium, Taiwan, on October 13, 2001. A total of 1,497 gal. (5,670 liters) of milk and 4,232 lb. (1,920 kg) of bread were consumed.

Largest religious feast A feast attended by 150,000 guests was held at Ahmedabad, India, on June 2, 1991, as part of the renunciation ceremony of Atul Dalpatlal Shah, when he became a monk.

Largest garlic festival The three-day Gilroy Garlic Festival, held each summer in Gilroy, California, U.S.A., attracts 130,000 people, who sample garlic-flavored food ranging from meat to ice cream.

Largest wedding banquet/reception Jayalalitha Jayaram (India), former Tamil Nadu chief minister and movie star, hosted a reception banquet for over 150,000 guests at her foster son's wedding in her 50-acre (20-

hectare) grounds in Madras, India, on September 7, 1995. The wedding is reported to have cost over 750 million rupees ($21,328,000).

☆**Largest picnic** At an open-air dinner held during the May Festival on May 2, 1999, 8,000 people gathered at the Plaza de Espana, Santa Cruz, Tenerife, Spain, to eat prepared meals brought from home.

Longest continuous table On March 22, 1998, a team of caterers set places for 15,000 people to eat at a table stretching over 3 miles (5.05 km) along the newly built Vasco da Gama bridge, Lisbon, Portugal—Europe's longest bridge at 11 miles (18 km).

WHERE IS THE WORLD'S LARGEST RELIGIOUS THEME PARK? FIND OUT ON P. 422

LARGEST GATHERING OF CLOWNS In 1991, the annual clown convention held in Bognor Regis in West Sussex, UK, attracted 850 clowns, including 430 from North America. The convention has been held since 1946 by Clowns International, which is the **largest** and **oldest clown organization** in the world.

LARGEST DONATION OF HAIR Pilgrims to the Tirupati temple in Andhra Pradesh, India, donate a tonsure of their hair as a form of sacrifice. An estimated 6.5 million people make donations of their hair every year, and more than $2.2 million is raised in temple funds through the annual auction of hair. The temple attracts an average of 30,000 visitors a day. Around 600 barbers are employed 24 hours a day by the temple to shave the pilgrims' heads, and the hair is auctioned to wig-makers as well as chemical and fertilizer factories.

DRINKS

Largest beer festival Oktoberfest, the annual beer festival in Munich, Germany (September 18 to October 5), was visited by a record 7 million people in 1999. What they consumed was also a record: 1.53 million gal. (5.8 million liters) of beer was "tasted" from 11 beer tents that stood on a site as large as 50 football fields.

Largest liquor tasting On November 24, 2001, at The World Trade Center in Stockholm, Sweden, 1,210 people took part in a whisky tasting, each participant sampling five different types.

Largest wine tasting event On November 22, 1986, approximately 4,000 wine tasters consumed 9,360 bottles of wine at a single wine tasting. The event was sponsored by local San Francisco television station KQED in California, U.S.A.

Largest simultaneous toast A total of 462,572 participants gathered in pubs, restaurants, bars, and concert sites across the U.S.A. on February 23, 2001, at 11:00 p.m. (EST) for The Great Guinness Toast.

POLITICS

GOVERNMENT

★ **Most votes cast in a national election** From April 20 to May 10, 2004, a total of 387.8 million votes were cast in India to elect the 543 members of the 14th Lok Sabha (the House of the People, which is the lower house of the Indian legislature). On May 13, the Bharatiya Janata Party conceded defeat to the new ruling party, the Indian National Congress under Prime Minister Manmohan Singh.

★ **Youngest voting age** Universal suffrage in Iran is at the age of just 15 years old.

☆ **Highest paid prime minister** In August 2000, the then prime minister of Singapore, Goh Chok Tong, earned an increase in annual salary of 14% to SG$1.94 million ($1.1 million). The current prime minister is Lee Hsien Loong, who was sworn in on August 12, 2004.

★ **Richest prime minister** Silvio Berlusconi, prime minister of Italy, has amassed a personal wealth of $10 billion according to *Forbes* in 2004.

☆ **Youngest appointed prime minister** Roosevelt Skerritt (b. June 8, 1972) was appointed prime minister of Dominica on January 8, 2004, at the age of 31.

The **oldest living prime minister** is King Fahd bin Abdul Aziz (b. 1921), who became king and prime minister of Saudi Arabia on June 13, 1982.

The **oldest appointed prime minister** was Morarji Ranchhodji Desai (India, 1896–1995), who took up his post in March 1977 aged 81. He served until 1979.

Youngest appointed president Jean-Claude Duvalier (b. July 3, 1951) succeeded his father, François Duvalier, as president of Haiti for life on April 22, 1971, at the age of 19 years 293 days. He served as president of Haiti until 1986.

Longest serving head of state Fidel Castro (b. August 13, 1927), president of Cuba's Council of State, has been the island-state's unchallenged revolutionary and political leader since July 26, 1959, when his guerrilla movement overthrew the military dictatorship headed by Fulgencio Batista.

☆ **Country with the most siblings in power** Saudi Arabia has five siblings holding powerful governmental offices. The current head of state is King Fahd bin Abdul Aziz, but owing to illness his half-brother, Crown Prince Abdullah bin Abdul Aziz, acts as regent, as well as being first deputy

★ **MOST ELECTION VOTES CAST IN ONE YEAR** A record total of 58 presidential and parliamentary elections were held in 2004, involving over 1.1 billion voters. The first that year was a presidential election in Georgia, held on January 4. The last was the third round of Ukraine's presidential elections on December 26. Pictured are voters in India (top left), the Philippines (top right), and South Africa (bottom).

prime minister and commander of the national guard. The king's full brother, Prince Sultan bin Abdul Aziz, is second deputy prime minister and minister of defense and aviation. Other (full) brothers include Prince Nayef bin Abdul Aziz (interior minister) and Prince Salman bin Abdul Aziz (governor of Riyadh).

Longest serving female prime minister Sirimavo Bandaranaike was prime minister of Sri Lanka for a total of 17 years 208 days. She served from July 21, 1960, to March 25, 1965; May 29, 1970, to July 22, 1977; and November 12, 1994, to August 10, 2000. Bandaranaike was also the world's **first female prime minister.**

MONARCHY

☆**Richest monarch** King Fahd bin Abdul Aziz (Saudi Arabia) has a personal wealth estimated by *Forbes* in 2004 to be $25 billion.

☆**Largest royal family** In 2002, the house of Al-Saud of Saudi Arabia had over 4,000 royal princes and 30,000 relatives. The kingdom was estab-

YOUNGEST CURRENT HEAD OF STATE The youngest current republican head of state is Lt. Yahya Jammeh (b. May 25, 1965), who became president of the provisional council and head of state of The Gambia following a military coup on July 26, 1994. On September 27, 1996, he was elected president following a return to civilian government. President Jammeh was reelected on October 18, 2001, for another five years.

lished by King Abdul Aziz in 1932. His 17 wives bore him 44 sons, four of whom have ruled the kingdom since the king's death in 1953.

Shortest reign ever Crown Prince Luis Filipe was king of Portugal (Dom Luis III) for just 20 minutes on February 1, 1908.

Longest reign ever Minhti, king of Arakan, part of Myanmar, is reputed to have reigned for 95 years from 1279 to 1374.

The **longest documented reign of any monarch** is that of Phiops II (also known as Neferkare or Pepi II), a Sixth-Dynasty pharaoh of ancient Egypt.

KING MSWATI III

King Mswati III of Swaziland was just 18 years and 6 days old when he took the throne. He talks to Guinness World Records about being the world's youngest reigning monarch.

What was it like to become king at such a young age? It was a great responsibility indeed. I was young with no experience, so I'm grateful to my mother and my advisors for their invaluable support and advice.

What is a typical day like as king? Always very busy with many problems to solve at both individual and government levels. A Swazi king must care for and support his people, who must always have access to him.

What is the most difficult thing about being king? The big responsibility of taking care of your nation and always making the right decision about the future.

If you were not king, what job would you like to do? I've never seriously thought about any career. I guess I was born to be king. Being king is, to me, a calling from God.

What are the biggest challenges facing Swaziland at this time? Unemployment, poverty, and HIV/AIDS are the biggest. We're addressing these problems through job creation programs aimed at reaching the people at the grass roots level. We have traditional and modern programs, such as the campaign for abstinence from premarital sex, to help our youth protect themselves from HIV/AIDS.

His reign began ca. 2281 B.C., when he was six years old, and lasted about 94 years.

Longest reign—current Bhumibol Adulyadej, king of Thailand succeeded to the throne following the death of his older brother on June 9, 1946.

The **most durable monarch** is the king of Cambodia, Norodom Sihanouk, who first became king on April 16, 1941. He abdicated on March 2, 1955, and returned to the throne on September 24, 1993.

★**Budget expenditure** In December 2003, the world's **lowest budget expenditure** was just $878,199—including capital expenditures—by the Pitcairn Islands in the South Pacific.

The **highest budget expenditure** (based on 2002 figures) was $2.052 trillion by the U.S. government.

WHICH QUEEN—THE LONGEST SERVING QUEEN ALIVE TODAY—VISITED THE GUINNESS WORLD RECORDS OFFICE IN 2004? FIND OUT ON P. XI

CRIME & PUNISHMENT

SENTENCES

★**Longest prison sentence for hacking** Brian Salcedo (U.S.A.) was sentenced to nine years in prison in Charlotte, North Carolina, U.S.A., on December 16, 2004, for computer hacking. Salcedo had pleaded guilty to conspiracy and numerous hacking charges in August 2004 after attempting to steal credit card information from the computer systems of Lowe's hardware stores (U.S.A.).

Longest prison sentence for fraud Chamoy Thipyaso (Thailand) and seven of her associates were each jailed for 141,078 years by the Bangkok Criminal Court, Thailand, on July 27, 1989. The "Queen of the Underground," as she was known, convinced over 16,000 Thais to put their life savings into a pyramid scheme. The government closed down Thipyaso's business—worth 4.6 billion baht ($204,984,268)—after it posed a threat to the Thai banking system.

★**Shortest jury deliberation** On July 22, 2004, Nicholas Clive McAllister (New Zealand) was acquitted of cultivating marijuana plants after the jury at Greymouth District Court, West Coast, New Zealand, had deliberated for just one minute. The jury would not have had time to take their seats at the deliberation table.

LONGEST SERVING PRISONER IN SOLITARY CONFINEMENT Mordecai Vanunu (Israel) spent nearly 12 years in a total isolation jail cell—the longest known term of solitary confinement in modern times. Born in 1954, Vanunu was convicted of treason for giving information about Israel's nuclear program to the UK's *Sunday Times* newspaper. He was held in isolation from 1986 until March 1998. However, Vanunu was sentenced to a total of 18 years in prison and remained incarcerated until he was released on April 21, 2004.

ROBBERY

Greatest art robbery On April 14, 1991, 20 paintings estimated to be worth $500 million were stolen from the Van Gogh Museum in Amsterdam, the Netherlands. However, only 35 minutes later they were found in an abandoned car not far from the museum.

Most valuable object stolen Arguably, Leonardo da Vinci's *Mona Lisa,* though never valued, is the most valuable object ever stolen. It disappeared from the Louvre, Paris, France, on August 21, 1911, and was recovered in Italy in 1913. Vincenzo Perugia (Italy) was charged with its theft.

Largest object stolen by an individual On the moonless night of June 5, 1966, N. William Kennedy slashed the mooring lines of the 10,639-dwt SS *Orient Trader* at Wolfes Cove, St. Lawrence Seaway, Canada. The vessel drifted to a waiting blacked-out tugboat, thus evading a ban on any shipping movements during a violent wildcat waterfront strike. It then set sail for Spain.

★LARGEST SPEEDING FINE Jussi Salonoja (Finland) was fined £170,000 ($223,000) for driving at 50 mph (80 km/h) in a 25-mph (40-km/h) zone in Helsinki, Finland, in February 2004. In accordance with Finnish law, speeders are fined in proportion to their annual incomes—and Mr. Salonoja, heir to a family-owned sausage empire, earned close to $11 million in 2002.

Largest train robbery

On August 8, 1963, a General Post Office mail train from Glasgow was ambushed at Sears Crossing and robbed at Bridego Bridge near Mentmore, Buckinghamshire, UK. A gang escaped with about 120 mailbags containing £2,631,784 ($7,369,784) in banknotes that were being taken to London for destruction. Only £343,448 ($961,757) was recovered.

Largest jewel robbery An estimated $100 million worth of gems were taken in a raid at the Antwerp Diamond Center, Belgium, sometime over the weekend of February 15–16, 2003. Although 123 of the 160 vaults were emptied, there was no sign of a break-in, alarms did not go off, and the bombproof vault doors were not tampered with.

★Oldest bank robber At the age of 92, J. L. Hunter Rountree was sentenced to 151 months in prison on January 23, 2004, after he pleaded guilty to robbing $1,999 from a bank in Texas, U.S.A., on August 12, 2003. In a newspaper interview, he said: "A bank that I'd done business with had forced me into bankruptcy. I have never liked banks since…I decided I would get even. And I have." He also claimed that prison food was better than what was served at some nursing homes.

WHICH IS THE WORLD'S LEAST CORRUPT COUNTRY? FIND OUT ON P. 248

LARGEST CRIMINAL ORGANIZATION According to Interpol, the centuries-old Six Great Triads of China has at least 100,000 members scattered around the world. (Pictured are suspected members of a Hong Kong triad gang.)

In terms of profits, the **largest organized crime syndicate** is the Mafia, with an estimated profit in March 1986 of $75 billion. It consists of up to 5,000 individuals in 25 "families," federated under "The Commission," involved in gambling, protection rackets, narcotics, bootlegging, loan-sharking, and prostitution.

MURDER

Most prolific murderer It was established at the trial of Behram, the "Indian Thug," that he had strangled at least 931 victims with his yellow and white cloth strip or "ruhmal" in the Oudh district (now in Uttar Pradesh, India) between 1790 and 1840. Thugs ("Thieves") were members of gangs who traveled around India on killing sprees from about 1550 until finally being suppressed in the mid-1800s.

Most prolific female murderer Historically, the most prolific murderer of the Western world was Elizabeth Bathori (Hungary), who practiced vampirism on girls and young women. Throughout the 17th century, she killed more than 600 virgins in order to drink their blood and bathe in it. When her murderous career was discovered, the countess was locked up in her castle from 1610 until her death in 1614.

Most prolific serial killer The most prolific substantiated modern serial killer is Pedro López (Colombia), who confessed to raping and killing 300 girls in Colombia, Peru, and Ecuador. Charged with 57 counts of murder in

Ecuador, the "Monster of the Andes" was sentenced to life imprisonment in 1980.

Most prolific murder partnership Sisters Delfina and María de Jesús Gonzáles (Mexico) abducted girls to work in brothels and are known to have murdered at least 90 of their victims. The sisters were sentenced to 40 years' imprisonment in 1964.

Country with the most murders According to the United Nations, from 1998 to 2000 the country with the most murders was India, with 37,170. However, Colombia has the **highest total recorded intentional homicides** per capita, with 65 murders per 100,000.

★ CAPITAL PUNISHMENT ★

EXECUTIONS

Most executions	China	726 legally sanctioned executions in 2003, according to Amnesty International
Most executions per capita	Saudi Arabia	1,409 executions from 1980 to 2002, a figure of 1 per 208,772 citizens
Most popular method of execution	Firing squad	Practiced in 73 countries, and sole method in 45; hanging comes next, practiced in 58 countries
First execution by injection	December 7, 1983	C. Brooke (U.S.A.), Huntsville, Texas, U.S.A.
First execution by electric chair	August 8, 1890	William Kemmler (U.S.A.), Auburn Prison, New York, U.S.A.
Greatest hanging at one gallows	38 Sioux natives	Hanged on December 26, 1862, outside Mankato, Minnesota, U.S.A.
First abolition	1798	Liechtenstein

DEATH ROW

Largest population	3,471	35 states of the U.S.A. (2004 figures)
Longest time on death row	39 years	Sadamichi Hirasawa (Japan, 1893–1987) lived out his life on death row in Sendai Prison, Japan, after poisoning 12 bank employees
Longest time on death row for a dog	8 years, 190 days	Word, a Lhasa apso incarcerated for biting in Seattle, Washington, U.S.A.

OBJECTS OF DESIRE

★**Most expensive pinball machine** A unique pinball machine produced in February 1992 is reported to have been sold for $120,000 in Los Angeles, California, U.S.A. This is equivalent to approximately $162,765 today.

Most complicated wristwatch The Piguet/Muller/Gerber Grand Complication watch has 1,116 individual parts and is owned by Willy Ernst Sturzenegger, Territorial Earl of Arran (Switzerland). It was last added to by master watchmaker Paul Gerber (Switzerland).

Most expensive cell phone A cell phone designed by David Morris International (UK) was sold for £66,629 ($113,256) in 1996. Made entirely from 18-karat gold, the unique cell phone had a keypad that was encrusted with pink and white diamonds.

Most expensive board game A deluxe version of Outrage!, which is based on stealing the Crown Jewels from the Tower of London, UK, retails at £7,995 ($15,400). The set includes mini-reproductions of the Crown Jewels, accurately made from solid, 18-karat gold with real diamonds, rubies, emeralds, and sapphires. Only 20 sets were ever produced.

Most expensive hotel suite In 2003, the Imperial Suite at the President Wilson Hotel in Geneva, Switzerland, could be reserved for CHF45,000 ($36,240) a night. This is equivalent to approximately $37,480 today. The suite is accessed by a private elevator and fills an entire floor. It has four bedrooms, all overlooking Lake Geneva. The dining room seats 26, the living room can hold 40 people, and all windows and doors are bulletproof.

Most expensive wallet A platinum-cornered, diamond-studded crocodile wallet made by Louis Quatorze of Paris, France, and Mikimoto of Tokyo, Japan, sold in September 1984 for $74,816. This figure is equivalent to approximately $137,030 today.

★ TOP 10 MOST VALUABLE ITEMS FROM THE GUINNESS WORLD RECORDS ARCHIVE ★

CATEGORY	DESCRIPTION
1. Jewelry collection	Owned by Duchess of Windsor
2. ★ Furniture	18th-century Italian Badminton cabinet
3. Illustrated manuscript	Leonardo da Vinci's *Codex Hammer.* Renamed *Codex Leicester,* its original title, after sale
4. Jewel	D color internally flawless pear-shaped diamond weighing 100.10 karats; named "Star of the Season" after sale
5. Car	1931 Bugatti Type 41 "Royale" Sports Coupe
6. Watch	Patek Phillipe watch, named *Supercomplication,* that belonged to Henry Graves Jr. (U.S.A.)
7. Stamp collection (single sale)	Kanai collection of 183 pages of the classic stamp issues of Mauritius
8. Book	An original four-volume subscriber set of J. J. Audubon's *The Birds of America*
9. Dinosaur bones	Largest and most complete *Tyrannosaurus rex* skeleton, known as "Sue"
10. Horse	Six-year-old broodmare called Cash Run

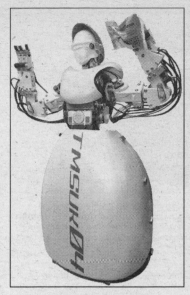

MOST EXPENSIVE COMMERCIALLY AVAILABLE DOMESTIC ROBOT The Japanese Thames company exhibited their TMSUK 04 robot in Tokyo, Japan, on January 23, 2000. The 180-lb. (82-kg) robot stands 4 ft. (1.2 m) tall and originally cost $44,800, the equivalent of approximately $49,508 today. The robot can run errands, massage humans, is totally obedient, and can be controlled remotely by phone.

☆ **Most expensive helmet** A British collector paid the sum of £156,450 ($277,292) for a Phrygian Chalcidian-type winged bronze helmet, dating from the 4th century B.C., at Christie's of London, UK, on April 28, 1994.

Most valuable philatelic item An 1847 letter to wine merchants in Bordeaux—franked with the 1d (one penny) and 2d (two penny) first issues of Mauritius—sold to an anonymous buyer in less than a minute for

PRICE PAID	LOCATION OF SALE	DATE OF SALE
£31,380,197 ($50,427,977)	Sotheby's, Geneva, Switzerland	April 3, 1987
£19,045,250 ($36,812,086)	Christie's, London, UK	December 9, 2004
$30,802,500	Christie's, New York City, U.S.A.	November 11, 1994
CHF19,858,500 ($16,561,171)	Sotheby's, Geneva, Switzerland	May 17, 1995
$15 million	NA	April 12, 1990
$11,002,500	Sotheby's, New York City, U.S.A.	December 2, 1999
CHF15,000,000 ($9,982,033)	Switzerland	November 3, 1993
$8,802,500	Christie's, New York City, U.S.A.	March 10, 2000
$8,362,500	Sotheby's, New York City, U.S.A.	October 4, 1997
$7,100,000	Lexington, Kentucky, U.S.A.	November 3, 2003

☆**LARGEST CUT DIAMOND** The world's largest cut diamond is an unnamed Fancy Black containing small red diamond crystals. It weighs 555.55 karats and was polished into 55 facets over several years and completed in June 2004. Ran Gorenstein (Belgium) commissioned this creation.

CHF6,123,750 ($4,075,165). The sale was conducted by auctioneer David Feldman (Ireland) in Zürich, Switzerland, on November 3, 1993. Feldman also auctioned the **most valuable stamp:** the Swedish "Treskilling" Yellow sold for CHF2,870,000 ($2,255,403) in Geneva, Switzerland, on November 8, 1996.

Most valuable baseball A baseball was sold at Guernsey's auction house, New York City, U.S.A., for $3,054,000 including commission, to Todd McFarlane on January 12, 1999. The ball had been hit by Mark McGwire (St. Louis Cardinals) for his 70th and final home run in his record-setting 1998 season.

MOST VALUABLE CRACKER
At Christie's in London, UK, on April 18, 2000, a cracker from Sir Ernest Shackleton's unsuccessful 1907–09 expedition to the South Pole sold for £4,935 (then $7,804). It was bought by art dealer Johnny Van Haeften (UK), whose great-uncle was Sir Philip Brocklehurst, a member of Shackleton's team.

WAGNER, PITTSBURG

MOST VALUABLE BASEBALL CARD
A rare 1909 card, known as T206 Honus Wagner, was sold during an online eBay auction for $1,265,000 to Brian Seigal (U.S.A.) on July 15, 2000.

☆**Most valuable guitar** Eric Clapton's (UK) "Blackie" Fender Stratocaster guitar sold for $959,500 to the U.S. chain The Guitar Center at Christie's in New York, U.S.A., on June 24, 2004. "Blackie" was made from the parts of various Strats bought in Nashville, Tennessee.

ART & ENTERTAINMENT

CONTENTS

ART & SCULPTURE

MOST VALUABLE . . .

Painting sold (privately) The seascape *Lost on the Grand Banks,* by Winslow Homer (U.S.A.), was sold for over $30 million on May 6, 1998, reportedly to Bill Gates (U.S.A.).

★**Moonscape painting** The most expensive moonscape was created by U.S. astronaut Alan Bean, who was lunar module pilot on *Apollo 12* (November 1969) and commander of *Skylab 2* (July–September 1973). It depicts a fictional scenario of Bean—who describes himself as an astronaut-explorer-artist—chasing a football, thrown by *Apollo 12* commander Pete Conrad, on the Moon. The painting, titled *If We Could Do It All Over Again—Are You Ready For Some Football?,* was sold to an unnamed buyer in 2004 for $182,369.60.

☆**Sculpture sold (auction)** A bronze sculpture titled *Danaïde* (1913), by Constantin Brancusi (Romania), was sold at Christie's, New York City, U.S.A., for $18,159,500 on May 7, 2002. It depicts a figure from Greek mythology—the Danaïdes were the 50 daughters of King Danaos of Argos, Greece.

Sculpture by a living artist *Michael Jackson and Bubbles,* a porcelain sculpture created by artist Jeff Koons (U.S.A.) in 1988, sold for $5,616,750 at Sotheby's, New York City, U.S.A., on May 15, 2001. The gold-and-white sculpture shows Michael Jackson reclining on a bed of roses with his arm around his pet chimp.

Great balls of . . . Alexandria, Indiana, home of the largest painted ball, also lays claim to the world's largest hairball record! In 1992, a "goat-sized mass of hair" was dredged from the town's sewers. A replica is often paraded through the town in the festive season.

While this is not an official record, GWR does recognize other world-beating balls, including:

Plastic wrap: Andy Martell (Canada) created a ball of plastic wrap 89.9 in. (228.5 cm) in circumference and weighing 155 lb. (70.3 kg).

Foil: Richard Roman (U.S.A.) made an aluminum foil ball weighing 1,615 lb. (0.45 kg) on September 17, 1987.

String: J. C. Payne (U.S.A.) tied a ball of string 41 ft. 6 in. (12.65 m) in circumference.

★ **MOST LAYERS OF PAINT ON A BALL** Michael Carmichael and his wife Glenda of Alexandria, Indiana, U.S.A., have covered a baseball with approximately 18,000 layers of paint. Since first painting the ball in 1977, they have added nearly two coats of paint a day and, as of June 2004, the ball had a circumference of 9 ft. 1 in. (2.77 m). The number of layers was estimated by taking a core sample (below) and analyzing it at a magnification of ×1,200.

The core sample from the Carmichaels' ball of paint!

Post-it note A Post-it note featuring a pastel and charcoal work called *After Rembrandt* was sold online on December 20, 2000, for $925. The artist, R. B. Kitaj (U.S.A.), was one of a group of celebrities invited to create mini-masterpieces to mark the 20th anniversary of the famous sticky notelet to raise money for charity.

LARGEST . . .

☆ **Stone sculpture** *God of Longevity,* a carved stone sculpture located in the Meng Shan mountains in Shandong, China, is so large that it can be seen from up to 19 miles (30 km) away. The sculpture is 715 ft. (218 m) high and

656 ft. (200 m) wide, and is represented with a long stick in one hand and an "immortal peach" in the other.

Popsicle stick sculpture Robert McDonald and his son Robbie (both U.S.A.) built *OlaBison*—a Viking ship 12.7 ft. (3.89 m) long and 3.8 ft. (1.18 m) wide—from 370,000 wooden Popsicle sticks. It floated for an hour in Urk harbor, the Netherlands, on September 12, 2003.

★**Indoor mural** A group of people sentenced to carry out community work completed a mural covering all internal walls and ceilings of the Police and Citizens' Youth Club in Bernie, Tasmania, Australia, on June 30, 2004. The work took 18 months to paint and was coordinated by a professional mural artist. It measures 7,830.96 ft.^{2} (727.52 m^2) and illustrates a cross-section of the terrain of Tasmania.

The **largest outdoor mural** is the *Pueblo Levee Project,* which measures 2 miles (3.21 km) long and 58 ft. (17.67 m) tall, and stretches along the Arkansas River levee in Pueblo, Colorado, U.S.A.

☆**Permanent coin mural** Staff at the PennySaver store in Rancho Cordova, California, U.S.A., created a permanent coin mural consisting of 100,000 pennies. It measures 191.75 ft.^{2} (17.8 m^2) and was completed in March 2004.

LARGEST SOAP SCULPTURE Artist Bev Kirk (U.S.A.) carved a winged pig titled *Sudsie, A Boar of Soap,* in Cincinnati, Ohio, U.S.A., in September 2003. Sudsie was made from a 5 × 5 × 6 ft. (1.5 × 1.5 × 1.8 m) bar of Ivory soap and weighs 7,000 lb. (3,175 kg)—the equivalent of 26,666 Ivory soap bars.

★ **MOST EXPENSIVE ELEPHANT PAINTING** The most expensive painting by a group of elephants is *Cold Wind, Swirling Mist, Charming Lanna I*, which sold for 1.5 million baht ($39,000) to Panit Warin (Sinanta), of Thailand, on February 19, 2005, at Maesa Elephant Camp, Chiang Mai, Thailand.

☆ **Painting by numbers** Great Ormond Street Hospital children's charity (UK) completed a 4,305-ft.^{2} (400-m^2) "painting by numbers" artwork at the Lindt Easter Bunny Event, Hyde Park, London, UK, on April 5, 2004, in support of the hospital.

☆ **Chalk sidewalk art** A chalk sidewalk artwork 35,509 ft.^{2} (3,298.95 m^2) in size was created by members of the Oosterhof-Niej Begin Scout Group, in Rijssen, the Netherlands, on June 12, 2004.

Largest sand painting A sand painting measuring 40 ft. 2 in. (12.24 m) by 40 ft. 2 in. (12.24 m) was created by the monks of the Golden Pagoda Buddhist Temple in the Singapore Expo Hall from May 15 to 22, 2004.

★ **Jell-O mosaic** A vast Jell-O mosaic measuring 42 × 65 ft. (12.8 × 19.8 m) was created by a group of students from the Imperial College Singapore Society, London, UK, on February 21, 2004. The 16,125-piece Jell-O mosaic depicts the flag of Singapore.

Pablo Picasso's (Spain) *Garçon à la Pipe* (1905) sold to an anonymous buyer for $104 million on May 5, 2004, at Sotheby's, New York City, U.S.A. With buyer's fees and premium, it cost $104,168,000, making it the first work of art to break the $100 million threshold. (It is also the most expensive image to reproduce in this book!)

★ **Bubble-gum mosaic** A mosaic of about 100,000 wrapped pieces of bubble gum was completed by TBWA Digerati and ID Productions in association with SABC 1 and Cadbury's Chappies (all South Africa) in Johannesburg, South Africa, on August 17, 2004. The mosaic, which took five days to create, was a portrait of former South African president Nelson Mandela and measured 209 ft.² (19.4 m²).

☆ LARGEST COMIC STRIP A colossal comic strip created by Norm Suchar (U.S.A.) and the Gentry High School Art Department, Indianola, Mississippi, U.S.A., was displayed on June 7, 2003. It measured 135 × 47 ft. 9.5 in. (41.15 × 14.56 m) and depicted the syndicated comic strip *Lucky Cow,* by Mark Pett (U.S.A.).

★ **Car mosaic** A collection of 192 Mini cars was formed into a mosaic depicting the Mini logo in Villafranca di Verona, Italy, on April 17, 2004, covering an area of 53,280 ft.² (4,950 m²).

PRINTED WORD

★ **Oldest known paper** A piece of paper thought to date from around A.D. 150 was found in Wuwei in China's Gansu province. It is made largely of cotton rags.

Paper as we understand it today (that is, a sheet formed on a screen from water suspension) was invented in China about 2,000 years ago. A court official called Ts'ai Lun is traditionally credited with its invention in about A.D. 100.

BOOKS

Wealthiest author According to the *Forbes World's Richest People 2005,* Harry Potter author J. K. Rowling (UK) has a net worth of $1 billion.

OLDEST AUTHORS

Sarah Louise Delany and A. Elizabeth Delany (both U.S.A.)
Book: *The Delany Sisters' Book of Everyday Wisdom*
Published: 1994
Age at publication: Sarah Louise, 105; A. Elizabeth, 103

Oldest male author:
Constantine Kallias (Greece)
Book: *A Glance of My Life*
Published: 2003
Age at publication: 101

YOUNGEST AUTHOR

Dorothy Straight (U.S.A.)
Book: *How the World Began*
Published: 1964
Age at publication: four

Youngest male author:
Dennis Vollmer (U.S.A.)
Book: *Joshua Disobeys*
Published: 1987
Age at publication: six

☆**LARGEST CATALOG** A replica of the Bon Prix S2 fashion catalog *Voila!* had 212 pages and measured 3 ft. 11 in. × 4 ft. 11 in. (1.2 m × 1.5 m) when unveiled in Hamburg, Germany, on August 30, 2003.

Rowling's annual earnings estimates for the period from June 2003 to June 2004 were $147 million—the **highest annual earnings by a children's author.** A total of 60 million Harry Potter books were sold in 2003, and so far 250 million books in the series have been sold worldwide.

★**Smallest printed book** An edition of *Chameleon* by the Russian author Anton Chekhov measuring 0.035 × 0.035 in. (0.9 × 0.9 mm) was published by Anatoliy Konenko (Russia) in 1996. Each book consists of 30 pages, has three color illustrations, and 11 lines of text to a page.

The book was printed in a limited edition of 100 copies, half in English, half in Russian. It is bound in gold, silver, and leather, and sewn in silk. Each copy retails at $500.

Most blank pages in a published book On September 9, 1999, fine art university lecturer Anne Lydiat (UK) published the 52-page *lost for words . . .* All of the book's pages are blank and are meant to be "a feminine place where there is silence," according to the author.

Best-selling cookbook *Betty Crocker's Quick and Easy Cookbook* has sold 50 million copies since 1950.

☆ **MOST FILMED AUTHOR** The plays and sonnets of William Shakespeare (England, 1564–1616) have been adapted into 420 feature film and TV-movie versions. *Hamlet* has appealed most to filmmakers, with 79 versions, followed by *Romeo and Juliet,* with 52, and *Macbeth,* filmed 36 times. The most recent feature film adaptations of Shakespeare plays have been *Huapango* (Mexico, 2004), a modern-day version of *Othello,* and *The Merchant of Venice* (U.S.A./Italy/Luxembourg/UK, 2004), starring Al Pacino (U.S.A.) as Shylock.

MAGAZINES & NEWSPAPERS

★ **Largest magazine** A scaled-up version of *Day & Night Jewellery and Watches Magazine* created by Naiem Jbara (UAE), consisting of 188 pages, measured 27.5 × 39.3 in. (70 × 100 cm) on October 14, 2003, at Jewellery Arabia 2003, Manama, Bahrain. In total, 150 copies of the large magazine were printed.

★ **Most syndicated columnist** Ann Landers's (U.S.A.) advice column appeared in over 1,200 newspapers, with an estimated readership of 90 million. She also wrote columns for Internet sites.

★ **Longest serving newspaper columnist** Jack Ingram (UK), a.k.a. White Eagle, contributed weekly articles on "Scouts and Scouting" to the *Heywood Advertiser* for 71 years, from December 29, 1933, until his final column on February 5, 2004.

Most letters published in a newspaper Subhash Chandra Agrawal (India) had 80 of his letters to the editor published in the *Kashmir Times* in 2003. This is also the ☆**most letters published in a single national newspaper in one year.**

Subhash has also had 319 letters published in the *Hindustan Times* since the early 1980s, the ☆**most letters to an editor of one newspaper in a lifetime.**

Madhu Agrawal (India) had 334 of her letters published during the year 2003 in 23 prominent Indian newspapers with circulations over 50,000, the ☆**most letters to editors published in one year in multiple newspapers.**

LIBRARIES

★**Most severe library penalty** Beverly Goldman (U.S.A.) was jailed in January 2000 on seven counts of failing to return overdue library books. Goldman was arrested after her local library in Clearwater, Florida, U.S.A., had tried for over 16 months to retrieve overdue materials valued at $127.86.

Largest library book fine paid A fine of $345.14 was due on the poetry book *Days and Deeds,* checked out of Kewanee Public Library, Illinois, U.S.A., in April 1955 by Emily Canéllos-Simms (U.S.A.). Emily found it in

LARGEST LIBRARY The Library of Congress in Washington, D.C., U.S.A., contains over 128 million items, including approximately 29 million books, 2.7 million recordings, 12 million photographs, 4 million maps, and 57 million manuscripts. These items are contained on about 530 miles (853 km) of shelves. The library was founded on April 24, 1800.

her mother's house 47 years
later and presented the library
with a check for overdue fines.

Most overdue library book
In 1667–68, Colonel Robert
Walpole (England) borrowed a
book about the Archbishop of
Bremen from Sidney Sussex
College, Cambridge, UK. Prof.
Sir John Plumb (UK) found the
book 288 years later in the li-
brary of the then Marquess
of Cholmondeley at Houghton
Hall, Norfolk, UK. He returned
it, but no fine was exacted.

LANGUAGE

Gorilla most proficient at sign language In 1972, a gorilla named
Koko was taught Ameslan (American Sign Language for the Deaf) by Dr.
Francine Patterson (U.S.A.). By 2000, Koko had a working vocabulary of
over 1,000 signs and understood approximately 2,000 words of spoken English. She can refer to the past and future, argue, joke, and lie. When Koko
was asked by Dr. Patterson whether she was an animal or a person, she
replied, "Fine animal gorilla."

Shortest alphabet Rotokas of central Bougainville Island, Papua New
Guinea, has the fewest letters, with 11 (a, b, e, g, i, k, o, p, ř, t, and u).

Longest alphabet The language with the most letters is Khmer (Cambodian), with 74 (including some without any current use).

★**LARGEST FICTIONAL LANGUAGE** Although it is impossible to know the number of speakers, there is little doubt that the Klingon language, invented for the *Star Trek* series by linguist Mark Okrand (U.S.A.), is the most widely used language of its kind. Participants at *Star Trek* conventions frequently converse in the language, and in addition to a Klingon dictionary there are translations of *Hamlet, Much Ado About Nothing,* and *Gilgamesh.* Amazon.com lists at least four other books written in Klingon or containing large tracts of the language, and the Google search engine is also available in Klingon. The greatest insult in this fictional language is "Hab SoSl'll' Quch!"—meaning "Your mother has a smooth forehead."

★**Fastest real-time court reporter (stenotype machine)** Mark Kislingbury (U.S.A.) is the National Court Reporters Association speed and real-time champion. At the association's 2003 summer convention, he typed at a rate of 360 words per minute with 92% accuracy.

Language with the most consonants The language with the largest number of distinct consonantal sounds was that of the Ubykhs in the Caucasus, with 81. Ubykh speakers migrated from the Caucasus to Turkey in the 19th century, and the last fully competent speaker, Tevfik Esenç, died in Istanbul, Turkey, in October 1992.

Longest scientific name The tryptophan synthetase A protein, an enzyme consisting of 267 amino acids, has a name 1,913 letters in length.

★**Language with the fewest speakers** According to the Ethnologue database of languages, over 400 of the world's languages are nearly extinct, meaning that "only a small number of elderly speakers are still living." It is thought that languages are disappearing at a rate of one every two weeks.

★**Language that is official in the greatest number of countries** English is an official language of 56 United Nations member states, more than a quarter of the total UN membership. However, it is not necessarily the most widely spoken language, or the only language, in these countries.

★**Largest Scrabble board** A Scrabble board with a surface area of 323 ft.^{2} (30 m^2) was created to celebrate the 50th birthday of the game and was played on October 13, 1998, in Wembley Stadium, London, UK, by teams made up of UK Scrabble champions helping the army v. the navy. The letter tiles, made from reinforced fiberglass, measured 16 ft.^{2} (1.5 m^2) and had to be maneuvered by two people at a time.

Most common language Chinese is spoken by more than 1.1 billion people. The "common speech" (Pûtônghuà) is the standard form, with pronunciation based on that of Beijing.

★ **HARD TO PRONOUNCE AND EVEN HARDER TO SPELL—
THE WORLD'S LONGEST WORDS** ★

Japanese—chinchinmogamaga **(16)**—meaning "hop on one leg, hopscotch"

Castilian (Spanish official language)—superextraordinarisimo **(22)**—meaning "highly extraordinary"

French—anticonstitutionnellement **(25)**—meaning "anticonstitutionally"

Italian—precipitevolissimevolmente **(26)**—meaning "as fast as possible"

Portuguese—inconstitucionalissimamente **(27)**—meaning "with the highest degree of unconstitutionality"

Icelandic— hæcstaréttarmalaflutningsmaður **(30)**—meaning "supreme court lawyer"

Russian— ryentgyenoelyektrokardiografichyeskogo **(33** Cyrillic letters)—transliterating as **38**, meaning "of the X-ray electrocardiographic"

German—Rechtsschutzversicherungsgesellschaften **(39)**—meaning "insurance companies that provide legal protection"

Hungarian— megszentségtelenithetetlenségeskedéseitekért **(44)**—meaning "for your unprofanable actions"

English— pneumonoultramicroscopicsilicovolcano-coniosis (-koniosis) **(45)**—meaning "a lung disease caused by the inhalation of very fine silica dust"

Dutch—kindercarnavalsoptochtvoorbereidingswerkzaamheden **(49)**—meaning "preparation activities for a children's carnival procession"

Danish— speciallægepraksisplanlægningsstabiliseringsperiode **(51)**—meaning "the stabilization period of the planning of medical specialists' practices"

Finnish— lentokonesuihkuturbiinimoottoriapumekaanikkoaliupseerioppilas **(61)**—meaning "apprentice corporal, working as assistant mechanic in charge of airplane turbine engines"

Swedish— nordöstersjökustartilleriflygspaningssimulatoranläggningsmateriel-underhållsuppföljningssystemdiskussionsinläggsförberedelse-arbeten **(130)**—meaning "preparatory work on the contribution to the discussion on the maintaining system of support of the material of the aviation survey device within the northeast part of the coast artillery of the Baltic"

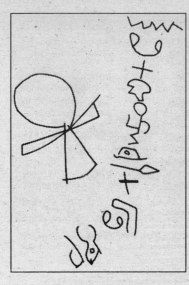

★ **EARLIEST ALPHABET** The earliest known example of an alphabet—that is, a writing system in which symbols are used to represent sounds rather than concepts—dates back to about 1800 B.C. It was found carved into limestone in Wadi el Hol near Luxor, Egypt, by Yale University archaeologists John and Deborah Darnell in the early 1990s. (Note that this is not the earliest known "writing.")

Most and fewest vowels

Sedang, a central Vietnamese language, has 55 distinguishable vowel sounds. By contrast, the Caucasian language Abkhazian has only two vowels.

LONGEST WORD IN THE ENGLISH LANGUAGE...

...With letters arranged in reverse alphabetical order
Spoonfeed (9 letters).

...Consisting only of vowels
Euouae (6). It is formed from the vowels of "seculorum amen," which is a religious chant.

...Consisting strictly of alternating consonants and vowels
Honorificabilitudinitatibus (27). It means "with honorableness" (a nonsense word from medieval literature).

...With letters arranged in alphabetical order
Aegilops (8), a plant family.

...With only one vowel
Strengths (9).

...Without any of the five main vowels
Twyndyllyngs (12), an archaic spelling of the word "twin."

Shortest word in the English language that contains all five main vowels
Eunoia (6). A little-used medical term that means "a normal state of mental health."

★ **LANGUAGE WITH THE MOST CLICK SOUNDS** The !Xú language, spoken by the Khoisan tribes of southern Africa, has 48 distinct click sounds.

Longest place name In its most scholarly transliteration, Krungthep Mahanakhon, the 167-letter official name for Bangkok, the capital of Thailand, has 175 letters. The official short version (without capital letters, which are not used in Thai) is krungthephphramahanakhon bowonratanakosin mahintharayuthaya mahadilokphiphobnovpharad radchataniburirom udomsantisug (six words, 111 letters).

★ **Most common language sound** No known language in the world lacks the vowel "a" (as in the English word "father").

Rarest speech sounds The rarest speech sound is "ř" in Czech and described as a rolled post-alveolar fricative. It occurs in very few languages and is the last sound mastered by Czech children.

Most succinct word The most challenging word for any lexicographer to define briefly is the Fuegian (southernmost Argentina and Chile) word mamihlapinatapai, meaning "looking at each other hoping that either will offer to do something which both parties desire but are unwilling to do."

WHO EARNED $928,000 PER MINUTE FOR STARRING IN A TV COMMERCIAL? FIND OUT ON P. 314

1. Mandarin Chinese—915 million speakers
2. English—354 million
3. Spanish—325 million
4. Hindi—300 million
5. Arabic—272 million
6. Bengali—194 million
7. Portuguese—170 million
8. Russian—164 million
9. Japanese—125 million
10. German—108 million

MOVIEGOING

THEATER ATTENDANCE

Highest total annual theater attendance The largest theater audience in one given year was 4.49 billion admissions in the U.S.A. in 1929.

☆**Highest theater attendance today** Theater admissions reached 2.8 billion in India in 2001, based on most recent figures.

☆**Highest annual theater attendance per capita** In 2004, Iceland registered a greater theater attendance per capita than any other country, with an average of 5.45 visits per person at 46 theaters. This is based on a figure for the Icelandic population of 280,798.

RECORD-BREAKING DRIVE-INS

At 216 ft. (65.8 m) wide and 4,800 ft.2 (445.9 m2) in area, the **largest drive-in theater screen ever** was the Algiers Drive-In, Detroit, Michigan, U.S.A., which opened on August 15, 1956, and closed in 1985.

With 1,200 seats, the All-Weather Drive-In, Copiague, New York, U.S.A., is the **largest drive-in theater (patron capacity)**. The Troy Drive-In, Detroit, Michigan, U.S.A., and the Panther Drive-In, Lufkin, Texas, U.S.A., have space for 3,000 cars, making them joint record holders for the **largest drive-in theater (car capacity)**.

LARGEST PERMANENT THEATER SCREEN The Panasonic IMAX Theatre in Darling Harbour, Sydney, Australia, holds the largest fixed projection screen in the world, measuring 117 × 97 ft. (35.72 × 29.57 m)—twice the width of a basketball court. It can seat 540 people.

LARGEST . . .

Theater complex by seats Kinepolis Madrid, which opened in Spain on September 17, 1998, is the world's largest theater complex. It has a seating capacity of 9,200 for its 25 screens that can, individually, seat from 211 to 996 people.

Drive-in by number of screens The Thunderbird Drive-In (also known as the Swap Shop Drive-In), Fort Lauderdale, Florida, U.S.A., which opened with a single screen on November 22, 1963, now has 13 screens of varying sizes.

☆**Annual movie output** India produces more feature-length movies than any other country. A record 1,200 movies were produced in 2002 and, in 1994, a total of 754 movies were produced in a record 16 languages.

FIRST . . .

★**Theater in operation** The Cinématographe Lumière at the Salon In-
dien, Paris, France, opened under the management of Clément Maurice
(France) on December 28, 1895. The opening performance, to an audience
of 35 who had paid one franc each, included *L'Arrivée d'un Train en Gare*
(France, 1895) by the Lumière brothers.

Drive-in theater The first patent for a "drive-in" was issued on May 16,
1933, to Richard Hollingshead (U.S.A.), who opened the first one on June 6,
1933, on a site for 400 cars in Camden, New Jersey, U.S.A., to show *Wife
Beware* (U.S.A., 1933).

Circular theater The first circular theater is located in the European Park
of the Moving Image at Futuroscope, near Poitiers, France. It consists of
nine projectors and nine screens covering a total surface area of 2,928 ft.^{2}
(272 m^2). The process enables the projection of nine electronically synchro-
nized films, offering a 360° field of vision.

OLDEST MOVIE THEATER IN OPERATION The Electric in London, UK,
first opened on February 24, 1911. Designed by Gilbert Seymour
Valentin in 1910, the theater had seating for 600 people. The historically
registered building was closed in the 1980s but reopened on February
22, 2001, with a seating capacity of 240.

SMALLEST MOVIE THEATER IN OPERATION Cinema dei Piccoli was built by Alfredo Annibali (Italy) in 1934 in the park of Villa Borghese, Rome, Italy, and today covers an area of 769.83 ft.² (71.52 m²). Originally called the Topolino Cinema, it used a Pathé-Baby 9.5-mm movie projector, had bed-sheets for a screen, and played 78s for background music. Restored in 1991, the theater has 63 seats, a 16.4 × 8.2-ft. (5 × 2.5-m) screen, stereo sound, and air-conditioning.

LONGEST . . .

Movie release *Titanic* (U.S.A., 1997) stayed in the charts from December 19, 1997, to September 25, 1998, in the U.S. market, a total duration of 281 days.

Commercial movie on general release *The Burning of the Red Lotus Temple* (China, 1928–31)—adapted by the Star Film Co. from a newspaper serial "Strange Tales of the Adventurer in the Wild Country" by Shang K'ai-jan—was released in 18 feature-length parts over a period of three years. Although never shown publicly in its 27-hour entirety, some theaters put on all-day performances of a half-dozen parts in sequence.

Nonstop theater show A 50-hour "B Movie Marathon" took place at The Variety Arts Center in Hollywood, U.S.A., from May 29 to 31, 1983. A $15 ticket enabled patrons to see 37 low-budget classics.

MISCELLANEOUS

★**Country with the least theaters per population** Suriname, with a population of 436,494, has only one theater, found in the capital Paramaribo. In 1997, this theater saw a total of 103,626 admissions.

★**Country with the most theater screens** According to the most recent statistics, China has 65,500 theater screens. By way of comparison, the U.S.A. has 35,280, India 11,962, and the UK 3,402.

LARGEST THEATER TODAY The Radio City Music Hall, New York City, U.S.A. (pictured above), opened on December 27, 1932, with 5,945 (now 5,910) seats.

The **largest theater by seat capacity** is the Roxy in New York City, U.S.A. It was built at a cost of $12 million and had a seating capacity of 6,214 when it opened on March 11, 1927. The theater employed 16 projectionists, an orchestra of 110 musicians led by four conductors, and three organists who rose from the orchestra pit playing simultaneously on Kimball organ consoles. It closed on March 29, 1960, and was demolished later that year.

The **smallest theater by seat capacity** to operate as a regular commercial venture has 21 seats. The Screen Room on Broad Street, Nottingham, UK, owned by Steven Metcalf (UK), opened on September 27, 2002, with the film *Lost in La Mancha* (Canada, 2002).

★ **Most expensive average admission price to a theater** The most expensive admission prices in the world are in Japan, where the average price of a theater ticket is $10.80.

The ★**lowest admission prices** are in India, with the average price of a theater ticket at $0.20.

AT THE BOX OFFICE

RECORD TAKINGS

Highest grossing movie *Titanic* (U.S.A., 1997) became the first film to take $1 billion at the international box office, with an unprecedented total gross of $1.834 billion. It also made a record 10-week gross of $918.6 million worldwide.

☆**Highest grossing film (inflation adjusted)** Rising theater ticket prices mean that the all-time top-grossing movies are nearly all recent films. However, *Gone with the Wind* (U.S.A., 1939)—which took just $393.4 million at the international box office when it was originally released—is first in an inflation-adjusted list, with a total gross of $5.362 billion. In the U.S.A. alone, *Gone with the Wind* had 283,100,000 admissions compared with 130,900,000 for *Titanic* (U.S.A., 1997).

Highest grossing movie on an opening day On its opening day, May 15, 2003, *The Matrix Reloaded* (U.S.A., 2003) took an unprecedented $42.5 million from a total of 3,603 theaters.

★ THE DECADES' BOX-OFFICE LEADERS ★

DECADE	FILM TITLE	BOX OFFICE	RANKING
1910s	*Mickey* (U.S.A., 1918)	*$18,000,000	10th
1920s	*The Big Parade* (U.S.A., 1925)	*$22,000,000	9th
1930s	*Gone with the Wind* (U.S.A., 1939)	$393,400,000	5th
1940s	*Bambi* (U.S.A., 1942)	$268,000,000	6th
1950s	*Lady and the Tramp* (U.S.A., 1955)	*$93,600,000	8th
1960s	*101 Dalmatians* (U.S.A., 1961)	$215,880,014	7th
1970s	*Star Wars* (U.S.A., 1977)	$797,998,007	3rd
1980s	*E.T. the Extra-Terrestrial* (U.S.A., 1982)	$704,804,539	4th
1990s	*Titanic* (U.S.A., 1997)	$1,834,165,466	1st
2000s	*The Lord of the Rings: The Return of the King* (U.S.A./NZ, 2003)	$1,129,219,252	2nd

*US domestic total available only

☆ **WIDEST MOVIE RELEASE ON AN OPENING DAY IN ONE COUNTRY**
Harry Potter and the Prisoner of Azkaban **(U.S.A., 2004) was given the widest release of any movie in history when it opened in the U.S.A. on June 4, 2004, at 3,855 theaters.**

★**Highest grossing documentary on an opening weekend**
Fahrenheit 9/11 (U.S.A., 2004) took $21.8 million in its opening weekend (June 25–27, 2004) and is the first documentary to top the U.S. box-office chart in its opening weekend.

☆**Highest grossing animation on an opening day** *The Incredibles* (U.S.A., 2004) took $20.5 million on its opening day at 3,933 locations across the U.S.A. on November 5, 2004, beating the previous record of $11.8 million that had been set by *Shrek 2* (U.S.A., 2004) on May 19, 2004.

Highest grossing movie in a single day *Spider-Man* (U.S.A., 2002) took $43.6 million on its second day of opening in the U.S.A. on May 4, 2002, from a total of 3,615 screens.

WHICH A-LIST HOLLYWOOD SUPERSTAR HOLDS THE RECORD FOR THE HIGHEST OVERALL BOX-OFFICE MOVIE GROSS? FIND OUT ON P. 298

☆ **HIGHEST GROSSING ANIMATION ON AN OPENING WEEKEND**
Shrek 2 (U.S.A., 2004) took an estimated $104.3 million over its opening
weekend of May 22, 2004, beating the original *Shrek* (U.S.A., 2001),
which took $42.3 million over the May 19, 2001, weekend. The film
opened at 3,737 screens on Wednesday May 19, 2004, and expanded to
4,163 by the weekend (defined as Friday to Sunday, May 21–23).

MOVIE RELEASE

☆**Largest simultaneous movie premiere** *Matrix Revolutions* (U.S.A.,
2003) was simultaneously released on 10,013 prints in a record 94 countries
by Warner Bros. on November 5, 2003.

★**Widest documentary release on an opening day** Michael
Moore's *Fahrenheit 9/11* (U.S.A., 2004) opened at 868 theaters on June 25,
2004, taking $23,920,637 on its first weekend. By comparison, his previous
film, *Bowling for Columbine* (U.S.A., 2002), opened at eight theaters to take
an initial weekend gross of $209,148.

★**Widest movie print run** Warner Bros. gave *The Matrix Reloaded*
(U.S.A., 2003) a print run of 8,517, the largest in history, when the movie
opened on May 15, 2003, at 3,603 theaters in the U.S.A.

★**Widest animation release on an opening day** *Shark Tale* (U.S.A.,
2004) was given the widest release of any animated movie in history when it
opened in the U.S.A. on October 1, 2004, at 4,016 theaters. This beat the
previous record—set by *Shrek 2* (U.S.A., 2004) on May 19, 2004—by 279
theaters.

★ MOST SUCCESSFUL MOVIES ★

★ RELIGIOUS
The Passion of the Christ
(U.S.A., 2004)
$604,300,000

★ ANIMATION
Finding Nemo
(U.S.A., 2003)
$844,400,000

★ MUSICAL
Grease (U.S.A., 1978)
$387,713,510

★ DRAMA
Titanic (U.S.A., 1997)
$1,834,165,466

★ ACTION
Jurassic Park
(U.S.A., 1993)
$920,067,947

HORROR
The Exorcist
(U.S.A., 1973)
$292,700,000

★ CRIME/GANGSTER
Ocean's Eleven
(U.S.A., 2001)
$446,180,493

★ WAR
Saving Private Ryan
(U.S.A., 1998)
$481,597,636

★ TV ADAPTATION
Mission Impossible II
(U.S.A., 2000)
$545,400,000

★ THRILLER
The Sixth Sense
(U.S.A., 1999)
$657,600,000

★ SCIENCE FICTION
*Star Wars: Episode I—
The Phantom Menace*
(U.S.A., 1999)
$923,136,824

★**Widest movie release in one country** *Shrek 2* (U.S.A., 2004) was given the widest release of any movie in history when, on May 21, 2004 (three days after its opening release), the number of engagements expanded from 3,737 to 4,163 theaters in the U.S.A.

FASTEST GROSSES

Fastest $100-million-grossing film Two films have surpassed the $100-million mark in just three days. The first was *Spider-Man* (U.S.A., 2002), which opened on May 3, 2002, at 3,615 theaters. This feat was equaled by *The Matrix Reloaded* (U.S.A., 2003), which opened on May 5, 2003, at 3,603 theaters.

Fastest $100-million-grossing animation *Finding Nemo* (U.S.A., 2003), the computer-animated film from Walt Disney and Pixar Animation Studios, reached the $100-million mark at the U.S. box office in just eight days from its release on May 30, 2003, at 3,374 theaters.

Fastest $200-million movie gross From its May 3, 2002, opening, *Spider-Man* (U.S.A. 2002) passed the $200-million mark in 10 days, taking $223.04 million by May 12.

MOVIE STARS

HIGHEST . . .

☆**Annual earnings by a movie actor** Mel Gibson (U.S.A.) earned an estimated $210 million in 2003, according to the 2004 *Forbes* Celebrity 100 list.

The ☆**highest annual earnings by a movie actress** is an estimated $33 million earned by Cameron Diaz (U.S.A.) in 2003.

☆**Box-office movie gross for an actor** By February 2005, Harrison Ford (U.S.A.) had starred in 27 movies with a record total box-office gross of $3,369,662,963, 10 of which took over $200 million.

The **highest box-office movie gross for an actress** is held by Julia Roberts (U.S.A.), who has starred in 33 movies since 1987, which have attained an overall box-office gross of $2.939 billion.

MOST . . .

★**Best Director Oscar nominations for an actor in the same movie** Woody Allen (U.S.A.) has been nominated for the category of Best

Director on five occasions for movies in which he also had a leading role: *Annie Hall* (U.S.A., 1977), *Interiors* (U.S.A., 1978), *Broadway Danny Rose* (U.S.A., 1984), *Hannah and her Sisters* (U.S.A., 1986), and *Crimes and Misdemeanors* (U.S.A. 1989). His sixth Best Director nomination was for *Bullets over Broadway* (U.S.A., 1993), in which he did not have an acting role.

★ **PUBLIC APPEARANCES— MOST IN 12 HOURS BY A MOVIE STAR** The greatest number of public appearances by a movie star at different cities in 12 hours promoting the same movie is three by Will Smith (U.S.A.). As set out in the rules, he walked the red carpet, signed autographs, and introduced the movie *Hitch* (U.S.A., 2005) at theaters in Manchester (bottom), Birmingham (middle), and London (top), UK, on February 22, 2005.

★ OLDEST OSCAR NOMINEES & WINNERS ★

NAME	AGE	MOVIE
★ Gloria Stuart (U.S.A.)	87 years 221 days	*Titanic* (U.S.A., 1997)
Ralph Richardson (UK)	82 years 49 days	*Greystoke: The Legend of Tarzan* (UK, 1984)
Jessica Tandy (UK)	80 years 295 days	*Driving Miss Daisy* (U.S.A., 1989)
George Burns (U.S.A.)	80 years 68 days	*The Sunshine Boys* (U.S.A., 1975)
Richard Farnsworth (U.S.A.)	79 years 167 days	*The Straight Story* (U.S.A., 1999)
★ Peggy Ashcroft (UK)	77 years 93 days	*Passage to India* (UK/U.S.A., 1984)
Henry Fonda (U.S.A.)	76 years 317 days	*On Golden Pond* (U.S.A., 1981)

★ YOUNGEST OSCAR NOMINEES & WINNERS ★

NAME	AGE	MOVIE
★ Jackie Cooper (U.S.A.)	9 years 20 days	*Skippy* (U.S.A., 1931)
Tatum O'Neal (U.S.A.)	10 years 148 days	*Paper Moon* (U.S.A., 1973)
Keisha Castle-Hughes (NZ)	13 years 309 days	*Whale Rider* (NZ/Germany, 2002)
★ Timothy Hutton (U.S.A.)	20 years 227 days	*Ordinary People* (U.S.A., 1980)
Marlee Matlin (U.S.A.)	21 years 218 days	*Children of a Lesser God* (U.S.A., 1986)
☆ Adrien Brody (U.S.A.)	29 years 343 days	*The Pianist* (France/Germany/UK/Poland, 2002)

★ **BEST DIRECTOR—MOST OSCAR WINS FOR AN ACTOR** Clint Eastwood (U.S.A.) has won the Oscar for Best Director twice for movies in which he also starred. The first was on March 29, 1993, for *Unforgiven* (U.S.A., 1992), followed by *Million Dollar Baby* (U.S.A., 2004) on February 27, 2005. In all, he has been nominated in this category three times; the second occasion was in 2004 for *Mystic River* (U.S.A., 2003), a movie he did not appear in.

OSCAR	NOMINEE/WINNER
Best Supporting Actress	Nominated February 10, 1998
Best Supporting Actor	Posthumously nominated 2/6/1985
Best Actress	Won March 29, 1990
Best Supporting Actor	Won March 29, 1976
Best Actor	Nominated February 15, 2000
Best Supporting Actress	Won March 25, 1985
Best Actor	Won March 29, 1982

OSCAR	NOMINEE/WINNER
Best Actor	Nominated October 5, 1931
Best Supporting Actress	Won April 2, 1974
Best Actress	Nominated January 27, 2004
Best Supporting Actor	Won March 31, 1981
Best Actress	Won March 30, 1987
Best Actor	Won March 23, 2003

Stars on the Hollywood Walk of Fame Gene Autry (U.S.A.)—a.k.a. the "Singing Cowboy"—has five stars on the Hollywood Walk of Fame strip, Los Angeles, U.S.A., for recording, motion pictures, television, radio, and theater.

Golden Globe nominations for an actor Jack Lemmon (U.S.A.) was nominated for a Golden Globe a total of 22 times from 1960 to 2000. In addition, he was also awarded the Cecil B. DeMille Award in 1991 and a Special Award for Best Ensemble Cast—along with the entire cast of *Short Cuts* (U.S.A., 1993)—in 1994.

★**Golden Globe nominations for an actress** Meryl Streep (U.S.A.) has been nominated for a Golden Globe a total of 19 times from 1979 to 2004, winning on five occasions (1980, 1982, 1983, 2003, and 2004).

OLDEST...

★**Golden Globe winner—actor** Henry Fonda (U.S.A., 1905–82) was aged 76 years 259 days when he was awarded the Golden Globe for Best Actor for playing Norman Thayer Jr. in *On Golden Pond* (U.S.A., 1981) on January 30, 1982.

★**Golden Globe winner—actress** Jessica Tandy (UK, 1909–94) was aged 80 years 227 days when she won the Golden Globe for Best Actress for her portrayal of Daisy Werthan in *Driving Miss Daisy* (U.S.A., 1989) on January 20, 1990.

MISCELLANEOUS

☆**Tallest actor in a leading role** Two actors hold this title, standing at 6 ft. 5 in. (1.94 m): Christopher Lee (UK), who has played most of the major horror characters in movies since 1958; and Vince Vaughn (U.S.A.), who has been in movies since the 1990s.

The **tallest actress in a leading role** is a record shared by Margaux Hemingway (d. 1996), Sigourney Weaver, Geena Davis (all U.S.A.), and Brigitte Nielson (Denmark), each of whom has been measured at 6 ft. (1.82 m).

★**First costars to win top acting oscars** At the 1934 Academy Awards held at the Biltmore Hotel, Hollywood, California, U.S.A., on February 27, 1935, the Best Actress and Best Actor Oscars went to costars Clark Gable and Claudette Colbert (both U.S.A.) for their performances in *It Happened One Night* (U.S.A., 1934). The most recent ceremony at which this has happened was on March 23, 1998, when both Jack Nicholson and Helen Hunt (both U.S.A.) won an Oscar for *As Good as it Gets* (U.S.A., 1997).

☆YOUNGEST BEST ACTOR OSCAR Adrien Brody (U.S.A., b. April 14, 1974) won the Best Actor Oscar on March 23, 2003, for his performance as Wladyslaw Szpilman in *The Pianist* (France/Germany/UK/Poland, 2002) aged 29 years 343 days.

★ **LONGEST PERFORMANCE CAPTURE MOVIE** *The Polar Express* (U.S.A., 2004)—the first movie to be created entirely via the performance capture technique, whereby the physical movements of actors are digitally recorded and translated into computer animation—was released on November 10, 2004, with a running time of 1 hr. 33 min. The film, based on Chris Van Allsburg's (U.S.A.) children's book, has Tom Hanks (U.S.A.) playing five of the characters and was made at a cost of $165 million.

★ **Only nonprofessionals to have won acting oscars** World War II veteran Harold Russell (Canada), who played the handless ex-soldier (he had both his arms blown off in combat) in *The Best Years of Our Lives* (U.S.A., 1946), and Cambodian refugee Dr. Haing S. Ngor, who played a victim of Cambodia's Pol Pot regime in *The Killing Fields* (UK, 1984), both received Best Supporting Actor Oscars for their performance.

STUNTS & SFX

STUNTS

★ **First movie stuntman** The first stuntman was ex-U.S. cavalryman Frank Hanaway (U.S.A.), who secured himself a part in Edwin S. Porter's (Italy/U.S.A.) *The Great Train Robbery* (U.S.A., 1903) thanks to his ability to fall off a horse without injuring himself.

Most prolific movie stuntman In a career spanning five decades, Vic Armstrong (UK) has been a stuntman, stunt coordinator, and director in

SHORTEST STUNTMAN Kiran Shah (UK) is the shortest professional stuntman working in movies, standing 4 ft. 1.7 in. (126.3 cm) when measured on October 20, 2003. He has appeared in 52 movies since 1976 and has performed stunts in 31 of them, including being perspective stunt-double for Christopher Reeve (U.S.A.) in *Superman* (UK, 1978) and *Superman II* (UK, 1980) and more recently for Elijah Wood (U.S.A.) in *The Lord of the Rings* trilogy (NZ/U.S.A., 2001–03).

more than 250 movies, and has doubled for every actor to have played the title role in the James Bond series.

Longest leap in a car propelled by its own engine In a stunt for *Smokey and the Bandit II* (U.S.A., 1980), Gary Davis (U.S.A.) raced a stripped-down Plymouth up a ramp, which was butted up against the back of a double-tiered car-carrier, at 80 mph (128 km/h) and cleared 163 ft. (49.6 m) before landing again safely.

★Greatest height range played by a stuntman Stuntman Riky Ash (UK) stands 5 ft. 3 in. (1.59 m) tall and has doubled for characters with a height differential of 34 in. (86 cm).

Largest movie explosion An explosion staged for *Blown Away* (U.S.A., 1994) used a scuttled ship beside an old wharf in East Boston, U.S.A., filled with 720 gal. (2,727 liters) of fuel and 32 bombs, each 16 oz. (453 g) in weight. The resultant explosion lasted nine seconds.

Highest base jump on film Dar Robinson (U.S.A.) performed a base-jump leap of 1,100 ft. (335 m) from a ledge at the summit of the CN Tower, Toronto, Canada, in a stunt for *Highpoint* (Canada, 1979). After six seconds of falling, his parachute opened just 300 ft. (91 m) from the ground.

★ **MOST BONES BROKEN IN A LIFETIME** Evel Knievel (U.S.A., b. Robert Craig Knievel), the pioneer of motorcycle jumping exhibitions, had suffered 433 bone fractures by the end of 1975. In the winter of 1976 he was seriously injured during a televised attempt to jump a tank full of sharks at the Chicago Amphitheater. Knievel, who suffered a brain concussion and two broken arms, decided to retire from major performances as a result.

SPECIAL EFFECTS

★ **Most digital artists on a film** A team of 320 visual effect artists worked on *Sky Captain and the World of Tomorrow* (U.S.A./UK/Italy, 2004), the first Hollywood feature film shot entirely against a blue screen with digital effects filled in. Directed by Kerry Conran (UK) and starring Jude Law (UK) and Gwyneth Paltrow (U.S.A.), the 106-minute movie completed principal photography on the blue set in 26 days. In all, over 2,000 digital shots were produced for the film over a period of eight months.

Largest movie budget for special effects A total of $6.5 million was budgeted for *2001: A Space Odyssey* (U.S.A., 1968), representing over 60% of the total production cost of $10.5 million. The modern equivalent of this in the year 2005 is approximately $49.1 million.

Longest stop-motion feature film *Chicken Run* (UK, 2000), directed by Peter Lord and Nick Park (both UK), was released with a running time of

LONGEST SPEEDBOAT JUMP IN A MOVIE A stunt sequence by Jerry Comeaux (U.S.A.) in *Live and Let Die* (UK, 1973)—in which James Bond is chased down Louisiana's bayou in a 1972 Glastron GT-150 speedboat and leaps over a road—set a world record distance of 120 ft. (36.5 m).

82 minutes and has 118,080 shots created using the stop-motion special effects technique. A normal live-action feature incorporates between 500 and 1,000 shots.

★**Most Oscar nominations for visual effects** Dennis Muren (U.S.A.) has been nominated for the Academy Award for Visual Effects a record 12 times, from *Dragonslayer* (U.S.A., 1981) in 1983 through to *Hulk* (U.S.A., 2003) in 2004.

In addition to winning the **most Oscars for visual effects,** with a total of six, he has also received two Special Achievement Awards, in 1981 for *Star Wars: Episode V—the Empire Strikes Back* (U.S.A., 1980) and in 1984 for *Star Wars: Episode VI—Return of the Jedi* (U.S.A., 1983), as well as the Technical Achievement Award in 1982.

Largest camera crane used on film In order to cover all angles of the 775-ft.-long (236-m) set of the movie *Titanic* (U.S.A., 1997), an Akela crane with a normal reach of 80 ft. (24 m) was adapted to have an expanded reach of almost 200 ft. (61 m). A gyro-stabilized camera was then mounted on the crane basket and the crane was able to move on tracks along the side of the ship in a water tank.

Titanic also had the **largest stunt budget**—more than $3 million of the $200-million budget went toward the stunts.

Most still cameras used in a sequence When shooting a "bullet time" sequence in *The Matrix* (U.S.A., 1999), 120 specially modified film cameras were used by directors Larry and Andy Wachowski (both U.S.A.) to achieve a panning shot of protagonist Neo (played by Keanu Reeves) as he dodged bullets from a pursuer. The effect is now more commonly called "time slicing."

TV STARS

★**Youngest actor to be nominated for an Emmy (lead category)**
At 15, Frankie Muniz (U.S.A.) was nominated for an Emmy award in the Outstanding Actor in a Comedy Series category for his role of Malcolm in *Malcolm in the Middle* (FOX, U.S.A.) in 2001.

First person to appear on a British TV ad On September 22, 1955—the opening night of the UK's Independent Television—Meg Smith (UK) beat 80 other actresses to become the UK's first "plug" girl—starring in a 60-second Gibbs toothpaste ad.

Most enduring TV commercial stars The PG Tips tea campaign (UK) starring chimpanzees began in December 1956. It eventually ran to more than 100 ads, with the final installment made in 1994. The chimpanzees, who are said to have earned more than £1,000 ($1,530) each per commercial, have a retirement fund set up by the company.

★**Longest broadcast career of a TV pet** George the tortoise, who first appeared on the children's television program *Blue Peter* (BBC, UK) in May 1982, made his final appearance 22 years later on April 14, 2004.

★**MOST HOURS ON CAMERA** Host Regis Philbin (U.S.A.) has logged 15,188 hours on camera. This is an average of almost an hour a day for every year of his 46-year career up to August 20, 2004.

Longest time in the same role in a TV series Helen Wagner (U.S.A.) has played the character of Nancy Hughes McClosky in *As the World Turns* (CBS, U.S.A.) since it premiered on April 2, 1956.

First virtual TV host "Maddy" cohosted *Tomorrow's World* (BBC, UK) on March 27, 2002, in realtime alongside the show's human hosts. Maddy was created by Digital Animations Group, Glasgow, UK.

Highest fine imposed on a TV broadcaster The Federal Communications Commission (U.S.A.) fined the CBS Television network $550,000 for the transmission of the American Super Bowl halftime performance broadcast on February 1, 2004, when singer Janet Jackson (U.S.A.) exposed her right breast during a dance routine.

DAVID HASSELHOFF

David Hasselhoff (U.S.A.) was the leading man in *Baywatch*—the most widely seen TV show, with a weekly audience of about 1.1 billion in 1996.

How does it feel to be in the book? It's really cool because it was presented to me by my children, who said, "Here Dad, you're on page 308." It meant more to me that it was brought to me by my children. They were really proud.

Why do you think *Baywatch* was so popular? Someone once said to me, "The whole world looks to America as the big lifeguard of the world." I kind of agree. *Baywatch* just came at the right time...The world was looking to America as a symbol of saving lives, and we were communicating that message around the world by television.

What are you most proud of? The thing that I'm most proud of is that I saved the name "Hasselhoff" because I took a lot of trouble for that name in high school! I look at my father now and I say, "The name you gave me—a billion people know that name." We walk down the street in South Africa or China or Vietnam and people walk by and say "David Hasselhoff" and I just grin.

If our readers wanted to be like you, what do they have to do? Whatever you feel you have a talent at, whatever you feel your dream is, go after it with a vision. Focus on what you want and stay focused. And then go for it.

LARGEST HOME IN HOLLYWOOD The 123-room house at Hollywood's 594 Mapleton Drive occupies an area of 56,550 ft.² (5,253 m²) and belongs to Aaron Spelling (U.S.A.), producer of such TV series as *Charlie's Angels* and *Beverly Hills 90210,* and the **world's most prolific TV drama producer.** The house is currently valued at $37 million and includes a gymnasium, bowling alley, and skating rink. Dubbed "The Manor" by the Spelling family, it was built after purchasing and demolishing the previous house on the site, which was owned by singer Bing Crosby (U.S.A.).

Longest screen kiss in a TV drama A kiss lasting for 3 min. 15 sec. was broadcast on *Hollyoaks* (Channel 4, UK) on July 2, 2002. It was incorporated into the story line when the characters Ellie Hunter and Ben Davies, played by Sarah Baxendale and Marcus Patric (both UK), won a kissing competition.

Longest TV talk show marathon Both Zoltán Kováry (Hungary) and Vador Lladó (Spain) have each broadcast for 30 hours. Kováry continually interviewed guests and hosted from 4:00 p.m. on February 13, 2003, until 10:00 p.m. on February 14, 2003, at the Fix.tv studios, Budapest, Hungary; Lladó of Flaix TV did the same from May 3 to 4, 2002, in Barcelona, Spain.

Most durable TV host With the exception of two episodes, the monthly *Sky at Night* (BBC, UK) has been hosted by Patrick Moore (UK) without a break or a miss since April 24, 1957. By December 2002, 600 shows had been broadcast, making it the world's **longest running TV show with the same host.**

★ TV CHEF
Jamie Oliver (UK),
£4.8 million ($8.9 million)
in 2004

TV NEWS BROADCASTER
(ANNUAL)
Katie Couric (U.S.A.), $13 million

☆ CHILD ACTRESS
Hilary Duff (U.S.A.),
$8 million in 2003

★ TV TALENT SHOW
JUDGE (ANNUAL)
Simon Cowell (UK),
£18 million ($34 million)
in 2004

★ REALITY TV HOST
Donald Trump (U.S.A.),
$7 million for appearing
on *The Apprentice,* 2003–04

ACTOR (ANNUAL)
Jerry Seinfeld (U.S.A.) earned
an estimated $267 million
in 1998

REALITY TV STARS
(OWN SHOW)
Jessica Simpson (pictured with
husband), $4 million in 2003

★ TV STYLISTS
Kyan Douglas, Ted Allen,
Carson Kressley, Jai Rodriguez,
and Thom Filicia (all U.S.A.),
stars of *Queer Eye for the
Straight Guy,* $4 million
in 2003

TV ACTRESS
(ANNUAL)
Helen Hunt (U.S.A.),
$31 million in 1999

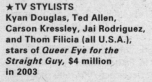

TALK SHOW HOST
Oprah Winfrey (U.S.A.),
$210 million in 2003

★ **TV PRODUCER EVER**
David E. Kelley (U.S.A.),
creator of *Ally McBeal,*
$300 million for a six-year
deal in 2000

TV ACTOR
Ray Romano (U.S.A.),
$1.8 million per episode
of *Everybody Loves
Raymond* in 2004–05

TV SHOWS & ADVERTISING

TV SHOWS

★**First prime-time animation show** *The Flintstones,* created by William Hanna and Joseph Barbera, was first aired on the ABC Television network (U.S.A.) in September 1960.

Largest producers of soap operas Brazil, Mexico, and Puerto Rico dominate the trade in "telenovelos," with the average running for more than 100 episodes. They supply them for stations throughout Latin America, Italy, and Portugal.

★**Most weddings in a TV soap opera** British soap *Coronation Street* has celebrated 59 weddings since it was first aired in December 1960.

★**Longest continuous TV shot** A continuous shot lasting 111 minutes—the entire episode of *C.I.D.*—was filmed by B. P. Singh (India) in Mumbai, India, on October 8, 2004, and broadcast on November 7, 2004.

★**Most consecutive wins on a game show** Ian Lygo (UK) celebrated 75 victories on UK game show *100%* in December 1998. Lygo also holds the record for the **most opponents defeated on a single TV game show,** with 150.

Most game show contestants on a single TV show A record 80,799 people took part in the All-Japan High-School Quiz Championship televised by NTV on December 31, 1983.

Most game show contestants in a series The quiz show *Trans-America Ultra Quiz* featured a total of 213,430 contestants throughout its 16-year run from 1977 to 1993. Only 31 contestants ever made it to the final stage.

Largest audience for a comedy program The final episode of *M*A*S*H* had an estimated audience of 125 million people when it was transmitted on February 28, 1983.

LONGEST RUNNING...

☆**Animated series**
The Simpsons (FOX, U.S.A.)
First aired: December 17, 1989
Episodes: 352 as of May 15, 2005

Children's program
Bozo the Clown (WGN TV, U.S.A.)
First aired: 1949
Episodes: over 150,000 as of August 2001

★**Science fiction series**
Doctor Who (BBC, UK)
First aired: November 23, 1963
Episodes: 709 (173 stories) as of June 18, 2005

☆**Soap opera**
Guiding Light (CBS, U.S.A.)
First aired: June 30, 1952
Episodes: 14,613 as of February 25, 2005

Talent show
Opportunity Knocks (ITV, UK/BBC, UK)
First aired: 1956
Episodes: unknown

Magic show
Magicland (WMC-TV, U.S.A.)
First aired: January 1966
Episodes: 1,200 as of January 1989

Comedy series
Last of the Summer Wine (BBC, UK)
First aired: November 12, 1973
Episodes: 235 as of April 18, 2004

MOST EXPENSIVE TV DOCUMENTARY SERIES PER MINUTE *Walking with Dinosaurs,* **the BBC TV series depicting how dinosaurs lived, reproduced, and became extinct, cost over $61,112 a minute to produce. It took more than two years to make the six 27-minute episodes at a total cost of $9.9 million.**

Largest audience for a TV series At its peak of popularity in 1996, *Baywatch* had an estimated weekly audience of more than 1.1 billion in 142 countries. Covering every continent except Antarctica, the show has since been seen in 148 countries and translated into 44 languages.

★Earliest TV series produced in color *The World Is Yours* began transmission on June 26, 1951. However, the predominance of black-and-white receivers in most U.S. homes at the time meant that many households did not receive it until color broadcasting was introduced in December 1953.

ADVERTISEMENTS

Largest simultaneous TV ad premiere The Ford Motor Company aired its Global Anthem advertisement on over 140 pan-regional or local market networks in 190 countries on November 1, 1999, at 9:00 p.m. local time. Featuring Charlotte Church (UK) and all seven of Ford's automobile brands, the ad was shot in nine countries.

★ **Most TV commercials shown for one product—single program** On August 17, 1996, Castlemaine XXXX screened nine different ads during the course of a program shown on ITV (UK). Three different versions of the ad were shown during each of three advertising breaks.

Highest advertising rate ever The highest TV advertising rate ever paid is $2.4 million for 30 seconds' airtime during the NBC network prime-time transmission of the Super Bowl XXXV game, broadcast on January 28, 2001.

First commercial filmed in space An advertising campaign for Tnuva Milk, showing cosmonaut Vasily Tsibliyev (Russia) drinking milk on board the Russian *Mir* space station, was first broadcast on August 22, 1997.

★ **MOST EXPENSIVE TV ADVERTISEMENT (PRODUCTION)** A four-minute feature film made by director Baz Luhrmann (Australia) advertising Chanel No. 5 perfume cost a total of $33 million to produce. Starring Nicole Kidman (Australia) as a Marilyn Monroe-style actress who is pursued by paparazzi, the ad made its debut on the big screen in theaters throughout the U.S.A. on November 1, 2004, and subsequently premiered on U.S. television on November 11, 2004. Kidman reportedly earned $3.71 million for this ad, the highest fee per minute by an actor for a TV commercial at $928,800 a minute.

GOODBYE, FRIENDS.
SERIES FINALE MAY 6

★ **HIGHEST ADVERTISING RATE FOR A TV SERIES** An average of $2 million was paid for a 30-second slot during the hour-long final episode of *Friends*, which aired in the U.S.A. on May 6, 2004.

Most commercials starring a company founder Between 1989 and 2002, Dave Thomas (U.S.A.), the founder of Wendy's Old Fashioned Hamburger Restaurants, made over 700 television commercial appearances for his company.

★ **LARGEST CASH PRIZE WON ON A TV GAME SHOW** Ken Jennings (U.S.A.) won $2,520,700 on *Jeopardy!* by winning 74 games during 75 episodes aired from June 2 to November 30, 2004. Jennings defeated 149 opponents, correctly answering over 2,000 questions in total.

TV Shows & Advertising

LONGEST RUNNING POP SHOW

The first edition of *Top of the Pops* (BBC, UK) was hosted by Jimmy Savile (top) on January 1, 1964. Artists featured were Dusty Springfield, the Rolling Stones, the Dave Clark Five, the Swinging Blue Jeans, and the Hollies. The Beatles and Cliff Richard and the Shadows were shown on film. The weekly show celebrated its 41st year on air in January 2005. Other hosts have included Bruno Brooks, Anthea Turner, and Gary Davis (center, left to right) and Fearne Cotton and Reggie Yates (bottom).

First public TV ad On June 27, 1941, the first open public TV advertisement was broadcast on NBC's WNBT station in New York, U.S.A., for a Bulova watch.

DIGITAL MUSIC

SALES

★**Biggest selling download single in a week in the UK** "Dogz Don't Kill People Wabbits Do" by Mouldy Looking Stain sold over 7,000 copies in the UK in a single week in October 2004.

★**Biggest selling download single in the U.S.A.** "Hey Ya" by Out-Kast (U.S.A.) is the only downloaded track to have received a multiplatinum Recording Industry Association of America (RIAA) award for sales of over 400,000 (as of October 2004).

★BIGGEST SELLING DOWNLOAD SINGLE IN THE UK "(Is This The Way To) Amarillo" by Tony Christie (UK, left) featuring Peter Kay (UK, right) was released on March 14, 2005. To date, it has recorded download sales of 57,804.

★LARGEST ILLEGAL FILE-SHARING SERVICE Before being shut down in 2001 after legal action by the RIAA, the illegal file-sharing service Napster (U.S.A.) had over 70 million users. Created by U.S. student Shawn Fanning, the service enabled members to swap MP3 music files online for free. The picture shows Shawn (far left) with his attorney David Boiesat at a press conference outside the federal court building in San Francisco, California, U.S.A., on March 2, 2001. Napster relaunched as a legal service in 2003.

WHAT IS DIGITAL MUSIC?

- Traditionally, music has been recorded and stored physically on **solid objects, such as in the grooves** on vinyl records or in the magnetized areas on audiocassettes.

- Digital music exists in a **binary digital format,** which is a series of **zeros and ones** that does the same job as the grooves on a record.

- Because digital music exists as data, you can **store it and play it on a computer**—often as an MP3 file.

- Development in personal computers, combined with the growth of the Internet, has meant that digital songs can be **easily transferred** around the world and from one type of playback device to another.

- It is **easier than ever** to get hold of your favorite tunes, but there are complex legal and copyright issues associated with this new way of buying and listening to music.

★**First download-only hit single** The first single to enter the U.S. Hot 100 chart on download singles sales alone was "Peacekeeper" by Fleetwood Mac (UK/U.S.A.) in March 2003.

First million-selling CD The first CD to sell a million copies worldwide was Dire Straits' *Brothers in Arms* in 1986. It subsequently topped a million sales in Europe alone, including over 250,000 in the UK.

TECHNOLOGY

★**Oldest multitrack digital recording studio** Sound 80 Studios, Minneapolis, Minnesota, U.S.A., was constructed in 1970 and—in a collaboration with the 3M Company, the developer of multitrack digital recording—became the world's first multitrack digital recording studio. The studio complex is now part of Orfield Laboratories.

First compact disk The standard for the compact disk was first proposed by Philips (Netherlands) and Sony (Japan) in 1980, and agreed upon in 1981 by the Compact Disk Standard Digital Audio Disk Committee. The first CDs became available to the public in Europe and Japan in the autumn of 1982, and the U.S.A. in 1983, where 800,000 disks were sold in the first

★**LARGEST ONLINE MUSIC STORE** The largest online collection of legally downloadable music is Apple's iTunes, which launched in May 2003. Since then, its catalog of songs has grown to over 1 million individual tracks, which can be paid for and downloaded over the Internet.

HIGHEST CAPACITY MULTIMEDIA JUKEBOX The highest capacity multimedia jukebox to date is the AV380, with 80 GB of storage space on its internal hard drive. Created by Archos (France), the AV380 can store and play MP3 music tracks as well as MPEG4 video files. It was launched in August 2003.

The 80-GB capacity of the AV380 is enough to hold about 2,000 CDs of music, or 160 hours of television, or about 120 full-length DVD movies.

year alone. Optical disks, which are written and read with a laser, have become the standard medium for home entertainment and computing.

★**First artist-created Internet Service Provider** BowieNet (www.davidbowie.com, U.S.A.) is the first musician-created ISP (Internet Service Provider) and was launched by David Bowie (UK) and Ultrastar Internet Services on September 1, 1998.

★**First MP3** The term MP3 is short for MPEG audio layer-3 and is a widely used digital music file type. It is audio-only and is a direct descendant of the MPEG-1, which is low-bandwidth video compression, commonly used over the Internet. The development of MP3 began in 1987 at the Fraunhofer Institut Integrierte Schaltungen in Germany, and in 1992 it became recognized as the global standard by the International Standards Organization.

★**Bestselling synthesizer** The most popular digital synthesizer of all time is the Korg M1 Music Workstation, which had a production run of 250,000 beginning in 1988.

INTERNET RADIO

★**First Internet radio show** The earliest Internet radio show was "Geek of the Week," produced by Internet Talk Radio (U.S.A.), which first aired on

★ **BIGGEST SELLING DOWNLOAD SINGLE IN A WEEK IN THE U.S.A.**
"Hollaback Girl" by Gwen Stefani (U.S.A.) recorded sales of 58,500 in
the week ending May 7, 2005.

April 1, 1993. The show was developed by Carl Malumud (U.S.A.) using
MBONE (IP Multicast Backbone on the Internet) technology. The show was
interview based, involved members of the nascent Internet community, and
was made available to listeners via FTP (File Transfer Protocol).

★ **First Internet radio station** The first full-time Internet-only radio station was Radio HK (U.S.A.), which began broadcasting music by independent bands in February 1995. The station, created by Norman Hajjar (U.S.A.)
in California, U.S.A., used a CU-SeeMe web conferencing reflector connected to a custom-created audio CD in endless loop.

CHART TOPPERS

★ **Fastest-selling compilation album** The 57th volume of the world's
most successful album series *Now!* sold a record 334,345 units in its first
week on sale in the UK in April 2004.

★ **Oldest record to reach No. 1 on the U.S. singles chart** In July
2004, the best-selling single in the U.S. was "That's Alright" by Elvis

★ MOST SWEARWORDS IN A NO. 1 SINGLE Topping the singles charts in the U.S., UK, Australia, and numerous European charts in early 2004, Eamon's (Eamon Doyle, U.S.A.) single "F*** It (I Don't Want You Back)" contained 33 swearwords.

Presley (U.S.A.). The track, which also made the UK Top 3, had been recorded and released (without success) 50 years earlier in 1954.

★ Highest debut position on U.S. singles chart The only artist to make their first chart appearance at No. 1 on the Hot 100 in the U.S.A. is Fantasia Barrino (U.S.A.), the winner of *American Idol 3,* with "I Believe" on July 10, 2004.

Most weeks spent simultaneously at No. 1 & 2 on U.S. singles chart OutKast (U.S.A.) simultaneously spent eight weeks at No. 1 & 2 on the U.S. singles chart, with "Hey Ya!" and "The Way You Move," from December 20, 2003, to February 7, 2004.

★ Lowest-selling U.S. No. 1 single *American Idol 3* runner-up Diana DeGarmo's (U.S.A.) single "Dreams" hit the No. 1 spot on the U.S. singles sales chart in September 2004 with a record-low weekly sale of under 3,000 copies.

★ Lowest-selling UK No. 1 single "Call On Me" by Eric Prydz (Sweden) sold just 21,749 copies in the week ending October 30, 2004, when it was the UK No. 1 hit single.

Most UK singles to debut at No. 1 Westlife, which included Shane Filan, Nicky Byrne, Bryan McFadden, Mark Feehily, and Kian Egan (all Ireland) had a record-breaking 12 singles debut at the No. 1 spot from May 1, 1999, to November 22, 2003.

★ **Most new entries on UK singles chart** On October 16, 2004, there were a record 17 new entries on the UK Top 40 singles chart.

★ **Most new entries on U.S. album chart** On October 16, 2004, there were a record 11 new entries on the U.S.A. Top 20 album chart.

★ **Most entries on U.S. adult contemporary chart** In September 2004, Elton John (UK) achieved a 64th entry on the U.S. adult contemporary chart with the track "Answer in the Sky." Barbra Streisand (U.S.A.) has 63 entries, making her the **female singer with the most appearances on the chart.**

Longest singles chart stay "How Do I Live" by LeAnn Rimes (U.S.A.) entered the Top 25 U.S. country singles sales chart on June 21, 1997, and was still there in February 2003—a record breaking 291 weeks (over 5.5 years) later.

BIGGEST-SELLING ALBUM *Thriller* by Michael Jackson (U.S.A.) has achieved global sales of over 51 million copies since 1982.

★ **LONGEST TIME SPENT AT NO. 1 ON U.S. SINGLES CHART IN A YEAR** Usher (Usher Raymond IV, U.S.A.) spent a total of 28 weeks at the top of the U.S. singles chart in 2004.

Longest U.S. chart span for a single Louis Armstrong (U.S.A., 1901–71) first appeared on a *Billboard* chart on April 6, 1946. His most recent entry to the listings came in 1988, a full 17 years after his death, with "What a Wonderful World" from the movie soundtrack to *Good Morning, Vietnam* (U.S.A., 1987). Armstrong also had over 50 hits before the "official" chart started in

ANDRE "3000" BENJAMIN

Andre 3000 (born Andre Benjamin, U.S.A.) is one half of OutKast, who hold a record for the most weeks at No. 1 & 2.

Did you always want to be a music artist? No, I'm a visual artist first. I wasn't interested in music until high school.

What's the best part of your job? Being able to hear and see an idea, and to bring it to the masses.

When you began your musical career did you think it would be as successful as it is? No, you hope your music resonates with people, but you never know how popular it will be.

What is your greatest achievement in music? Reaching the point where the audience was just as excited about something new and challenging as I was.

What advice would you give to youngsters wanting to make music their career? Make sure you're having fun or getting enjoyment from what you're doing. Learn the business as well as the craft. Know your worth. Diversify. Let the music almost be your hobby because in today's climate it's hard to make real money from it.

1940, his first being "Muskrat Ramble" in 1926, thus taking his span of hits to more than 61 years.

★ **Most multinational UK No. 1 album group** The group Il Divo had four different nationalities making up their numbers when their album *Il Divo* reached the No. 1 spot on November 13, 2004. The quartet is made up of Carlos Marin (Spain), David Miller (U.S.A.), Urs Buhler (Switzerland), and Seb Izambard (France). The album features both classical and pop numbers and is sung in English, Spanish, and Italian.

★ **Most successful UK song title** The most successful song title to appear on the UK singles chart is "Angel," with 11 appearances in the Top 40, the latest coming from The Corrs (Ireland) in September 2004.

WHERE IS THE WORLD'S LARGEST JAZZ FESTIVAL HELD EACH YEAR? FIND OUT ON P. 351

MOST UK NO. 1S BY A CHRISTMAS SONG "Do They Know It's Christmas?" has topped the UK singles chart at Christmas on three separate occasions—in 1984, 1989, and 2004. The first version sold a

then-record 3.6 million copies in the UK alone, and the latest version by Band Aid 20 was the UK's top selling single in 2004, with over 1 million sold. It was written by Bob Geldof (Ireland) and Midge Ure (UK).

Chart Toppers   **325**

BIG STUFF

☆ **BOOT** The largest leather boot measures 20 ft. (6 m) long, 7 ft. (2.1 m) wide, and 16 ft. (4.8 m) tall, and was made by the staff of the Red Wing Shoe Company at their premises in Red Wing, Minnesota, U.S.A., and unveiled on February 5, 2005. It weighs 2,300 lb. (1,043 kg), used 80 hides of leather and is equivalent to a size 638½; (European size 850).

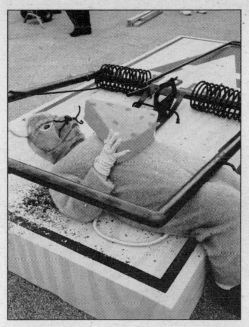

☆ **MOUSETRAP** A mousetrap built by Truly Nolen, a U.S.-based pest control company, measured 11 ft. 7 in. (3.53 m) long and 5 ft. 6 in. (1.67 m) wide when unveiled in Miami Gardens, Florida, U.S.A., on November 5, 2003.

★ SCISSORS The world's largest pair of functional scissors were created in July 2001 by Mike Stephenson (U.S.A.), and measure 36 in. (0.9 m) tip to handle when closed, and 32.5 in. (0.82 m) blade tip to blade tip when fully open.

★ SKATEBOARD The Foundation Skateboards WBS (World's Biggest Skateboard) is 12 ft. (3.66 m) long, 4 ft. (1.2 m) wide, and 2 ft. 6 in. (0.76 m) high, and was designed and produced by Tod Swank, Greg Winter, Dana Hard, and Damon Mills (all U.S.A.) in San Diego, California, U.S.A. Its wheels are car tires and it has scaled-up trucks that turn when the board is tilted, as on a regular-sized skateboard.

★POPCORN MACHINE Greg Scott Abbott (a.k.a. Rev Gadget), Wink Eller, Lisa Lejohn, Eric Scarlett, Christoff Koon, and Charles Cretors (all U.S.A.) built a popcorn machine measuring 22 ft. 2.75 in. (6.77 m) tall, 9 ft. 7 in. (2.92 m) wide, and 8 ft. 1.1 in. (2.46 m) deep in Santa Clarita, California, U.S.A. It took five days to construct and was unveiled in June 2004 on Discovery Channel's *BIG!* television show.

★SURFBOARD A surfboard made by Nev Hyman (Australia) was 39 ft. 4 in. (12 m) long, 9 ft. 10 in. (3 m) wide, and 11.8 in. (30 cm) thick and was launched at Snapper Rocks, Queensland, Australia, on March 5, 2005. It took 79 gal. (300 liters) of resin and nearly 1,102 lb. (500 kg) of foam to make and weighed nearly 1,760 lb. (800 kg).

RUBBER BAND BALL John J. Bain (U.S.A.) constructed a ball made of rubber bands that weighed 3,120 lb. (1,415.2 kg) when measured on October 22, 2003, in Delaware, U.S.A. It has a circumference of 15 ft. 1 in. (4.59 m).

★BURGER The largest hamburger commercially available weighs 9 lb. (4 kg) and is available on the menu at Denny's Beer Barrel Pub, Inc., Clearfield, Pennsylvania, U.S.A. It costs $23.95, and anyone who can finish it within three hours receives a refund, together with their name on a plaque and a $65 gift certificate to use for a future visit. To date, no one has managed the feat.

★GOLF TEE HARIBO GmbH & Co. KG (Germany) created a wooden golf tee measuring 10 ft. 9.25 in. (3.30 m) long with a head diameter of 29.25 in. (74.5 cm) and a shaft width of 11.75 in. (30 cm). It was made of spruce wood and was completed in July 2004 as part of the HARIBO Children and Young Persons Golf Series.

COLOSSAL CONSTRUCTIONS

What's taller: the Empire State Building or the Great Pyramid at Giza? Did you know that the tallest recorded iceberg could have towered over the London Eye observation wheel? Or that the world's tallest tree dwarfs the Statue of Liberty?

On the following special feature pages we've gathered a selection of structures, each the tallest of their kind, to help give you a better idea of how some well-known—and some less well-known—objects compare with one another. Most are manmade, but we've included some natural giants, such as the tallest iceberg and the tallest tree, as these can often be a lot larger than you might imagine.

Finally, we look at two superstructures under construction—the Freedom Tower on the site of the World Trade Center in New York City, U.S.A., and the Burj Dubai in the United Arab Emirates. Soon one, then the other, will be the tallest building in the world. But for how long?

TALLEST SNOWMAN
Residents of Bethel, Maine, U.S.A., and nearby towns, built a snowman measuring 113 ft. 7.5 in. (34.63 m) tall over a period of 14 days, completing him on February 17, 1999.

Art & Entertainment

TRILITHONS The tallest of the trilithons ("three stones") at Stonehenge, to the south of Salisbury Plain, UK, is **22 ft. (6.7 m)** high, with another 8 ft. (2.4 m) below ground. The sarsen blocks weigh more than 99,200 lb. (49.6 tons) and would require over 550 men to drag them up a 9° gradient.

CACTUS (ARMLESS) An armless cactus in Cave Creek, Arizona, U.S.A., measured in April 1978 by Hube Yates, was found to be **78 ft. (24 m)** tall. It was toppled in a windstorm in July 1986 at an estimated age of 150 years.

MONOLITHIC OBELISK Once 118 ft. 1 in. (36 m) tall, the "skewer" or "spit" (from the Greek *obeliskos*) of Tuthmosis III—now repositioned in the Piazza San Giovanni in Laterano, Rome, Italy—currently stands **107 ft. 7 in. (32.81 m)** high.

SNOWMAN **113 ft. 7.5 in. (34.63 m)** (*see page 332*)

STATUE OF LIBERTY **305 ft. 1 in. (92.99 m)**

CHRISTMAS TREE A 221-ft. (67.36 m) Douglas fir (*Pseudotsga menziesii*) was erected and decorated at Northgate Shopping Center, Seattle, Washington, U.S.A., in December 1950.

SCULPTURE **180 ft. 5 in. (55 m)**

TREE The tallest living tree is the Stratosphere Giant—a coast redwood (*Sequoia sempervirens*) discovered by Chris Atkins (U.S.A.) in August 2000 in the Rockefeller Forest of the Humboldt Redwoods State Park, California, U.S.A. The tree measured 370 ft. (112.7 m), as of July 2004.

VERTICAL DROP AMUSEMENT RIDE The Giant Drop at Dreamworld in Queensland, Australia, drops from a height of 390 ft. (119 m), giving riders five seconds of free-fall time before being brought to a halt by electromagnetic brakes.

STATUE A bronze statue of Buddha measuring 393 ft. 8 in. (120 m) high was completed in Tokyo, Japan, in January 1993.

ROLLER COASTER Kingda Ka at Six Flags Great Adventure near Jackson, New Jersey, U.S.A., reaches a maximum height of 418 ft. (127.4 m) above ground level, making it the world's tallest. It opened in spring of 2005 and is also the **world's fastest coaster**, with riders reaching 128 mph (206 km/h) just seconds after launch.

UNSUPPORTED FLAGPOLE The world's tallest unsupported flagpole stands 416 ft. (126.8 m) tall and was erected by Trident Support Corporation (Jordan).

AIRPORT CONTROL TOWER The 425-ft. (130-m) tower at Kuala Lumpur International Airport (KLIA), Malaysia, is the tallest air-traffic control tower in the world. It is shaped like a giant Olympic torch and was designed by a local architect. The tower houses air-traffic controllers, radar systems, and a high-tech air-space computer system.

OBSERVATION WHEEL The British Airways London Eye, designed by architects David Marks and Julia Barfield (both UK), has a diameter and height of 443 ft. (135 m). Constructed at Jubilee Gardens on London's South Bank, UK, it made its first "flight" on February 1, 2000, with regular service commencing the following month.

HOSPITAL The world's tallest hospital building is Guy's Tower at Guy's Hospital in London, UK, which is 468 ft. (142.6 m) tall. It was completed in 1974 and has 34 floors.

PYRAMID The pyramid of Khufu at Giza, Egypt, is the world's tallest. Also known as the Great Pyramid, it was 481.4 ft. (146.6 m) high when completed around 4,500 years ago, but erosion and vandalism have reduced its height to 451 ft. 4 in. (137.5 m) today.

FLAGPOLE The flagpole at Panmunjom, North Korea, near the border with South Korea, is 525 ft. (160 m) high and flies a flag 30 m (98 ft. 6 in.) long. The flagpole is the result of a propaganda war between the two countries and is said to have been erected in reply to a tall flagpole erected in a nearby South Korean village.

CATHEDRAL SPIRE The tallest cathedral spire in the world is that of the Protestant Cathedral of Ulm in Germany. The building is early gothic and was begun in 1377. The tower, in the center of the west facade, was not finally completed until 1890 and is 528 ft. (160.9 m) high.

ICEBERG An iceberg reported off western Greenland by the U.S. icebreaker East Wind in 1958 measured 550 ft. (167 m) tall.

OBELISK The Washington Monument in Washington D.C., U.S.A., stands 555 ft. (169 m) tall and was completed in 1884 to honor George Washington, the first president of the United States. An obelisk is a tapered four-sided column, usually with a pointed top.

MONUMENT The stainless-steel Gateway Arch in St. Louis, Missouri, U.S.A., is a sweeping arch spanning 630 ft. (192 m) and rising to the same height. It was completed on October 28, 1965, to commemorate the westward expansion after the Louisiana Purchase of 1803. The arch was designed in 1947 by the Finnish-American architect Eero Saarinen.

MINARET The tallest minaret belongs to the Great Hassan II Mosque in Casablanca, Morocco, and measures 656 ft. (200 m). The cost of construction of the mosque was 5 billion dirhams ($513.5 million).

RESIDENTIAL BUILDING The tallest purely residential building in the world is the 21st Century Tower in Dubai, UAE, which has 54 floors and tops out at 882 ft. (269 m).

HOTEL The all-suite Burj Al Arab ("The Arabian Tower"), situated 9 miles (15 km) south of Dubai, UAE, is the tallest hotel in the world, standing at 1,052 ft. (320.94 m) high from ground level to the top of its mast, when measured on October 26, 1999. The hotel is shaped like a sail and was built on a manmade island.

BRIDGE The 8,070-ft.-long (2,460-m) Millau Viaduct (France) is supported by seven concrete piers, the tallest of which measures 1,095 ft. 4.8 in. (333.88 m) from the ground to its highest point.

CHIMNEY The coal power-plant No. 2 stack at Ekibastuz, Kazakhstan, completed in 1987, is 1,378 ft. (420 m) tall. The diameter tapers from 144 ft. (44 m) at the base to 46 ft. 7 in. (14.2 m) at the top, and it weighs 66,000 tons.

EMPIRE STATE BUILDING (tallest building, 1931–74) 1,250 ft. (381 m) to roof; 1,472 ft. (449 m) to tip of antenna.

BUILDING Also known as the Taipei Financial Center, Taipei 101 (Taiwan) tops out at 1,666 ft. (508 m). The building's design incorporates an "active damper"—essentially a 1.98 million-lb. (990-ton) iron pendulum suspended within the interior of the building—to stabilize it.

TOWER The tallest freestanding tower (as opposed to a guyed mast) in the world is the CN Tower in Toronto, Canada, which rises to 1,815 ft. 5 in. (553.34 m).

Colossal Constructions

FREESTANDING STRUCTURE The Petronius oil-and-gas drilling platform, which stands 1,870 ft. (570 m) above the ocean floor in the Gulf of Mexico, began commercial production on July 21, 2000. The highest point on the platform, the vent boom, stands more than 2,000 ft. (610 m) above the ocean floor.

STRUCTURE The KVLY-TV tower in North Dakota, U.S.A., is a stayed television transmitting mast 2,063 ft. (629 m) tall.

SKY'S THE LIMIT?

While Taipei 101 (Taiwan) is currently the world's **tallest building,** two new skyscrapers under construction seem destined to ensure that it holds the title for less than five years. The Freedom Tower in New York is set to be a symbolic **1,776 ft. (541 m)** tall—1776 being the date of the U.S. Declaration of Independence. Due for completion in 2009, it may, however, be beaten to the post in 2008 by a monster that will be the **tallest ever manmade structure.** The Burj Dubai ("Dubai Tower"), UAE, is set to be **2,313 ft. (705 m)** tall and will tower over all other manmade structures, whether on land or at sea, and whether self-supported or not.

☆**TALLEST SCULPTURE** *B of the Bang* by Thomas Heatherwick (UK) is 180 ft. 5 in. (55 m) tall and was unveiled by athlete Linford Christie (UK) on January 12, 2005, in Manchester, UK. The sculpture takes its name from a quotation by Christie, who said that he started his races not merely at the "bang" of the starting pistol, but at "the B of the Bang." The structure is taller— and leans at a greater angle—than the Leaning Tower of Pisa!

Art & Entertainment

X GAMES

SKATEBOARD

- STREET PARK—a concrete course with stairs, rails, banks, and ledges
- BIG AIR—a roll-in from a height of 60–80 ft. (18–24 m), launching over a gap to land in a 27-ft. (8-m) quarter-pipe
- VERT—big air and tricks performed off a half-pipe
- VERT BEST TRICK—best half-pipe trick

MOTO X
(125cc/250cc DIRT BIKES)

- STEP-UP—a 25-ft. (7.6-m) run-up to a vertical dirt face used as a launchpad for a high jump over a bar
- FREESTYLE—tricks using ramp-to-dirt and dirt-to-dirt jumps
- BEST TRICK—a jump trick off a giant dirt ramp
- SUPER MOTO—a combination of street racing, motocross, and freestyle on a dirt and asphalt track

BIKE STUNT (BMX)

- VERT—big air and tricks off a half-pipe
- PARK—tricks using launch and sub boxes, wall rides, and rails

AGGRESSIVE INLINE SKATE

- VERT—big air and tricks off a half-pipe
- SURFING THE GAME—two teams compete for overall score
- WAKEBOARD—jumps and tricks performed off a boat's wake around a course of water obstacles

FOR A COMPLETE LIST OF X GAMES MEDAL RECORDS, PLEASE REFER TO THE SPORTS REFERENCE SECTION, P. 560

X GAMES HISTORY

The X Games (originally called Extreme Games) were first held in Rhode Island and Vermont, U.S.A., in July 1995, and have been staged annually ever since. In 1997, the first Winter X Games were held at Snow Summit Mountain Resort in California, U.S.A.

The X Games are the brainchild of the sports TV network ESPN (Entertainment and Sports Programming Network), which was looking to create an international forum for action sport athletes. Its popularity has continued to grow around the world, with top athletes now battling it out in various qualifying rounds for limited spots in the X Games.

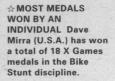

☆ **MOST MEDALS WON BY AN INDIVIDUAL** Dave Mirra (U.S.A.) has won a total of 18 X Games medals in the Bike Stunt discipline.

☆ **MOST GOLD MEDALS WON BY AN INDIVIDUAL** Dave Mirra (U.S.A.) also holds the record for the most X Games gold medals won by an individual, with 13 in the Bike Stunt category.

SNOWBOARDING MOST MEDALS WON (WOMEN) The most X Games snowboarding medals won by a woman is 10 by Barrett Christy (U.S.A.).

★ YOUNGEST ATHLETE Takeshi Yasutoko (Japan) was 11 years 50 days old when he made his X Games debut in the 1998 Aggressive Inline Skate Vert.

TONY HAWK

"Birdman" Tony Hawk (U.S.A., page 340) has won a record 16 X Games skateboard medals, and was also the first to pull off a "900" (see page 340).

How does it feel to be a Guinness World Record holder?
It's huge! I would never have believed it if you'd told me when I was a kid that I would be included in the book, especially for skateboarding. It's a big honor.

What's been your greatest achievement so far? Making the "900" for the first time in any contest was a great feat for me, because it was the one trick I had pursued for the longest—probably about five years up to that point. But I'd had the idea long before that without having the guts to try it. It'd been this thorn in my side since I'd thought about trying it.

Beyond that, being on *The Simpsons* was a major event for me. It's such a measure of pop-culture status, especially if they have you play yourself.

Did you ever expect to be where you are now? I'm still in disbelief that I get to skateboard for a living. Even when skateboarding wasn't very big and when it was difficult to make a living, I was still doing it. Now it's bigger and better than ever and I still get to do it—just on a bigger scale!

What advice do you give to kids who are starting out?
Don't get too frustrated with yourself—these things take a long time to learn. Also, enjoy it. Don't do it if you think it's some tool to get fame or fortune, because you have to be enjoying it to be successful.

★ **SNOWBOARD SUPERPIPE—MOST MEDALS WON** Danny Kass (U.S.A.) has won a total of four medals in the snowboard Superpipe discipline: gold in 2001, silver in 2003 and 2004, and bronze in 2005.

FIRST "900" ON A SKATEBOARD Skateboard legend Tony Hawk (U.S.A.) became the first person to achieve a "900" (two and a half airborne rotations) in competition at the X Games in San Francisco, California, U.S.A., on June 27, 1999. The "900" (so-called because the skater spins through 900°) is one of the most difficult tricks in skateboarding. Hawk was successful on his 11th attempt of the evening.

★ **MOTO X MOST MEDALS WON BY AN INDIVIDUAL** Brian Deegan (U.S.A.), known as the Metal Mulisha, has won a total of nine X Games medals (two of them gold) during his career in the discipline of Moto X.

★ X GAMES—WINTER EVENTS ★

MOTO X

■ BEST TRICK—midair trick performed over a gap between takeoff and landing ramps

SKI

■ SKIER X—racers follow a downhill course
■ SLOPESTYLE—tricks performed through a course of obstacles, rails, and jumps
■ SUPERPIPE—tricks performed off a half-pipe

SNOCROSS

A race combining oval-track racing and cross-country

SNOWBOARD

■ SNOWBOARDER X—racers follow a downhill course
■ SLOPESTYLE—(see SKI)
■ SUPERPIPE—(see SKI)

ULTRACROSS

A downhill relay race in pairs of one skier and one snowboarder

★ SNOCROSS MOST MEDALS WON (MEN) Blair Morgan (Canada) has won a record seven medals for snocross. He took gold in 2001, 2002, 2003, and 2005, silver in 1999 and 2000, and bronze in 2004. He came back to win the gold in 2005 after recovering from a broken back and leg.

★ MOST SKIING MEDALS Jon Olsson (Sweden) has won eight Winter X Games skiing medals: four in the Superpipe discipline and four in the Slopestyle, 2002–05.

MOTO X HIGHEST STEP-UP JUMP The greatest height achieved in the X-Games Moto X Step-Up event is 35 ft. (10.67 m), by Tommy Clowers (U.S.A.) in August 2000. Essentially a "high jump" on a motorcycle, riders must try to clear a bar placed at the top of a steep takeoff ramp. The height obtained is the equivalent of jumping onto the roof of a two-story building.

SEE P. xxvii FOR AN INTERVIEW WITH RYAN SHECKLER, THE YOUNGEST X GAMES GOLD MEDALIST

ARTISTS & REPERTOIRE

BIGGEST SELLING . . .

★**Contemporary jazz album** The Norah Jones (U.S.A.) album *Come Away With Me* headed the U.S. contemporary jazz chart for 143 successive weeks, selling 16 million copies around the world. It debuted at No. 1 in March 2002, before finally slipping to No. 2 in December 2004.

World music album The 1998 Grammy Award–winning album *Buena Vista Social Club* (Cuba, 1997) has sold more than 4 million copies.

Female Latin artist Gloria Estefan (Cuba) has achieved world sales estimated at more than 70 million by her record company. She amassed eight gold albums in the U.S.A., four of which have passed the 3 million sales mark: *Primitive Love* (1985), *Let It Loose* (1987), *Cuts Both Ways* (1989), and *Greatest Hits* (1992).

Male Latin artist Vocalist Julio Iglesias (Spain) has achieved reported global sales of more than 200 million albums. His album *Julio* (1983) was the first foreign-language album to sell more than 2 million copies in the U.S.A., and the only foreign-language record to go double platinum there.

★**HIGHEST CHART POSITIONS FOR SIMULTANEOUS U.S. ALBUM RELEASES** Two albums by rap artist Nelly (U.S.A., b. Cornell Haynes)— *Suit* and *Sweat*—simultaneously entered the U.S. album chart at No. 1 and No. 2 in October 2004.

★ **MOST PUBLIC APPEARANCES BY A POP ARTIST IN 24 HOURS** Rachel Stevens (UK) made seven public appearances on September 8 and 9, 2004. The cities visited were, in order: Salford, Liverpool, Stoke-on-Trent, Birmingham, Bristol, Oxford, and London (all UK). All appearances lasted a minimum of 15 minutes.

Rap artist Rap legend 2Pac (U.S.A., b. Tupac Shakur) has certified U.S. album sales of 36 million. He has had more hits since he died (at the age of 25 in September 1996) than he managed to amass while he was alive, including three No. 1 albums.

Country artist Garth Brooks (U.S.A.) has achieved album sales of over 100 million since 1989.

Music video *The Making of Michael Jackson's Thriller,* released in December 1983, has sold over 900,000 units.

★ **Longest credit on a single** The single "Was Ist Passiert?" released by PUR (Germany) on October 20, 2003, lists the names of 1,491 people. Those credited are fans who registered via the band's website.

WHAT ALBUM HAS SOLD MORE THAN 51 MILLION COPIES SINCE ITS RELEASE IN 1982? FIND OUT ON P. 323

MOST...

☆**BRIT Awards won by an individual** Robbie Williams (UK) has won 15 BRIT (British Record Industry Trust) Awards. His most recent win was for Best Song (of the last 25 years) Award, received for "Angels," at the ceremony held on February 10, 2005.

BRIT Awards won in a year by a group Blur won four BRIT Awards in 1995. At the time, the group—which formed in 1988—included Damon Albarn, Graham Coxon, Alex James, and Dave Rowntree (all UK).

Grammy Awards won by an individual The classical music conductor Sir Georg Solti (UK) won 31 Grammy Awards (including a special Trustees award in 1967) from 1958 to 1997.

Grammy Awards won by a female artist Aretha Franklin (U.S.A.) has won 15 Grammys since receiving her first in 1967 for Best R&B Vocal Performance with "Respect." She then went on to win the female category of the same award 11 times from 1967 to 1987.

Grammy Awards won by a solo pop performer Stevie Wonder (U.S.A.) has won 19 Grammy Awards, including Best Male R&B Vocal Performance six times, since 1973.

Grammy Awards won in a year by a group Rock group Santana, formed in the 1960s, won eight Grammy Awards on February 23, 2000.

★**MOST ALBUMS CONSECUTIVELY SIGNED BY THE ARTIST** Yahir Othön Parra (Mexico) signed a record 2,852 copies of his album *Otra historia de amor* at Plaza Cuicuilco, Mexico City, on July 6 and 7, 2004. He signed CDs nonstop for 8 hr. 13 min. 49 sec.

★YOUNGEST FEMALE TO TOP UK ALBUM CHART Joss Stone (UK) reached No. 1 with her second album *Mind, Body & Soul* on October 9, 2004, aged 17 years and 181 days.

Grammy Awards won in a year by an individual Michael Jackson (U.S.A.) won eight Grammy Awards in 1984.

People to share a Grammy Award The 46 members of the Chicago Symphony Orchestra won a Grammy Award in February 1978 for Best Choral Performance–Classical with its recording of Verdi's *Requiem*.

MOST EXPENSIVE . . .

Pop star clothing An outfit worn by Geri Halliwell (UK) for the Spice Girls' 1997 BRIT Awards performance was bought for £41,320 (then $66,112) at Sotheby's, London, UK, on September 16, 1998. The outfit had been made by the singer's sister Karen Davis who, on a budget, made a corset onto which she stitched a Union Jack.

Music video Directed by Mark Romanek (U.S.A.), the video for Michael and Janet Jackson's hit single "Scream" (1995) cost $7 million to make.

MUSIC FACTS & FEATS

VOCAL POWER

Fastest rap MC Rebel XD, otherwise known as Seandale Price (U.S.A.), is the world's fastest rap artist. On June 24, 1998, he rapped 683 syllables in 54.501 seconds, which works out at just over 12.5 syllables a second, beating his own previous record of 674 syllables in 54.9 seconds, or 12.2 syllables a second, which was set in 1992.

★Longest continuous vocal note David McFetridge (Ireland) held a single vocal note continuously for 29.03 seconds on the children's radio program *Big Toe Radio Show* in London, UK, on July 29, 2003. David was placed exactly 3 ft. 2 in. (1 m) from the measuring instrument and chose his own pitch, which was checked for deviation from the original starting note by two qualified musical experts.

MARATHONS

☆**Elvis** Franz Nübel (Germany), the "Eifel-Elvis," held an Elvis Presley singing marathon lasting 42 hr. 16 min. 8 sec. in Kall, Germany, from January 29 to 30, 2004.

☆**Radio DJ** Arulanantham Suresh Joachim (Sri Lanka) broadcast for 120 hours on Geethavaani Tamil Radio in Scarborough, Ontario, Canada, from June 23 to 28, 2003.

Club DJ DJ Martin Boss (U.S.A.) held a 74-hour mixing session at Vinyl Frontier in Orlando, Florida, U.S.A., from February 1 to 4, 2002.

★ LARGEST MUSICAL INSTRUMENT ENSEMBLES ★

INSTRUMENT	NUMBER	PLACE	DATE
Bell (campanology)	10,000	Gdansk, Poland	December 31, 2000
Violin	4,000	London, UK	June 15, 1925
Recorder	3,337	Hong Kong, China	March 4, 2001
Drum	3,140	Hong Kong, China	July 13, 2003
★Panpipes	2,317	La Paz, Bolivia	October 24, 2004
Kazoo	1,791	Quincy, U.S.A.	June 30, 2004
★Erhu	1,490	Jiangsu, China	October 17, 2004
Guitar	1,322	Vancouver, Canada	May 7, 1994
Cello	1,103	Kobe, Japan	November 29, 1998
☆Harmonica	851	Poznan, Poland	September 13, 2003
Shamisen	815	Tokyo, Japan	November 27, 1999

☆ **LONGEST CONCERT BY A GROUP** From February 20 to 22, 2004, the Grand Boys—a.k.a. Paul Bromley, John Griffin, Bob and Robert Kelly, Alan Marshall, Adrian Robertson, Colin Sinclair, and Alan Stewart (all UK)—played for 42 hr. 38 min. at Smith's Restaurant in Stirling, UK.

★**Karaoke** Mark Pearson (UK) sang for 25 hr. 45 min. at Keighley Cougars Rugby Club, Keighley, UK, on June 25–26, 2004. The ★**longest group karaoke session** featured 399 acts and lasted for 100 hours in an event held at the Guangzhou Victory Plaza, China, from December 26 to 30, 2004.

MOST . . .

★**DJs in relay** The most DJs to consecutively mix one record each is 59 at D-Train, Bridge & Tunnel Club, London, UK, on June 18, 2003. Each DJ played one record, one after the other, with every mix being continuous, synchronous and to a professional standard.

★**Turntables in a mix** DJ Trixta (Andrew Cooper, UK) used six records on six turntables in a synchronous mix at the Phoenix Centre, Exeter, Devon, UK, on September 26, 2002.

★**Instruments in a piece of music** A total of 147 different musical instruments were played by children from Caistor Primary School in a recital held on July 3, 2002, at Caistor, Lincolnshire, UK. The piece—entitled *Caistor Symphony*—lasted 30 minutes.

Drumbeats in a minute Oliver Butterworth (UK) played 1,080 single-stroke drumbeats in one minute on June 13, 2002, at the University of Lincoln, UK.

LARGEST...

Band On June 28, 1964, a total of 20,100 bandsmen from Norges Musikkorps Forbund assembled at the Ullevaal Stadium in Oslo, Norway.

★Carillon A carillon consists of brass bells fixed to a frame, played by keyboard and pedals. The largest (minimum 23 bells) is the five-octave Hyechon College Carillon in Seo-ku, Taejon, South Korea, with 78 bells, which took two years to build. The heaviest bell, the Bourdonbell, weighs 22,046 lb. (11 tons).

Choir A choir of 60,000 sang at a choral contest finale in Breslau, Germany, on August 2, 1937.

★Human beatbox A human beatbox made up of 106 people, mostly residents of Laburnham Road, Maidenhead, Berkshire, UK, came together on June 3, 2002. They kept to a set rhythm for over three minutes.

☆Jazz festival The world's largest jazz festival is the *Festival International de Jazz de Montréal* in Quebec, Canada. For its 25th anniversary festival in July 2004 it attracted 1,913,868 people.

★Music lesson Len Collins (UK) held a guitar class for 211 students at Middleton Hall, Milton Keynes, Buckinghamshire, UK, on May 11, 2004.

Organ The largest and **loudest musical instrument** ever constructed is the now only partially functional Auditorium Organ in Atlantic City, New Jersey, U.S.A. Completed in 1930, it had two consoles, 1,477 stop controls,

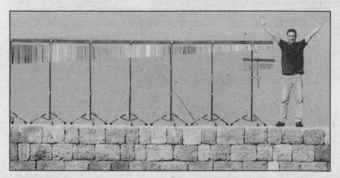

★LARGEST PLAYABLE BAR CHIMES Bar chimes built by George Barbar (Lebanon) and played at the Byblos-off Festival in Byblos, Lebanon, on June 17, 2004, measured 49 ft. (15 m) in length and consisted of 1,000 chimes. They varied in length from 2 in. (5.1 cm) to 41 in. (105 cm), and were attached to 20 wooden bars fixed to 20 cymbal stands.

LARGEST DRUM ENSEMBLE The largest drum ensemble consisted of 3,140 participants who gathered to play at the opening ceremony of the Hong Kong Drum Festival at Victoria Park, Hong Kong, China, on July 13, 2003. Among those leading the group were the 100-piece drum troupe of the Hong Kong Chinese Orchestra.

and 33,112 pipes. It had a range of seven octaves and the volume of 25 brass bands.

Orchestra A total of 6,452 musicians—made up of the Vancouver Symphony Orchestra and music students from British Columbia, Canada—played "Ten Minutes of Nine" for 9 min. 44 sec. at Place Stadium, Vancouver, Canada, on May 15, 2000.

★**Sing-along (one site)** On May 9, 2004, Freddy Quinn (Germany) led 88,600 people in a rendition of "La Paloma" from the museum ship *Rickmer Rickmers* in Hamburg, Germany.

THE STAGE

MUSICALS

★**Shortest theatrical run in the West End** A production of *Oscar Wilde* closed after its opening night performance on October 22, 2004, due to only five seats having been sold for the second night at the 466-seater Shaw Theatre in London, UK.

★ **MOST CONCURRENT MUSICAL PRODUCTIONS** As of February 2005, the musical *Mamma Mia!* had the most global productions playing at the same time with 12, consisting of nine resident productions (UK; two in the U.S.A.; Spain; Japan; Sweden; Germany; Canada; Holland) along with three tours in Europe, South Africa, and the U.S.A.

Cameron Mackintosh's production of *Les Misérables* had the **most concurrent productions ever**, with 15 being staged around the world at one time.

★**LARGEST BUDGET (PREPRODUCTION)** The largest preproduction budget allocated to a stage show before its world premiere has so far been in excess of $22.3 million for the musical *The Lord of the Rings*. Directed by Matthew Warchus (UK) and produced by Kevin Wallace Ltd., the show is due to premiere at the Prince of Wales Theatre, Toronto, Ontario, Canada, in 2006.

★**Highest paid actor in a Broadway musical** Michael Crawford (UK) was given a reported $180,000-a-week contract for the role of Count Von Krolock in the Broadway production of *Dance of the Vampire*. The show opened on December 9, 2002, at the Minskoff Theater, New York City, U.S.A., and closed on January 25, 2003, after playing more previews (61) than performances (56), securing the record for the greatest theatrical loss on Broadway.

★**Most prolific composer** With various collaborators, Richard Rodgers (U.S.A.) wrote 51 musicals for theater and movies in a career that spanned seven decades, beginning with *You'd Be Surprised* (1920) and ending with

---

MOST TONY AWARD NOMINATIONS

★**Actor:** eight, Jason Robards (U.S.A.), 1957–1978

★**Actress:** 10, Julie Harris (U.S.A.), 1952–1997

Play: nine for *Angels in America: Millennium Approaches* (1993) and *Indiscretions* (1995)

★**Play (without winning):** nine for *Indiscretions* (1995)

★**Musical (without winning):** 11 for *Chicago* (1976) and *Steel Pier* (1997)

I Remember Mama (1979). Perhaps the most popular production was *South Pacific,* first produced in 1949 and made into a movie in 1958. The soundtrack holds the record for the **most weeks at No. 1 on the UK album chart,** with 70.

Most expensive stage production in the West End Eon Productions' *Chitty Chitty Bang Bang,* which opened on April 16, 2002, at the London Palladium, UK, starring Michael Ball (UK), cost £6.2 million ($8.9 million) to stage, beating the previous record set by *Cats* of £6 million ($12.69 million) on May 11, 1981.

Most Tony Awards won by a musical *The Producers* won a record 12 awards from 15 nominations—including Best Musical—at the 2001 Tony Awards. Directed by Susan Stroman (U.S.A.), it broke the previous record of 10 wins held since 1964 by *Hello Dolly!*

Highest theatrical box office gross Since first opening in London on October 9, 1986, Andrew Lloyd Webber's musical *The Phantom of the Opera* has played over 65,000 performances in 20 countries and has taken over $3.2 billion at the box office.

WHICH POP STAR MADE THE MOST PUBLIC APPEARANCES IN 24 HOURS? FIND OUT ON P. 345

THEATER

★**Most characters played by one actor in a single production** Laxman Deshpande (India) plays all 52 parts in the three-hour one-man play *Varhad Nighalay Londonla.* He has performed 2,125 times since the first paying production in December 1979 in Aurangabad, India.

☆**Fastest production** On September 27, 2003, the cast and crew of Dundee University Musical Society, in association with Apex Productions, produced and performed *Seven Brides for Seven Brothers* at the Gardyne Theatre, Dundee, UK, in a time of 23 hr. 30 min. from first receiving the script. The time includes auditions, casting, rehearsals, publicity design, rigging, stage and set design, and construction.

★**Most plays by one writer running simultaneously on Broadway** For a period of 186 days from December 21, 1966, to June 25, 1967, Neil Simon (U.S.A.) had four plays running on Broadway: *Barefoot in the Park* at the Biltmore (October 23, 1963, to June 25, 1967), *The Odd Couple* at the Eugene O'Neill (August 1, 1966, to July 2, 1967), *The Star-Spangled Girl* at the Plymouth (December 21, 1966, to August 5, 1967), and *Sweet Charity* at the Palace (January 9, 1966, to July 15, 1967).

MOST THEATRICAL APPEARANCES ON A SINGLE NIGHT On February 24, 2004, Jerry Hall (U.S.A.) took on recognized scripted roles in six different London West End theater productions during the course of a single night.

★**Longest theatrical run of a comedy** Since first opening at the Edinburgh Festival Fringe, Scotland, UK, on August 18, 1979, *NewsRevue* has continued its run in London, UK, at the Kings Head Theatre (1979), Gate Theatre (1980–85), and the Canal Café Theatre (1985 to present) as well as producing a concurrent production every August for the Edinburgh Festival Fringe.

★**Youngest theater producer in the West End** Gary Sullivan (UK) was 20 years 152 days old when his variety showcase, *Energy,* played at Her Majesty's Theatre, London, UK, on March 18, 2001. It featured 200 performers, consisting of solo singers, dance groups, bands, and choirs.

★**Largest live entertainment company** Clear Channel Entertainment, Inc. is the world's largest producer, promoter, and operator of live entertainment events such as concerts, touring Broadway shows, and sports events. It operates in 65 countries, with sales of $2.6469 billion in 2003.

Largest theater cast A total of 2,100 children appeared in the finale of the Rolf Harris Schools Variety Spectacular, which was held in Sydney, Australia, in November 1985.

JERRY HALL'S THEATER SCHEDULE, FEBRUARY 24, 2004

Phantom of the Opera
Character: Monsieur André
On stage: 7:30 p.m.
Off stage: 7:40 p.m.

Les Misérables
Character: a prostitute
On stage: 7:59 p.m.
Off stage: 8:04 p.m.

Fame
Character: Mr. Myers
On stage: 8:30 p.m.
Off stage: 8:35 p.m.

Blood Brothers
Character: Brenda
On stage: 8:55 p.m.
Off stage: 9:00 p.m.

Anything Goes
Character: one of six "Swings"
On stage: 9:25 p.m.
Off stage: 9:40 p.m.

Chitty Chitty Bang Bang
Character: one of the 24 members of the ensemble
On stage: 10:09 p.m.
Off stage: 10:18 p.m.

Total time: 2 hr. 42 min.

CIRCUS SKILLS

LARGEST . . .

Traveling circus tent The Ringling Bros. and Barnum & Bailey Circus (U.S.A.) traveled with a circus tent covering 91,407 ft.^{2} (8,492 m^2). Consisting of a round top 200 ft. (61 m) in diameter with five middle sections each 59 ft. (18 m) wide, it was used on tours from 1921 to 1924. The biggest circus tents now in use have a floor area just over half this size.

★ MOST EXPENSIVE STAGE PRODUCTION ON BROADWAY The stage adaptation of Disney's 1994 movie *The Lion King* is the most expensive theatrical production ever, with the Broadway show—which opened on November 13, 1997—costing an estimated $15 million.

★MOST PEOPLE STILT-WALKING SIMULTANEOUSLY As part of Cirque de Soleil's 20th anniversary celebrations on June 16, 2004, 544 of their employees simultaneously walked a distance of 328 ft. (100 m) on stilts at their headquarters in Montreal, Quebec, Canada.

★ MOST CONSECUTIVE FOOT-JUGGLING FLIPS Stiv and Roni Bello (Italy) performed 45 consecutive foot-juggling flips during their performance in "Varekai," Cirque du Soleil's North American tour in San Jose, California, U.S.A., on February 15, 2003.

Big tops The two largest big tops measure 396 × 124 ft. (120.7 × 37.8 m)—slightly longer and narrower than a football field—and are used by Carson and Barnes Circus, and Clyde Beatty-Cole Brothers' Circus, both in the U.S.A. The Carson and Barnes tent is moved seven days a week for a record 36 consecutive weeks every year. The Clyde Beatty-Cole Brothers' tent seats 3,000 people.

JUGGLING—DURATION

Three objects:
Terry Cole (UK)
11 hr. 4 min. 22 sec. (1995)

★ Three objects underwater:
Ashrita Furman (U.S.A.)
48 min. 36 sec. (2002)

★ Three shot puts (male):
Milan Roskopf (Slovakia)
52.02 sec. (2002)

Five clubs:
Anthony Gatto (U.S.A.)
45 min. 2 sec. (1989)

Circus tent audience An audience of 16,702 (15,686 paid) assembled for the Ringling Bros. and Barnum & Bailey Circus in Concordia, Kansas, U.S.A., on September 13, 1924.

Animal circus act: lions "Captain" Alfred Schneider (UK) mastered and fed 70 lions in a cage, unaided, at Bertram Mills' Circus, London, UK, in 1925.

Animal circus act: polar bears Willy Hagenbeck (Germany) worked with 70 polar bears in a presentation at the Paul Busch Circus, Berlin, Germany, in 1904.

Clown boots Circus clown Coco (Latvia, b. Nicolai Poliakoff) took an enormous size 58½ boot.

FIRE BREATHING Robert Milton (UK, pictured) blew a flame 13 ft. 5 in. (4.1 m) high to achieve the ☆**highest flame blown**. The greatest distance blown by a fire-breather is 31 ft. (9.4 m) by Reg Morris (UK) on October 29, 1986.

Matthew "Matt the Knife" Cassiere (U.S.A.) held a lit torch vertically in his teeth for 23 seconds on October 30, 2004—the **longest duration for fire torch teething**. Antti Karvinen (Finland) extinguished 36 torches by mouth on October 9, 2000, to claim the record for ★**most torches extinguished in one minute**.

LONGEST...

★Running circus The Ringling Bros. and Barnum & Bailey Circus' "Greatest Show on Earth" has run for 135 years. Barnum started the show in 1870 and merged with the Ringling Brothers in 1919.

Serving circus bandmaster Merle Evans (U.S.A.) served with the Ringling Bros. and Barnum & Bailey Circus for 50 years. From 1919 to 1969 he led the band for about 30,000 performances.

MOST...

★Foot-juggling flips in 30 seconds Cirque du Soleil's Bello Brothers—Stiv and Roni Bello (Italy, pictured on p. 360)—achieved 38 consecutive foot-juggling flips in 30 seconds during a performance in California, U.S.A., on February 15, 2003.

★Elephants performing at a circus The Ringling Bros. and Barnum & Bailey Circus toured 55 elephants around the U.S.A. in the 1920s and 1930s. The **most performers in a circus act** ever was 263 people plus around 175 animals, in the 1890 Barnum & Bailey Circus tour of the U.S.A.

★Inventive clown From 1927 to 1937, Charlie Cairoli (Italy) and his father devised over 700 different routines at the Cirque Medrano in Paris, France. He then played 40 consecutive seasons without repeating a routine.

★Saddle rolls in one minute Ami Miller (UK) and the Funky Fools achieved 19 saddle rolls on horseback in Newcastle-Upon-Tyne, UK, on September 1, 2004.

★FASTEST 10 KM JOGGLE WITH THREE OBJECTS Paul-Erik Lillholm (Norway) jogged 6.2 miles (10 km) while juggling three beanbags without dropping them in 41 min. 18 sec. in Skansemyrer, Bergen, Norway, on July 9, 2000.

★**Consecutive skips on a tightrope** Juan Pedro Carrillo (U.S.A.) managed 1,323 consecutive skips with a rope on a 27-ft.-high (8.2-m) wire at the Big Apple Circus Big Top in Massachusetts, U.S.A., on April 26, 2004.

☆**Swords swallowed** Natasha Verushka (U.S.A.) swallowed 13 swords at the Third Annual Sideshow Gathering and Sword Swallowers Convention in Wilkes-Barre, Pennsylvania, U.S.A., on September 3, 2004.

FARTHEST . . .

★**Human arrow shot** Vesta Gueschkova (Bulgaria) was fired 75 ft. (22.9 m) from a crossbow at the Ringling Bros. and Barnum & Bailey Circus in Tampa, Florida, U.S.A., on December 27, 1995.

★ JUGGLING AND FLASHING ★

OBJECTS	NUMBER	HOLDER	DATE
Balls (juggled)	10	Enrico Rastelli (Italy)	1920
		Bruce Sarafian (U.S.A.)	1996
Balls (flashed)	12	Bruce Sarafian (U.S.A.)	1995
Balls (bounced)	10	Tim Nolan (U.S.A.)	1998
Flaming torches	7	Anthony Gatto (U.S.A.)	1989
Clubs	7	Albert Petrovski (USSR)	1963
		Sorin Munteanu (Romania)	1975
		Jack Bremlov (Czechoslovakia)	1985
		Albert Lucas (U.S.A.)	1996
		Anthony Gatto (U.S.A.)	1988
		Bruce Tiemann (U.S.A.)	1995
Clubs (flashed)	8	Anthony Gatto (U.S.A.)	1989
		Scott Sorensen (U.S.A.)	1995
Batons	7	Françoise Rochais (France)	1999
Rings	11	Albert Petrovski (USSR)	1963
		Eugene Belaur (USSR)	1968
		Sergei Ignatov (USSR)	1973
Rings (flashed)	13	Albert Lucas (U.S.A.)	2002

Note: In **juggling**, the number of catches made equals the number of objects multiplied by the number of hands. When **flashing**, the number of catches made equals at least the number of objects but less than a juggle.

MAGIC & ILLUSION

★**Most prolific quick-change illusion artist** Arturo Brachetti (Italy) changed costume 22,500 times during 250 performances of the show *L'Homme Aux Mille Visages,* Paris, France, in 2001–02. His quickest

SLOWLY
BRING THE STAMP
TO YOUR NOSE

RUB SPOTTED SCARF
WITH YOUR FINGER

★ **FIRST MAGIC SOCIETY TO BE FEATURED ON A NATIONAL STAMP**
The UK's Royal Mail issued a series of five interactive stamps on March
15, 2005, marking the centennial of The Magic Circle (UK), one of the
oldest societies of magicians in the world. The issue features another
first—a "scratch and reveal" first-class stamp. Rubbing it with a coin
reveals either a "heads" or "tails" image.

costume change, including shoes, took two seconds, from black tail suit to
white in full view of the audience.

★ **Most magic shows playing at one time in one city** Excluding re-
vues and variety shows, as of March 1, 2005, there were 11 magic shows
playing in Las Vegas, Nevada, U.S.A.

★ **Largest displayed magic poster collection** There are 587 stone
lithograph magic posters on display within the collection belonging to
Norm and Lupa Nielsen (both U.S.A.). The collection, which was started in

DAVID COPPERFIELD

David Copperfield (U.S.A.) has 11 Guinness World Records—more than any other magician. He talks to us about his achievements.

Who inspired you to become a magician? Magic was something that I always had a feeling for, and I just seemed to be good at it. I love movies and all the fantasy and wonder that they create, but magic is what I did well. So I tried to combine the two. So the answer would be a lot of people who were working in film, including Walt Disney, Orson Welles, Frank Capra, and Victor Fleming.

What is your favorite magic illusion of all time? I'm very proud of Flying, especially flying into the Plexiglas box. I also like the Death Saw and the Lottery piece with the car that appears surrounded by the audience.

Of your career so far, what are you most proud of? The one thing I'm proudest of is Project Magic. It's a program that I created which uses magic as a form of therapy for people who have disabilities. It's currently being used in 1,000 hospitals in 30 countries around the world.

Can you see yourself ever retiring or slowing down? Why? My work is my play. I get to enjoy one of my passions every time I do a show. Why would I want to give that up?

What's it like to be a Guinness World Record holder? It's a great honor to be in the same company as the fastest baked bean eater! I remember reading *Guinness World Records* as a kid. To be recognized by it is amazing.

1991, includes 34 Houdini posters—14 of which are colored lithographs—and 64 different Chung Ling Soo lithographs.

★ **Largest stone lithograph magic poster** A 28-sheet poster printed in 1895 by the Strobridge Lithograph Company (U.S.A.) for Frederick Bancroft (U.S.A.) measured 9 × 25 ft. (2.74 × 7.62 m).

★ **Highest suspension straitjacket escape** Scott Hammell (Canada) escaped from a regulation straitjacket while suspended by a rope hanging inverted below the basket of a hot-air balloon traveling at a height of 7,200 ft. (2,194.5 m) over Knoxville, Tennessee, U.S.A., on August 13, 2003. The rope hung 50 ft. (15.24 m) from the basket.

★ **Deadliest magic trick** At least 11 people have been killed during the bullet-catching trick, where at least one gun loaded with a marked bullet is fired at a magician, who appears to catch the bullet in his teeth or on a plate. Although the feat involves illusionary elements, it is fraught with danger. The most famous death has been Chung Ling Soo (U.S.A., b. William Elsworth Robinson), who was shot on stage at the Wood Green Empire, London, UK, on March 23, 1918.

★ **MOST VALUABLE MAGIC POSTER** There are two holders of this record. A Houdini *Water Torture Cell* lithograph by Strobridge was sold by CRG Auctions in Las Vegas, U.S.A., on October 30, 2004, for $55,000 to David Copperfield (U.S.A.).

Houdini's *Water Torture Cell* (pictured), a lithograph printed by Dangerfield (UK), was auctioned on May 25, 2000, at Christie's, London, UK, and purchased by Norm Nielsen (U.S.A.) for £30,000 ($44,669).

MOST LIVING CREATURES PRODUCED DURING A MAGIC PERFORMANCE Penn & Teller (U.S.A.) produced more than 80,000 bees during their television special, *Don't Try This at Home,* filmed in 1990.

★**Most consecutive multi-coin rolls** Jeff McBride (U.S.A.) simultaneously rolled eight silver dollars around the fingers of both his hands (four coins per hand) using the classic coin-roll technique, each completing 18 consecutive revolutions in a time of 5 min. 43 sec. at the Magical Arts Center, Las Vegas, Nevada, U.S.A., on July 17, 2004.

★**Most tickets sold worldwide by a solo entertainer** From the period 1984 to 2004, the magician David Copperfield (U.S.A.) sold approximately 39,690,000 tickets to his shows.

★**Most generations of magicians** The Bamberg family consisted of six generations who excelled in the art of magic for over 200 years.

Longest running theater of magic John Nevil Maskelyne and George Cooke (both UK) founded, produced, and starred in the Maskelyne & Cooke magic theater at the Egyptian Hall, Piccadilly, London, UK, from May 26, 1873, to December 10, 1904. After Maskelyne and business partner David Devant moved the show to St. George's Hall, Langham Place, London, UK, the daily shows were continued by the Maskelyne family until October 14, 1933.

LOWEST DEATH-DIVE ESCAPE In 1997, Robert Gallup (U.S.A.) was leg-manacled, handcuffed, chained, sealed in a secured mailbag, and locked in an 8-ft.² (0.74-m²) jail cell cage before being thrown out of a plane at 18,000 ft. (5,485 m) above the Mojave Desert, California, U.S.A. A minute before impact, and traveling at 150 mph (240 km/h), he escaped to reach his parachute—secured on the outside of the cage—and deployed it safely at 1,200 ft. (366 m), just five seconds before impact.

Most expensive magic show ever staged

Siegfried and Roy at the Mirage, Las Vegas, Nevada, U.S.A., starring Siegfried Fishbacher and Roy Horn (both Germany), cost over $28 million to stage when it opened on February 1, 1990. The show, which featured dozens of wild animals, a giant mechanical dragon that breathed fire, and a cast of 60, closed after its 5,750th performance on October 3, 2003.

Fastest transformation illusion

Internationally renowned illusionists The Pendragons (U.S.A.) present Houdini's metamorphosis illusion at a speed that would have fooled its inventor. Jonathan Pendragon is locked in a trunk on top of which his wife, Charlotte, stands. She conceals herself behind a curtain, which drops after just 0.25 seconds to reveal her husband. Charlotte is now locked in the trunk.

COMPUTER GAMES

★**Most ported computer game** *Tetris,* invented by Alexey Pajitnov (Russia) in 1987, is regarded as one of the most original yet simple ideas in game history. Since launch, its code has been translated onto more than 70 different platforms, including cell phones.

★**Largest game of *Tetris*** In November 1995, students at Delft University of Technology, Delft, Netherlands, temporarily converted the building of the university's Faculty of Electrical Engineering into a huge version of the computer game *Tetris*. They installed a series of lights (which turned on and off to represent falling blocks) in each room of the 314-ft.-tall (96-m) building. In total, the giant *Tetris* game used 15 stories, each 10 rooms wide, to create a playable area of about 21,500 ft.^{2} (2,000 m^2).

★**Largest video arcade** The Gran Prix Race-O-Rama Arcade in Fort Lauderdale, Florida, U.S.A., contained 844 individual video arcade games in 1984, increasing to about 950 before being demolished in 1986 to make way for a new highway. Afterwards, it was rebuilt at a new location in Fort Lauderdale, where it contained about 1,200 games in separate buildings.

★**Largest cash prize won by an individual in a gaming event** On October 19, 2004, Meng "RocketBoy" Yang (China) won $125,000 for

☆ **MOST COMPLEX CHARACTER IN A COMPUTER GAME** In *Black and White II* by Lionhead Studios, due for release in late 2005, the player controls a character that trains an artificially intelligent creature. During the game, the creature learns from the player and develops its own distinct personality. The mind of a mature creature can take up to 1.2 MB of physical hard-drive space.

defeating Jonathan "Fatal1ty" Wendell in the ACON Fatal1ty Shootout at the Great Wall of China.

★**Largest LAN party** DreamHack Winter 2004 was the world's largest Local Area Network party. It was hosted in Jönköping, Sweden, from November 25 to 28, 2004. A total of 5,272 gamers attended, and the maximum number of computers on the LAN during the party was 5,852. It was organized by Martin Öjes and Kenny Eklund (both Sweden).

★**Longest serving professional gaming referee** Walter Day (U.S.A.), founder of Twin Galaxies, has been refereeing world computer game high scores since 1982, when his database of high-score statistics was first made available to the public. He has refereed high scores ever since and has been recognized by most of the major games manufacturers.

★**Largest cash prize for a tournament** The Cyberathlete Professional League (CPL) began hosting professional game tournaments in 1997. The CPL tournament, held in Texas, U.S.A., in August 2004, awarded $250,000 to gamers as prize money.

★**Most action gamers playing on a single server** On November 27, 2004, a team from Microsoft and Unisys (both Sweden) sustained 1,073 computer gamers playing *Counterstrike* on a single Unisys ES7000 server. The event took place as part of DreamHack Winter 2004 in Jönköping, Sweden.

★**Largest online game economy** According to research by Prof. Edward Castronova at Indiana University, U.S.A., the Kingdom of Norrath in the game *Everquest* has a gross national product per capita of $2,266. This is based on a market exchange rate between virtual Norrath gold coins sold on online auction sites and real world currency. This places the Kingdom of Norrath as the world's 73rd largest economy, between the actual economies of Turkey (GNP per head: $2,451) and Ghana (GNP per head: $2,174).

★**MOST VALUABLE VIRTUAL OBJECT** On December 11, 2004, David Storey (Australia), a.k.a. Deathifier, paid 265,000 PEDs (Project Entropia Dollars) for an island in the MMORPG (massively multi-player online role-playing game) *Project Entropia.* Because the game allows a real exchange rate between virtual and real money, the Amethera Treasure Island was sold to Deathifier by auction for the equivalent of $26,500.

☆ **BEST-SELLING CONSOLE GAMES PlayStation 2:** According to *Screen Digest,* the best-selling game is *Grand Theft Auto Vice City* (pictured), which had sold 9 million units as of December 2003. **GameCube:** *Mario Sunshine* had sold a record 3.5 million units as of December 2003. **Xbox:** *Halo* had sold 4 million units as of December 2003.

Most advanced battle-field simulator The most sophisticated battlefield computer simulator is the Combined Arms Tactical Trainer. Situated at Warminster, UK, and Sennelager, Germany, it is capable of training more than 850 personnel at once in an integrated, realistic combat scenario involving vehicles, aircraft, soldiers, and weapons. Simulated combat arenas of more than 3,800 miles² (10,000 km²) are used. It became operational on September 1, 2002.

☆ **Most expensive computer game development** *Enter the Matrix,* published by Atari in 2003, has a story that runs parallel to the *Matrix* movies, and features original material written and directed by brothers Andy and Larry Wachoski (U.S.A.), who wrote and directed the movies. The game includes two hours of original live action footage not seen in the movie series. Its development was reported to have cost more than $30 million.

★ **Longest running online subscription game** *Ultima Online* was first launched in May 1997 by Electronic Arts, and helped define the emerging category of MMORPGs. It is now played by millions of gamers in more than 100 countries.

Most successful coin-operated game From its launch in 1981 until 1987, a total of 293,822 *PAC-MAN* arcade machines were built and installed around the world. Designed by Tohru Iwatani (Japan) of Namco, it is estimated that *PAC-MAN* has been played more than 10 billion times in its 25-year history.

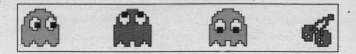

★**First perfect *PAC-MAN* score** The first person ever to achieve a perfect score on *PAC-MAN* was Billy Mitchell (U.S.A.). On July 3, 1999, he played the game for nearly six hours continuously, on one quarter-coin, eating every dot, energizer, blue man, and fruit on each of the 256 boards, after which the game runs out of memory and ends with a split screen. Billy used only one life and his final perfect score was 3,333,360 points. The event was monitored by Twin Galaxies, the world's authority on computer game high scores.

★ FIRST ... ★

COMPUTER GAME *Spacewar!* (1961–62)
M.I.T., U.S.A.

VIDEO ARCADE GAME *Computer Space* (1971)
By Nolan Bushnell (U.S.A.), founder of Atari

PLATFORM ARCADE GAME *Donkey Kong* (1981)
Nintendo

★**MULTIUSER DUNGEON (MUD)** *MUD1* (1980)
Conceived by Roy Trubshaw (UK) of Essex University

★**FULL-ANIMATION LASER DISK GAME** *Dragon's Lair* (1983)
Cinematronics

★ "GOD" GAME *Populous* (1989) by Peter Molyneux (UK) of Bullfrog

★ REAL-TIME STRATEGY (RTS) *Dune 2* (1992) by Westwood, U.S.A.

★ FIRST-PERSON SHOOTER (PC VERSION) *Wolfenstein 3D* (1992/3) by ID Software, U.S.A.

★ MMORPG (MASSIVELY MULTIPLAYER ONLINE ROLE-PLAYING GAME) *Meridian 59* (1996) by 3DO Studios, U.S.A.

       Art & Entertainment

ENGINEERING

CONTENTS

MONSTER MACHINES

LARGEST...

Ambulance Articulated Alligator Jumbulances are 59 ft. (18 m) long. Operated by the Across Trust (UK), these outsized vehicles are designed to convey the sick and disabled on vacations and pilgrimages across Europe.

Car engine The greatest engine capacity of a production car was 13.5 liters (823.8 in.³) for the U.S. Pierce-Arrow 6–66 Raceabout of 1912–18, the U.S. Peerless 6–60 of 1912–14, and the Fageol of 1918. Despite their size, these giants from the early days of automobiles were very inefficient compared with their modern counterparts.

The ★**largest production car engine currently in use** is the 8.275-liter (505-in.³) V10 engine of the Dodge Viper SRT-10. It produces 500 hp (373 kW) and 525 lb.-ft. (712 Nm) of torque—enough to power it to 60 mph (96.5 km/h) in four seconds.

LAND VEHICLE The 31.3 million-lb. (15,648-ton) RB293 bucket wheel excavator is an earthmoving machine 722 ft. (220 m) long and 310 ft. (94.5 m) tall at its highest point. It is capable of moving 8.475 million ft.³ (240,000 m³) of earth a day. The 18 buckets—each with a volume of 1,743 gal. (6,600 liters)—are attached to the outside of a huge wheel (the bucket wheel) at the front of the vehicle, which is as tall as a four-story building.

★ **RACING VEHICLES** The trucks in the FIA European Truck Racing Championship weigh at least 12,125 lb. (5,500 kg). They typically sport 12-liter (732-in.³) turbocharged engines that generate over 1,000 hp (746 kW) and 2,200 lb.-ft. (3,000 Nm) of torque. Despite this huge power, their top speed is limited to 99 mph (160 km/h) for safety reasons.

Crane (revolving pedestal) The revolving pedestal crane at the Yantai Raffles shipyard in Yantai, China, can lift 4.4 million lb. (2,200 tons) to a height of 311 ft. (95 m) from its main hook, and 440,000 lb. (220 tons) to 443 ft. (135 m) from its secondary arm. It is used in the construction of oil rigs and tall vessels.

The **largest tower crane** is the Kroll K-10000, which is capable of lifting a weight of 264,500 lb. (132 tons) at a 269-ft. (82-m) radius (i.e. the distance from the central supporting column to the weight being lifted). The Kroll K-10000 tower crane stands 393 ft. (120 m) high on a rotating cylinder 39 ft. 4 in. (12 m) in diameter without support wires, but has 491,630 lb. (245 tons) of counterweights to balance its 275-ft.-long (84-m) boom.

★ **Diesel engine** The 14-cylinder Wärtsila Sulzer RTA96C two-stroke diesel engine has a rated maximum output of 108,920 hp (80,080 kW), weighs 5.07 million lb. (2,530 tons), and is 44 ft. 4 in. (13.5 m) tall and 89 ft. 6 in. (27.3 m) wide. Each of the engine's pistons is 37.8 in. (960 mm) in diameter and has an 8-ft. 2-in. (2.5-m) stroke. The Wärtsila Sulzer RTA96C is designed to be used in the world's largest container ships.

Dragline excavator *Big Muskie,* a walking earthmoving machine weighing 29.1 million lb. (14,500 tons)—nearly as much as 10,000 cars—moved 127 million ft.³ (3.6 million m³) of earth during its operational life. That's nearly twice the amount excavated in the creation of the Panama Canal.

☆**Dump truck** The Liebherr T 282 B has a payload capacity of 800,000 lb. (400 tons). It is 47 ft. 6 in. (14.5 m) long, 28 ft. 10 in. (8.8 m) wide, 24 ft. 3 in. (7.4 m) high, and weighs over 441,000 lb. (220 tons) empty. Its tires are twice as tall as an average man.

Monster truck *Bigfoot 5* is 15 ft. 6 in. (4.7 m) tall with 10-ft.-tall (3-m) tires and weighs 38,000 lb. (17,236 kg). Built in 1986 as one in a series of 17 created by Bob Chandler of St. Louis, U.S.A., *Bigfoot 5* is now permanently parked in St. Louis, U.S.A., and makes occasional appearances at local shows.

★**Tractor** In 1978, Northern Manufacturing of Havre, Montana, U.S.A., built a tractor weighing around 95,000 lb. (47 tons) without ballast. A unique vehicle, the 900-hp (670-kW) *Big Bud* 16V-747 is powered by a 16-cylinder, 24-liter (1,46-in.³), dual turbo Detroit Diesel engine and has eight giant tires, each 94 in. (2.4 m) in diameter.

★**AUTOMATED PARKING FACILITY** The two 157-ft.-tall (48-m) "car towers" at Volkswagen's Autostadt in Wolfsburg, Germany, can each store 400 cars. Car buyers at the Autostadt are treated to the sight of their new car being retrieved and delivered to them from one of the 20-story towers (inset, left) by an automated system that travels at up to 6.6 ft./s (2 m/s).

★LONGEST TRICYCLE *Anaconda* measures 19 ft. 6 in. (5.94 m) long and seats up to 10 riders. It was constructed by Stephen McGill (U.S.A.), weighs 1,420 lb. (644 kg), and consists of a 1998 Harley Davidson Electra-Glide with a custom-built rear end. It is licensed for road use.

The ★ **most powerful tractor** record is held by the John Deere 9620T and the Caterpillar Challenger MT865, both of which have a claimed power output of 500 hp (373 kW).

The 9620T has four-wheel drive, with four sets of double wheels, and weighs 39,000 lb. (19.5 tons) without ballast. The MT865 is powered by a 14.6-liter (890-in.^{3}) engine and runs on tracks.

Tunnel boring machine The boring machine being used to carve the 4.3-mile-long (7-km) Groene Hart Tunnel from Amsterdam to Rotterdam, the Netherlands, measures 48 ft. 9 in. (14.87 m) in diameter by 393 ft. (120 m) long, and weighs 7,760,271 lb. (3,880 tons).

WHAT'S THE MOST POWERFUL PRODUCTION MOTORCYCLE IN THE WORLD? FIND OUT ON P. 385

CARS

PRODUCTION

★**Most produced automobile** The Ford F-series nameplate has appeared on more vehicles than any other, with more than 29.3 million F-series pickup trucks having been produced. The first in the series, the F1, was first produced in 1948, and an F-150 truck provided the bodywork for the original *Bigfoot* monster truck.

Between 800,000 and 900,000 F-series trucks are sold annually, largely in North America, accounting for nearly one eighth of Ford's global sales.

☆ **FASTEST PRODUCTION CAR** A standard Koenigsegg CCR achieved an average speed of 240.387 mph (387.866 km/h) over a measured kilometer at the Nardo Prototipo proving ground in Italy on February 28, 2005. The 806-hp (601-kW) supercar, which is powered by an aluminum V8 engine, was driven by test driver Loris Bicocchi (Italy).

☆ **MOST FUEL-EFFICIENT CAR** Team FANCY CAROL-NOK (Japan) achieved a fuel consumption of 11,524.915 mpg (0.0245 liters/100 km) around a 11.9-mile (19.2-km) course during the Super Mileage Car Contest 2004 at the Hiroshima License Center, Japan, on August 29, 2004.

☆ **Most produced car** Toyota Corolla is the name that has appeared on more cars than any other, with in excess of 28.2 million units produced worldwide.

However, the vehicle itself has undergone a total of nine transformations since it was first produced in 1966 and cannot, strictly speaking, be said to be the same car.

☆**Best-selling hybrid (dual-fuel) car** Over 250,000 Toyota Prius hybrid cars have been sold globally since 1997. In 2004, Toyota announced that global production would rise from 10,000 to 15,000 units a month to meet growing demand, especially in the U.S. market, where about 100,000 were expected to be sold in 2005 alone.

☆**Best-selling two-seater sports car** Mazda Motor Corporation (Japan) has produced in excess of 700,000 units of the Mazda roadster (known as the Miata in North America and the MX-5 in Europe), an open two-seater sports car, since production began in April 1989 at Mazda's production plant in Hiroshima, Japan.

WHEEL SKILLS

Greatest distance driven on side wheels Sven-Eric Soderman (Sweden) covered 214.7 miles (345.6 km) driving a car on two side wheels at Mora Siljan Airport, Dalarna, Sweden, on September 25, 1999. In an event lasting 10 hr. 38 min., he covered 108 laps of a circuit 1.9 miles (3.2 km) long.

★**LARGEST PRODUCTION PICKUP TRUCK** The International Truck & Engine Company's (U.S.A.) 7300 CXT is the world's largest standard pickup truck, weighing in at 14,500 lb. (6,577 kg). Although it is 21 ft. 6 in. (6.55 m) long and 9 ft. (2.74 m) high, it can be driven with a standard driver's license.

LONGEST OWNERSHIP OF VEHICLE John P. O'Hara (U.S.A.) bought a new 1953 Chevrolet Bel-Air in Detroit, Michigan, U.S.A., in June 1953 and has owned the vehicle ever since. It remains in mint condition.

☆**Longest ramp jump with trailer** Professional stuntman Derek Lea (UK) jumped a distance of 187 ft. 8 in. (57.2 m) in a car towing a full-size trailer at Bentwaters Parks, Suffolk, UK, on May 5, 2004, for the TV car show *5th Gear.*

Longest horizontal power slide On July 29, 2001, at the MIRA Proving Ground, Nuneaton, UK, Simon de Banke (UK) performed a slide that lasted 2 hr. 11 min. 18 sec. He was driving a standard Subaru Impreza WRX 2001. The road surface was Bridgeport pebbles, which, when wet, have similar handling characteristics to compacted snow.

★**Fastest time to do 10 donuts in a car** On September 11, 2004, Russ Swift (UK) performed 10 donuts in 16.07 seconds in a Mitsubishi Lancer Evo VIII on the set of *Guinness World Records: 50 Years, 50 Records* at London Studios, UK.

★**Most simultaneous donuts by the same driver** Terry Grant (UK) had three cars performing donuts (360° spins) at the MPH '04 show at Earl's Court, London, UK, on November 20, 2004.

FASTEST . . .

☆**Trailer tow** On October 24, 2003, a Mercedes Benz S600 driven by Eugene Herbert (South Africa) reached a speed of 139.113 mph (223.881 km/h) while towing a standard trailer at Hoedspruit Air Force Base, South

Africa. The record attempt was organized by Risk Administrative Consultants.

★**Diesel-engined car** Virgil W. Snyder (U.S.A.) reached a speed of 235.7 mph (379.4 km/h) in a streamliner called *Thermo King-Wynns* at Bonneville Salt Flats, Utah, U.S.A., on August 25, 1973.

☆**Wheel-driven vehicle** Al Teague (U.S.A.) reached an average speed of 409.986 mph (659.808 km/h) over two runs, with a peak speed of 432.692 mph (696.331 km/h), in *Spirit of '76,* at Bonneville Salt Flats, Utah, U.S.A., on August 21, 1991.

MISCELLANEOUS

Largest production car The Bugatti "Royale" type 41, known in the UK as the "Golden Bugatti," was built in 1927 and measures over 22 ft. (6.7 m) in length, with the hood itself more than 7 ft. (2.13 m) long.

Longest car Jay Ohrberg (U.S.A.) designed a 100-ft.-long (30.5-m), 26-wheeled limo. The car incorporates many features, including a swimming pool with diving board, a king-sized water bed, and a helipad.

☆**Most powerful production car** The Bugatti Veyron, due to go into production in September 2005, has a claimed output of 988 hp (736 kW) from its 8-liter (488-in.³), 16-cylinder engine. The engine has four turbochargers. The top speed has not been officially tested, but Bugatti claims it is capable of speeds of over 248 mph (400 km/h).

★**Longest running car pool** M. te Lindert, A. Hogendoorn, J. Kalisvaart, and J.J. Kooy (all Netherlands) belong to a car pool that began on January 1, 1972, and has been running ever since between their homes and their workplace.

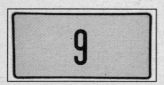

MOST EXPENSIVE REGISTRATION
License plate No. 9 was sold at a Hong Kong government auction for HK$13 million ($1.7 million) on March 19, 1994, to Albert Yeung Sau-shing (China). In Cantonese, the pronunciation of the word "nine" is identical to the word "dog" and was considered lucky because 1994 was the Year of the Dog.

BIKES & MOTORCYCLES

MOTORCYCLES

★**Longest side-wheel ride on a quad bike** Ron Flerlage (U.S.A.) covered a distance of 12.8 miles (19.3 km) on two side wheels of his quad bike around a track-and-field track at Scott High School, Covington, Kentucky, U.S.A., on October 5, 2003.

★**Highest speed on a quad bike** Graham "G-Force" Hicks (UK) reached a speed of 133.02 mph (214.07 km/h) on a quad bike at RAF Wittering, UK, on August 14, 2004. Because Hicks is deaf and blind, Brian Sharman (UK) rode "pillion" and communicated steering instructions to him through a touch system.

☆**Highest motorcycle speed (riding backwards)** Dave Coates (UK) reached a speed of 151.7 mph (244.1 km/h) on a motorcycle sitting with his back to the handlebars at Elvington airfield, Yorkshire, UK, on October 28, 2002.

☆**Fastest motorcycle wheelie over a kilometer** Dave Rogers (UK) reached a speed of 136.9 mph (220.3 km/h) while performing a motorcycle wheelie over 3,281 ft. (1 km) at Elvington airfield, Yorkshire, UK, on October 28, 2002.

★**Most powerful production motorcycle with a piston engine** Based on manufacturers' claims, the most powerful piston-powered motorcycle in production is the 73.1-cu.-in. (1,198-cc) Kawasaki Ninja ZX-12R, which has a power output of 175.6 hp (131 kW) without a forced-air system

---

DEFINITIONS

cu. in. (cc): cubic inch (cubic cm). A measure of volume capacity used to define engine size.

hp (kW): horsepower (kilowatts). A measure of power.

N-m (lb.-ft.): Newton-meters (foot-pounds). A measure of torque. One Newton-meter is the force required to give a mass of 1 kilogram an acceleration of 1 meter per second at a distance of 1 meter from the fulcrum.

Torque: a measure of the "twisting" force an engine can apply to its crankshaft (and therefore to a vehicle's wheels).

★ MOST PEOPLE ON A QUAD BIKE WHEELIE Roger LeBlanc (Canada) wheelied an unmodified Honda 350 Fourtrax ATV carrying 16 people over 165 ft. (50 m) at Riverglade Speedway, New Brunswick, Canada, on May 15, 2004.

(RAM), and 187.7 hp (140 kW) with RAM air. However, rivals Honda, Suzuki, and Yamaha all produce sports bikes with claimed power outputs in excess of 170 hp (127 kW).

★ Most expensive production motorcycle The MTT Turbine Superbike, powered by a Rolls-Royce Allison gas-turbine engine, went on sale in 2004 for $185,000.

★ Largest simultaneous motorcycle burn-out A total of 37 motorcycles took part in a "burn-out" organized by IBM Klub Motobiking at Heidesheim, Germany, on August 28, 2004. A burn-out consists of spinning the rear wheel of the motorcycle while it is stationary, burning rubber and creating smoke.

★ Longest forks William Longest, Rick Dozer, Bill Decker, and Rob Moore (all U.S.A.) built a rideable chopper-style motorcycle—the world's **longest motorcycle**—with 15-ft.-long (4.57-m) forks. It is 6 ft. (1.8 m) tall at its highest point and measures 29 ft. 3 in. (8.9 m) wheel to wheel. William Longest rode it on a public road near Georgetown, Kentucky, U.S.A., on June 15, 2003.

★ SPEED RECORDS *all records: Fédération Internationale de Motocyclisme

CLASS*	RIDER	MOTORCYCLE
★ 50 cc	Jan Huberts (Netherlands)	Casal Plompen
★ 125 cc	A.J. Smit (Netherlands)	Cagiva Plompen
★ 250 cc	Fabrizio Braccini Lazari (Italy)	Aprilia
★ 500 cc	Ron Haslam (UK)	Honda Elf 3
★ 1,000 cc	Christian Le Liard (France)	Holda Elf
★ 1,300 cc	Nicolas Brisset (France)	Suzuki GSX
"Absolute"	Dave Campos (U.S.A.)	Easyriders

★**MOST POWERFUL PRODUCTION MOTORCYCLE** The $185,000 MTT Turbine Superbike's Rolls-Royce Allison gas-turbine engine is claimed by its manufacturer to supply 286 hp (213 kW) at the rear wheel, with 425 lb.-ft. (576 N-m) of torque at 2,000 rpm. This makes the Superbike the most powerful motorcycle ever to enter series production.

★**Most pirouettes on a motorcycle in 30 seconds** Horst Hoffman (Germany) pulled off 16 pirouettes (360° spins) on the rear wheel of his motorcycle in 30 seconds on the set of *Guinness World Records: Die Grössten Weltrekorde* in Cologne, Germany, on January 23, 2004.

BICYCLES

☆**Longest bicycle** The longest true bicycle—with two wheels and no supporting wheels—is 92 ft. 2 in. (28.1 m) long, and was built by students at Delft University of Technology. It was ridden over 328 ft. (100 m) at Delft, the Netherlands, on December 11, 2002.

**all speeds average over 1 km [flying start] ★

PLACE	DATE	SPEED**
Lelystad, Netherlands	08/03/81	139.547 mph (224.580 km/h)
Lelystad, Netherlands	08/03/81	159.762 mph (257.113 km/h)
Nardo, Italy	08/27/95	157.841 mph (254.021 km/h)
Nardo, Italy	09/14/86	173.271 mph (278.853 km/h)
Nardo, Italy	09/14/86	190.444 mph (306.491 km/h)
Nardo, Italy	06/23/02	210.160 mph (338.221 km/h)
Bonneville, U.S.A.	07/14/90	322.150 mph (518.450 km/h)

☆**Tallest bicycle** Terry Goertzen (Canada) rode a true bicycle 18 ft. 2.5 in. (5.55 m) tall—without supporting wheels—for over 1,000 ft. (300 m) at North Kildonan Mennonite Brethren Church, Canada, on June 26, 2004.

☆**Largest pedal-powered vehicle** Jacques Frechette (Canada) built a pedal-powered vehicle capable of carrying 74 riders. It was ridden for 2.17 miles (3.5 km) through the town of Laurierville in Quebec, Canada, on July 31, 2004. Also, 72 of the 74 passengers shared the same last name: Bergeron.

★**Greatest depth bicycled underwater** Vittorio Innocente (Italy) bicycled to a depth of 172.2 ft. (52.5 m) on the ocean floor off Genoa, Italy, on July 23, 2002. He used scuba gear and a standard mountain bike modified with small, lead weights and a plastic wing behind the seat. The tires were

★**FASTEST MONOWHEEL Kerry McLean (U.S.A.) reached 57 mph (91.7 km/h) on a monowheel at Irwindale Speedway, California, U.S.A., on January 10, 2001. His 48-in.-diameter (1.22-m) monowheel was powered by a 20.7-cu.-in. (340-cc) snowmobile engine generating 40 hp (30 kW). A monowheel consists of a wheel that revolves around a track, which houses the rider and engine.**

★**FASTEST DOWNHILL WHEELIE (FLYING START)** Gilles Cruchaud (Switzerland) covered 1,640 ft. (500 m) of a downhill course on the back wheel of his bicycle in 26.341 seconds, averaging a speed of 42.45 mph (68.33 km/h) at Col de l'Aiguillon, Switzerland, on July 12, 2004.

also flooded to reduce buoyancy.

On May 4, 2003, Innocente also set the ★**farthest underwater bicycling** record by pedalling for 1.24 miles (2 km) on the bottom of the Naviglio canal in Milan, Italy. It took him 36 min. 38.15 sec.

☆**Lightest racing bike** *Sub 4.0* is a rideable full-size racing bicycle—built by Mirko Glöckner (Germany)—weighing just 8 lb. 9.2 oz. (3.89 kg). It has a carbon-fiber frame weighing 1 lb. 14.7 oz. (873 g) and components made largely of aluminum, titanium, and carbon fiber.

★**Fastest bicycle wheelie** Bobby Root (U.S.A.) reached a speed of 86.1 mph (138.56 km/h) while riding on the rear wheel of his bicycle at Palmdale, California, U.S.A., on January 31, 2001 for *Guinness World Records: Primetime*. The **highest speed ever** achieved on a bicycle is 166.944 mph (268.831 km/h).

Farthest distance bicycled (no hands) in one hour Shai Hadar (Israel) bicycled a distance of 12.92 miles (20.8 km) in one hour without his hands touching the handlebars at the Wingate Institute near Netanya, Israel, on October 18, 2002.

Bicycle balancing Rudi Jan Jozef De Greef (Belgium) stayed stationary on his bicycle—without any means of support—for a total of 10 hours at Meensel-Kiezegem, Belgium, on November 19, 1982.

TRAINS

★ **Busiest national railroad system** Japan's railroads carried an estimated 8.6 billion passengers during 2003, making the system the world's busiest in terms of the number of people using it, according to the International Union of Railways (UIC). India was second with nearly 5.2 billion passengers, and Germany third with nearly 1.7 billion passengers.

★ **Busiest railroad company** In 2003, the East Japan Railway Company carried 5.846 billion passengers, with an average of 16 million a day. The company operates 4,679 miles (7,530 km) of network in the east of Japan, including the busy Tokyo metropolitan area.

★ **Busiest underground railroad** The Moscow Metro in Russia carries 8–9 million passengers each day. By comparison, the New York City Subway, the world's **largest urban railroad system,** carries 4.5 million people each day, and the London Underground—the **oldest subway system**—just under 3 million.

★ **Most frequent travelers by train** Swiss citizens cover an average distance of 1,290 miles (2,077 km) by train each year, closely followed by the Japanese, who travel 1,180 miles (1,900 km) on railroads annually.

★ **Smallest armored train** During World War II, the 15-in.-gauge (381-mm) Romney, Hythe & Dymchurch Railway, which runs between Hythe and Dungeness along the coast of Kent, UK, was requisitioned by the British government. One steam locomotive, *Hercules,* and several coaches

LONGEST STRAIGHT RAILROAD The Trans-Australian line over the Nullarbor Plain runs dead straight, though not level, for 297 miles (478 km). The section runs from Mile 496—between Nurina and Loongana, Western Australia—to Mile 793—between Ooldea and Watson, South Australia. The word "nullarbor" literally means "no trees," and is a reflection of the lack of vegetation on this virtually uninhabited limestone plateau.

Engineering

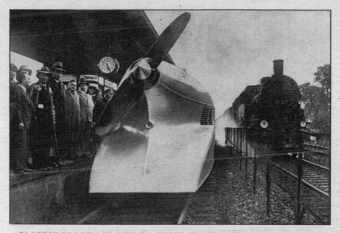

★ **FASTEST PROPELLER-DRIVEN TRAIN** The "Rail Zeppelin" built by the German engineer Franz Kruckenberg reached a speed of 143 mph (230 km/h) during a test run on June 21, 1931, between Hamburg and Berlin, Germany. The vehicle received its nickname because of the large propeller mounted behind the passenger compartment and its lightweight steel and canvas construction. It was powered by a 580-hp (433-kW) BMW aircraft engine but never entered regular service.

were given steel armor and machine guns were mounted on the train, both as a defense against invasion and to protect trains transporting war goods. With a track gauge roughly one quarter the width of standard gauge, the locomotives and coaches are correspondingly diminutive.

★ **Highest altitude railroad tunnel** The Fenghuo Mount railroad tunnel is situated at 16,092 ft. (4,905 m) on the Qinghai-Tibet Railway as it passes over the Qinghai-Tibet Highland between China and Tibet. It is 4,390 ft. (1,338 m) long and was built from October 18, 2001, to September 30, 2003.

★ **Largest high-speed rail network** According to the UIC, Japan has the world's largest high-speed rail network, with 1,678 miles (2,700 km) of high-speed lines in operation or under construction. The country opened the world's first dedicated high-speed line—between Tokyo and Osaka—in 1964.

Fastest steam locomotive The London North Eastern Railway "Class A4" No. 4468 *Mallard* recorded a speed of 125 mph (201 km/h) while hauling seven coaches weighing 535,722 lb. (220 tons) down Stoke Bank, near Essendine, between Grantham, Lincolnshire, and Peterborough, Cambridgeshire, UK, on July 3, 1938.

FASTEST RAILED VEHICLE (ROCKET SLED) A four-stage rocket sled system accelerated a 192-lb. (87-kg) payload to a speed of 9,468 ft./s (2,886 m/s) in 6.031 seconds at Holloman High Speed Test Track, Holloman Air Force Base, New Mexico, U.S.A., on April 30, 2003. This is equivalent to 6,453 mph (10,385 km/h).

Fastest train journey (average speed) The West Japan Railway Company operates its 500-Series-Nozomi bullet trains (Shinkansen) at an average speed of 162.7 mph (261.8 km/h) on the 119-mile (192-km) line between Hiroshima and Kokura on the island of Honshu, Japan.

Fastest train in regular public service The magnetically levitated (maglev) train linking China's Shanghai International Airport and the city's financial district reaches a top speed of 267.8 mph (431 km/h) on each 18.6-mile (30-km) run. The train had its official maiden run on December 31, 2002.

Fastest maglev train The MLX01, a manned maglev train, reached a speed of 361 mph (581 km/h) on December 2, 2003. It was operated by the Central Japan Railway Company and Railway Technical Research Institute and ran on the Yamanashi Maglev Test Line, Yamanashi Prefecture, Japan.

★First maglev train to enter public service A maglev train ran for 1,968 ft. (600 m) between Birmingham International Airport and the nearby Birmingham International Interchange in West Midlands, UK, from 1984 to 1995. It was taken out of service owing to the high cost of replacing worn parts.

Fastest train on a national rail system On May 18, 1990, a French SNCF high-speed TGV Atlantique train (No. 325) reached 320.2 mph (515.3 km/h) on a national rail track (as opposed to a dedicated test track) between Courtalain and Tours, France.

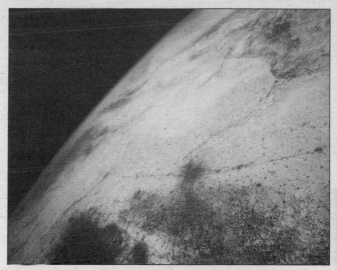

LONGEST TRAIN JOURNEY WITHOUT CHANGING TRAINS A continuous 6,346-mile (10,214-km) train journey can be taken from Moscow, Russia, to Pyongyang, North Korea. One train a week makes the journey by this route, which includes sections of the famous Trans-Siberian line. It is scheduled to take 7 days 20 hr. 25 min. Pictured top, the Trans-Siberian stretch is shown as a thin lateral line; the dark area near the center of this line is the Russian city of Omsk.

Fastest diesel train A British Rail InterCity 125 train achieved a speed of 148 mph (238 km/h) on a test run between Darlington and York, UK, on November 1, 1987.

Heaviest freight train On June 21, 2001, a train assembled by BHP Iron Ore (Australia) was weighed at 220 million lb. (90,476.3 tons). At 4.5 miles (7.35 km) long, it was also the **longest freight train ever.**

SHIPS & BOATS

LARGEST . . .

★**Passenger-carrying capacity for a ship** The vessels with the largest standard passenger loads are the Staten Island ferry (New York City, U.S.A.) sister ships *Andrew J. Barberi* and *Samuel I. Newhouse*. Each can carry

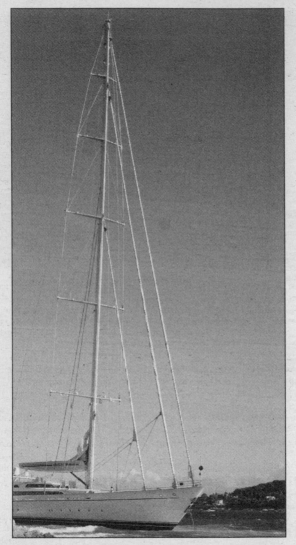

★LONGEST SLOOP The 246.7-ft. (75.2-m) luxury vessel *Mirabella V* is the world's longest sloop, or single-masted yacht. The state-of-the-art ship has a composite hull, a 330,000-lb. (136-ton) lifting keel, and, at 295 ft. (90 m) high, the world's **tallest mast.**

★ **LARGEST OPEN-DECK TRANSPORT SHIP** The semisubmersible *Blue Marlin* has a flat open cargo deck 584 ft. (178.2 m) long and 206 ft. 8 in. (63 m) wide and is capable of carrying oversized cargo weighing 167.6 million lb. (69,000 tons). The giant carrier, which is operated by Dockwise of the Netherlands, is able to submerge its deck to a depth of 52 ft. 6 in. (16 m) to allow it to load its giant cargoes—typically oil and gas platforms—by floating underneath them.

6,000 passengers and is 310 ft. (95 m) long and 69 ft. 10 in. (21 m) wide with a speed of 16 knots (19 mph, or 30 km/h).

★**Dry bulk carrier ship** The *Berge Stahl* can carry 804.1 million lb. (330,914 tons) of cargo (typically iron ore). The vessel, owned by Bergesen of Norway, is 1,125 ft. (343 m) long and 208 ft. (63.5 m) wide.

Passenger liner The Cunard Line's *Queen Mary 2* which made its maiden voyage in January 2004, is 1,132 ft. (345 m) long, and has a beam of 135 ft. (41 m). At 150,000 gross registered tons (grt), *Queen Mary 2* is nearly three times larger than *Titanic* (46,000 grt), with space for 2,620 passengers and 1,253 crew.

★**Drillship** *Discoverer Enterprise, Discoverer Spirit,* and *Discoverer Deep Seas* each displace 227 million lb. (93,440 tons). The vessels are owned by Transocean, Inc. (U.S.A.) and are capable of drilling in more than 10,000 ft. (3,050 m) of water, and to depths of 35,000 ft. (10,650 m). The ships are 835 ft. (255 m) long and 125 ft. (38 m) wide.

Icebreaker The 1,007-ft. (306.9-m) long SS *Manhattan* was converted into a 335 million-lb. (138,262-ton) icebreaker, equipped with steel armor 9 ft. (2.7 m) thick, 30 ft. (9.1 m) deep, and 670 ft. (204 m) long. It made a double voyage through the Northwest Passage in arctic Canada in August 1969.

★**Rescue operation by a single ship** During the Korean War, the freighter SS *Meredith Victory* evacuated 14,000 civilian refugees to safety from Hungnam, North Korea, to Pusan, South Korea, in a single voyage from December 22 to 25, 1950.

Cargo vessel The oil tanker *Jahre Viking* (formerly the *Happy Giant* and *Seawise Giant*) can carry 1.245 trillion lb. (512,349 tons) of cargo, fuel, and stores (deadweight tonnage). It is 1,504 ft. (458.45 m) long and has a beam of 226 ft. (68.8 m) and a draft of 80 ft. 9 in. (24.61 m).

Private yacht The Saudi Arabian royal yacht *Abdul Aziz* is 482 ft. (147 m) long. Completed on June 22, 1984, at Vospers Yard, Southampton, UK, it was estimated in 1987 to be worth more than $100 million.

★Racing trimaran (yacht) The trimaran *Geronimo,* skippered by Olivier de Kersauson (France), is 111 ft. (34 m) long and has a 72-ft. (22-m) beam. It was built at the Multiplast yard at Vannes, France, from 1999 to 2001.

★ WATER SPEED RECORDS ★

RECORD	PILOT/CAPTAIN (NATIONALITY)	VESSEL NAME (DATE)	SPEED
Human-powered vessel	Mark Drela (U.S.A.)	*Decavitator* (1991)	18.5 knots (21.2 mph; 34.2 km/h)
Passenger liner	U.S.A.	*United States* (1952)	44 knots (50.63 mph; 81.4 km/h)
Destroyer (warship)	France	*Le Terrible* (1935)	45.25 knots (52 mph; 83.42 km/h)
Sailing vessel	Simon McKeon (Australia)	*Yellow Pages Endeavour* (1993)	46.5 knots (53.5 mph; 86.1 km/h)
Windsurfer	Finian Maynard (Ireland)	—	46.82 knots (53.87 mph; 86.71 km/h)
Aquabike (PWC)	Forrest Smith (U.S.A.)	Yamaha GP1200R (2002)	76.17 mph (122.79 km/h)
Propeller powerboat	Dave Villwock (U.S.A.)	*Miss Budweiser* (2004)	220.49 mph (354.84 km/h)
Overall water speed	Ken Warby (Australia)	*Spirit of Australia* (1977)	275.97 knots (317.5 mph; 511.1 km/h)

FASTEST . . .

★Passenger liner The SS *United States* reached speeds in excess of 44 knots (50.63 mph; 81.4 km/h) during sea trials and cruised across the Atlantic at an average speed of 34.51 knots (39.7 mph; 63.9 km/h) in 1952. It was 990 ft. 6 in. (301.9 m) long, but its speed was due to its light weight (aluminum was used in its construction) and powerful 241,000-hp (180,000-kW) engines.

☆**Highest speed under sail on water** The highest speed reached under sail on water is 46.82 knots (53.87 mph; 86.71 km/h) by Finian Maynard (Ireland) on a windsurfer at Saintes-Maries-de-la-Mer, France, on November 13, 2004. By way of comparison, the **fastest animal on land over long distances,** the pronghorn (*Antilocapra americana*), reaches speeds of 35 mph (56 km/h).

★**Greatest distance covered in a monohull in 24 hours** The monohull yacht *Mari-Cha IV,* captained by Robert Miller (UK) and sailed by a crew of 24, covered a distance of 525.7 nautical miles (604.96 miles; 973.59 km) under sail on October 6–7, 2003.

Distance sailed in 24 hours The greatest distance covered by sail power alone in a 24-hour period is 694.78 nautical miles (799.5 miles; 1,286.73 km)—more than 1.2 times the entire length of the UK—by the 110-ft. (33.5-m) maxi catamaran *Maiden 2* in the North Atlantic on June 12–13, 2002.

☆**Propeller-driven boat** Dave Villwock (U.S.A.) reached a top speed of 220.493 mph (354.849 km/h) in *Miss Budweiser,* an unlimited-class hydroplane, on March 23, 2004, at Thermalito Afterbay, Oroville, California, U.S.A. The boat is powered by a Lycoming T-55 L-7 turbine engine from a Chinook helicopter, which is rated at 2,650 hp (1,976 kW).

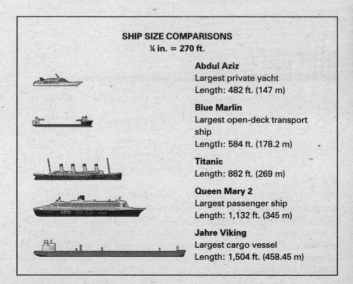

SHIP SIZE COMPARISONS
¼ in. = 270 ft.

Abdul Aziz
Largest private yacht
Length: 482 ft. (147 m)

Blue Marlin
Largest open-deck transport ship
Length: 584 ft. (178.2 m)

Titanic
Length: 882 ft. (269 m)

Queen Mary 2
Largest passenger ship
Length: 1,132 ft. (345 m)

Jahre Viking
Largest cargo vessel
Length: 1,504 ft. (458.45 m)

★ OLDEST COMMISSIONED WARSHIP AFLOAT The USS *Constitution*—also known as "Old Ironsides"—was commissioned on October 21, 1797, and remains on the U.S. Navy ship roster with a crew of between 50 and 80 active duty navy sailors. *Constitution*'s home port is Charlestown, Massachusetts, U.S.A., and it makes occasional trips to sea.

AIRCRAFT

FLIGHTS

Highest altitude by an aircraft The Fédération Aéronautique Internationale (FAI) altitude record is 123,523 ft. (37,650 m), by Alexandr Fedotov (USSR) flying a highly modified MIG-25 "Foxbat" (designated E266M) from Podmoskovnoe Aerodrome, Russia, on August 31, 1977.

Highest altitude flight by a helicopter Jean Bouletan (France) reached an altitude of 40,820 ft. (12,442 m) in an Aérospatiale SA315B "Lama" helicopter over Istres, France, on June 21, 1972.

★ Fastest air-breathing aircraft On November 16, 2004, NASA's unmanned Hyper-X (X-43A) aircraft reached Mach 9.68, almost 10 times the speed of sound. It was boosted to an altitude of 115,000 ft. (33,000 m) by a

Pegasus rocket launched from beneath a B52-B aircraft. The "scramjet" aircraft then burned its engine before crashing into the Pacific Ocean.

★ Longest flight by a model aircraft Maynard Hill, Barrett Foster, and David Brown (all U.S.A.) flew a piston-engined radio-controlled model aircraft a distance of 1,882.7 miles (3,030 km) from Cape Spear, Newfoundland, Canada, to Mannin Beach, Ireland, without refueling or landing, in 38 hours from August 9 to 11, 2003.

Lightest aircraft to cross the Atlantic On May 7, 1933, Capt. Stanislaw Skarzynski (Poland) flew a RWD-5bis 2,225 miles (3,582 km) from St. Louis, Senegal, to Maceio, Brazil, in 20 hr. 30 min. At the time this was an FAI record for straight-line distance for single-seater aircraft with a top weight of 992 lb. (450 kg), less than half the weight of a new Mini Cooper.

Highest hot-air balloon flight On June 6, 1988, Per Lindstrand (UK) rose to a height of 64,997 ft. (19,811 m) over Laredo, Texas, U.S.A., in a Colt 600 hot-air balloon.

Highest altitude reached by a balloon The greatest altitude ever reached by a manned balloon is 113,740 ft. (34,668 m), by Commander

---

SPEED RECORDS

★ Paraglider: Edel Energy 30/Patrick Berod (France)
17.55 mph (28.26 km/h)

★ Hang-glider: Moyes Delta Gliders Litespeed 4/Tomas Suchanek (Czech Republic)
31.57 mph (50.81 km/h)

★ Microlight: B-612/Pavel Skarytka (Czech Republic)
120.67 mph (194.2 km/h)

★ Glider: Jantor STD11/Horacio Miranda (Argentina)
154.77 mph (249.09 km/h)

Helicopter: Westland Lynx/John Trevor Eggington (UK)
249.08 mph (400.86 km/h)

Production jet aircraft: Lockheed Martin SR-71/Capt. E. Joersz and Maj. G. Morgan (both U.S.A.)
2,193.17 mph (3,529.56 km/h)

Rocket aircraft: X-15A2/Pete Knight (U.S.A.)
4,520 mph (7,274 km/h)

★ Air-breathing (jet) aircraft: X-43A/unmanned
6,400 mph (10,300 km/h)

Malcolm D. Ross and Lieutenant Commander Victor A. Prather of the U.S. Navy over the Gulf of Mexico, U.S.A., on May 4, 1961. Their gas-filled non-pressurized, polyethylene balloon was called *Lee Lewis Memorial*.

SIZE & WEIGHT

★**Largest biplanes** The biggest ever aircraft were four aircraft built for the U.S. Navy in 1918 by the Curtiss company (designated NC 1–4). They had a wingspan of 126 ft. (38.4 m), were 68 ft. 3 in. (20.8 m) long and had an operational weight of around 26,400 lb. (12,000 kg).

The ★**biggest double-wing aircraft currently in common use** is the Antonov An-2/An-3, first manufactured in 1947, which has a wingspan of 61 ft. 7 in. (18.8 m) and a maximum takeoff weight of 12,790 lb. (5,800 kg). It has a 12-person capacity in typical configuration and was first manufactured in 1947.

★**Largest flying boat** The Martin JRM-3 "Mars" has a wingspan of 200 ft. (61 m) and a maximum takeoff weight of 162,000 lb. (73,500 kg). Five were built by the Glenn L. Martin Company for the U.S. Navy in the 1940s, and two remain in service as water bombers with the Canadian company Flying Tankers.

Heaviest production aircraft The Ukrainian Antonov An-124 "Ruslan" has a maximum takeoff weight of 893,000 lb. (367.4 tons). Its cargo hold has a usable volume of 35,800 ft.^{3} (1,014 m^3).

Longest passenger aircraft in service The Airbus A340–600 is 246 ft. 11 in. (75.3 m) long. It has a maximum takeoff weight of 804,700 lb. (331.1 tons), a wingspan of 208 ft. 2 in. (63.45 m), and can carry 419 passengers.

★**Largest airborne telescope** NASA's Stratospheric Observatory for Infrared Astronomy (Sofia) is a Boeing 747SP fitted with an infrared tele-

HEAVIEST AIRCRAFT The aircraft with the highest standard maximum takeoff weight is the Antonov An-225 "Mriya" (Dream), at 1.32 million lb. (544.3 tons). Only two of these behemoths were ever built. With a wingspan of 290 ft. (88.4 m)—almost as long as four tennis courts—it was designed to "piggyback" the Russian Buran space shuttles into launch position. The "Mriya" is a heavylift version of the standard Antonov An-124 "Ruslan" cargo plane.

LARGEST CARGO AIRCRAFT BY VOLUME
The Airbus A300-600ST Super Transporter
"Beluga" has a cargo deck with a volume of
49,440 ft.^{3} (1,400 m^3), and is 123 ft. 8 in.
(37.7 m) long, with a maximum height and
width of 23 ft. 3 in. (7.1 m). Its maximum
payload weight is 103,610 lb. (42.6 tons).
The schematic (left) shows how the plane is
front-loaded.

scope with an 8-ft. 10-in.-wide (2.7-m) primary mirror. "First light" (the
moment it was first successfully tested) occurred on August 18, 2004.

Largest passenger aircraft The Boeing 747–400 has a wingspan of 211
ft. 3 in. (64.4 m), a length of 231 ft. 7 in. (70.6 m), and a maximum takeoff

HIGHEST FLIGHT BY PROPELLER-DRIVEN AIRCRAFT The unmanned
solar-powered *Helios* prototype flying wing achieved an altitude of
96,863 ft. (29,524 m) over the Hawaiian island of Kauai on August 13,
2001. Developed by AeroVironment, Inc. of Monrovia, California, U.S.A.,
for NASA, *Helios* is a new breed of slow-flying, high-altitude aircraft
that could be an alternative to communications satellites.

weight of 875,000 lb. (360 tons). However, the Airbus A380, unveiled on January 18, 2005 and due to enter service by 2007, will have a wingspan of 261 ft. 10 in. (79.8 m), a length of 239 ft. 6 in. (73 m), and a maximum take-off weight of 1.23 million lb. (508 tons).

★**Largest working airship** Manufactured by Zeppelin Luftschifftechnik of Germany, the 246-ft.-long (75-m) Zeppelin NT has an envelope volume of 290,463 ft.^{2} (8,225 m^2) and can carry 14 people. The **largest airships ever** were the 471,500-lb. (235.75-ton) German *Hindenburg* (LZ 129) and *Graf Zeppelin II* (LZ 130). Each had a length of 803 ft. 10 in. (245 m).

Largest production helicopter The five-man Russian Mil Mi-26 has a maximum takeoff weight of 123,460 lb. (56,000 kg). Unladen it weighs 62,170 lb. (28,200 kg) and it is 131 ft. 4 in. (40.03 m) long. The eight-bladed rotor has a diameter of 105 ft. (32 m) and is powered by two 11,400-hp (8,500-kW) turbine engines.

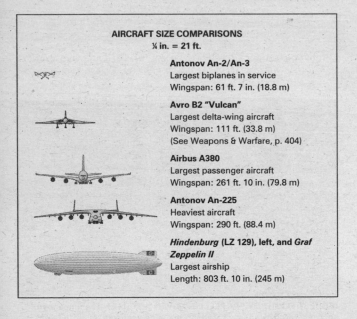

AIRCRAFT SIZE COMPARISONS
¼ in. = 21 ft.

Antonov An-2/An-3
Largest biplanes in service
Wingspan: 61 ft. 7 in. (18.8 m)

Avro B2 "Vulcan"
Largest delta-wing aircraft
Wingspan: 111 ft. (33.8 m)
(See Weapons & Warfare, p. 404)

Airbus A380
Largest passenger aircraft
Wingspan: 261 ft. 10 in. (79.8 m)

Antonov An-225
Heaviest aircraft
Wingspan: 290 ft. (88.4 m)

Hindenburg **(LZ 129), left, and** *Graf Zeppelin II*
Largest airship
Length: 803 ft. 10 in. (245 m)

WEAPONS & WARFARE

★ **Most aircraft on a submarine** The three Japanese I-400 Sen Toku-class submarines built during World War II each carried three Aichi M6A1 "Sieran" seaplanes, which were stored folded in a 115-ft. (35-m-long) hangar on the submarines' decks and launched along the deck by catapult. The subs displaced about 13,228,000 lb. (6,614 tons) submerged and were 400 ft. (122 m) long, making them the largest ever at that time.

★ **Largest gun on a submarine** The three British Royal Navy M-Class submarines developed toward the end of World War I were equipped with a deck-mounted 12-in. (30-cm) gun, a weapon more commonly found on bat-tleships. The diesel-electric-powered submarines were 297 ft. (90.5 m) long, had a surface displacement of 3.5 million lb. (1,750 tons), and could travel at 8 knots (9 mph; 15 km/h) submerged and at 14 knots (16 mph; 26 km/h) on the surface.

★ **Most produced military jet aircraft** It is estimated that over 8,000 Russian MIG-21 "Fishbed" jet fighters have been produced since the first prototype flew in 1955, making it the most common jet-powered military aircraft ever and the military aircraft produced in the greatest numbers in the post-World War II era. The aircraft has been produced in over 30 different variants and has seen service with about 50 air forces around the world.

Largest ever bomber wingspan The American 10-engined Convair B-36J "Peacemaker" had a wingspan of 230 ft. (70.1 m). The aircraft had a maximum takeoff weight of 410,000 lb. (205 tons)—equivalent to the weight of 120 average cars, and about 15 such cars could be parked end to end along its wings. Its top speed was 435 mph (700 km/h).

★ **First use of military balloons in warfare** Military balloons were first used by the French in 1794 for reconnaissance observations of their en-emy, Austria, during the French Revolutionary Wars of 1792–1801.

INTERNATIONAL WARS

Shortest: 9:00 a.m. to 9:45 a.m. on August 27, 1896, between Zanzibar and Britain

Longest: Thirty Years War between various European countries from 1618 to 1648, after which the map of Europe was radically changed

---

★**LARGEST DELTA WING** The British RAF's Avro B2 "Vulcan" delta-wing nuclear bomber had a wingspan of 111 ft. (33.8 m) and a top speed of 645 mph (1,038 km/h) thanks to its four Bristol Siddeley Olympus 201 engines. The B2 version of the Vulcan first entered service in 1958 and the last was retired by the RAF in 1986.

★**First use of a fixed-wing aircraft in warfare** On October 22, 1911, during the Italo-Turkish War of 1911–12, Captain Carlo Piazza of the Italian army flew a Blériot monoplane from Tripoli to Azzia in Libya during a reconnaissance mission over Turkish forces.

HEAVIEST TANKS The M1A2 Abrams main battle tank, produced by General Dynamics Land Systems (U.S.A.), has a combat weight of 138,900 lb. (69.4 tons), making it the ★**heaviest tank currently in operational service.** Equipped with a 4.7-in. (120-mm) gun, it has a top speed of 42 mph (68 km/h).

The heaviest operational tank ever was the 165,780-lb. (82.9-ton) 13-man French Char de Rupture 2C bis of 1922. It carried a 6.1-in. (15.5-cm) howitzer and was powered by two 250-hp (186-kW) engines giving a top speed of 7.5 mph (12 km/h).

LARGEST AMPHIBIOUS SHIP The U.S. Navy's Wasp-class vessels have a full load displacement of 80.5 million lb. (40,250 tons) and a length of 844 ft. (257 m). Capable of carrying aircraft, landing vessels of various kinds, and large numbers of personnel, their primary role is to put troops onto enemy shores.

★ **First offensive strike by an Unmanned Aerial Vehicle (UAV)** On November 3, 2002, in Yemen, an AGM-114 Hellfire missile was fired from a CIA-operated General Atomics RQ-1 "Predator" at six alleged Al-Qaeda operatives traveling in a car.

Largest tank battle The Battle of Kursk was fought on July 12, 1943, in the Prokhorovka region near the Russian town of Kursk. A total of 1,500 German and Russian tanks amassed for close-range fighting. By the end of the day both sides had lost more than 300 tanks each.

★ **Longest range tank hit** The longest documented range at which a tank has scored a hit on another is 2.54 miles (4.1 km) by a British Challenger tank of the Royal Scots Dragoon Guards during the land offensive of the Gulf War (February 24–28, 1991). The Iraqi tank was a Russian-made T-55.

★ **Longest range hit by ship's guns** On two occasions during World War II, one ship's guns hit another vessel at a distance of 15 miles (24 km). On June 8, 1940, the German "pocket battleship" *Scharnhorst* hit the British aircraft carrier HMS *Glorious* at that range in the North Atlantic, while a month later on July 9, during the battle of Calabria, the British battleship HMS *Warspite* hit the Italian flagship *Guilio Cesare* at a similar distance. Both are remarkable feats of gunnery, considering that in each case both vessels involved in the exchange were moving at high speed.

★ **FASTEST WORLD WAR II FIGHTER AIRCRAFT** Germany's Messerschmitt ME 163 was a rocket-powered aircraft with a top speed of 597 mph (960 km/h). It entered service with the Luftwaffe in May 1944 but, because of its very limited flight time, was never a great success operationally.

★ MILITARY ROBOTS: FIRST USE IN COMBAT The first time robots were used in ground combat occurred during the war in Afghanistan in July 2002. A robot named Hermes was deployed to search a network of caves in Qiqay, Afghanistan. Hermes—and the other three prototypes, Professor, Thing, and Fester—are heavy enough (42 lb.; 19 kg) to trigger mines, tall enough (1 ft.; 30 cm) to trip booby-traps at foot level, and long enough (1 ft.; 30 cm) to carry 12 cameras, a grenade launcher, and a 12-gauge shotgun.

★ FIRST FILMING OF A WAR The first war to be filmed was the Battle of Volo in Thessaly, Greece, in April 1897. This war between Turkey and Greece was filmed by the British war correspondent and cinematographer Frederick Villiers (UK), but never publicly broadcast. The earliest footage of war that still exists was filmed on November 12, 1899, by John Bennett (UK) during the British campaign at Orange River, South Africa, during the Boer War.

★ **MOST POWERFUL LASER WEAPON** The Airborne Laser (ABL), developed by Boeing, Lockheed Martin, and Northrop Grumman, is designed to fit inside a modified Boeing 747 and will ultimately be used to track and destroy ballistic missiles. Although still in development, its power output measures about one megawatt. The ABL's chemical oxygen iodine laser (COIL) was first fired in a ground test at Edwards Air Force Base, California, U.S.A., in November 2004; the first aerial test of shooting a ballistic missile is scheduled for late 2005.

Most widely used firearm During the Cold War, the USSR supplied Automatic Kalashnikov 1947s (AK-47s) to anti-Western insurgents and thus the rifle became a popular symbol of left-wing revolution. Between 50 and 80 million copies and variations of the AK-47 have been produced globally.

★ **First aerial bombardment** The first aerial bombardment was attempted in 1849 when Austrians launched 200 pilotless hot-air balloons to drop timed-release bombs over enemy defenses in Venice, Italy. Unpredictable winds meant that there were few casualties.

The ★ **first aerial bombardment by airplane** occurred on November 1, 1911, during the Italo-Turkish War of 1911–12. Second Lieutenant Giulio Gavotti of the Italian Air Flotilla threw four small 4.5-lb. (2-kg) grenades over a Turkish camp stationed in Ain Zara, Libya, from his Taube monoplane, which was flying at an altitude of 600 ft. (185 m).

★**SMALLEST MAMMAL USED IN DETECTING LAND MINES** The Gamgian (or African) giant pouch rat (*Cricetomys gambianus*) measures 30 in. (76 cm) long (including the tail) and weighs 3 lb. (1.35 kg), i.e., light enough not to trigger an explosion. According to APOPO, the Belgian company that developed this idea, a single rat and its handler can search 1,614 ft.^{2} (150 m^2) in a day. The rats are trained to respond to the smell emitted by the explosive by biting or scratching at the location until they are rewarded with food.

★**Heaviest cannon** A cannon built in 1868 at Perm, Russia, weighs 317,685 lb. (158.8 tons), has a bore of 20 in. (50.8 cm) and a barrel 15 ft. 1 in. (4.6 m) long. Its cannonballs weighed approximately half a ton. Known as the Czar Cannon, it is on display in the Museum of the Lenin Works in Moscow, Russia.

★**Fastest torpedo** Russia's rocket-propelled Shkval (Squall) torpedo releases a stream of bubbles from its nose and skin, surrounding it with a sheath of gas and dramatically reducing its friction with seawater. This allows it to reach velocities estimated at 200 mph (360 km/h), with a range of about 4.2 miles (6.8 km).

Heaviest nuclear bomb The MK 17, which was carried by U.S. B-36 bombers in the mid-1950s, weighed 41,998 lb. (19,050 kg) and was 24 ft. 6 in. (7.49 m) long.

★**First test of a laser weapon** In a test that took place in November 1973, a 100-kW carbon dioxide laser destroyed a 12-ft. (3.6-m) airborne drone above the Sandia Optical Test Range of Kirtland Air Force Base, New Mexico, U.S.A.

Highest rate of fire by a ballistic weapon A prototype 36-barrel gun built by Metal Storm Limited of Brisbane, Australia, has a firing rate in excess of one million rounds a minute. Such high rates of fire are possible because the rounds are stacked in the barrels of the gun and fired electronically by computer, rather than by a hammer detonator.

Largest non nuclear conventional bomb in existence The Massive Ordnance Air Blast (MOAB) is a guided weapon weighing 21,500 lb. (9,752 kg). It was first tested at the Eglin Air Force Armament Center, Florida, U.S.A., on March 11, 2003.

★Longest range missile ever The U.S. Atlas missile entered service in 1959 and had a range of 10,357 miles (16,669 km)—about 3,000 miles (4,828 km) more than was needed to hit any point in Soviet territory from launch sites in the West.

Highest rate of fire by a machine gun in service The 0.3-in. (7.62-mm) caliber M134 Minigun has a firing rate of 6,000 rounds a minute, or 100 a second—about 10 times that of an ordinary machine gun.

★Country with the most troops deployed overseas As of May 2004, the U.S.A. had approximately 370,000 land-based military personnel on active duty. This is out of a global total of over 500,000 soldiers from 47 countries serving abroad in all capacities, including war, peacekeeping, and disaster relief.

First use of a crossbow The earliest use of a crossbow was in 341 B.C. at the Battle of Ma-Ling, Linyi, China.

MOST INTELLIGENT HANDGUN The O'Dwyer Variable Lethality Law Enforcement (VLe) prototype pistol, made by Metal Storm Limited of Brisbane, Australia, has no moving parts. Instead, projectiles are fired electronically by a built-in computer processor. It can only be fired by someone wearing an authorized transponder ring, and is capable of firing up to three shots in extremely quick succession (within 1/500th of a second).

PROJECTILES

MOST POTATOES LAUNCHED IN 3 MINUTES Tom Pringle (UK), a.k.a. Dr. Bunhead, successfully fired eight potatoes manually from a potato launcher in three minutes. The attempt occurred on December 14, 2004, in London, UK. Dr. Bunhead is a professional science communicator dedicated to "bringing science out of the laboratory and into the classroom, theaters, and TV."

FARTHEST DISTANCE . . . The objects on the following pages represent those that have been hurled, spat, tossed, popped, or thrown farther than any others.

TOBACCO SPIT *Wad (mouthful) of tobacco* 53 ft. 3 in. (16.23 m) David O'Dell (U.S.A.), World Tobacco Spitting Championships, Calico Ghost Town, California, U.S.A., March 22, 1997

WATERMELON SEED SPIT 75 ft. 2 in. (22.91 m) Jason Schayot (U.S.A.) De Leon, Texas, U.S.A., August 12, 1995

CHERRY STONE SPIT 93 ft. 6.5 in. (28.51 m) Brian "Young Gun" Krause (U.S.A.) 2004 International Cherry Pit-Spitting Championships, Eau Claire, Michigan, U.S.A.

HOUSE BRICK THROW *5-lb. (2.27-kg) house brick*
146 ft. 1 in. (44.54 m) Geoff Capes (UK), Orton
Goldhay, Cambridgehire, UK, July 19, 1978

ROLLING PIN THROW *Weighing 2 lb. (907 g)*
175 ft. 5 in. (53.47 m), Lori La Deane Adams
(U.S.A.), Iowa State Fair, U.S.A., August 21,
1979

CHAMPAGNE CORK FLIGHT *Cork from an untreated and
unheated Champagne bottle,* 177 ft. 9 in. (54.18 m),
Heinrich Medicus (U.S.A.), Woodbury Vineyards Winery,
New York, U.S.A., June 5, 1988

HAGGIS HURL *Minimum weight of 1 lb. 8 oz.
(680 g),* 180 ft. 10 in. (55.11 m), Alan Pettigrew (UK),
Inchmurrin, Argyll and Bute, Scotland, UK, May 24,
1984

RUBBER BOOT THROW (MAN)
Size 9 Challenger Dunlop boot
209 ft. 9 in. (63.98 m)
Teppo Luoma (Finland)
Hämeenlinna, Finland
October 12, 1996

RUBBER BOOT THROW (WOMAN)
Size 9 Challenger Dunlop boot
134 ft. 1 in. (40.87 m)
Sari Tirkkonen (Finland)
Hämeenlinna, Finland
April 19, 1996

PAPER AIRCRAFT *Made from a single sheet of 8.5 × 11 in. paper, and a specified length of standard Scotch tape,* 207 ft. 4 in. (63.19 m), Stephen Krieger (U.S.A.), Near Moses Lake, Washington, U.S.A., September 6, 2003

COW PIE TOSS *Not molded into a spherical shape, 100% "organic"*
226 ft. (81.1 m)
Steve Urner (U.S.A.)
Mountain Festival
Tehachapi, California, U.S.A.
August 14, 1981

EGG THROW *Fresh, raw, hen's egg—must remain intact when caught*
323 ft. 2 in. (98.51 m)
Johnny Fell to Keith Thomas (both U.S.A.) Jewett, Texas, U.S.A.
November 12, 1978

BASEBALL THROW (MAN) 445 ft. 10 in. (135.88 m)
Glen Edward Gorbous (Canada)
August 1, 1957
BASEBALL THROW (WOMAN) 296 ft. (90.2 m)
Mildred Ella "Babe" Didrikson (U.S.A.)
July 25, 1951

FLYING DISC THROW (MAN) 820 ft. (250 m)
Christian Sandstrom (Sweden)
El Mirage, California, U.S.A.
April 26, 2002
FLYING DISC THROW (WOMAN) 454 ft. 6 in. (138.56 m)
Jennifer Griffin (U.S.A.)
Fredericksburg, Virginia, U.S.A.
April 8, 2000

OBJECT WITH NO TAIL *Flying ring*
1,333 ft. (406.29 m)
Erin Hemmings (U.S.A.)
Fort Funston, California, U.S.A.
July 14, 2003

MOST PAINTBALLS CAUGHT IN TWO MINUTES Fired from a distance of 65 ft. (20 m), Anthony Kelly (Australia) caught 28 intact in two minutes at Ultimate Skirmish paintball field, Helensburgh, New South Wales, Australia, on May 30, 2003.

★ **LARGEST TREBUCHET WITH A PROJECTILE WEIGHT OF 20 KG (44 LB.) AND OVER** The *Car Thrower* threw a 7,496-lb. (3,400-kg) steel block over a distance of 50 ft. 3 in. (15.32 m), creating a power output of 376,623 lb.-ft. (52,088 kg-m). The trebuchet was built by Angus Robson and team of Rocktec Ltd. (New Zealand) and fired on February 19, 2004, in Matamata, New Zealand.

Pictured is the *Car Thrower* throwing a car!

BUILDINGS

Largest administrative building The Pentagon in Arlington, Virginia, U.S.A., has a floor area of 6.5 million ft.² (604,000 m²). Each of the outermost sides is 921 ft. (281 m) long and the perimeter of the building is about 4,610 ft. (1,405 m). Its corridors total 17.5 miles (28 km) in length and there are 7,754 windows to be cleaned. More than 26,000 military and civilian employees work in the building.

☆**Fastest elevator** Two high-speed elevators installed by Toshiba Elevator and Building Systems (Japan) in Taipei 101, the world's **tallest building**, situated in Taipei, Taiwan, have a maximum speed of 3,313 ft./min. (1,010 m/min.), equivalent to 37.6 mph (60.6 km/h). The elevators take just 40 seconds from ground level to the 89th floor, situated at 1,253 ft. (382 m), and have atmospheric pressure regulatory systems to avoid discomfort (ear popping) for the occupants.

★**Largest mixed-use building** Berjaya Times Square KL in Kuala Lumpur, Malaysia, has a total floor area of 7.3 million ft.² (678,000 m²) and features a 3.45 million-ft.² (320,000-m²) shopping mall, an indoor theme park, and two 48-story towers containing offices and a hotel. It opened in 2003.

COMPARE THE WORLD'S TALLEST STRUCTURES
BY TURNING TO P. 332–36

TALLEST HOTEL The all-suite Burj Al Arab ("The Arabian Tower"), situated 9 miles (15 km) south of Dubai, UAE, was 1,052 ft. (320.94 m) high from ground level to the top of its mast when measured on October 26, 1999. Pictured is its helipad, which was temporarily converted into a tennis court in 2005 for a noncompetition match between Roger Federer (Switzerland) and Andre Agassi (U.S.A.).

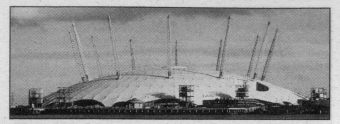

★**LARGEST DOME STRUCTURE** Although not a true "dome," in the sense that it is not self-supporting, the Millennium Dome at Greenwich in London, UK, is the largest dome-shaped structure. It has an overall diameter of 1,181 ft. (365 m), an internal diameter of 1,050 ft. (320 m), and a roof height of 164 ft. (50 m). It consists of a polytetrafluorethylene-(PTFE-) coated fiberglass membrane, suspended from twelve 312-ft.-tall (95-m) steel masts, and covers 861,000 ft.² (80,000 m²).

★**Tallest unoccupied building** Although it had reached its full height of 1,082 ft. (330 m), the Ryugyong Hotel in Pyongyang, North Korea, was not finished when construction was halted in 1992. It is the world's 18th tallest building, and would be the world's tallest hotel if completed.

★**First building to have a safety elevator** On March 23, 1857, the first modern "safety elevator" went into service at the Haughwout Department Store in New York City, U.S.A. It was installed by Elisha Otis and was powered by a steam engine.

☆**Heaviest building moved intact** The 10-story, 29.2 million-lb. (12,023-ton) Talent Exchange Center in Wuzhou, Guangxi, China, was moved 99 ft. (30.2 m) on a specially built roller system, from May 25 to June 3, 2004. Dalian Jiuding Special Construction Engineering carried out the move, which happened at a rate of 10–23 ft. (3–7 m) a day. The building's occupants continued to live and work in it during the move.

★**Highest mosque above ground level** The Prince Abdulla Mosque on the 77th floor of the Kingdom Center building in Riyadh, Saudi Arabia, is 600 ft. (183 m) above ground level and was completed on July 5, 2004.

★**Largest underground shopping complex** The PATH Walkway in Toronto, Canada, has 16.7 miles (27 km) of shopping arcades with 4 million ft.² (371,600 m²) of retail space for about 1,200 shops and services. Over 50 buildings, five subway stations, and a rail terminal are accessible through the complex.

★**Largest kaleidoscope** The Nagoya City Pavilion "Earth Tower," erected for the Aichi Expo 2005 near Nagoya, Japan, stands 154 ft. (47 m)

★**LONGEST SINGLE-SPAN ROOF STRUCTURE** The giant steel arch supporting the roof of the north stand of the new Wembley Stadium in London, UK, has a span of 1,033 ft. (315 m), making it the world's longest unsupported roof structure. It weighs 3.85 million lb. (1,587 tons) and is 23 ft. (7 m) in diameter. The Eiffel Tower (1,063 ft.; 324 m) is just a shade taller than the steel arch's span.

tall and projects a kaleidoscopic image 131 ft. (40 m) to viewers at the base of the triangular tower.

★**Tallest hospital building** The 34-story Guy's Tower at Guy's Hospital in London, UK, is 468 ft. (142.6 m) tall.

★**Largest single free-span wooden structure** The Odate Jukai Dome in Odate, Japan, is a dome-shaped building that measures 584 ft. (178 m) on its longest axis and 515 ft. (157 m) on its shortest axis. It consists of an opaque membrane stretched over a frame constructed from 25,000 Akita cedar trees.

Largest pyramid The Quetzalcóatl pyramid at Cholula de Rivadavia, 63 miles (101 km) southeast of Mexico City, Mexico, is both the largest pyramid and the **largest monument** ever built. It is 177 ft. (54 m) tall, and its base covers nearly 45 acres (18.2 hectares). Its total volume has been estimated at 116.5 million ft.³ (3.3 million m³), compared with the current volume of 84.7 million ft.³ (2.4 million m³) for the Great Egyptian Pyramid of Khufu or Cheops, the **tallest pyramid.**

Largest religious structure The Angkor Wat (City Temple) in Cambodia encloses 401 acres (162.6 hectares). It was built in honor of the Hindu god Vishnu by the Khmer King Suryavarman II in the period A.D. 1113–50.

Its curtain wall measures 4,200 ft. (1,280 m) and its population, before it was abandoned in 1432, was 80,000. The temple forms part of a complex of 72 major monuments that extends across 15.4 miles (24.8 km).

Largest surviving ziggurat Although not the largest ever ziggurat (rectangular stepped pyramid), the largest surviving ziggurat is the Ziggurat of Ur (now Muqayyar, Iraq) with a base 200 × 150 ft. (61 × 45.7 m), built to three stories, and surmounted by a summit temple. The first story and part of the second story now survive to a height of 60 ft. (18 m).

The ziggurat was constructed during the reign of Ur-nammu (ca. 2113–2095 B.C.).

STRUCTURES

HIGHEST . . .

Bridge The bridge over the Royal Gorge of the Arkansas River in Colorado, U.S.A., is 1,053 ft. (321 m) above water level. It is a suspension bridge with a main span of 880 ft. (268 m) and was finished on December 6, 1929, after six months' construction.

Dam The Nurek dam, 984 ft. (300 m) high, on the Vakhsh River, Tajikistan, is currently the highest dam, but this should be surpassed by the Rogunskaya dam, at 1,098 ft. (335 m), also across the Vakhsh River. However, the breakup of the former Soviet Union has delayed its completion.

Concrete dam Grande Dixence, on the Dixence River in Switzerland, was built from 1953 to 1961 to a height of 935 ft. (285 m), with a crest length of 2,297 ft. (700 m), using 210,400,000 ft.³ (5,960,000 m³) of concrete.

Causeway Once the road bridge at the highest altitude in the world at 18,380 ft. (5,602 m), Bailey bridge, erected in August 1982 over Khardungla Pass, Ladakh, India, was

LONGEST TIBETAN BRIDGE The bridge connecting the islands of Procida and Vivara, Italy, has a span of 1,187 ft. (362 m). It was completed on July 15, 2001.

★ **TALLEST BRIDGE FROM GROUND TO HIGHEST POINT** The Millau Viaduct in France was constructed to relieve heavy traffic in the old town of Millau. Stretching for 8,070 ft. (2,460 m) across the Tarn River in the Massif Central mountains, the road deck is supported by seven concrete piers, the tallest of which measures a record 1,125 ft. (343 m) from the ground to the tip—more than twice the original height of the Great Pyramid at Giza, Egypt. The bridge was designed by Foster and Partners (UK) and opened to the public in December 2004.

replaced by a causeway—a raised road—in the mid-1990s owing to damage from avalanches.

LARGEST . . .

★ **Tidal barrier** The Oosterscheldedam, a storm-surge barrier in the southwest of the Netherlands, is the world's largest tidal river barrier. It has 65 concrete piers and 62 steel gates and covers a total length of 5.6 miles (9 km).

Reservoir (by volume) The most voluminous fully man-made reservoir is the Bratskoye reservoir on the river Angara in Russia, with a volume of 40.6 miles^3 (169.3 km^3) and an area of 2,112 miles^2 (5,470 km^2).

Reservoir (by surface area) The world's largest artificial lake is Lake Volta in Ghana, formed by the Akosombo dam, completed in 1965. By 1969, the lake had filled to an area of 3,275 miles^2 (8,482 km^2), with a shoreline 4,500 miles (7,250 km) in length.

Cooling tower The largest cooling tower is 590 ft. (180 m) tall and stands adjacent to the nuclear power plant at Uentrop, Germany. It was completed in 1976.

Road tunnel (diameter) The road tunnel blasted through Yerba Buena Island, San Francisco, California, U.S.A., is 79 ft. (24 m) wide, 56 ft. (17 m) high, and 541 ft. (165 m) long. More than 280,000 vehicles pass along its two decks every day.

LONGEST . . .

Road and rail bridge system The Seto-Ohashi bridge in Japan consists of six bridge sections and stretches across a total distance of 5.8 miles (9.4 km).

Bridge The Second Lake Pontchartrain causeway bridge, which joins Mandeville and Metairie, Louisiana, U.S.A., is 23.87 miles (38.42 km) long.

LONGEST WALL The Great Wall of China has a main-line length of 3,460 km (2,150 miles)—nearly three times the length of Britain—plus 3,530 km (2,195 miles) of branches and spurs. Construction began during the reign of Qin Shi Huangdi (221–210 B.C.). Its height varies from 4.5 to 12 m (15 to 39 ft.) and it is up to 9.8 m (32 ft.) thick. It runs from Shanhaiguan to Yumenguan and Yangguan, and was kept in repair up to the 16th century. Some 51.5 km (32 miles) of the wall have been destroyed since 1966, and part of the wall was blown up to make way for a dam in July 1979.

LONGEST SPAN OF A CABLE SUSPENSION BRIDGE The main span of the Akashi-Kaikyo road bridge, which links Honshu and Shikoku, Japan, is 6,532 ft. (1.24 miles; 1,990.8 m) long. The overall suspended length with side-spans totals 12,831 ft. 8 in. (2.43 miles; 3,911.1 m).

Cable suspension bridge (road and rail) The Tsing Ma bridge in Hong Kong opened to the public in May 1997. It has a main span of 4,518 ft. (1,377 m), a width of 130 ft. (40 m), and a length of 1.36 miles (2.2 km), making it the longest suspension-bridge span for combined road and railroad traffic.

Its shipping clearance reaches 203 ft. (62 m) and the tower height is 675 ft. (206 m).

Cantilever bridge The Quebec bridge (Pont de Quebec) over the St. Lawrence River in Canada has a cantilever truss span measuring 1,800 ft. (549 m) between the piers and 3,239 ft. (987 m) overall. It carries a railroad track and a divided highway. Work started in 1899 and it was finally opened to traffic on December 3, 1917.

Concrete girder bridge The Raftsundet bridge in Norway is 978 ft. (298 m) long—approximately the length of four 747 jumbo jets laid end to end. It links the main islands of the Norwegian Lofoten group and was completed in 1997.

Floating bridge Second Lake Washington bridge, Washington State, U.S.A., has a total length of 2.39 miles (3.8 km), with its floating section measuring 7,518 ft. (2,291 m). It was completed in August 1963.

Steel arch bridge The Lupu bridge in Shanghai, China, has a span of 1,804 ft. (550 m) over the Huangpu River. It was constructed over a period of three years and opened on June 28, 2003.

Longest wooden bridge Lake Pontchartrain Railroad Trestle, Louisiana, U.S.A., made of creosoted yellow pine timber, spans 5.82 miles

LARGEST CONCRETE DAM The Grand Coulee dam (begun in 1933 and operational on March 22, 1941) on the Columbia River, Washington State, U.S.A., had a concrete volume of 285,760,000 ft.³ (8,092,000 m³) to a weight of 43.2 billion lb. (17,776,467 tons). It was finally completed in 1942 at a cost of $56 million. It has a crest length of 4,173 ft. (1,272 m) and is 550 ft. (168 m) high.

(9.36 km). Construction began in February 1882 and finished in September of that year. When it opened in 1883, it originally spanned 21.49 miles (34.6 km).

THEME PARKS

LARGEST . . .

LARGEST RELIGIOUS THEME PARK The Holy Land Experience, a 15-acre (6-hectare) site in Orlando, Florida, U.S.A., opened on February 5, 2001, and is a re-creation of Jerusalem, Israel, during the period from 1450 B.C. to A.D. 66.

OLDEST CONTINUALLY OPERATING ROLLER COASTER The Scenic Railway at Luna Park, St. Kilda, Melbourne, Australia, opened to the public on December 13, 1912, and has remained in operation ever since.

★**Theme park operator** Walt Disney Parks & Resorts is the world's largest operator of theme parks, with an estimated 101 million people visiting its attractions in 2004, according to *Amusement Business* magazine. By comparison, France, the ☆**most popular tourist destination,** only receives about 75 million international tourists each year. In 2004, eight of the world's top 10 theme parks were operated by Disney.

Indoor amusement park Galaxyland, located in West Edmonton Mall, Alberta, Canada, covers 400,000 ft.² (37,200 m²). It has 30 skill games and 27 rides and attractions.

Observation wheel The British Airways London Eye designed by architects David Marks and Julia Barfield (both UK), has a diameter of 443 ft. (135 m). Constructed at Jubilee Gardens on London's South Bank, it made its first "flight" on February 1, 2000, with regular services commencing the following month.

Wave pool According to the World Waterpark Association, the largest wave pool (often called an artificial sea) covers 172,000 ft.² (16,000 m²) and can be found at Siam Park, Bangkok, Thailand.

LONGEST . . .

Roller coaster Steel Dragon 2000 at Nagashima Spaland, Mie, Japan, is 8,133 ft. (2,479 m) long. A steel-track out-and-back coaster, it has a maximum height of 311 ft. 8 in. (95 m) and a top speed of 92.5 mph (149 km/h). It opened on August 1, 2000.

★Flying roller coaster Batwing at Six Flags America in Maryland, U.S.A., and X-Flight at Geauga Lake, Ohio, U.S.A., are both 3,340 ft. (1,018 m) long. Flying roller coasters are rides in which the occupants are suspended horizontally beneath the coaster parallel to the track, giving the sensation of flying.

★Stand-up roller coaster Riddler's Revenge at Six Flags Magic Mountain in California, U.S.A., is 4,370 ft. (1,332 m) long. Riders stand rather

☆ **FASTEST ROLLER COASTER** Kingda Ka at Six Flags Great Adventure near Jackson, New Jersey, U.S.A., has a design speed of 128 mph (206 km/h) and opened in the spring of 2005. It is also the ☆**tallest roller coaster**, with riders reaching 418 ft. (127.4 m) above ground level.

than sit during the ride, which is also the fastest of its kind, reaching a top speed of 65 mph (104 km/h).

Wooden roller coaster Beast, built in 1979 at Paramount's Kings Island in Ohio, U.S.A., is the longest traditional wooden laminated track roller coaster at 7,400 ft. (2,286 m). Rides last 3 min. 40 sec. and reach a top speed of 65 mph (104 km/h).

MOST . . .

Rides in an amusement park Cedar Point Amusement Park near Sandusky, Ohio, U.S.A., dates back to 1870 and has a total of 68 different mechanical rides—the most of any single theme or amusement park in the world today.

☆**Visited theme park** The world's most visited theme park is the Magic Kingdom at Walt Disney World in Florida, U.S.A., which in 2004 attracted more than 15.1 million visitors, according to *Amusement Business* magazine. It was followed by Disneyland in Anaheim, California, U.S.A., which had 13.36 million guests, and Tokyo Disneyland in Japan, which had 13.2 million visitors.

THE FERRIS WHEEL.

Roller coasters in one theme park Both Six Flags Magic Mountain in Valencia, California, and Cedar Point near Sandusky, Ohio, U.S.A., opened their 16th roller coaster during 2003, making them jointly the theme parks with the largest number of roller coasters.

★**Naked riders on a theme park ride** On August 27, 2004, 32 naked people took a ride on Nemesis at Alton Towers, Staffordshire, UK, for *Guinness World Records: 50 Years, 50 Records* (UK).

FIRST FERRIS WHEEL The Ferris wheel was designed by George Washington Gale Ferris Jr. (U.S.A., 1859–96) and was erected for the World's Columbian Exposition of 1893 in Chicago, Illinois, U.S.A., at a cost of $385,000. It was 264 ft. (80 m) high and had a circumference of 790 ft. (240 m).

ROY VOCKING

Roy Vocking is vice-president at Intamin AG, a leading roller coaster manufacturer.

What does a top-spec roller coaster cost? Easily in excess of $10 million, which includes the factory cost as well as decoration and park infrastructure, etc.

How are coasters developed? We develop many of the ideas ourselves with well-established parks in the U.S.A. and UK, who either approach us to see what's new or present us with an idea to see if it's feasible.

How do you start a design? Everything's done on computers, and the calculations and drawings can run into hundreds of thousands of dollars, even for a simple coaster.

What's the biggest challenge when designing a coaster? Finding customers who are willing to buy the first example of a new coaster. You just don't know whether the public will like the ride.

What's the next big thing? A lot of parks have problems with space and noise thanks to the growth of nearby towns and we now have to address this. The more restrictions you put on us, the more interesting our ride will become, so we're developing some compact, high-impact thrill rides.

SPORTS & GAMES

CONTENTS

AIR SPORTS

AEROBATICS

Most world championship wins Petr Jirmus (Czechoslovakia, now Czech Republic) is the only man to become world champion twice, in 1984 and 1986.

★**Oldest world champion** Henry Haigh (U.S.A., b. December 12, 1924) was aerobatics world champion at the age of 64 in 1988.

BALLOONING

★**Longest duration flown by a balloon (solo)** Steve Fossett (U.S.A.) flew for 14 days 19 hr. 50 min., from June 19 to July 4, 2002, while piloting his balloon, *Bud Light Spirit of Freedom,* around the world solo.

GLIDING

Highest speed James and Thomas Payne (both U.S.A.) recorded an FAI average top speed of 153.78 mph (247.49 km/h) over a course of 310.6 miles (500 km) when setting the out-and-return speed record at California City, U.S.A., on March 3, 1999.

The **highest speed in a glider by a woman** was reached by Pamela Kurstjens-Hawkins (UK), with an FAI average top speed of 98.83 mph (159.06 km/h) over a triangular course of 62 miles (100 km) at McCaffrey's Airfield, Australia, on December 14, 2002.

MOST PEOPLE TO TANDEM PARACHUTE IN 24 HOURS A total of 128 tandem parachute jumps were made from Hibaldstow Airfield, Lincolnshire, UK, on June 28, 2004, at a charity event for the Echo Trust children's charity.

**FÉDÉRATION AÉRONAUTIQUE INTERNATIONALE (FAI)
DEFINITIONS OF AIRCRAFT:**

Hang glider
A glider capable of being carried, foot-launched, and landed solely by
the use of the pilot's legs

Paraglider
A hang glider with no rigid primary structure

Microlight
A one or two-seat airplane with a specified maximum mass and a very
low wing loading

Glider
A fixed-wing aerodyne (a heavier-than-air aircraft deriving lift from
motion) capable of sustained flight and having no means of propulsion

HANG GLIDING

Greatest height gain Larry Tudor (U.S.A.) rose to an altitude of 14,250 ft. (4,343 m) over Owens Valley, California, U.S.A., on August 4, 1985.

The **greatest height gain in a hang glider by a woman** was achieved by Judy Leden (UK), who reached 13,025 ft. (3,970 m) in Kuruman, South Africa, on December 1, 1992.

★Highest speed Thomas Suchanek (Czech Republic) achieved a top speed of 31.57 mph (50.81 km/h) over a 15.5-mile (25-km) triangular course at Riverside, Australia, on December 15, 2000.

The **★highest speed for a hang glider by a woman** over the same distance was achieved by Jenny Ganderton (Australia), who reached a top speed of 16.15 mph (26 km/h) at Forbes, New South Wales, Australia, on February 14, 1990.

PARACHUTING

Largest FAI-approved free-fall formation A group of 357 sky divers from over 40 countries formed above Takhli, Thailand, on February 6, 2004. The event was organized by World Team 04 and formed part of the Thailand Royal Sky Celebration, in honor of the Thai royal family.

★FIRST HOT-AIR BALLOON WORLD CHAMPIONSHIPS This form of ballooning was revived in the U.S.A. in 1961, and the first World Championships were held in Albuquerque, New Mexico, U.S.A., from February 10 to 17, 1973. The greatest mass ascent of hot-air balloons took place at the 2000 event when 329 balloons were launched in the space of an hour.

MOST PARACHUTISTS TO JUMP FROM A BALLOON SIMULTANEOUSLY A group of 20 members of the Paraclub Flevo of Lelystad (Netherlands) jumped simultaneously at 6,500 ft. (2,000 m) over Markelo, the Netherlands, on May 10, 2003.

Longest free-fall jump (unofficial) Capt. Joseph W. Kittinger (U.S.A.) dropped 84,700 ft. (25,820 m) from a balloon at 102,800 ft. (31,330 m) above Tularosa, New Mexico, U.S.A., on August 16, 1960. The maximum speed reached in rarefied air was 625.25 mph (1,006 km/h)—just faster than the speed of sound—at 90,000 ft. (27,400 m). He fell for 4 min. 37 sec. before his parachute was deployed automatically.

★**MOST PARACHUTE JUMPS IN 24 HOURS** Jay Stokes (U.S.A.) made 534 successful parachute jumps in a 24-hour period on November 11 and 12, 2003, above Lake Elsinore, California, U.S.A. This required Jay to make a parachute jump every two-and-a-half minutes.

PARAGLIDING

★**Longest flight (distance)—tandem** André Luis Grosso Fleury and Claudia Otila Guimaraes Ribeiro (both Brazil) traveled 186.2 miles (299.7 km) without landing from Patu to Varzea da Cacimba, Brazil, on October 17, 2003.

★**Most powered paragliders airborne simultaneously** A total of 78 powered paragliders were airborne above the Fantasy of Flight Museum, Polk City, Florida, U.S.A., on April 12, 2003.

SKYDIVING

Speed skydiving—greatest speed Speed skydiving involves jumping from an aircraft at 13,000 ft. (4,000 m) and accelerating in a near vertical headfirst position into the "measuring zone," which extends from 8,850 ft. (2,700 m) altitude to 5,570 ft. (1,700 m).

Michael Brooke (France) reached a speed of 325.67 mph (524.13 km/h)

ESTRID GEERTSEN

Estrid Geertsen (Denmark, b. August 1, 1904) became the ☆oldest tandem parachute jumper on September 30, 2004, leaping from an altitude of 13,100 ft. (4,000 m) over Roskilde, Denmark, at the age of 100 years 60 days.

What was it like? There was a lot of noise from the parachute but it was still a great experience.

What inspired you to make your first jump? After reading in a newspaper that the record belonged to an American woman, I wanted to do everything I could to get Denmark the record.

Do you get scared before you make your jumps? Not at all—don't forget, I'm 100 years old!

What do your family think about your hobby? They think it's wonderful. At first I wasn't going to tell them—I thought they would try to talk me out of it.

Do you intend to keep making parachute jumps? Only if my record is taken by somebody else!

at the Millennium Speed Skydiving Competition over Gap, France, on September 19, 1999.

The **fastest female speed skydiver** is Lucia Bottari (Italy), who reached 268.5 mph (432.12 km/h) in Bottens, Switzerland, on September 16, 2002.

Largest free-fall event The World Freefall Convention 2000, held in Quincy, Illinois, U.S.A., from August 4 to 13, attracted 5,732 registered sky divers from 55 countries, who made in excess of 63,000 jumps.

FOOTBALL

NFL

Highest score in an NFL regular season game The Washington Redskins scored 72 against the New York Giants (41) in Washington, D.C., U.S.A., on November 27, 1966. The aggregate score of 113 is also a record.

★Longest NFL interception return The longest interception return in an NFL game is 106 yards by Ed Reed (U.S.A.) for the Baltimore Ravens against the Cleveland Browns on November 7, 2004.

★Most postseason wins by a head coach Two National Football League head coaches have won ten postseason games—Vince Lombardi (U.S.A.), coach of the Green Bay Packers from 1961 to 1967; and Bill Belichick (U.S.A.), coach of the New England Patriots from 1994 to 2005. Of the two coaches, Belichick has the better over-

★HIGHEST PAID FOOTBALL PLAYER The highest paid NFL player is Atlanta Falcons quarterback Michael Vick (U.S.A.), who signed a 10-year $130-million deal on December 23, 2004, including a $27-million signing bonus.

★ **MOST CONSECUTIVE GAME WINS** The New England Patriots had 18 consecutive regular season game wins from September 28, 2003, to October 24, 2004. Head coach Bill Belichick (U.S.A., pictured) holds the Vince Lombardi trophy after the team won Super Bowl XXXVIII on February 1, 2004, at Reliant Stadium in Houston, Texas, U.S.A.

all record with 10 victories and one loss to Lombardi's 10 victories and two losses.

Most NFL career interceptions Paul Krause (U.S.A.), a free safety from the University of Iowa, U.S.A., is the leading pass interceptor of all time with 81 steals during a 16-season career, playing for the Washington Redskins (1964–67) and Minnesota Vikings (1968–79).

Longest pass completion A pass completion of 99 yd. has been achieved on eight occasions and has always resulted in a touchdown. The most recent was a pass from Brett Favre to Robert Brooks of the Green Bay Packers against the Chicago Bears on September 11, 1995.

Most NFL titles The Green Bay Packers have won 12 titles (1929–31, 1936, 1939, 1944, 1961–62, 1965–67, and 1996).

★ **Most passes received in a game** Terrell Owens (U.S.A.) caught a record 20 passes in an NFL game playing for the San Francisco 49ers v. the Chicago Bears on December 17, 2000.

Most field goals by an individual in a career Gary Anderson (U.S.A.), playing for Pittsburgh Steelers (1982–94), Philadelphia Eagles (1995–96), San Francisco 49ers (1997), and Minnesota Vikings (1999–2001), kicked 465 field goals in his NFL career.

Most yards gained receiving in a season Jerry Rice (U.S.A.) gained 1,848 yd. receiving in the 1995 NFL season, playing for the San Francisco 49ers.

☆ **MOST PASSES RECEIVED IN A SUPER BOWL GAME** **Three players share the record of 11 passes received: Dan Ross (U.S.A.) for the Cincinnati Bengals in 1982, Jerry Rice (U.S.A.) for the San Francisco 49ers in 1989, and Deion Branch (U.S.A., pictured) for the New England Patriots in 2005.**

Most games played by an individual George Blanda (U.S.A.) played in a record 340 games in a record 26 seasons in the NFL (Chicago Bears 1949–58, Baltimore Colts 1950, Houston Oilers 1960–66, and Oakland Raiders 1967–75).

Most touchdowns in a game The most touchdowns scored in an NFL game is six by Ernie Nevers (U.S.A.) playing for the Chicago Cardinals v. the Chicago Bears on November 28, 1929; William Jones (U.S.A.) for the Cleveland Browns v. the Chicago Bears on November 25, 1951; and Gale Sayers (U.S.A.) for the Chicago Bears v. the San Francisco 49ers on December 12, 1965.

☆ **Most touchdowns in a career** Jerry Rice (San Francisco 49ers, Oakland Raiders, and Seattle Seahawks) scored a record 197 touchdowns from 1985 to 2004. He also holds the Super Bowl career records for **most points**

★ **MOST POINTS SCORED IN A SUPER BOWL QUARTER** The most points scored by both teams in a quarter of Super Bowl play is 37 by the New England Patriots and Carolina Panthers in the fourth quarter of Super Bowl XXXVIII held in Houston, Texas, U.S.A., on February 1, 2004.

scored (48), **most yards gained receiving** (589), and **most passes received** (33).

Most yards gained rushing by a quarterback in a game The most yards rushed by a quarterback in a single NFL game is 173 yd. by Michael Vick (U.S.A.) for the Atlanta Falcons against the Minnesota Vikings in the 30–24 victory on December 1, 2002, in Minneapolis, Minnesota, U.S.A.

☆ **Most yards gained rushing in a career** Emmitt Smith (U.S.A.) gained 18,355 yd. in a career lasting from 1990 to 2004 playing for the Dallas Cowboys and Arizona Cardinals.

★ **Worst start by an NFL franchise** The worst start by a new National Football League franchise is 26 consecutive regular season losses by the Tampa Bay Buccaneers after they joined the league in 1976.

☆ **MOST TOUCHDOWN PASSES IN A SEASON** Peyton Manning (U.S.A.) threw a record 49 touchdown passes playing for the Indianapolis Colts in 2004.

SUPER BOWL

Highest team score The highest team score and record victory margin was achieved when the San Francisco 49ers beat the Denver Broncos 55–10 in New Orleans, Louisiana, U.S.A., on January 28, 1990.

Longest touchdown in a Super Bowl Muhsin Muhammad (U.S.A.) scored on an 85 yd. play for the Carolina Panthers in Super Bowl XXXVIII on February 1, 2004.

Most Super Bowl MVPs (Most Valuable Player) Joe Montana, quarterback with the San Francisco 49ers, was voted Most Valuable Player in three Super Bowls: 1982, 1985, and 1990.

ANIMAL & SADDLE SPORTS

DOG RACING

★**Most consecutive wins** From April 15, 1985, to December 9, 1986, Ballyregan Bob (UK) won a total of 32 consecutive greyhound races.

★**Most money won at a race** The richest greyhound race in the world is the Great American Greyhound Futurity Race, held every year at The Woodlands Racetrack, Kansas, U.S.A. On May 28, 2001 (the eighth year of the race), it had a net purse of $344,762.25, of which $155,143 was claimed by the winner, Tom S. Green Mile.

Fastest greyhound The highest speed at which any greyhound has been timed is 41.83 mph (67.32 km/h) by Star Title at Wyong, New South Wales, Australia, on March 5, 1994.

★LONGEST RIDE ON A MECHANICAL RODEO BULL Jamie Manning (Australia, pictured) rode a mechanical rodeo for 2 min. 4.49 sec. on the set of *Guinness World Records* at Seven Network Studios, Sydney, Australia on April 2, 2005. This record involves staying on the bull at level 1 for 8 seconds, and if successful, progressing to level 2 for 8 seconds, and every subsequent level for 8 seconds until the top level is reached. At this point, the participant must stay on at the top level—which must be set at 50 Hz—for as long as possible.

DRESSAGE

★**Most individual World Championship wins** Dr. Reiner Klimke (West Germany) won two titles, on Mehmed in 1974 and Ahlerich in 1982. Isabell Werth (Germany) achieved the same feat on Gigolo in 1994 and 1998.

Most team World Championship wins Germany won nine times from 1966 to 2002 (as West Germany from 1968 to 1990).

★**Largest parade of horse-drawn carriages** A total of 208 horse-drawn carriages rode in a 3.5-mile (5.7-km) parade through the streets of Lingen, Germany, on August 1, 2004. The event was organized by the Dressurclub Hanekenfähr as part of the city's International Dressage Festival.

HORSE RACING

Most career wins Laffit Pincay Jr. (U.S.A.) won 9,531 races in his career, from his first win on May 16, 1964, to March 1, 2003.

Oldest race-winning horse Al Jabal, a purebred Arab ridden by Brian Boulton and owned by Andrea Boulton (both UK), won The Three Horseshoes Handicap Stakes (over 6 furlongs) on June 9, 2002, at Barbury Castle, Wiltshire, UK, aged 19 years.

Most runners in a race There were 66 runners in the Grand National at Aintree, Merseyside, UK, on March 22, 1929. The record for a race on the flat is 58 in the Lincolnshire Handicap in Lincoln, UK, on March 13, 1948.

☆**Most steeplechase wins in a career** Tony McCoy (UK) won 2,211 races from 1992 to 2004. He also holds the record for **most steeplechase wins in a season,** with 289 in 2001–02.

RODEO

★**Highest earnings at a single rodeo** Ty Murray (U.S.A.) earned $124,821 at the National Finals Rodeo in Las Vegas, Nevada, U.S.A., in 1993.

Most all-around World Championship wins Ty Murray (U.S.A.) won seven all-around titles (awarded to the leading money winner in a single season in two or more events) at the Professional Rodeo Cowboy Association (PRCA) World Championships from 1989 to 1998.

★**Most combined World Championship titles won** Jim Shoulders (U.S.A.) won 16 combined events at PRCA World Championships from 1949 to 1959.

HIGHEST EARNINGS IN A RODEO CAREER Ty Murray (U.S.A.) amassed career earnings of $2,931,227 from 1989 to 2002.

★**Most money won by a rookie in a year** Will Lowe (U.S.A.) won $149,690 in 2002 (his debut year) in the bareback competition.

★**Most World Championship wins** Guy Allen (U.S.A.) won 18 championships in steer roping in 1977, 1980, 1982, 1984, 1989, a record 11 consecutively from 1991 to 2001, and 2003–04.

SHOW JUMPING

Highest jump The official Fédération Equestre Internationale (FEI) record for high jump is 8 ft. 1.25 in. (2.47 m) by Huaso ex-Faithful, ridden by Alberto Larraguibel Morales (Chile) at Viña del Mar, Santiago, Chile, on February 5, 1949.

Farthest jump The official FEI record for a long jump over water is 27 ft. 6.7 in. (8.4 m). The feat was achieved on April 25, 1975, by Something, ridden by André Ferreira (South Africa) in Johannesburg, South Africa.

Most World Championship wins Two men have won a total of two titles each—Hans Günter Winkler (Germany), who won in 1954 and 1955, and Raimondo d'Inzeo (Italy), in 1956 and 1960.

The **most show-jumping World Championships won by a woman** is also two. The feat was achieved by Janou Tissot (née Lefebvre, France), who won two titles on Rocket in 1970 and 1974.

LARGEST PRIZE FOR A SINGLE HORSE The Dubai World Cup, held in Dubai, United Arab Emirates, has a total purse of $6 million, $3.6 million of which goes to the race winner. Pictured is jockey Jerry Bailey, riding atop Balletto from the United Arab Emirates.

Most team World Championship wins Three teams each hold two show-jumping World Championship titles: France in 1982 and 1990, Germany in 1994 and 1998, and the U.S.A. in 1986 and 2002.

★ FLAT-RACING RECORDS ★

RACE (FIRST RUN)	FASTEST TIME/HORSE
Epsom Derby (1780)	2 min. 32.3 sec., Lammtarra (1995)
Prix de L'Arc de Triomphe (1920)	2 min. 24.6 sec., Peintre Célèbre (1997)
Dubai World Cup (1996)	1 min. 59.5 sec., Dubai Millennium (2000)
VRC Melbourne Cup (1861)	3 min. 16.3 sec., Kingston Rule (1990)
Kentucky Derby (1875)	1 min. 59.4 sec., Secretariat (1973)

★ **MOST WORLD THREE-DAY EVENTING WINS BY AN INDIVIDUAL** Bruce Davidson (U.S.A.) has won two World Championship titles, on Irish Cap in 1974 and Might Tango in 1978. Blyth Tait (New Zealand, left) matched this record on Messiah in 1990 and Ready Teddy in 1998.

MOST WINS/JOCKEY

9, Lester Piggott (UK), 1954–83

4, Jacques Doyasbère (France), 1942–51
4, Frédéric Head (France), 1966–79
4, Yves Saint Martin (France), 1970–84
4, Pat Eddery (Ireland), 1980–87

4, Jerry Bailey (U.S.A.), 1996–2003

4, Bobby Lewis (Australia), 1902–27
4, Harry White (Australia), 1974–79

5, Eddie Arcaro (U.S.A.), 1938–52
5, Bill Hartack (U.S.A.), 1957–69

MOST WINS/TRAINER

7, Robert Robson (UK), 1793–1823

5, Andre Fabre (France), 1987–98

4, Saeed bin Suroor (UAE), 1999–2003

11, Bart Cummings (Australia), 1965–99

6, Ben Jones (U.S.A.), 1938–52

TRACK & FIELD

CROSS-COUNTRY

Most World Championship individual wins (men) John Ngugi (Kenya) won five World Championships from 1986 to 1989 and in 1992. Paul Tergat (Kenya) also won five times, from 1995 to 1999.

Most World Championship individual wins (women) Grete Waitz (Norway) won five times from 1978 to 1981 and in 1983.

☆ **Most World Championship team wins (men)** Kenya won 18 team victories in the official World Championships from 1986 to 2003.

Most World Championship team wins (women) The USSR won a total of eight women's team victories, in 1976–77, 1980–82, and 1988–90.

HOW YOUNG IS THE YOUNGEST OLYMPIC GOLD MEDALIST? FIND OUT ON P. 514

OLYMPIC GAMES

Most track-and-field medals (men) Paavo Nurmi (Finland) has won a total of 12 medals (nine gold and three silver), which he secured at the Games of 1920, 1924, and 1928.

Most track-and-field medals (women) Merlene Ottey (Jamaica) won eight medals—three silver and five bronze—over the course of the Games in 1980, 1984, 1992, 1996, and 2000.

FARTHEST TRIPLE JUMP (WOMEN) During the International Association of Athletics Federations (IAAF) World Indoor Championships at the Budapest Sportarena in Budapest, Hungary, on March 6, 2004, Tatyana Lebedeva (Russia) won the triple-jump final with a jump that measured 50 ft. 4.5 in. (15.36 m).

★ **MOST COMPETING COUNTRIES AT THE HALF MARATHON WORLD CHAMPIONSHIPS** Athletes from 64 nations attended the 13th International Association of Athletics Federations (IAAF) World Half Marathon Championships in New Delhi, India, on October 3, 2004.

Most track-and-field gold medals won (women) Four athletes have won four golds. Francina "Fanny" Elsje Blankers-Koen (Netherlands) in the 100 m, 200 m, 80 m hurdles, and 4 × 100 m relay in 1948; Elizabeth "Betty" Cuthbert (Australia) in the 100 m, 200 m, and 4 × 100 m relay in 1956 and 400 m in 1964; Bärbel Wöckel (née Eckert, GDR) in the 200 m and 4 × 100 m relay in 1976 and 1980; and Evelyn Ashford (U.S.A.) in the 100 m in 1984 and 4 × 100 m relay in 1984, 1988, and 1992.

FOR A FULL LIST OF TRACK-AND-FIELD RECORDS, SEE P. 560

WORLD ATHLETICS CHAMPIONSHIPS

Most gold medals The World Championships—which are distinct from the Olympic Games—were inaugurated in 1983, when they were held in Helsinki, Finland. The most golds won is nine by Michael Johnson (U.S.A.): the 200 m in 1991 and 1995; the 400 m in 1993, 1995, 1997, and 1999; and the 4 × 400 m relay in 1993, 1995, and 1999.

Gail Devers (U.S.A.) has won the **most gold medals by a woman** with five: the 100 m in 1993, the 100 m hurdles in 1993, 1995, and 1999, and the 4 × 100 m in 1997.

☆ **Most gold medals for individual events** Iván Pedroso (Cuba) has won five gold medals, in the long jump in 1993, 1995, 1997, 1999, and 2001.

The **most individual golds won by a woman** is five by Stefka Kostadinova (Bulgaria) in the high jump of 1985, 1987, 1989, 1993, and 1997, and Maria Mutola (Mozambique) in the 800 m races of 1993, 1995, 1997, 2001, and 2003.

Most medals (men) Carl Lewis (U.S.A.) won 10 medals: eight gold (the 100 m, long jump, and 4 × 100 m relay in 1983; the 100 m, long jump, and 4 × 100 m relay in 1987; the 100 m and 4 × 100 m relay in 1991), one silver (the long jump in 1991), and one bronze (the 200 m in 1993).

Most medals (women) Merlene Ottey (Jamaica) won 14 medals—three gold, four silver, and seven bronze—in the 100 m, 200 m, and 4 × 100 m from 1983 to 1997.

MISCELLANEOUS

★**Oldest road race** The Red Hose Five Mile Race has been held annually in Carnwath, UK, since 1508. It is named after its original prize—a pair of hose, or stockings, traditionally red.

☆**Most participants in a relay race** On April 24, 2004, the Batavieren-race relay race (an annual race from Nijmegen to Enschede, the Netherlands) featured a total of 7,375 runners.

Fastest 100-mile relay (team of 10) On September 21, 2003, 10 cadets from the 2331 (St. Ives) Squadron Air Training Corps (UK) set a time of 10 hr. 21 min. 35 sec. in the 100-mile relay at the St. Ivo Outdoor Centre, Cambridgeshire, UK.

☆**MOST MARATHON COMPETITORS A total of 36,562 out of an initial 37,257 starters in the New York City Marathon, New York, U.S.A., managed to complete the race on November 7, 2004. Pictured is the Verrazano Narrows Bridge at the start of the marathon in Brooklyn. The first race in 1970 had only 55 finishers, who completed just over four laps of Central Park. The race increased in popularity following the decision in 1976 to move the route onto the city's streets.**

HIGHEST ALTITUDE MARATHON The highest start to a marathon is that of the Everest Marathon, first run on November 27, 1987. It begins at Gorak Shep, 17,100 ft. (5,212 m), ending at Namche Bazar, 11,300 ft. (3,444 m). The fastest time to complete this race by a man is 3 hr. 50 min. 23 sec. by Hari Roka (Nepal) in 2000. The record for a woman is 5 hr. 16 min. 3 sec., by Anne Stentiford (UK) in 1997.

Most world records set on one day Jesse Owens (U.S.A.) set six world records in 45 minutes in Ann Arbor, Michigan, U.S.A., on May 25, 1935. In order, by times, they were:
1 3:15 p.m.: 100 yd. in 9.4 seconds
2 3:25 p.m.: 26-ft. 8.25-in. (8.13-m) long jump
3 & 4 3:45 p.m.: 220 yd. (and 200 m) in 20.3 seconds
5 & 6 4:00 p.m.: 220 yd. low hurdles (and 200 m) in 22.6 seconds.

Longest winning sequence in a track event Edwin Corley Moses (U.S.A.) won 122 consecutive races at the 400 m hurdles. The winning sequence began on September 2, 1977, and ended when Moses was beaten by Danny Lee Harris (U.S.A.) at Madrid, Spain, on June 4, 1987.

Most finishers in a 5 km road race A total of 35,957 people finished the 5 km Race for the Cure, held in Washington, D.C., U.S.A., on June 6, 1998. The race is organized by the Susan G. Komen Breast Cancer Foundation.

☆**Longest annual running race** The longest race staged annually is the Sri Chinmoy 3,100-mile (4,989-km) race, which is held in Jamaica, New York, U.S.A. The fastest time to complete the race is 42 days 13 hr. 24 min. 3 sec., a feat achieved by Wolfgang Schwerk (Germany) in 2002.

Longest winning streak in a field event Iolanda Balas (Romania) won 150 consecutive competitions at the high jump from 1956 to 1967.

Oldest woman to set a world record Marina Styepanova (USSR, b. May 1, 1950) was 36 years 139 days old when she set the record of 52.94 seconds for the 400 m hurdles in Tashkent, USSR, on September 17, 1986.

Fastest 10 km run wearing a British pantomime costume (two person) Simon Wiles and Les Morton (both UK) ran the Percy Pud 10 km race in a time of 44 min. 2 sec. in Loxley, Sheffield, South Yorkshire, UK, on December 2, 2001, while wearing a camel costume.

ATHLETICS & ENDURANCE

ENDURANCE

☆ **Greatest lifetime mileage run by a man** Dr. Ron Hill (UK), who is the 1969 European and 1970 Commonwealth marathon champion, has trained every day since December 20, 1964. His training log shows a total of over 145,511 miles (234,177 km) from September 3, 1956, to March 23, 2005. He has competed in 115 marathons, with all but his last sub 2:52, and has raced in 88 nations.

★ **Greatest lifetime mileage run by a woman** Kathy Pycior (U.S.A.) has not missed a day's training since December 31, 1980. She has kept a detailed log of route and distance for every single run from January 1, 1981 to June 30, 2004, and has run a total distance of 48,656.5 miles (78,305 km).

Longest ever running race The 1929 transcontinental race from New York City to Los Angeles, California, U.S.A., was competed over a total of 3,635 miles (5,850 km). Finnish-born Johnny Salo was the winner, in 79 days from March 31 to June 17. In a "two horse" race, his elapsed time of 525 hr. 57 min. 20 sec. (averaging a speed of 6.91 mph, or 11.12 km/h) put him only 2 min. 47 sec. ahead of Pietro "Peter" Gavuzzi (UK).

LONGEST ESTABLISHED MAJOR MARATHON The Boston Marathon (U.S.A.) was first held on April 19, 1897, when it was run over a distance of 39 km (24 miles). John A. Kelley (U.S.A.) finished the Boston Marathon 61 times from 1928 to 1992, winning in 1935 and 1945.

HIGHEST POLE VAULT The highest pole vault by a man is 20 ft. 2 in. (6.15 m) by Sergei Bubka (Ukraine) in Donetsk, Ukraine, on February 21, 1993. Yelena Isinbayeva (Russia, pictured) cleared 16 ft. 0.75 in. (4.9 m) in Madrid, Spain, on March 6, 2005 to take the record for the ★highest indoor pole vault by a woman.

☆ **Most 100 km races in a lifetime** Henri Girault (France) ran 517 races at 100 km—an International Association of Athletics Federations (IAAF) recognized distance—from 1979 to November 6, 2004.

HALF MARATHONS

Fastest (men) The best time on an officially measured course is 59 min. 5 sec. by Paul Tergat (Kenya) in Lisbon, Portugal, on March 26, 2000. The official world's best recognized by the IAAF is 59 min. 17 sec., also by Paul Tergat, in Milan, Italy, on April 4, 1998.

Fastest (women) Masako Chiba (Japan) ran a half marathon in 66 min. 43 sec. in Tokyo, Japan, on January 19, 1997.

Largest The BUPA Great North Run, between Newcastle upon Tyne and South Shields, Tyne and Wear, UK, had 36,822 finishers out of 50,173 entries for the event held on October 22, 2000.

★**Deepest** On March 4, 2004, 11 participants made 8.5 circuits of an 8,000-ft. (2,438-m) running track at a depth of 695 ft. (212 m) in Bochnia salt mine, Poland.

☆ **Most individual wins at the World Championships** Two runners have won three times: Tegla Loroupe (Kenya) in 1997, 1998, and 1999 and Paula Radcliffe (UK) in 2000, 2001, and 2003.

FASTEST TIME TO COMPLETE THE HAWAIIAN IRONMAN (WOMEN) Paula Newby-Fraser (Zimbabwe) completed the Hawaiian Ironman in a time of 8 hr. 55 min. 28 sec. in 1992. She has also achieved the most wins in the Hawaiian Ironman, with a total of eight victories in 1986, 1988–89, 1991–94, and 1996.

☆**Most team medals at the World Championships** Kenya has won eight medals in the men's World Championships, from 1992 to 1995, 1997, 2000, 2002, and 2004.

The **most medals in the women's World Championships** is six, by Romania, from 1993 to 1997 and in 2000.

☆**Most individual medals at the World Championships** Lidia Simon-Slavuteanu (Romania) won eight medals—three team gold, one team silver, one individual silver, and three individual bronze—from 1996 to 2000.

Fastest speed march with 40-lb. pack William Hugh MacLennan (UK) ran a half marathon wearing full military combat gear and carrying a 40-lb. (18-kg) backpack in 1 hr. 43 min. 42 sec. at the Redcar Half Marathon, North Yorkshire, UK, on March 25, 2001.

MARATHONS

Fastest aggregate time to run a marathon on each continent (men) Tim Rogers (UK) ran a marathon on each continent in 34 hr. 23 min. 8 sec. from February 13 to May 23, 1999. He also holds the record for the **shortest duration to complete a marathon on each continent (men):** 99 days, from February 13 to May 23, 1999.

★**Fastest aggregate time to run a marathon on each continent (women)** Amie Dworecki (U.S.A.) completed a marathon on all seven continents in a total time of 32 hr. 24 min. 29 sec. from February 25, 2002, to August 2, 2003. She also holds the record for the **shortest duration to complete a marathon on each continent (women)**—523 days, from February 25, 2002, to August 2, 2003.

☆**Most completed** Horst Preisler (Germany) has run 1,305 races of 26 miles 385 yd. (42.195 km) or longer from 1974 to December 31, 2004.

★**Most northerly** The North Pole Marathon has been held annually since 2002, and the course at the geographic North Pole has been certified by the Association of International Marathons and Road Races (AIMS). The fastest men's time is 3 hr. 43 min. 17 sec. by Sean Burch (U.S.A.); the fastest woman is Stevie Matthews (UK), with a time of 7 hr. 55 min. 32 sec.

Fastest time to complete three marathons in three days Raymond Hubbard (UK) ran three marathons in three days with a total time of 8 hr. 22 min. 31 sec. He ran in Belfast in 2 hr. 45 min. 55 sec., London in 2 hr. 48 min. 45 sec., and Boston in 2 hr. 47 min. 51 sec. from April 16 to 18, 1988.

TRIATHLON

Most wins in the Hawaiian Ironman (men) Dave Scott (U.S.A.) won six races, in 1980, 1982–1984, and 1986–87. He shares this record with Mark Allen (U.S.A.), who has also won six races in 1989–93 and in 1995.

☆**MOST TRIATHLON WORLD CHAMPIONSHIP VICTORIES (MEN)** Simon Lessing (UK) has won the triathlon World Championships a total of four times, in 1992, 1995, 1996, and 1998. In addition to his victories, he has also won the greatest number of medals overall to date in the World Championships, with two silver medals (in 1993 and 1999) and one bronze (in 1997).

Fastest time to complete the Hawaiian Ironman (men) Luc van Lierde (Belgium) set a time of 8 hr. 4 min. 8 sec. in 1996.

BALL SPORTS

AUSTRALIAN FOOTBALL (AFL)

★**Most Brownlow medal wins** A record three wins is shared by Haydn Bunton, in 1931, 1932, and 1935; Dick Reynolds, in 1934, 1937, and 1938; and Ian Stewart, in 1965, 1966, and 1971 (all Australia).

★**Most Premierships won by a player** Michael Tuck (Australia) won seven titles with Hawthorn, from 1972 to 1991.

Most games played Michael Tuck (Australia) played 426 games for Hawthorn from 1972 to 1991.

Most Premiership titles Two teams have amassed 16 AFL Premiership titles: Carlton from 1906 to 1995, and Essendon from 1897 to 2000.

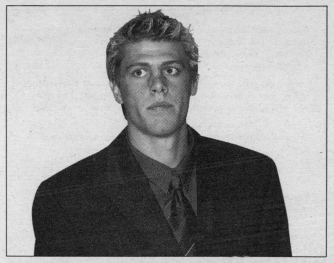

DISCIPLINARY FINES LARGEST FOR A SINGLE AFL MATCH A fine of AUS$67,500 ($49,773) was imposed in an AFL match between the Western Bulldogs and St. Kilda on May 4, 2003. Nine players from each side were fined, but only one player was suspended. The Bulldogs' Ryan Hargrave (above) was banned for three games for kicking St. Kilda's Heath Black (both Australia) in the face during a brawl.

BEACH VOLLEYBALL

☆**Most men's World Championships** The Brazil men's pair has won the title three times, in 1997, 1999, and 2003.

★**Most world tour titles by a pair** Sinjin Smith and Randy Stoklos (both U.S.A.) won four men's titles, in 1989–90 and 1992–93.
   Shelda Bede and Adriana Behar (both Brazil) won six titles, from 1997 to 2001, and, in 2004, the **most women's world tour titles by a pair.**

CANADIAN FOOTBALL (CFL)

★**Highest scoring Grey Cup final** In 1989, the Saskatchewan Roughriders beat the Hamilton Tiger-Cats 43–40, to give an aggregate score of 83.

Longest field goal Paul McCallum (Canada) scored a goal from 62 yards for the Saskatchewan Roughriders v. the Edmonton Eskimos on October 27, 2001.

★ **AFL GRAND FINAL WINS—MOST CONSECUTIVE** From 2001 to 2003, the Brisbane Lions had three consecutive wins. The Lions were formed in the first ever union of two AFL clubs, when the Brisbane Bears merged with the Fitzroy Lions. The new club was formed in 1996, before entering national competition in 1997.

★**Most yards receiving in one game** Hal Patterson (U.S.A.) received passes totaling 338 yards for the Montreal Alouettes v. the Hamilton Tiger-Cats on September 29, 1956.

★**Most touchdowns by a player in one game** Two players have scored six touchdowns: Eddie James (Canada) for Winnipeg St. Johns v. Winnipeg Garrison on September 28, 1932; and Bob McNamara (U.S.A.) for the Winnipeg Blue Bombers v. British Columbia Lions (a.k.a. the B.C. Lions) on October 13, 1956.

FIELD HOCKEY

Most men's champions' trophy wins The greatest number of wins is eight by Germany, in 1986–88 (as West Germany), 1991–92, 1995, 1997, and 2001.

Highest score in an international match (women) England defeated France 23–0 at Merton, Greater London, UK, on February 3, 1923.

☆**Most goals scored in international hockey** Sohail Abbas (Pakistan) scored a total of 274 goals from 1998 to 2004.

Highest attendance at a match A total of 65,165 people attended the match between England and the U.S.A. at Wembley, London, UK, on March 11, 1978.

MOST WOMEN'S FIELD HOCKEY CHAMPIONS' TROPHIES Australia (Wendy Alcorn, pictured far left) has won this trophy a record six times, in 1991, 1993, 1995, 1997, 1999, and 2003. The trophy was first contested in 1987.

GAELIC FOOTBALL

Highest combined score in an All-Ireland final The highest combined score by both teams is 45 points, when Cork (26, 3–17)* beat Galway (19, 2–13) in 1973.

☆**Most All-Ireland final wins** Kerry won 33 All-Ireland Championships from 1903 to 2004.

★**Most consecutive All-Ireland final wins** Wexford had four wins from 1915 to 1918. Kerry equaled the feat twice, from 1929 to 1932, and 1978 and 1981.

---

*Note: In the Gaelic football records, the aggregate score is listed first. The goals and points, respectively, are given separately afterwards.

WHICH BALL SPORT IS CONSIDERED TO BE THE FASTEST IN THE WORLD? FIND OUT ON P. 460

HANDBALL

Highest score in an international match The USSR beat Afghanistan 86–2 in the "Friendly Army Tournament" in Miskolc, Hungary, in August 1981.

MOST MEN'S HANDBALL WORLD CHAMPIONSHIPS Romania has won four times, in 1961, 1964, 1970, and 1974; Sweden matched this achievement with their fourth victory in 1999 to follow wins in 1954, 1958, and 1990. Pictured is the Swedish captain, Stefan Lovgren, celebrating Sweden's victory in 1999.

Target shooting Jonas Källman (Sweden) hit eight handball targets in 30 seconds in Stockholm, Sweden, on November 27, 2001.

HURLING

★**Highest combined score in an All-Ireland final** The greatest aggregate score is 64 points, achieved when Cork beat Wexford 39 (6–21) 25 (5–10) in the 1970 final in Dublin, Ireland.

Highest team score in an All-Ireland final This stands at 41 and was achieved by Tipperary (4–29) when they beat Antrim's score of 18 (3–9) at Croke Park, Dublin, Ireland, in 1989.

★**Lowest combined score in an All-Ireland final** The lowest total is 4, scored when Tipperary 4 (1–1) beat Galway (zero) in the first championship held at Birr, Ireland, in 1887.

☆**Most All-Ireland final victories** Cork has won 29 championships from 1890 to 2004.

Most consecutive All-Ireland final wins Cork had four successive wins from 1941 to 1944, all at Croke Park, Dublin, Ireland.

Note: In the hurling records, the aggregate score is listed first. The goals and points, respectively, are given separately afterwards, in brackets.

HOW FAST WAS THE FASTEST SHUTTLECOCK EVER STRUCK? FIND OUT ON P. 518

KORFBALL

Highest score in a World Championship final The highest team score is 23, by the Netherlands against Belgium (11) in 1999.

★**Largest tournament** On June 14, 2003, 2,571 men and women participated in the Kom Keukens/Ten Donck international youth korfball tournament in Ridderkerk, the Netherlands.

Most victories at the World Championships The Netherlands has won six times, in 1978, 1984, 1987, 1995, 1999, and 2003.

MOST COMMONWEALTH NETBALL TITLES Netball has been contested twice at the Commonwealth Games, first in Kuala Lumpur, Malaysia, in 1998 and then in Manchester, UK, in 2002. Australia won both times. Pictured are Sherelle McMahon (Australia, left) battling Sherly Clarke (New Zealand) in the 2002 final of the Commonwealth Games.

CANADIAN FOOTBALL—MOST GAMES PLAYED Lui Passaglia (Canada) played in 408 CFL games for the British Columbia Lions (a.k.a. the B.C. Lions) from 1976 to 2000. He also scored a CFL career record 3,991 points for the B.C. Lions during that time.

LACROSSE

Longest throw Barnet Quinn of Ottawa, Canada, achieved a throw of 488 ft. 6 in. (148.91 m) on September 10, 1892.

★Most indoor World Championship wins The inaugural indoor lacrosse World Championships held in Ontario, Canada, in 2003 were won by Canada, who beat the Iroquois Nationals 21–4 for the gold medal. The winning team was undefeated in the competition.

NETBALL

Highest team score at a World Championship On July 9, 1991, during the World Championships in Sydney, Australia, the Cook Islands beat Vanuatu 120–38.

FASTEST SPORT The fastest projectile speed in any ball game is 187.6 mph (302 km/h) in jai alai. This compares with 169.6 mph (273 km/h) for an electronically timed golf ball driven off a tee.

Most World Championship wins Australia has won a record eight times, in 1963, 1971, 1975, 1979, 1983, 1991, 1995, and 1999.

Most points scored by one player at a World Championship Irene van Dyk (South Africa) scored 543 goals in the 1995 tournament.

SHINTY

★**Most consecutive Camanachd Cup wins** Kingussie (Scotland) won seven times from 1997 to 2003.

Highest team score in a Camanachd final This record was set in 1997 when Kingussie beat Newtonmore 12–1 in Fort William, Highland, UK.

VOLLEYBALL

★**Most World Championship wins (men)** The USSR has won six titles, in 1949, 1952, 1960, 1962, 1978, and 1982.

☆**Most World Championship wins (women)** The USSR has won five titles, in 1952, 1956, 1960, 1970, and 1990.

★**Most consecutive World Championship wins (men)** Italy has won three times—in Brazil (1990), Greece (1994), and Japan (1998).

★**Most World Cup wins (men)** The USSR has won the volleyball World Cup four times, in 1965, 1977, 1981, and 1991. Russia also won the title in 1999.

★**Most World Cup wins (women)** Cuba had four consecutive victories in the volleyball World Cup, in 1989, 1991, 1995, and 1999.

BEACH VOLLEYBALL—MOST WORLD TITLE WINS (WOMEN) The Brazil women's pair has won the World Championships three times, in 1997, 1999, and 2001. Pictured are Shelda Bede (left) and Adriana Behar (both Brazil) celebrating their victory in a 2004 World Tour semifinal match in Rio de Janeiro, Brazil, in September 2004.

MOST CFL GREY CUPS The Toronto Argonauts have won 15 Grey Cups, in 1914, 1921, 1933, 1937–38, 1945–47, 1950, 1952, 1983, 1991, 1996–97, and 2004. Damon Allen (U.S.A.) is pictured above, holding the Grey Cup after the win in 2004.

★**Beach volleyball: most consecutive passes** The most consecutive passes of a beach volleyball—one touch per person—is 29, on the set of *L'Été de Tous les Records,* Biscarrosse, France, on July 1, 2004.

BASEBALL

World Series—most wins Played annually between the winners of the National League and the American League, the World Series was first staged unofficially in 1903, and officially from 1905. The most wins to date is 26 by the New York Yankees, from 1923 to 2000.

Most consecutive games Cal Ripken Jr. (U.S.A., Baltimore Orioles) played 2,632 consecutive games from May 30, 1982, to September 19, 1998.

Most runs in a Major League season Billy Hamilton (U.S.A., Philadelphia Phillies) scored 192 runs in 1894.

Most runs batted in in a Major League season Hack Wilson (U.S.A., Chicago Cubs) drove in a total of 191 runs in the 1930 season. The **most runs batted in in a Major League career** is 2,297, by Henry "Hank" Aaron (U.S.A.) for the Milwaukee Braves from 1954 to 1976.

★**Most doubles hit in a Major League season** Earl Webb (U.S.A.) hit 67 playing for the Boston Red Sox in 1931.

Most doubles hit in a Major League career Tris Speaker (U.S.A., Boston Red Sox, Cleveland Indians, Washington Senators, and Philadelphia Athletics) hit 792 doubles from 1907 to 1928.

Most triples hit in a Major League season Chief Wilson (U.S.A.) hit 36 triples in a season playing for the Pittsburgh Pirates in 1912.

HISTORY OF BASEBALL

Baseball is descended from the English games of cricket and rounders, although the exact origins of America's national pastime are unclear.

The first set of rules were published for the Knickerbocker Club of New York in 1845 by Alexander Cartwright (U.S.A.), often referred to as "The Father of Modern Baseball."

The professional game began in 1865 in the United States, with the first World Series contested between the National and American Leagues in 1903.

☆ **MOST HITS IN A MAJOR LEAGUE SEASON** Ichiro Suzuki (Japan) had 262 base hits playing for the Seattle Mariners in 2004.

★ **FASTEST TIME TO VISIT ALL MAJOR LEAGUE BASEBALL STADIUMS**
Joe Pfeiffer of Irvine, California, U.S.A., watched a complete baseball game at all 30 Major League stadiums in the U.S.A. and Canada in 30 days, from July 22 to August 20, 2004. He began in San Francisco, California, and finished in Houston, Texas, U.S.A.

★ **Most triples hit in a Major League career** Sam Crawford (U.S.A., Cincinnati Reds and Detroit Tigers) hit 309 triples from 1899 to 1917.

Longest home run hit On September 10, 1960, Mickey Mantle (U.S.A.) hit a home run of 633 ft. (193 m) for the New York Yankees against the Detroit Tigers at Briggs Stadium, Detroit, Michigan, U.S.A.

Most home runs in a season Barry Bonds (U.S.A.) hit 73 home runs playing for the San Francisco Giants in 2001.

Most home runs in a career Hank Aaron (U.S.A.) hit 755 in his career: 733 for the Milwaukee (1954–65) and Atlanta (1966–74) Braves in the National League, and 22 for the Milwaukee Brewers in the American League, 1975–76. On April 8, 1974, he beat the previous record of 714 set by George Herman "Babe" Ruth (U.S.A.) in 1935.

Most runs in a career At the close of the 2003 season, Rickey Henderson (U.S.A.) had scored 2,295 runs.

★ **Highest slugging percentage in a season** A batter's slugging percentage is calculated by dividing the total number of bases gained by the total number of at bats. Barry Bonds (U.S.A.) registered an unprecedented .863 playing for the San Francisco Giants in 2001.

★Highest slugging percentage in Major League history Babe Ruth (U.S.A.) recorded .690 playing for the Boston Red Sox and the New York Yankees from 1914 to 1935.

Highest batting average in a Major League career Tyrus Raymond "Ty" Cobb (U.S.A., Detroit Tigers, Philadelphia Athletics) had a batting average of .367 from 1905 to 1928.

Most base hits in a Major League career Pete Rose (U.S.A., Cincinnati Reds, Philadelphia Phillies, Montreal Expos, Cincinnati) had a total of 4,256 base hits from 1963 to 1986.

Most total bases in a career From 1954 to 1976, Hank Aaron (U.S.A.) achieved the highest number of total bases in a career, with 6,856.

Most innings pitched in a career Denton True "Cy" Young (U.S.A.) pitched a record total of 7,356 innings from 1890 to 1911.

MOST MAJOR LEAGUE GAMES PITCHED By the end of the 2003 season, Jesse Orosco (U.S.A.) had pitched 1,251 games for the New York Mets, L.A. Dodgers, Cleveland Indians, Milwaukee Brewers, Baltimore Orioles, St. Louis Cardinals, Minnesota Twins, New York Yankees, and San Diego Padres.

MOST WINS OF THE MOST VALUABLE PLAYER AWARD Barry Bonds
(U.S.A.) has won more Most Valuable Player (MVP) awards than anyone
else in Major League baseball, with seven. He won in 1990, 1992, 1993,
and 2001–03, winning his seventh award while playing with the San
Francisco Giants in the 2004 season.

Most games won by a pitcher in a career Cy Young (U.S.A.) won
511 games playing for the Cleveland Spiders, St. Louis Perfectos/Cardinals,
Boston Americans/Somersets/Pilgrims/Red Sox, Cleveland Naps and
Boston Braves from 1890 to 1911.

★**Most games lost by a pitcher in a career** Cy Young (U.S.A.) lost
316 games from 1890 to 1911.

★**Most games saved by a pitcher** A save is credited to a relief pitcher
if he is the last pitcher in a game won by his team. Lee Smith (U.S.A.) saved
478 games from 1980 to 1997 playing for the Chicago Cubs, Boston Red
Sox, St. Louis Cardinals, New York Yankees, Baltimore Orioles, California
Angels, Cincinnati Reds, and Montreal Expos.

★**Most batters hit by a pitcher** Gus Weyhing (U.S.A.) hit 277 batters
from 1887 to 1901 while pitching for the Philadelphia Athletics, Brooklyn
Ward's Wonders, Philadelphia Phillies, Louisville Colonels, Pittsburgh
Pirates, Washington Senators, St. Louis Cardinals, Brooklyn Superbas,
Cincinnati Reds, and Cleveland Blues.

★**Most wild pitches** A wild pitch is a ball pitched beyond the area usually covered by the catcher. Tony Mullane (U.S.A.) threw 343 wild pitches playing for the Detroit Wolverines, Louisville Eclipse, St. Louis Browns, Toledo Blue Stockings, Cincinnati Red Stockings/Reds, Baltimore Orioles, and Cleveland Spiders from 1881 to 1894.

HOW MUCH DID THE MOST VALUABLE BASEBALL CARD SELL FOR? FIND OUT ON P. 271

BASKETBALL

Highest point scoring average in an NBA career For players exceeding 10,000 points (the minimum at which an average is calculated), the record for average points per game is 30.1 by Michael Jordan (U.S.A.), who scored 32,292 points in 1,072 games for the Chicago Bulls (1984–98) and the Washington Wizards (2001–03).

Highest scoring average in an NBA season Wilt Chamberlain (U.S.A.) scored an average of 50.4 points a game for the Philadelphia Warriors in the 1961–62 season.

Most rebounds in an NBA career Wilt Chamberlain (U.S.A.) made 23,924 rebounds in 1,045 games playing for the Philadelphia Warriors (1959–62), San Francisco Warriors (1962–64), Philadelphia 76ers (1964 -68), and Los Angeles Lakers (1968–73).

Most blocks in an NBA career Hakeem Olajuwon (U.S.A.) made 3,830 blocks in 1,238 games while playing for the Houston Rockets (1984–2001) and the Toronto Raptors (2001–02).

HISTORY OF BASKETBALL

Basketball was invented in 1891 by Dr. James Naismith (Canada) in Springfield, Massachusetts, U.S.A., in an attempt to provide sports activity for his charges at the local YMCA during the long winter months. Using a soccer ball, he established some basic rules and nailed a peach basket to the wall of the indoor gym.

One of his students then came up with the name "basket ball" and, after the first official game on January 20, 1892, the new sport spread quickly across the U.S.A.

★LONGEST SUSPENSION FOR AN ON-COURT INCIDENT The longest non-drug-related suspension given out by the NBA to an individual player is 72 days to Ron Artest (U.S.A., pictured far left) of the Indiana Pacers following a game with the Detroit Pistons on November 19, 2004. Artest was banned from playing the rest of the 2004–05 season after sparking a mêlée in which Pacers players brawled with Pistons fans.

Most field goals in an NBA season Wilt Chamberlain (U.S.A.)—voted in 1996 as one of the 50 greatest players in NBA history—scored a record 1,597 field goals for the Philadelphia Warriors in the 1961–62 season.

Most assists in an NBA career John Stockton (U.S.A.) has the most assists in an NBA career, with 15,806 in 1,504 games playing for 19 seasons for the Utah Jazz (1984–2003).

Most consecutive NBA games played A. C. Green (U.S.A.) played 1,177 games for the Los Angeles Lakers, Phoenix Suns, Dallas Mavericks, and Miami Heat from November 19, 1986, to March 20, 2001.

Most points scored by a team in an NBA game The Detroit Pistons—the 2003–04 NBA Champions—scored a record 186 points in a game against the Denver Nuggets (who scored an impressive 184) in Denver, Colorado, U.S.A., on December 13, 1983.

Most consecutive NBA wins The Los Angeles Lakers won 33 NBA games in succession from November 5, 1971, to January 7, 1972.

☆**Most free throws in an NBA career** Karl Malone (U.S.A.) made 9,787 free throws in 1,476 games playing for the Utah Jazz from 1985 to 2003 and the Los Angeles Lakers in 2003–04.

Most points in NBA All-Star games Michael Jordan (U.S.A.) scored 262 points in NBA All-Star games, scoring 20 points in his 14th appearance in Atlanta, Georgia, U.S.A., on February 9, 2003.

☆ **MOST THREE-POINTERS IN AN NBA CAREER** Reggie Miller (U.S.A.) scored 2,491 three-point field goals for the Indiana Pacers from 1987 to 2005. He also broke the record for the **most three-pointers in a rookie season** with 61 in 1987–88.

MOST CAREER MINUTES PLAYED IN THE NBA Kareem Abdul-Jabbar (U.S.A.) played for a record 57,446 minutes during the course of his career from 1969 to 1989.

Most points scored by an individual in an NBA game Wilt Chamberlain (U.S.A.) scored 100 points when he played for the Philadelphia Warriors against the New York Knicks on March 2, 1962.

Most games played in an NBA career Robert Parish (U.S.A.) played 1,611 regular season games from 1976 to 1997.

Most NBA championship titles The Boston Celtics have won 16 titles, in 1957, 1959–66, 1968–69, 1974, 1976, 1981, 1984, and 1986.

★Longest field goal made in a women's game Allyson Fasnacht (U.S.A.) scored a field goal measured at 81 ft. 6 in. (24.85 m) for the Glenvar Highlanders against J.J. Kelly at Salem Civic Center, Salem, Virginia, U.S.A., on December 6, 2002.

★Most miniature basketball shots made in one minute Jay Kleicum (U.S.A.) made 139 miniature basketball shots in one minute in Willoughby Hills, Ohio, U.S.A., on July 11, 2004.

★ MOST NBA GAMES WON BY A COACH During the NBA's golden anniversary celebrations in 1996, Lenny Wilkens (U.S.A.) was named one of the 10 greatest coaches in NBA history. To date, he has won a record 1,315 games as an NBA coach. He is also one of only two men to be inducted into the Hall of Fame as both a player and a coach.

★ Farthest distance slam-dunked from a trampoline Jonathon Thibout (France) slam-dunked a basketball from a trampoline placed 19 ft. 2 in. (5.86 m) from the backboard on August 3, 2004.

Longest time to spin a basketball on one finger Zhao Guang (China) spun a regulation basketball on one finger for a total time of 3 hr. 59 min. on January 29, 2003, in Shenyang, China.

☆ Greatest distance to dribble a basketball in 24 hours Tyler Curiel (U.S.A.) dribbled a basketball for a distance of 108.4 miles (174.46 km) in 24 hours at Tulane University, New Orleans, Louisiana, U.S.A., on December 15–16, 2003.

WHAT'S THE FASTEST TIME FOR ONE PERSON TO WATCH COMPLETE GAMES AT ALL THE MAJOR LEAGUE BASEBALL STADIUMS? FIND OUT ON P. 464

COMBAT SPORTS

BOXING

Longest reign by a world heavyweight Joe Louis (U.S.A.) was champion for 11 years 252 days, from June 22, 1937, when he knocked out James Joseph Braddock (U.S.A.), until announcing his retirement on March 1, 1949.

☆ MOST MEN'S TEAM KARATE KUMITE WORLD TITLES Two nations
have won six World Championships (instituted 1970) at the men's
kumite team event: the UK in 1975, 1982, 1984, 1986, 1988, and 1990;
and France in 1972, 1994, 1996, 1998, 2000, and 2004. Karate is
Japanese for "open hand"; kumite means "sparring."
  Pictured is the French team after winning the title at the 17th
Championships on November 19, 2004.

Most knockdowns Vic Toweel (South Africa) knocked down Danny
O'Sullivan (UK) 14 times in 10 rounds in their world bantamweight fight in
Johannesburg, South Africa, on December 2, 1950.

Shortest world title fight Gerald McClellan (U.S.A.) beat Jay Bell
(U.S.A.) in 20 seconds in a World Boxing Council (WBC) middleweight
bout in Puerto Rico on August 7, 1993.

Most world title recaptures The only boxer to win a world title five
times at one weight is "Sugar" Ray Robinson (U.S.A.), who beat Carmen
Basilio (U.S.A.) in the Chicago Stadium on March 25, 1958, to regain the
world middleweight title for the fourth time.

Most rounds Jack Jones defeated Patsy Tunney (both UK) in a boxing
match that lasted 276 rounds in Cheshire in 1825. The fight lasted 4 hr.
30 min.

★**Boxing announcer: most bouts in one week** Hank Kropinski
(U.S.A.) announced 240 bouts during the 1998 U.S. Championships in
Colorado Springs, Colorado, U.S.A., from March 16 to 21, 1998.

JUDO

Most throws in one hour by a pair Dale Moore and Nigel Townsend (both UK) completed 3,786 judo throws in one hour at Esporta Health Club, Chiswick Park, London, UK, on February 23, 2002.

Most throws in 10 hours Csaba Mezei and Zoltán Farkas (both Hungary) of the Szany Judo Sport Team completed 57,603 judo throws in a 10-hour period at the Szany Sports Hall, Szany, Hungary, on May 1, 2003. The pair threw 27 members of their club.

Most women's World Championships Ingrid Berghmans (Belgium) won six women's world titles: the Open in 1980, 1982, 1984, and 1986, and the Under 72 kg in 1984 and 1989.

KARATE

Most competitors at a World Championships A total of 1,157 competitors took part in the ninth staging of the World Championships, in Cairo, Egypt, in 1988.

Most kicks in one minute using one leg Fabian Cuenca Pirroti (Spain) completed 128 karate kicks in one minute, using only one leg, on November 11, 2001, on the set of *El Show de los Records* in Madrid, Spain.

OLDEST WRESTLING COMPETITION The Kirkpinar Wrestling Festival has been held since 1460. The event is currently staged on the Sarayici Peninsula, near Edirne, Turkey.

★**LARGEST MONGOLIAN WRESTLING TOURNAMENT** A total of 2,048 competitors participated in a Mongolian Wrestling tournament that took place in Bayanwula, Xiwuzhumuqinqi, Inner Mongolia, China, from July 28 to August 1, 2004.

Most individual kumite World Championship titles Guusje van Mourik (Netherlands) has won a total of four karate kumite World Championship titles—in the Female Over 60 kg category—in 1982, 1984, 1986, and 1988.

KICKBOXING

Most world titles Don "The Dragon" Wilson (U.S.A.) won 11 world titles in three weight divisions (light-heavyweight, super light-heavyweight, and cruiserweight) and for six sanctioning organizations from 1980 to 1999. The organizations are the World Kickboxing Association (WKA), Standardized Tournaments And Ratings (STAR), Karate International Council of Kickboxing (KICK), International Sport Karate Association (ISKA), Professional Kickboxing Organization (PKO), and International Kickboxing Federation (IKF).

WRESTLING

★**Largest attendance** A total of 190,000 people attended the Pyongyang Stadium, Pyongyang, North Korea, for the International Sports and Cultural Festival for Peace on April 29, 1995.

Largest sumo wrestler (*yokozuna*) In January 1993, Chad Rowan (Hawaii), alias Akebono, became the first foreign *rikishi* (sumo wrestler) to be promoted to the top rank of *yokozuna*. He is also the **tallest *yokozuna*—**

at 6 ft. 8 in. (204 cm)—and **heaviest** *yokozuna*—at 501 lb. (227 kg)—in sumo history.

Most consecutive wins at sumo wrestling *(yokozuna)* The *yokozuna* Sadaji Akiyoshi (Japan), alias Futabayama, had 69 consecutive wins, 1937–39.

MISCELLANEOUS

★**Most plates broken in one minute by nunchaku** Thierry Guyon (France) broke 51 clay sporting targets in one minute using nunchaku (Japanese martial arts weapons made from two hardwood sticks linked by a chain or strap) on the set of *L'Été de Tous les Records* in Bénodet, France, on August 2, 2004.

★**Most speedball hits in one minute** Michael Benham (Australia) registered 373 hits in one minute at Melbourne's Crown Casino, Australia, on May 7, 2001.

★**Most full-contact kicks in one hour** Suzanne Nobles (U.S.A.) performed 2,180 full-contact kicks in one hour in Deep Creek Baptist Church Gymnasium, Chesapeake, Virginia, U.S.A., on May 22, 2004.

☆**GREATEST COMBINED WEIGHT FOR A WORLD TITLE FIGHT On December 11, 2004, at the Mandalay Bay Resort, Las Vegas, Nevada, U.S.A., defending champion Vitali Klitschko (Ukraine, above right) met Danny Williams (UK, above left) for the World Boxing Council heavyweight title. The combined weight of both fighters was 520 lb. (235.8 kg), with Klitschko weighing in at 250 lb. (113.3 kg) and Williams at 270 lb. (122.4 kg). Klitschko retained his title, knocking out Williams in the eighth round.**

CRICKET

BATTING

Highest batting average in Test Cricket After playing for Australia in 52 Tests from 1928 to 1948, Sir Don Bradman finished his career with a batting average of 99.94 (6,996 runs in 80 innings).

Most ducks in Test cricket The player who has the dubious honor of scoring the most ducks in Test cricket is Courtney Walsh (Jamaica) with 43 in 185 innings for the West Indies, from November 1984 to April 2001.

Most runs in Test cricket Allan Border (Australia) scored 11,174 runs in 156 Tests (averaging 50.56) from 1978 to 1994.

☆ **MOST CENTURIES IN A CAREER (ONE-DAY INTERNATIONALS)** Sachin Tendulkar (India) has scored 37 centuries, having played 342 matches from 1989 to 2005.

★**MOST TEST MATCHES UMPIRED BY AN INDIVIDUAL** Steve Bucknor (Jamaica) umpired 102 Test matches from 1989 to 2005.

☆**Most runs in a career (one-day internationals)** Sachin Tendulkar (India) scored 13,497 runs in 342 one-day international matches (at an average of 44.84) from 1989 to 2005.

Most runs by an individual in a Test match Graham Gooch (UK) scored 456 runs in the 1st Test against India at Lords, Middlesex, UK, from July 26 to 31, 1990. Gooch, who was England captain at the time, scored 333 in the first innings and 123 in the second.

★**Most runs off a Test match over** Brian Lara (Trinidad and Tobago) scored 28 off one over playing for the West Indies against South Africa, at the Wanderers, Johannesburg, South Africa, on December 14, 2003. The runs were taken off the bowling of Robin Peterson (South Africa), and the scoring sequence ball by ball was 466444. Lara scored 202 in his innings.

Highest cricket innings score Brian Lara scored 501 not out in 7 hr. 54 min. for Warwickshire v. Durham in Edgbaston on June 3 and 6, 1994. His innings included the **most runs in a day** (390 on June 6) and the **most runs from strokes worth four or more** (308, 62 fours and 10 sixes).

★**Highest partnership in cricket (one-day internationals)** Indian captain Sachin Tendulkar (186*) and Rahul Dravid (153) scored 331 runs

★HIGHEST INNINGS IN A LIMITED-OVERS MATCH (TEAM) Surrey scored 438 in a limited 50-over Cheltenham and Gloucester Trophy match against Glamorgan at The Oval, London, UK, on June 19, 2002. Pictured is Surrey batsman Alistair Brown (UK), whose score of 268, shown on the scoreboard, is the **highest innings by an individual in a limited-overs match.**

against New Zealand in Hyderabad, India, on November 8, 1999, with both batsmen making their highest scores in limited-overs internationals.

Highest partnership in Test cricket Sanath Jayasuriya (340) and Roshan Mahanama (225) put on a stand of 576 for the second wicket for Sri Lanka v. India in Colombo on August 4–6, 1997.

CRICKET TERMINOLOGY

* indicates a "not out" score

bye: a run scored other than by using the bat

duck: a score of zero by a batsman

leg-bye: a run scored off the batsman's body

no-ball: a ball that has been bowled illegally. It must be bowled again; 1 run is added to the batting team's score

wide: a ball that is bowled too far away from the batsman for him to strike it. It must be bowled again; 1 run is added to the batting team's score

---

Sports & Games

☆**Most centuries in Test cricket** Two Indian batsmen have scored 34 Test match centuries: Sunil Gavaskar from 1971 to 1987, and Sachin Tendulkar from 1989 to 2005.

☆**Highest Test innings** Brian Lara (Trinidad and Tobago) scored 400* for West Indies v. England at the Antigua Recreation Ground, St. John, Antigua, from April 10 to 12, 2004. The innings included four sixes and 43 fours in a team total of 751–5.

WHO HAS SCORED THE MOST GOALS IN INTERNATIONAL SOCCER—A MAN OR A WOMAN? FIND OUT ON P. 486

BOWLING

Fastest ball bowled The highest electronically measured speed for a ball bowled by any bowler is 100.23 mph (161.3 km/h) by Shoaib Akhtar (Pakistan) against England on February 22, 2003, in a World Cup match at Newlands, Cape Town, South Africa. The World Cup communications director has stated: "ICC has always said there is not enough uniformity in the various speed guns around the world for any one performance to be designated official." Many believe this to have been the fastest ball bowled, though.

Most wickets in a career (one-day internationals) Wasim Akram (Pakistan) took 502 wickets (at an average of 23.52) in 356 matches, from 1984 to 2003.

WICKETKEEPING

Most catches by a wicketkeeper in Test cricket Ian Healy (Australia) took 366 catches in 119 Tests, playing for Australia from 1988 to 1999.

Most dismissals by a wicketkeeper in Test cricket Ian Healy made 395 dismissals in 119 Tests—366 caught and 29 stumped—playing for Australia from 1988 to 1999.

Most stumpings by a wicketkeeper in Test cricket William Oldfield (Australia) claimed 52 stumpings in 54 Tests from 1920 to 1937.

TEAMS

Highest cricket Test score Sri Lanka scored 952–6 against India in Colombo on August 4–6, 1997. England scored 903–7 declared in 15 hr. 17 min. against Australia at The Oval, London on August 20, 22, and 23, 1938.

Lowest innings total in Test cricket New Zealand scored 26 against England in Auckland on March 28, 1955.

Most World Cup victories Australia won in 1987, 1999, and 2003. The cricket World Cup competition began in 1975, and is held every four years.

MISCELLANEOUS

★**Most durable cricket scorer** Mike Garwood (UK, b. February 24, 1928) has been keeping score regularly for Old Minchendenians Cricket Club, Southgate, UK, for 50 years.

★**Most matches played in a career (one-day internationals)** Wasim Akram (Pakistan) played 356 one-day international matches from 1984 to 2003.

Most extras in a one-day international Two teams have conceded 59 extras in a one-day international: West Indies (8 byes, 10 leg-byes, 4 no-balls, and 37 wides) v. Pakistan in Brisbane, Australia, on January 7, 1989; and Scotland (5 byes, 6 leg-byes, 15 no-balls, and 33 wides) v. Pakistan in Chester-le-Street, Durham, UK, on May 20, 1999.

The **most extras conceded in a Test match** is 71 by West Indies in Pakistan's first innings in Georgetown, Guyana, on April 3–4, 1988 (21 byes, 8 leg-byes, 4 wides, and 38 no-balls).

☆**MOST TEST MATCH WICKETS Shane Warne (Australia) is the leading Test match wicket-taker, with 583 (at an average of 25.51 runs a wicket) in 123 matches, from August 1992 to March 2005.**

BICYCLING

TOUR DE FRANCE

Most stage wins Eddy Merckx (Belgium) won 34 stages from 1969 to 1978.

Closest race The closest Tour de France race was in 1989, when after 2,030 miles (3,267 km) over 23 days (July 1–23), Greg LeMond (U.S.A.)—who completed the Tour in 87 hr. 38 min. 35 sec.—beat Laurent Fignon (France) in Paris by only 8 seconds.

Youngest winner Henri Cornet (France) was 19 years 350 days when he won in 1904. He actually finished fifth, but was awarded victory after the first four riders—Maurice Garin, Lucien Pothier, César Garin, and Hippolyte Aucouturier (all France)—were disqualified.

Oldest winner Firmin Lambot (Belgium) was 36 years 4 months when he won the Tour de France in 1922.

★MOST WINS—KING OF THE MOUNTAINS The "best climber" in the Tour de France is awarded a polka-dot jersey and the title King of the Mountains. Richard Virenque (France) has won the polka-dot jersey seven times from 1994 to 2004.

Fastest average speed During the 1999 Tour, Lance Armstrong (U.S.A.) bicycled at an average speed of 25.026 mph (40.276 km/h). The **fastest average speed in a single stage** was 31.29 mph (50.355 km/h) by Mario Cipollini (Italy) on July 7, 1999 (during stage 4).

Largest attendance for a sporting event An estimated 10 million people gather over a period of three weeks to watch the annual Tour de France race.

Biggest winning margin The greatest gap between winner and runner-up at the finish of a Tour de France is 28 min. 27 sec., between Fausto Coppi (Italy) and Stan Ockers (Belgium) in 1952.

HOW FAST WAS THE FASTEST BICYCLE WHEELIE? FIND OUT ON P. 389

GREAT DISTANCES

★**Fastest time to bicycle the length of South America** Giampietro Marion (Italy) bicycled the South American portion of the Pan-American Highway, starting in Chigorodo, Colombia, and finishing in Ushuaia, Argentina, in a time of 59 days from September 17 to November 15, 2000.

Greatest distance cycled in 24 hours The 24-hour record behind pace is 1,216.8 miles (1,958.196 km) by Michael Secrest (U.S.A.) at Phoenix International Raceway, Arizona, U.S.A., on April 26–27, 1990. Solo and unpaced, he achieved a distance of 532.74 miles (857.36 km) at the Olympic Velodrome, California State University, Carson, U.S.A., on October 23–24, 1997.

★ ABSOLUTE TRACK BICYCLING WORLD RECORDS ★

MEN	TIME/DISTANCE	NAME & NATIONALITY
200 m	9.865	Curt Harnett (Canada)
500 m	25.850	Arnaud Duble (France)
1 km	58.875	Arnaud Tournant (France)
4 km	4:11.114	Chris Boardman (UK)
Team 4 km	3:56.610	Australia (Graeme Brown, Brett Lancaster, Bradley McGee, Luke Roberts, pictured right)
1 hour	49 km 441 m	Chris Boardman (UK)

WOMEN	TIME/DISTANCE	NAME & NATIONALITY
200 m	10.831	Olga Slioussareva (Russia)
500 m	29.655	Erika Saloumiaee (USSR)
3 km	3:24.357	Sarah Ulmer (New Zealand)
1 hour	48 km 159 m	Jeannie Longo-Ciprelli (France)

Greatest distance (backward) in one hour Markus Riese (Germany) bicycled 18 miles (29.1 km) backward in one hour at the VC Darmstadt 1899 eV cycling club, Darmstadt, Germany, on May 24, 2003.

MOUNTAIN BIKING

★**Most cross-country World Cups (men)** Thomas Frischknecht (Switzerland) won three cross-country World Cup titles, in 1992–93 and 1995.

★**Most cross-country World Cups (women)** Juli Furtado (U.S.A.) won three cross-country mountain-bike World Cup titles from 1993 to 1995, equaled by Alison Sydor (Canada) between 1996 and 1999.

☆**Most downhill world titles (women)** Anne-Caroline Chausson (France) won 11 World Championships—three in the junior championship from 1993 to 1995, and eight in the senior class from 1996 to 2003.

★**Most downhill World Cups (men)** Nicolas Vouilloz (France) won five downhill World Cup titles, in 1995–96 and 1998–2000.

★**Most World Cup titles by a woman** Anne-Caroline Chausson (France) won five titles from 1998 to 2002.

PLACE	DATE
Bogota, Colombia	September 28, 1995
La Paz, Bolivia	October 10, 2001
La Paz, Bolivia	October 10, 2001
Manchester, UK	August 29, 1996
Athens, Greece	August 22, 2004
Manchester, UK	August 27, 1996

PLACE	DATE
Moscow, Russia	April 25, 1993
Moscow, USSR	August 6, 1987
Athens, Greece	August 22, 2004
Mexico City, Mexico	October 26, 1996

MISCELLANEOUS

★ **Most cyclo-cross world titles (women)** Two women have won the World Championships twice: Hanka Kupfernagel (Germany) in 2000 and 2001, and Laurence Leboucher (France) in 2002 and 2004.

★ **Most vertical feet in 24 hours** Alessandro Forni (Italy) bicycled 57,782 vertical ft. (17,612 m) on October 19–20, 2002 in Trento, Italy. The height—nearly twice the height of Mt. Everest—was gained by completing

LANCE ARMSTRONG

Between 1994 and 2005, Lance Armstrong (U.S.A.) won the Tour de France a record seven times. In October 1996, he was diagnosed with testicular cancer and given less than 50% chance of survival. Against all the odds, he returned to claim the yellow jersey on his first Tour out of recovery.

Who inspired you most when you were growing up? Easy answer—my mom! If I had to name the bicyclists I most admire, I'd have to say Eddy Merckx...my idol and the greatest bicyclist of all time.

When you began your bicycling career, did you think it would be so successful? I knew I'd be successful, but never to the level that I'm fortunate to be at now.

Did you always want to be a professional bicyclist? I started off in triathlons but switched to bicycling as a teenager.

What's been your greatest achievement in bicycling? Without a doubt, winning the Tour de France seven times. It's my favorite race.

How do you motivate yourself each season after the amazing successes you've had? I look at each season as a new one. Whatever's happened in the previous years doesn't matter when the new season starts.

What advice would you give to young sportsmen and women? Just never take anything for granted!

MOST MEN'S TRIALS WORLD CHAMPIONSHIPS Two riders have won a record two elite trials bicycling World Championships: Marco Hösel (Germany) in 1999 and 2002, and Benito Ros Charral (Spain, pictured) in 2003 and 2004.

23 laps of a 14.16-mile (22.8-km) circuit with a 2,528-ft. (770.5-m) difference between its lowest and highest points.

★**Longest static bicycling marathon** The Netherlands' Niels Rietveld and Edwin Snijders continuously and simultaneously bicycled for 77 hr. 15 min. at Sportstudio Buiten, Almere, the Netherlands, from April 30 to May 3, 2004.

☆**Most gyrator spins in one minute—BMX** Sam Foakes (UK) executed 33 spins in one minute at the offices of Guinness World Records in London, UK, on July 20, 2004.

SOCCER

GOALS & GAMES

Most international appearances Kristine Lilly (U.S.A.) made 270 international appearances from 1987 to 2004.

The **most international appearances by a man** is 171 by Claudio Suarez (Mexico), from 1992 to 2003.

Highest score in an international soccer match Australia won 31–0 against American Samoa in a World Cup qualifying match at Coffs Harbour, New South Wales, Australia, on April 11, 2001.

The **highest score in an international women's soccer match** is 21–0 and has occurred on four occasions: Japan v. Guam at Guangzhou, China, on December 5, 1997; Canada v. Puerto Rico at Centennial Park, Toronto, Canada, on August 28, 1998; and Australia v. American Samoa and New Zealand against Samoa, both at Mt. Smart Stadium, Auckland, New Zealand, on October 9, 1998.

MOST INTERNATIONAL GOALS SCORED BY A WOMAN Mia Hamm (U.S.A.) has scored 144 international match goals. Widely regarded as the best female soccer player ever, her senior international career began in 1987 aged just 15 years old. In 2001, she was voted FIFA World Footballer of the Year and currently plays for the Washington Freedom in WUSA, the U.S. women's professional league.

★ **MOST INTERNATIONAL GOALS SCORED BY A MAN** The most international match goals scored by a man is 103 by Ali Daei (Iran, pictured right) from 1993 to 2005.

INTERNATIONAL TOURNAMENTS

Most European Championship wins Germany has won the European Championships three times, in 1972, 1980, and 1996 (the first two as West Germany). A women's version was first held in 1984 and the **most wins in women's soccer** is four, also by Germany (1989, 1991, 1995, and 1997).

Most Africa Cup of Nations wins The most wins is four by Ghana (1963, 1965, 1978, and 1982), Egypt (1957, 1959, 1986, and 1998), and Cameroon (1984, 1988, 2000, and 2002).

Most South American championship wins Argentina has won the South American Championship (Copa America since 1975) a record 15 times from 1910 to 1993.

"FOOTBALL" V. "SOCCER"

The world's first governing body for "football" was founded in 1863 with the formation of the Football Association in England after the split between rugby football and association football. The international organization *Fédération Internationale de Football Association* (FIFA) was established in 1904 with seven founding members: France, Belgium, Denmark, the Netherlands, Spain, Sweden, and Switzerland.

The name "soccer," as the sport is known in some parts of the world, derives from the shortening of "association" to "assoc" and then "soccer."

☆**MOST ASIAN CUP WINS** The most wins in the Asian Cup is three by Iran (1968, 1972, and 1976), Saudi Arabia (1984, 1988, and 1996), and Japan (1992, 2000, and 2004, pictured).

Fastest international hat trick Japanese international Masashi "Gon" Nakayama scored a hat trick in 3 min. 15 sec. against Brunei during an Asian Cup qualifying match played on February 16, 2000. Nakayama netted on 1 min., 2 min., and 3 min. 15 sec., bettering the 62-year-old mark set by England's George William Hall, who scored three in 3 min. 30 sec. against Ireland at Old Trafford, Manchester, UK, on November 16, 1938.

★ **BALL CONTROL** ★

RECORD	DURATION/ TOUCHES	HOLDER
Feet, legs, head (male)	19 hr. 30 sec.	Martinho Eduardo Orige (Brazil)
Feet, legs, head (female)	7 hr. 5 min. 25 sec.	Cláudia Martini (Brazil)
Head	8 hr. 12 min. 25 sec.	Goderdzi Makharadze (Georgia)
Head, seated	3 hr. 59 min.	Andrzej Kukla (Poland)
Chest	30.29 sec.	Amadou Gueye (France)
☆ Lying down	8 min. 27 sec.	Tomas Lundman (Sweden)
☆ Spinning, forehead	12.9 sec.	Tommy Baker (UK)
Fastest marathon distance	7 hr. 18 min. 55 sec.	Jan Skorkovsky (Czech Republic)
Most touches 1 min. (male)	266	Ferdie Adoboe (U.S.A.)
Most touches 1 min. (female)	269	Tasha-Nicole Terani (U.S.A.)
Most touches 30 sec. (male)	141	Ferdie Adoboe (U.S.A.)
Most touches 30 sec. (female)	137	Tasha-Nicole Terani (U.S.A.)
Most people, simultaneous	446	FA Centres of Excellence Festival

WORLD CUPS

★**Most penalty shootout saves** Two goalkeepers have saved four penalties in World Cup finals match penalty shootouts: Harald Schumacher playing for West Germany in 1982 and 1986, and Sergio Goycochea playing for Argentina in 1990.

Largest soccer match attendance A record 199,854 people attended the Brazil v. Uruguay World Cup match in the Maracanã Municipal Stadium, Rio de Janeiro, Brazil, on July 16, 1950.

Most goals in a World Cup finals Just Fontaine (France) scored a record 13 goals during the 1958 World Cup finals in Sweden.

★**Most goals scored by an individual in a game** Oleg Salenko (Russia) scored five goals playing for Russia against Cameroon in a 1994 finals match at Stanford Stadium, San Francisco, U.S.A., on June 28, 1994.

★**Longest World Cup finals clean sheet** The longest time played in World Cup finals matches by a goalkeeper without conceding a goal is 518 minutes by Walter Zenga playing for Italy in the 1990 tournament staged in Italy.

Most goals scored in an international match by an individual During Australia's record-breaking 31–0 defeat of American Samoa in a World Cup qualifying match at Coffs Harbour, New South Wales, Australia, on April 11, 2001, Archie Thompson (Australia) scored an international record 13 goals.

PLACE	DATE
Ararangua, Brazil	August 2–3, 2003
Caxias do Sul, Brazil	July 12, 1996
Tbilisi, Georgia	May 26, 1996
Biala Podlaska, Poland	March 20, 1998
Paris, France	September 7, 2001
Bankery, Sweden	October 31, 2004
Newcastle, UK	December 4, 2004
Prague, Czech Republic	July 8, 1990
Blaine, Minnesota, U.S.A.	July 19, 2000
Atlanta, Georgia, U.S.A.	September 4, 2003
New York City, U.S.A.	August 27, 2003
New York City, U.S.A.	August 27, 2003
Warwick, UK	June 19, 1999

★ **MOST WORLD CUP FINALS APPEARANCES BY A TEAM** Brazil appeared in a record 17 World Cup finals tournaments from 1930 to 2002. Pictured above is the 1958 team lining up for the national anthems on June 29, 1958, before the final where Brazil defeated Sweden, attaining their first title.

EUROPEAN

Most European Cup wins The European Champions Cup has been won nine times by Real Madrid (Spain) in 1955–56, 1956–57, 1957–58, 1958–59, 1959–60, 1965–66, 1997–98, 1999–2000, and 2002–03.

Most consecutive Champions League match victories The longest winning streak in UEFA Champions League matches is 11 games by FC

MOST GOALS IN THE ENGLISH PREMIERSHIP The most goals scored in the English Premiership is 250 by Alan Shearer (UK). Shearer began his career with Southampton before moving to Blackburn Rovers and finally to Newcastle United in July 1996 for a record fee (at that time) of £15.6 million ($22.4 million). Shearer continues to play for Newcastle United and is still scoring goals.

★ **HIGHEST AGGREGATE SCORE IN A CHAMPIONS LEAGUE MATCH**
The most goals scored by both teams is 11, when French team Monaco beat Deportivo La Coruña of Spain 8–3 at the Stade Louis II, Monaco, France, on November 5, 2003. Pictured are Monaco forward Dado Prso (Croatia, right) and Deportivo La Coruña defender Jorge Andrade (Portugal).

Barcelona in the 2002–03 season. The Catalan team posted a perfect record from the start of the competition before registering a goalless draw with Inter Milan (Italy).

Fastest Champions League goal Gilberto Silva (Brazil) scored in 20.07 seconds playing for Arsenal against PSV Eindhoven in Eindhoven, the Netherlands, on September 25, 2002. Arsenal went on to win the game 4–0.

WHO IS THE HIGHEST PAID NFL PLAYER? FIND OUT ON P. 434

OTHER COMPETITIONS

★ Longest Premiership clean sheet The longest time played by a Premiership goalkeeper without conceding a goal is 781 minutes by Peter Cech (Czech Republic) playing for Chelsea FC (UK) from November 27, 2004, to February 2, 2005.

Most domestic league titles won Rangers FC (UK) won 50 titles in the Scottish Division 1 and Premier Division Championships from 1891 to 2003.

☆ Most FA Cup wins The greatest number of wins is 11 by Manchester United (UK) in 1909, 1948, 1963, 1977, 1983, 1985, 1990, 1994, 1996, 1999, and 2004.

★ Longest FA Cup playoff The FA Cup playoff between Alvechurch and Oxford City (both UK) in November 1971 lasted for six games and 11 hours. The match results sequence was 2–2, 1–1, 1–1, 0–0, 0–0, with Alvechurch finally winning 1–0.

Highest score in a National Cup Final In 1935, Lausanne-Sports beat Nordstern Basel 10–0 in the Swiss Cup Final. Two years later, they suffered defeat by the same score at the hands of Grasshopper-Club (Zurich) in the 1937 Swiss Cup Final.

★ Longest running charity game The Football Association Charity Shield was inaugurated in 1908 and has been played annually since 1924 at Wembley Stadium, London, UK, and more recently the Millennium Stadium in Cardiff, Wales.

MISCELLANEOUS

★ Longest serving soccer club manager Roly Howard (UK) of Marine Football Club managed his first game on August 12, 1972, and continued to 2004–05, his 33rd and final season.

Most expensive soccer player The highest transfer fee for a player is 13 billion Spanish pesetas ($66 million) for Zinédine Zidane (France) for his transfer from Juventus to Real Madrid on July 9, 2001.

Fastest time to visit all Soccer League grounds Ken Ferris (UK) watched a League match at all 92 League grounds in England and Wales (including Berwick Rangers) in just 237 days, from September 10, 1994, to May 6, 1995. He began at Carlisle Utd. and finished at Everton.

Most soccer management rejection letters Richard Dixon (UK) applied for—and received rejection letters for—29 jobs as a soccer manager.

★LONGEST UNBEATEN PREMIERSHIP RUN The most games unbeaten in the English Premier League is 49 by Arsenal from May 7, 2003, to October 16, 2004. This total includes the last two games of the 2002–03 season, 38 games unbeaten for the whole 2003–04 season, and the first nine games of the 2004–05 season.

This also means that Arsenal has the record for the **★longest unbeaten run in top-division English soccer.**

Richard applies only for jobs that are available and has received official letters from clubs such as Tottenham Hotspur, Manchester United, Atlético de Madrid, and the English and Cypriot national sides. The hobby began in 2000 when physical education teacher Dixon contracted infectious mononucleosis and applied for the Millwall job.

★Longest tour From July 3 to August 3, 2004, Lenton Griffins Football Club (UK) visited a total of 12 countries. The team played games in Wales, Belgium, Luxembourg, Germany, Austria, Liechtenstein, Switzerland, Italy, France, Andorra, Spain, and Morocco. There were also inadmissable games played in England and Ireland.

★Youngest hat trick scorer in women's soccer Amy Wilding (UK) was 15 years 220 days old when she scored three goals for Camberley Town Ladies against CTC Ladies in Croydon, Surrey, UK, on March 30, 2003.

Fastest goal Goals scored in 3 seconds and less after the kickoff have been claimed by a number of players. From video evidence, Ricardo Olivera (Uruguay) scored in 2.8 seconds for Rio Negro against Soriano at the José Enrique Rodó stadium, Soriano, Uruguay, on December 26, 1998..

☆ **MOST MAJOR LEAGUE CHAMPIONSHIP WINS** The most Major League soccer titles won by a team is four by D.C. United (U.S.A.) in 1996, 1997, 1999, and 2004. Pictured is star player Freddy Adu (U.S.A., middle).

GOLF

Most World Cup team wins The World Cup (instituted as the Canada Cup in 1953) has been won by the U.S.A. 23 times from 1955 to 2000.

Most U.S. Open titles Four U.S. golfers have won the U.S. Open four times: Willie Anderson (1901, 1903–05); Bobby Jones Jr. (1923, 1926, 1929, and 1930); Ben Hogan (1948, 1950, 1951, and 1953); and Jack Nicklaus (1962, 1967, 1972, and 1980).

Most British Open titles Harry Vardon (UK) won six British Open titles (1896, 1898, 1899, 1903, 1911, and 1914).

Most U.S. Masters wins Jack Nicklaus (U.S.A.) won the Masters title six times (1963, 1965, 1966, 1972, 1975, and 1986).

In 1973, Nicklaus became the **first player ever to have career earnings of $2 million,** and in 1986 he became the **oldest player to win the Masters,** aged 46.

★ **Most World Match play championships won by an individual** Ernie Els (South Africa) won six championships (1994–96 and 2002–04).

Most Solheim Cup wins by a team The female equivalent of the Ryder Cup is contested every two years between the top professional players of Europe and the U.S.A. The U.S.A. has won five times (1990, 1994, 1996, 1998, and 2002), with Europe winning in 1992, 2000, and 2003.

Most individual Curtis Cup ties and wins Carole Semple-Thompson (U.S.A.) has played in 12 ties and won 18 matches from 1974 to 2002.

Highest career earnings on U.S. PGA tour The all-time top career earner on the U.S. PGA circuit is Tiger Woods (U.S.A.) who won $46,356,737 from August 1996 to January 2005.

★Biggest margin of victory in a major golf tournament Tiger Woods (U.S.A.) won the 2000 U.S. Open by 15 strokes. He finished with a

★MOST ROUNDS OF GOLF PLAYED IN DIFFERENT COUNTRIES IN ONE DAY Eric Kirchner and Patrick Herresthal (both Germany) played six rounds of golf in six different countries on June 19, 2004. The pair played a full 18-hole round at the following courses: Golfpark Riefensberg (Austria), Golfclub Waldkirch (Switzerland), Golf de Soufflenheim (France), Five Nations Golfclub (Belgium), Golf de Clervaux (Luxembourg), and the Golfclub Heddesshiem (Germany).

★ **LARGEST GOLF FACILITY** Mission Hills Golf Club, China, has had 10 fully operational 18-hole courses since April 2004. In addition, the extensive facilities can accommodate up to 3,000 guests.

round of 67 to add to rounds of 65, 69, and 71 for a 12-under-par total of 272.

Lowest score over 18 holes (women) Annika Sorenstam (Sweden) scored 59 in the 2001 Standard Register PING at Moon Valley Country Club, Phoenix, Arizona, U.S.A., on March 16, 2001.

RYDER CUP—MOST WINS BY A TEAM The biennial Ryder Cup professional match between the U.S.A. and Europe was instituted in 1927. The U.S.A. has won 24 to 9 (with 2 draws) to 2004. Pictured is U.S. Ryder Cup team captain Ben Crenshaw accepting the trophy on September 26, 1999, in Brookline, Massachusetts, U.S.A.

Lowest below-age score At the age of 89, James D. Morton (U.S.A.) hit a 72 at Valleybrook Golf and Country Club, Hixson, Tennessee, U.S.A., on April 21, 2001, setting the lowest score below a player's age at 17.

★Fastest round by a four-ball A four-ball consisting of Kenny Crawford, Colin Gerard, John Henderson, and Joe McParland (all UK) completed 18 holes in 1 hr. 32 min. 48 sec. on the Torrance Course at St. Andrews Bay Golf Resort & Spa, St. Andrews, Fife, UK, on June 12, 2004.

Most participants in a lesson A total of 478 people were taught by Andrew Carnall (UK), a PGA-qualified golf professional, at Chesterfield, Derbyshire, UK, on September 26, 2003.

Fastest round of golf by a team The WBAP News/Talk 820 team of golfers completed 18 holes in 8 min. 47 sec. at Bridlewood Golf Club, Flower Mound, Texas, U.S.A., on August 12, 2003.

Most consecutive holes in one There are at least 20 cases of people achieving two aces consecutively, but the greatest was Norman L. Manley's unique double albatross on the par-4 330-yd. (301-m) seventh and par-4 290-yd. (265-m) eighth holes on the Del Valle Country Club course, Saugus, California, U.S.A., on September 2, 1964. The first woman to achieve this feat was Sue Prell (Australia) on the 13th and 14th holes at Chatswood GC, Sydney, Australia, on May 29, 1977.

★Greatest distance between two rounds of golf played on the same day John Knobel (Australia) played two full 18-hole rounds—the first at The Coast Golf Club, Sydney, Australia, and the second 9,223 miles (14,843 km) away at White Pines Golf Club, Bensenville, Illinois, U.S.A., on September 15, 2004.

GOLF TERMINOLOGY

albatross: three strokes under par for a specific hole. Also called a double eagle

handicap: the number of strokes given to a player to enable him or her to complete a round on scratch

hole in one: a ball that is holed directly from the tee in one shot. Also called an "ace"

par: the number of strokes it should take a golfer with a low handicap to complete a hole or a round. The par for a hole is made up of the number of strokes taken to reach the green, plus two strokes to putt the ball

scratch: a player who has no handicap, and can therefore complete a course in par

---

Longest golf drive at an altitude below 1,000 m Karl Woodward (UK) drove a ball a distance of 408 yd. (373 m) at Golf del Sur, Tenerife, on June 30, 1999.

★ **Most holes in seven days with a cart** Using a golf cart for transportation, Troy Grant, a.k.a. Rusty Gate, (Australia) completed 1,800 holes at Tenterfield Golf Club, New South Wales, Australia, February 3–10, 2004.

★ **Largest golf cart parade** A total of 1,138 golf carts took part in a parade at the Timber Pines retirement community in Spring Hill, Florida, U.S.A., on March 15, 2004.

HOW TALL IS THE WORLD'S LARGEST GOLF TEE?
FIND OUT ON P. 331

ICE HOCKEY

NHL

★ **Most goals scored by a team in a game** The Montreal Canadiens scored 16 goals in their 16–3 victory over the Quebec Bulldogs on March 3, 1920.

Most goals scored by a team in a season The Edmonton Oilers scored 446 goals in the 1983–84 season. The Oilers also achieved a record 1,182 scoring points the same season.

Most goals scored by an individual in a game Joe Malone (Canada) scored seven goals for the Quebec Bulldogs in their game against the Toronto St. Patricks in Quebec City, Canada, on January 31, 1920.

★ **Fastest hat trick** Bill Mosienko (Canada) scored a hat trick within 21 seconds for the Chicago Blackhawks against the New York Rangers on March 23, 1952.

Most career wins by a goaltender Up to the end of the 2003 regular season, Patrick Roy (Canada) achieved 551 wins, playing for the Colorado Avalanche (having begun his career with the Montreal Canadiens in 1985).

Most goals scored by an individual in a season Wayne Gretzky (Canada) scored a record 92 goals for the Edmonton Oilers in the 1981–82 season.

Most goals scored by a rookie in a season Teemu Selanne (Finland) scored 76 goals playing for the Winnipeg Jets in the 1992–93 season.

MOST HAT TRICKS IN AN NHL CAREER Wayne Gretzky (Canada) scored 50 hat tricks during his NHL career, playing for the Edmonton Oilers, Los Angeles Kings, St. Louis Blues, and New York Rangers from 1979 to 1999.

Most goaltending shutouts in a career Terry Sawchuk (Canada) achieved 103 goaltending shutouts for the Detroit Red Wings, Boston Bruins, Toronto Maple Leafs, Los Angeles Kings, and New York Rangers from 1949 to 1970.

★Most Lady Byng trophies Frank Boucher (Canada) has won seven times, in 1928–31 and in 1933–35, playing for the New York Rangers.

Most penalty minutes in a career The player with the most penalty minutes in NHL history is Dave "Tiger" Williams (Canada) with 3,966, in 17 seasons (1971–88), playing for the Toronto Maple Leafs, Vancouver Canucks, Detroit Red Wings, Los Angeles Kings, and the now defunct Hartford Whalers.

Ice Hockey

Most Stanley Cup wins by a team The Montreal Canadiens won the cup 24 times from a record 32 finals, in 1916, 1924, 1930–31, 1944, 1946, 1953, 1956–60, 1965–66, 1968–69, 1971, 1973, 1976–79, 1986, and 1993.

Most All-Star selections Gordie Howe (Canada) was selected 21 times for the NHL All-Star game while playing for the Detroit Red Wings from 1946 to 1979. He was selected for the first team on 12 occasions and the second team on nine.

NHL HISTORY & AWARDS

An ice hockey league began in Canada in 1885 and featured four teams. The Stanley Cup (named after the English Governor General of Canada, Lord Stanley of Preston) was introduced in 1892, and was awarded to the team that won the playoffs. The National Hockey League (NHL), as it is known today, played its first game on December 19, 1917.

Today, the NHL awards many different cups and trophies, including:

Art Ross Trophy: Top point scorer in the NHL

Bill Masterton Memorial Trophy: Qualities of perseverance and sportsmanship

Calder Memorial Trophy: Rookie of the year

Clarence S. Campbell Bowl: Western Conference champion

Conn Smythe Trophy: Most Valuable Player in the Stanley Cup playoffs

Frank J. Selke Trophy: Top defensive forward in the NHL

Hart Memorial Trophy: NHL Most Valuable Player

Jack Adams Award: Coach of the year

James Norris Memorial Trophy: Top defenseman in the NHL

King Clancy Memorial Trophy: Leadership and humanitarian contribution

Lady Byng Memorial Trophy: Player who displays gentlemanly conduct

Lester B. Pearson Award: Most Valuable Player as selected by the NHLPA

Lester Patrick Trophy: Top goal scorer in the NHL

Presidents' Trophy: Best overall record

Prince of Wales Trophy: Eastern Conference champion

Vezina Trophy: Top goaltender in the NHL

William M. Jennings Trophy: Goaltender(s) with the fewest goals scored against them

---

★ MOST NHL TEAMS PLAYED FOR Two players who began their careers with the Vancouver Canucks have played for 10 National Hockey League (NHL) teams. J. J. Daigneault (Canada, pictured) left the Canucks at the end of the 1985–86 season and went on to play for the Philadelphia Flyers, Montreal Canadiens, St. Louis Blues, Pittsburgh Penguins, Anaheim Mighty Ducks, New York Islanders, Nashville Predators, Phoenix Coyotes, and Minnesota Wild.

Michael Petit (Canada) left the Canucks during the 1987–88 season and went on to play for the New York Rangers, Quebec Nordiques, Toronto Maple Leafs, Calgary Flames, Los Angeles Kings, Tampa Bay Lightning, Edmonton Oilers, Philadelphia Flyers, and Phoenix Coyotes.

★**Most penalty minutes in a season** Dave "The Hammer" Schultz (Canada) had 472 penalty minutes playing the Philadelphia Flyers in 1974–75.

Most penalties against an individual in a game Chris Nilan (U.S.A.), playing for the Boston Bruins against the Hartford Whalers on March 31, 1991, had 10 penalties called against him, made up of six minors, two majors, one 10-minute misconduct, and one game misconduct.

★**Most penalty minutes in a playoff game** The most penalty minutes accrued by an individual player in a Stanley Cup playoff game is 42 by

MOST GOALS SCORED IN A STANLEY CUP GAME Five goals were scored in a Stanley Cup game by Newsy Lalonde (Canada) for Montreal against Ottawa on March 1, 1919; by Maurice Richard in Montreal's 5–1 win over Toronto on March 23, 1944; by Darryl Glen Sittler for Toronto (8) v. Philadelphia (5) on April 22, 1976; by Reggie Leach for Philadelphia (6) v. Boston (3) on May 6, 1976; and by Mario Lemieux (pictured) for Pittsburgh (10) v. Philadelphia (7) on April 25, 1989.

Dave "The Hammer" Schultz (Canada) for the Philadelphia Flyers against the Toronto Maple Leafs on April 22, 1976.

MISCELLANEOUS

★**Largest ice hockey tournament by players** The Quikcard Edmonton Minor Hockey Week, held from January 10 to 19, 2003, in Edmonton, Canada, was contested by 471 teams totaling 7,127 players.

★**Most durable ice hockey player** John Burnosky (U.S.A.) began playing in 1929 and continued for a total of 76 years.

Highest score in an ice hockey game Australia beat New Zealand 58–0 in Perth on March 15, 1987.

☆**Most women's ice hockey World Championships** World Championships for women have been held since 1990, and have been won eight times by Canada, in 1990, 1992, 1994, 1997, 1999, 2000, 2001, and 2004.

MOST MEN'S ICE HOCKEY WORLD CHAMPIONSHIPS Canada won 23 World Championships, in 1920–32 (held irregularly), 1934–35, 1937–39, 1948, 1950–52, 1958–59, 1961, 1994, 1997, and 2003–04.

MOTOR SPORTS

DRAG RACING

☆**Fastest speed in a Top Fuel drag racer** The highest terminal velocity at the end of a 440-yd. run is 333.41 mph (536.57 km/h) by Brandon Bernstein (U.S.A.) in Lake Forest, California, U.S.A., on May 22, 2004, in a McKinney dragster.

Lowest elapsed time in a Top Fuel drag racer Anthony Schumacher (U.S.A.) covered 440 yd. in 4.441 seconds in a McKinney dragster in Long Grove, Illinois, U.S.A., on October 4, 2003. Top Fuel cars run on 90% nitromethane and 10% methanol, also known as racing alcohol. As a result, the engine is about 2.4 times as powerful as a similar displacement engine running gasoline, and produces at least 8,000 horsepower.

☆**Lowest elapsed time in a Funny car** John Force (U.S.A.) covered 440 yd. in 4.665 seconds driving a Ford in Yorba Linda, California, U.S.A., on March 10, 2004.

☆**Fastest speed in a drag racing Pro Stock car** For a gasoline-driven piston-engined car (Pro Stock), the highest terminal velocity is 207.75 mph

MOST WINS BY A CONSTRUCTOR IN A SEASON McLaren (UK, 1988) and Ferrari (Italy, 2002 and 2004) have both had 15 wins by a constructor in a single F1 season.

☆ **GRAND PRIX: MOST WINS BY A DRIVER** Michael Schumacher (Germany) won 83 races, 1991–2004. He has also won the most World Championships in Formula One with seven (1994–95, 2000–04).

(334.34 km/h), set by Greg Anderson (U.S.A.) in a Pontiac in Concord, North Carolina, U.S.A., on February 10, 2004.

☆ **Lowest elapsed time in a drag racing Pro Stock car.** Greg Anderson (U.S.A.) covered 440 yd. in 6.661 seconds in a Pontiac Grand Am in Concord, North Carolina, U.S.A., on February 10, 2004.

Fastest speed on a drag racing Pro Stock motorcycle Matt Hines (U.S.A.) reached 194.10 mph (312.37 km/h) on a Suzuki in Englishtown, New Jersey, U.S.A., in May 2001.

DRAG RACING

Drag racing is a form of motorsport where cars and motorcycles compete on short tracks, usually a quarter of a mile (440 yd.), with the objective of finishing the course as quickly as possible. The National Hot Rod Association, or NHRA, was founded in 1951 in California by Wally Parks (U.S.A.) to provide a governing body for the sport.

★ **FASTEST SPEED BY A FUNNY CAR (DRAG RACING)** John Force (U.S.A.) reached a terminal velocity of 333.58 mph (536.84 km/h) from a standing start over 440 yd. in a Ford in Yorba Linda, California, U.S.A., on March 10, 2004.

☆ **Lowest elapsed time on a drag racing Pro Stock motorcycle** Andrew Hines (U.S.A.) covered 440 yd. in 7.016 seconds on his Harley V-rod, in Brownsburg, Indiana, U.S.A., on June 19, 2004.

FORMULA ONE

★ **Fastest average speed in a Grand Prix** Michael Schumacher achieved an average speed of 153.842 mph (247.585 km/h) in a Ferrari in Monza at the Italian Grand Prix on September 14, 2003.

★ **Most consecutive Grand Prix victories** Alberto Ascari (Italy), driving for Ferrari, won nine consecutive Formula One Grands Prix in 1952–53. He won all six races of the 1952 season and the first three of 1953, winning the World Championship in both years.

☆ **Most constructors' World Championship titles** Ferrari won 14 Formula One constructors' World Championship titles (1961, 1964, 1975–77, 1979, 1982–83, and 1999–2004).

☆ **Most points by a constructor in a season** In the 2004 Formula One season, the Ferrari team amassed an overall total of 262 World Championship points.

☆ **Most points by a driver in a season** Michael Schumacher scored 148 points in the 2004 Formula One season.

☆**Most Grand Prix wins by a manufacturer** Ferrari has had 166 Grand Prix race wins.

☆**Most points scored by a driver** Michael Schumacher scored a record 1,186 points from 1991 to 2004. (This total includes 78 points from the 1997 season when he was excluded from the final standings.)

★**Youngest driver to claim a World Championship point** Jenson Button (UK, b. January 19, 1980) was 20 years 67 days old when he finished in sixth place in the Brazilian Grand Prix on March 26, 2000.

MOTORCYCLE WORLD CHAMPIONSHIPS

Most 50-cc titles Angel Roldán Nieto (Spain) won six 50-cc titles (1969, 1970, 1972, and 1975–1977).

☆**YOUNGEST DRIVER TO WIN A WORLD CHAMPIONSHIP RACE** Fernando Alonso (Spain, b. July 29, 1981) was 22 years 26 days old when he won the Hungarian Formula One Grand Prix on August 24, 2003, driving for Renault. He is pictured here, in April of the same year, holding the third-place trophy that he won in the Brazilian Grand Prix.

Most 80-cc titles Jorge Martinez (Spain) won three 80-cc motorcycle World Championships from 1986 to 1988.

Most 125-cc titles Angel Roldán Nieto (Spain) won seven 125-cc titles (1971, 1972, 1979, and 1981–84).

Most 250-cc titles Phil Read (UK) won four 250-cc titles (1964, 1965, 1968, and 1971). Max Biaggi (Italy) equaled this record from 1994 to 1997.

Most 350-cc titles Giacomo Agostini (Italy) won seven 350-cc titles from 1968 to 1974.

Most 500-cc titles Giacomo Agostini (Italy) won eight titles in 1966–72 and 1975.

HOW FAST IS THE WORLD'S FASTEST PRODUCTION CAR? FIND OUT ON P. 381

NASCAR

Most consecutive Championship wins Eight drivers have won back-to-back NASCAR—National Association for Stock Car Auto Racing—Championships, but Cale Yarborough (U.S.A.) has won three consecutively, from 1976 to 1978.

★**Most titles by an owner** Richard Petty (U.S.A.) won six titles from 1964 to 1979, as did Junior Johnson (U.S.A.) in 1976–85, and Richard Childress (U.S.A.) in 1986–94.

MOST DAKAR RALLY WINS Ari Vatanen (Finland) has won the Dakar Rally a record four times, first in 1987 and then on three more occasions from 1989 to 1991. Vatanen is pictured near Barcelona, Spain, on December 31, 2004.

☆ **MOST RACE WINS BY A MANUFACTURER** The superbike World Championships were first held in 1988. Since that time, Ducati has won a record 235 World Championship races, 1988–2004. Pictured is Carlos Checa (Spain).

Most titles by a driver Richard Petty (U.S.A.) won seven times, 1964–79. Dale Earnhardt (U.S.A.) equaled this feat, 1980–94.

Most wins in a season Richard Petty (U.S.A.) won 27 races in the 1967 NASCAR season, when he also set the mark for the **most consecutive wins**, with 10.

★**Most titles by a car make** Chevrolet (U.S.A.) provided the winning car for the NASCAR champion 21 times from 1957 to 2001.

Most NASCAR pole positions in a career Richard Petty (U.S.A.) achieved pole position 126 times, 1958–92.

RALLYING

★**Most Dakar rally truck category wins** Karel Loprais (Czech Republic) won six times in the truck category of the Dakar rally (1988, 1994–95, 1998–99, and 2001).

Most Dakar rally bike category wins Stéphane Peterhansel (France) won six times in the bike category of the Dakar rally (1991–93, 1995, and 1997–98).

Youngest rally World Championship driver Jari-Matti Latvala (Finland) was 18 years 61 days old when he drove in the 50th Acropolis Rally, Athens, Greece, from June 6 to 8, 2003.

HIGHEST EARNINGS IN A NASCAR CAREER Jeff Gordon (U.S.A.) won a record $66,956,249 during his NASCAR career from 1992 to 2005.

☆**Most World Championship race wins** From 1990 to 2004, Carlos Sainz (Spain) won 26 World Championship races.

Most World Championship wins by a manufacturer Lancia (Italy) won the rally World Championships 11 times from 1972 to 1992.

Most World Championship title wins Juha Kankkunen and Tommi Makinen (both Finland) have four title wins each, the former for the championships in 1986–87, 1991, and 1993; the latter for the championships in 1996–99.

★**Longest rally** The Singapore Airlines London-Sydney Rally covers 19,329 miles (31,107 km). The rally was won on September 28, 1977, by Andrew Cowan, Colin Malkin, and Michael Broad (all UK) in a Mercedes 280E.

SUPERBIKE

Most pole positions by a manufacturer Ducati (Italy) achieved 126 pole positions in superbike World Championship races from 1988 to 2005.

Most superbike World Title wins The most titles won is four by Carl Fogarty (UK) in 1994, 1995, 1998, and 1999.

☆**Most titles won by a manufacturer** Ducati has won 13 titles, in 1991–96 and 1998–2004.

MISCELLANEOUS

★**Youngest stock car driver** At just 12 years old, Amanda "A.K." Stroud (U.S.A., b. March 21, 1989) was a regular competitor in the Papa John's Pizza Pro-Cup racing division at Hickory Motor Speedway, North Carolina, U.S.A., during the 2001 racing season.

☆**Oldest racing driver** On February 5–6, 2005, the actor Paul Newman (U.S.A., b. January 26, 1925) competed in a Pixar/Newman Prod/Silverstone Racing/Ford Crawford car during the Rolex 24 at Daytona International Speedway, Florida, U.S.A., aged 80 years 10 days.

★**Most auto races in 24 hours** The most auto races driven by one racing driver in 24 hours is five by Fiona Leggate (UK) at Silverstone Circuit, Northamptonshire, UK, on July 25, 2004. The races were part of the MG Car Club Silverstone MG 80 Race Meeting, and Leggate won the last race.

MOST LE MANS RACE WINS Tom Kristensen (Denmark, pictured) won the Le Mans 24-hour race six times (1997 and 2000–04), equaling the record set by Jacky Ickx (Belgium) in 1969, 1975–77, and 1981–82.

Most Cart championship titles won The most wins in the National Championship—formerly the AAA (American Automobile Association, 1909–55), USAC (US Auto Club, 1956–78), CART (Championship Auto Racing Teams, 1979–91), IndyCar (1992–97) and currently the FedEx Series Championship—is seven by A. J. Foyt Jr. (U.S.A.) in 1960–61, 1963–64, 1967, 1975, and 1979.

Most wins in the Indianapolis 500 The most Indianapolis 500 wins is four and is shared by A. J. Foyt Jr. (U.S.A.; 1961, 1964, 1967, 1977); Al Unser Sr. (U.S.A.; 1970–71, 1978, 1987); and Rick Mears (U.S.A.; 1979, 1984, 1988, and 1991).

HOW POWERFUL IS THE WORLD'S MOST POWERFUL PRODUCTION MOTORCYCLE? FIND OUT ON P. 387

OLYMPICS

INDIVIDUALS

Most medals won Gymnast Larisa Latynina (USSR, now Ukraine) won a total of nine gold, five silver, and four bronze medals from 1956 to 1964, a total of 18 medals.

The **most Olympic medals won by a man** is 15, by gymnast Nikolay Andrianov (USSR), who collected seven gold, five silver, and three bronze medals from 1972 to 1980.

Most gold medals won Three men have won nine gold medals at the Olympic Games. Paavo Nurmi (Finland) won three in 1920, five in 1924, and one in 1928 for track-and-field; Mark Spitz (U.S.A.) won two in 1968

THE INTERCALATED GAMES

Intended as an interim tournament to be held in Athens every four years, the Intercalated Games of 1906 were the only ones ever held.

The Intercalated Games were due to fit neatly into the gaps between the regular Olympics (1904, 1908, 1912, etc., the four-year span known as an olympiad) but scheduling problems meant that the tournament was abandoned. Medals won in the 1906 Games are no longer recognized by the International Olympic Committee (IOC).

(The only other Olympics to be canceled were the 1916, 1940, and 1944 Games, owing to the world wars.)

MOST MEDALS WON AT A WINTER OLYMPIC GAMES (COUNTRY)
Germany won 35 medals at the XIX Winter Games held in Salt Lake City, Utah, U.S.A., in 2002. Pictured above is Stephan Hocke, a member of Germany's gold medal-winning ski-jumping team.

and seven in 1972 for swimming; and Carl Lewis (U.S.A.) won four in 1984, two in 1988, two in 1992, and one in 1996 for track-and-field.

If the Intercalated Games of 1906 are included, the record is 10, by Raymond Ewry (U.S.A.), who won three in 1900, three in 1904, two in 1906, and two in 1908. He competed in standing high, standing long, and standing triple jumps, all of which were dropped from the Olympic program after 1912.

Larisa Latynina (USSR, now Ukraine) holds the record for **most gold medals won by a woman,** with nine Olympic gold medals for gymnastics: four in 1956, three in 1960, and two in 1964.

Most consecutive gold medals won The only Olympians to win four consecutive individual titles in the same event are Al Oerter (U.S.A.), discus 1956–68, and Carl Lewis (U.S.A.), long jump 1984–96. However, Raymond Ewry (U.S.A.) won both the standing long jump and the standing high jump at four games in succession (1900, 1904, 1906, and 1908)—if the Intercalated Games of 1906, which were staged officially by the IOC, are included. Also, Paul Elvstrøm (Denmark) won four successive gold medals at monotype yachting events, 1948–60, but there was a class change (1948 Firefly class, 1952–60 Finn class).

★Most consecutive individual event medals George Hackl (Germany) won a medal in luge at five consecutive Olympic Games (1988–2002).

Longest span as an Olympic competitor The longest span of an Olympic competitor is 40 years. The record is shared by: Dr. Ivan Joseph

☆ **MOST GOLD MEDALS WON AT THE GAMES (COUNTRY)** The U.S.A. has won 976 gold medals at the Winter and Summer Olympic Games, from 1896 to 2004. Pictured from left to right are Tina Thompson, Tamika Catchings, Lisa Leslie, and Ruth Riley, shown after receiving the gold medal for women's basketball on August 28, 2004, during the Summer Olympic Games in Athens that year.

Martin Osiier (Denmark) in fencing, 1908–32 and 1948; Magnus Andreas Thulstrup Clasen Konow (Norway) in yachting, 1908–20, 1928, and 1936–48; Paul Elvstrøm (Denmark) in yachting, 1948–60, 1968–72, and 1984–88; and Durward Randolph Knowles (GB 1948, then The Bahamas) in yachting, 1948–72 and 1988.

The **longest span as a female Olympic competitor** is 28 years by Anne Jessica Ransehousen (née Newberry, U.S.A.) in dressage (1960, 1964, and 1988) and Christilot Hanson-Boylen (Canada), also in dressage (1964–76, 1984, and 1992).

Youngest gold medalist Kim Yun-mi (South Korea, b. December 1, 1980) was aged 13 years 85 days when she became champion in the 1994 women's 3,000 m short-track speed-skating relay event.

COUNTRIES

Most gold medals won at a Summer Games The U.S.A. won 83 gold medals at the XXIII Olympic Games in Los Angeles, California, U.S.A., in 1984.

The U.S.A. also holds the overall records for the ☆**most gold medals** won at the Summer Games (907), the ☆ **most medals won at the Games** (2,399), and the ☆ **most medals won at the Summer Games** (2,215).

★ **Most gold medal-winning countries at a Summer Games** An unprecedented 57 countries took home at least one gold medal from the 28th olympiad held in Athens, Greece, in 2004. During the same Games, a total of 931 medals (consisting of 303 gold, 301 silver, and 327 bronze) were awarded—the ☆ **most medals awarded at one Games.**

★ **Most gold medal-winning countries at a Winter Games** Eighteen countries took home at least one gold medal from the XIX Olympic Winter Games held in Salt Lake City, Utah, U.S.A., in 2002.

The **most countries to win a medal at a single Winter Games** is 25 in 2002 in Salt Lake City, Utah, U.S.A.

Most medals won at the Winter Games Norway has won 263 medals in the history of the Winter Games.

MISCELLANEOUS

★ **Most events featured at a Games** A total of 301 events were on the program at the 28th olympiad held in Athens, Greece, in 2004.

☆ **MOST COUNTRIES TO PARTICIPATE IN THE SUMMER OLYMPIC GAMES** A total of 201 countries' NOCs (National Olympic Committees) participated in the Summer Olympic Games held in Athens, Greece, from August 13 to 29, 2004.

☆ **MOST SWIMMING MEDALS WON BY A MAN (SINGLE GAMES)** Michael Phelps (U.S.A.) won six gold medals (100 m and 200 m butterfly, 200 m and 400 m medley, 4 × 200 m freestyle, and 4 × 100 m medley) and two bronze medals (200 m freestyle and 4 × 100 m freestyle) at the Athens Olympics in 2004.

Greatest attendance The overall spectator attendance at the Olympic Games held in Los Angeles, California, U.S.A., in 1984 was given as 5,797,923 people.

Most participants at a Summer Games The Games in Sydney, Australia, in 2000 featured a total of 10,651 athletes (4,069 of them women).

Most participants at a Winter Games The Games in Salt Lake City, Utah, U.S.A., in 2002 drew 2,550 competitors from 77 countries.

RACKET SPORTS

BADMINTON

Most World Championship singles titles Four Chinese players have each won two individual world titles: the men's singles title was won by Yang Yang in 1987 and 1989; the women's singles title was won by Li Lingwei in 1983 and 1989; Han Aiping in 1985 and 1987; and Ye Zhaoying in 1995 and 1997.

Most Thomas Cup wins The most wins at the men's team badminton World Championships for the Thomas Cup is 13 by Indonesia (1958, 1961, 1964, 1970, 1973, 1976, 1979, 1984, 1994, 1996, 1998, 2000, and 2002).

Most Sudirman Cup wins The most wins at the mixed team World Championships for the Sudirman Cup is four by China (1995, 1997, 1999, and 2001).

Most World Cup women's singles won Susi Susanti (Indonesia) won five women's singles tournaments (1989, 1993–94, and 1996–97).

☆ **MOST MEN'S TABLE TENNIS TEAM WORLD WINS** Instituted in 1926, the most men's team titles for the Swaythling Cup is 14 by China (1961, 1963, 1965, 1971, 1975, 1977, 1981, 1983, 1985, 1987, 1995, 1997, 2001, and 2004, pictured).

Shortest match On May 19, 1996, Ra Kyung-min (South Korea) beat Julia Mann (England) 11–2, 11–1 in 6 minutes during the Uber Cup in Hong Kong.

WHO HAS THE FASTEST TENNIS SERVE IN THE WORLD? FIND OUT ON P. 531

RACQUETBALL

★**Most women's doubles World Championships by an individual** Jackie Paraiso (U.S.A.) won six racquetball World Championships from 1990 to 2004.

☆**Most women's World Championships by an individual** The record of three championships is shared by two women. Michelle Gould (U.S.A.) won in 1992, 1994, and 1996; and Cheryl Gudinas (U.S.A.) won in 2000, 2002, and 2004.

★**Most men's doubles World Championships by a pair** Doug Ganim and Dan Obremski (both U.S.A.) won in 1988 and 1990. The record was equaled by Adam Karp and Bill Sell (both U.S.A.) after winning the championships in 1996 and 1998.

★**Most men's World Championship wins** Three people share this record—Egan Inoue (U.S.A.) won in 1986 and 1990; Sherman Greenfeld (Canada) in 1994 and 1998; and Jack Huczek (U.S.A.) in 2002 and 2004.

FASTEST SHUTTLECOCK SPEED OFF A BADMINTON RACKET In tests at Warwickshire Racquets and Health Club on November 5, 1996, Simon Archer (UK, pictured near left) hit a shuttlecock at a speed of 162 mph (260 km/h).

REAL TENNIS

Most women's World Championships Instituted in 1985, the women's World Championships have been won six times by Penny Lumley (née Fellows, UK), in 1989, 1991, 1995, 1997, 1999, and 2003.

★ Most women's doubles World Championships by a pair Penny Lumley and Sue Haswell (both UK) won the women's doubles real tennis World Championships three times (1995, 1997, and 1999).

Most men's World Championship wins Pierre Etchebaster (France) successfully defended the championship title eight times from 1928 to 1952.

Jacques Edmond Barre (France) had the **longest Real Tennis World Championship career.** Although, at the time, the championships were not held every year, he was world champion over a period of 33 years (1829–62).

★ Largest prize money for a tournament Rob Fahey (Australia) was awarded $57,400 when he won the real tennis World Championships held at Newport, Rhode Island, U.S.A., on May 20, 2004.

SQUASH

Most World Championship wins by a men's team Australia has won an unprecedented eight men's world team titles, in 1967, 1969, 1971, 1973, 1989, 1991, 2001, and 2003.

Badminton is played with a shuttlecock on a court with a high net. As with tennis, it is contested in five events: men's singles, women's singles, men's doubles, women's doubles, and mixed doubles.

Racquetball is played mainly in the U.S.A. with rackets and a hollow rubber ball on an indoor court, with walls, floor, and ceiling inbounds.

Real tennis (pictured) is the original racket sport from which lawn tennis is descended. It is played with a ball, handmade from cork or felt and wrapped in cloth, on a specialized court with walls on all sides, three of which have sloping roofs.

Squash, similar to racquetball, is played with slightly bigger rackets and a softer hollow rubber ball on an indoor court.

Table tennis, also known as Ping-Pong, is played on a rectangular table with small rubber-coated wooden bats and a cellulose ball.

Most World Championship wins by a woman Sarah Fitzgerald (Australia) won five World Open titles in 1996–98 and 2001–02.

☆**Most World Championship wins by a women's team** The women's title has been won eight times by Australia in 1981, 1983, 1992, 1994, 1996, 1998, 2002, and 2004.

MOST UBER CUP WINS (BADMINTON) The most wins at the women's team badminton World Championships for the Uber Cup is nine by China, from 1984 to 2004. Pictured is Dai Yun (China) holding the Uber Cup trophy on May 20, 2000.

Most World Open titles Jansher Khan (Pakistan) has won a record eight World Open titles in 1987, 1989, 1990, and 1992–96.

TABLE TENNIS

☆**Most women's team World Championships** Instituted in 1926, the Corbillon Cup has been won by China a record 16 times—1965, 1971, 1975–89 (eight successive, every two years), 1993, 1995, 1997, 2000, 2001, and 2004.

★**Longest rally** Leif Alexis (Sweden) and Mat Hand (UK) achieved a 5 hr. 8 min. 22 sec. rally at the Bonington Gallery, Nottingham, UK, on December 9, 2003.

RUGBY

RUGBY LEAGUE

Most NRL titles The National Rugby League is Australia's premier rugby league competition. The Brisbane Broncos have won two titles, in 1998 and 2000.

Most Challenge Cup wins The UK's rugby league Challenge Cup has been won 17 times by Wigan (1924, 1929, 1948, 1951, 1958–59, 1965, 1985, 1988–95, and 2002).

Most Super League titles The Super League is the UK's premier rugby league competition, instituted in 1996. The most titles won by a team is four by St. Helens (1996, 1999, 2000, and 2002).

☆ **MOST IRB SEVENS SERIES TITLES** The International Rugby Board Sevens series, which began in 1999, has been won five times (and every year) by New Zealand. The series is a competition made up of between seven and 11 separate Sevens tournaments, played around the world each season. New Zealand's captain Orene Ai'i is pictured performing the traditional Maori dance called the *haka* to celebrate their 34–5 defeat of Argentina in the final of the Los Angeles tournament in Carson, California, U.S.A., on February 13, 2005.

★MOST STATE OF ORIGIN SERIES WINS New South Wales has won Australia's rugby league State of Origin series 11 times from 1980 to 2004. Pictured above is New South Wales captain Brad Fittler (Australia).

Most World Cups won The World Cup competition was first held in 1954. Australia has won eight times (1957, 1968, 1970, 1977, 1988, 1992, 1995, and 2000), and also won the International Championship of 1975.

Fastest hat trick The fastest hat trick of tries scored from the start of a match is 6 min. 54 sec. by Chris Thorman (UK) playing for Huddersfield Giants against Doncaster Dragons in the semifinal of the Buddies National League Cup in Doncaster, South Yorkshire, UK, on May 19, 2002.

Highest score in an international match Australia beat Russia 110–4 in a rugby league World Cup match in Hull, East Riding of Yorkshire, UK, on November 4, 2000.

RUGBY UNION

★**Youngest rugby union international** Edinburgh Academy pupils Ninian Jamieson Finlay (1858–1936) and Charles Reid (1864–1909) were both 17 years 36 days old when they played for Scotland v. England in 1875 and 1881 respectively. However, as Finlay had one less leap year in his lifetime up to his first cap, the record must be credited to him. Semi Taupeaafe (Tonga) was reportedly aged 16 when he played in a 1989 Test for Tonga v. Western Samoa.

★**Oldest rugby union competition** The United Hospitals Cup was first played in 1875 between teams representing hospitals in England.

Biggest rugby World Cup match win The largest winning margin recorded in rugby union World Cup matches is 142 points, a feat achieved when host nation Australia beat Namibia 142–0 in Adelaide, Australia, on October 25, 2003.

☆**Most Tri-Nations titles** The Tri-Nations—an international competition inaugurated in 1996 and played annually between Australia, New Zealand, and South Africa—has been won a record five times by New Zealand (1996–97, 1999, and 2002–03). Australia has won it twice (2000–01), as has South Africa (1998 and 2004).

Most Six Nations championships The Six Nations replaced the Five Nations in 2000 when Italy was invited to join the historic competition. England has won three Six Nations Championships—more than any other country—in 2000–01 (when they failed to complete the grand slam in either year) and in 2003 (when they achieved the clean sweep of victories).

★**Most Super 12 titles** The Super 12 is an annual tournament contested by teams from Australia, South Africa, and New Zealand. The most Super 12 tournament victories by a team is four by the Canterbury Crusaders (New Zealand) from 1998 to 2000 and 2002.

Fastest World Cup try Elton Flatley scored a try after only 18 seconds on October 18, 2003, playing for Australia against Romania at the Suncorp Stadium, Brisbane, Queensland, Australia.

Most tries in an international career David Campese scored 64 tries in 101 internationals for Australia from 1982 to 1996.

Most international appearances for British and Irish Lions William James "Willie John" McBride (Ireland) made a record 17 test appearances for the British Isles, as well as 63 for Ireland.

Most international appearances Jason Leonard (UK) appeared 114 times for England from 1990 to 2004.

MOST GOALS KICKED IN SIX NATIONS Jonny Wilkinson (UK) kicked a record 13 goals—nine conversions and four penalty goals—for England during its match against Italy in Twickenham, London, UK, on February 17, 2001. Wilkinson also holds the record for the **most points scored by an individual in a season,** with 78 points (12 conversions and 18 penalty goals) in the five games of the 2000 International Championship series.

Most points in an international career In all internationals, Neil Jenkins (UK) has scored 1,049 points in 87 matches for Wales (1,008 points in 83 matches) and the British Lions (41 points in four matches), from 1991 to March 2001.

IRB SEVENS

★**Most individual IRB Sevens tournament appearances** Shane Thompson (Canada) appeared 46 times in International Rugby Board Sevens tournaments from 1999 to 2005.

★**MOST HEINEKEN CUP TITLES** Inaugurated in 1995, European club rugby's premier competition, the Heineken Cup, has been won twice by two teams: Toulouse (France) in 1996 and 2003, and Leicester Tigers (UK) in 2001 and 2002. Pictured above is Martin Johnson (UK), the Leicester captain.

★**Most points scored by an individual in IRB Sevens tournaments** Ben Gollings (UK) scored 1,120 points for England from 1999 to 2005

★**Most tries scored by an individual in IRB Sevens tournaments** Karl Te'Nana (New Zealand) scored 113 tries in IRB Sevens tournaments from 1999 to 2004.

TARGET SPORTS

ARCHERY

★**Heaviest longbow draw weight** Mark Stretton (UK) drew a longbow to the maximum draw weight of 200 lb. (90 kg) on an arrow of 32.5 in. (82.5 cm) at The Bath Archers, Somerset, UK, on August 15, 2004.

★**Most bull's-eyes in 90 seconds** Jeremie Masson (France) scored three bull's-eyes in 90 seconds, from a distance of 59 ft. (18 m) from the target, in Argeles Gazost, France, on July 15, 2004.

FARTHEST ARROW SHOT USING FEET Claudia Gomez (Argentina) shot an arrow into a target at a distance of 18.04 ft. (5.5 m) using only her feet on the set of *El Show de los Récords,* Madrid, Spain, on November 15, 2001.

Highest score in 24 hours Michael Howson and Stephen Howard (both UK) scored 26,064 points at Oakbank Sports College, Keighley, West Yorkshire, UK, on November 11–12, 2000.

Most crossbows triggered—arrow relay The most arrows triggered by a single crossbow shot, with the final arrow hitting a marked target, is nine. Ross and Elisa Hartzell performed the feat on December 18, 1998, on the set of *Guinness World Records: Primetime* in Los Angeles, California, U.S.A.

**FOR A LIST OF ARCHERY WORLD RECORDS
RECOGNIZED BY THE FÉDÉRATION INTERNATIONALE
DE TIR À L'ARC (FITA), TURN TO THE SPORTS
REFERENCE SECTION ON P. 560**

CROQUET

Most national titles Bob Jackson (New Zealand) won the New Zealand Open Championship Singles title 14 times, in 1975, 1978, 1982–84, 1989, 1991–92, 1995, 1997–99, and 2002–03.

Most World Championship wins by an individual The most wins by an individual is five by Robert Fulford (UK) in 1990, 1992, 1994, 1997, and 2002.

DARTS

Youngest player in a competitive tournament Nick Stoekenbroek (Netherlands, b. May 11, 1989) played in the Dutch Open, Veldhoven, the Netherlands, on February 5–7, 2002, at the age of 12.

★Highest score by inner and outer bull's-eyes in two minutes Josette Kerdraon and Yannick Geay

SHOOTING RIFLE 50 M PRONE (MEN) Numerous competitors have scored the maximum 600 points in this discipline, but this is without "finals," which are points awarded in a final round. (The top eight shooters advance to a 10-shot final; the final is scored in tenths of a point and added to the match score to determine winners.) The record score of 704.8 points with finals was set by Christian Klees (Germany) at the 1996 Olympic Games in Atlanta.

MOST DARTS WORLD CHAMPIONSHIP TITLES The most World Championship titles won is 12 by Phil Taylor (UK): with the World Darts Organization (WDO) in 1990 and 1992, and the Professional Darts Council (PDC) in 1995–2002 and 2004–2005.

(both France) achieved a record with a score of 475 (15 × 25 and 2 × 50) on August 5, 2004, on the set of *L'Été de Tous les Records* in Bénodet, France.

☆**Largest electronic darts tournament** A tournament took place in Barcelona, Spain, from March 26 to 28, 2004, that featured 5,099 individual players.

Least darts 100,001 A total of 100,001 was achieved in 3,579 darts by Chris Gray (UK) at the Dolphin, Cromer, Norfolk, UK, on April 27, 1993.

POOL

★**Most world titles** Ralph Greenleaf (U.S.A.) won the world professional pool title 19 times from 1919 to 1937.

Speed pocketing on one U.S. table (men) Dave Pearson (UK) pocketed all 15 balls on a table in 26.5 seconds at Pepper's Bar and Grill, Windsor, Ontario, Canada, on April 4, 1997.

★**Speed pocketing on two U.S. tables (men)** On October 14, 2002, Dave Pearson (UK) pocketed two consecutive racks of 15 pool balls in 1 min. 22 sec. in Natick, Massachusetts, U.S.A.

★**Speed pocketing on 10 U.S. tables (men)** Dave Pearson (UK) cleared 10 tables of 15 balls in 8 min. 57 sec. on October 12, 2002, in Natick, Massachusetts, U.S.A.

FASTEST 147 IN A PROFESSIONAL SNOOKER TOURNAMENT Ronnie O'Sullivan (UK) achieved a 147 in 5 min. 20 sec. during the World Championships in Sheffield, South Yorkshire, UK, on April 21, 1997.

SNOOKER

Highest break Wally West (UK) made a break of 151 in a match at the Hounslow Lucania, Middlesex, UK, in October 1976. The break involved a free ball, which therefore created an "extra" red, when all 15 reds were still on the table. In these very exceptional circumstances, the maximum break is 155.

Youngest world champion On April 29, 1990, Stephen Hendry (UK, b. January 13, 1969) became world professional snooker champion at 21 years 106 days.

Youngest player to score 147 Ronnie O'Sullivan (UK, b. December 5, 1975) scored a competitive maximum of 147 at the age of 15 years 98 days during the English Amateur Championship at Aldershot, Hampshire, UK, on March 13, 1991.

Fastest colors clear Ken Doherty (Ireland) pocketed all of the colors in sequence on a snooker table in 23.4 seconds at The Chase Centre, Staffordshire, UK, on August 29, 1997.

MISCELLANEOUS

★**Casting—most world titles (women)** Jana Maisel (Germany) won 36 gold medals at the International Casting Sport Federation World Championships from 1990 to 2002. In total, she has won 46 world medals (36 gold) and 42 European medals (30 gold).

ISSF

Shooting with a **rifle, pistol, or shotgun** has been included in the Olympic Games since 1896 and is monitored by the International Shooting Sport Federation (ISSF). The governing body administers records for both men and women as well as teams.

For **rifle, pistol, and running target events,** shooters fire at round black areas displayed on white backgrounds. The targets are divided into 10 concentric scoring zones or rings. Targets are electronic and a computer system instantly scores each shot.

For **shotgun events,** each time the shooter fires and hits the target so that at least one visible piece is broken, it is scored as a hit and counts as one point.

★**Most casts made in 24 hours** Brent Olgers (U.S.A.) made 6,358 casts in 24 hours on Lake Michigan at Chicago, Illinois, U.S.A., on July 9–10, 1999.

★**Fastest time to shoot 25 clay pigeon targets** Jose Lopes (France) shot 25 clay pigeon sporting targets in 1 min. 11 sec. on the set of *L'Été de Tous les Records* in Argeles Gazost, France, on July 12, 2004.

☆**Highest bowling pin-fall in 24 hours using one lane** Twelve bowlers achieved a pin-fall of 37,129 at REVS Bowling & Entertainment Centre, Burnaby, Canada, in 24 hours on February 20–21, 2004.

★**Most bowling strikes in a minute** Tomas Leandersson (Sweden) achieved six bowling strikes in a minute at Sundbybergs Bowling Hall, Sweden, on October 24, 2001.

FOR A LIST OF INDIVIDUAL EVENTS AND DISCIPLINES THAT THE ISSF MONITORS AT OLYMPIC LEVEL, TURN TO THE SPORTS REFERENCE SECTION ON P. 574–576

TENNIS

GRAND SLAM TOURNAMENTS

Most tournament wins (singles) Margaret Court (Australia) won 24 grand slam tournament singles titles from 1960 to 1973.

Most tournaments won (doubles) Two women's partnerships have won 20 grand slam tournaments: Althea Louise Brough and Margaret Evelyn Du Pont (both U.S.A.) from 1942 to 1957; and Pam Shriver and Martina Navratilova (both U.S.A.) from 1981 to 1989.

The **most grand slam wins by a men's doubles partnership** is 12, by John Newcombe and Tony Roche (both Australia) from 1965 to 1976.

☆**Longest match** In 2004, Fabrice Santoro and Arnaud Clément (both France) played for a total of 6 hr. 33 min. in the first round of the French Open.

FASTEST SERVE The fastest service by a woman (measured by modern equipment) is 127.4 mph (205 km/h) by Venus Williams (U.S.A.) in Zurich, Switzerland, on October 16, 1998. The ☆**fastest service by a man** is 153 mph (246.2 km/h) by Andy Roddick (U.S.A.) at the Queen's Club, London, UK, on June 11, 2004.

★MOST CONSECUTIVE FINALS WINS From October 2003 to February 2005, Roger Federer (Switzerland) won 16 consecutive Open finals: Vienna, Houston Masters, Australian Open, Dubai, Indian Wells Masters, Hamburg Masters, Halle, Wimbledon, Gstaad, Canadian Masters, U.S. Open, Bangkok, Houston Masters, Qatar Open, Rotterdam, and Dubai Open.

Most Wimbledon singles titles won Pete Sampras (U.S.A.) won seven Wimbledon singles titles in 1993–95 and 1997–2000.

The **most Wimbledon singles titles won by a woman** is nine by Martina Navratilova (U.S.A.) in 1978–79, 1982–87, and 1990.

★ **Most Wimbledon doubles titles won** Todd Woodbridge (Australia) won nine Wimbledon men's doubles tennis titles from 1993 to 2004. He won the first six playing with Mark Woodforde (Australia) and the last three with Jonas Bjorkman (Sweden).

Most U.S. Open singles titles Three men have won a record seven U.S. Open singles titles: Bill Tilden (U.S.A.) in 1920–25 and 1929; Richard Sears (U.S.A.) in 1881–87; and William Larned (U.S.A.) in 1901, 1902, and 1907–11.

The **most U.S. Open singles titles won by a woman** is eight by Molla Mallory (née Bjurstedt, Norway) in 1915–18, 1920–22, and 1926.

Most French Open singles titles Björn Borg (Sweden) won six French Open singles titles in 1974–75 and 1978–81. The **most French Open singles titles won by a woman** is seven by Chris Evert (U.S.A.) in 1974, 1975, 1979, 1980, 1983, 1985, and 1986.

ROGER FEDERER

The men's tennis No. 1 seed—and winner of a record 16 consecutive tournaments—talks about his world-beating achievements.

Who inspired you as a child? I looked up to two athletes. One was Michael Jordan and the other was Björn Borg.

What do you think your greatest achievement in tennis is? It has to be winning three grand slam tournaments, the Masters Cup, plus six additional events, and only losing six matches throughout the year . . . all in one year (2004).

What are your future goals? Stay No. 1 . . . and Wimbledon is always a goal! I'd also like to do charity work. I set up the Roger Federer Foundation to promote sport for young people and fund projects for disadvantaged children, which I'd like to do more work with. I'd definitely like to stay in sports in some capacity.

What advice would you give to young sportsmen and women? You're going to go through ups and downs, but you learn a lot during the down periods. You have to keep to your long-term goals and love what you're doing. You also need a lot of support around you, from parents and family.

Most Australian Open singles titles Roy Emerson (Australia) won the Australian Open singles tennis title six times (1961 and 1963–67). The **most Australian Open singles titles won by a woman** is 11 by Margaret Court (Australia) in 1960–66, 1969–71, and 1973.

DAVIS CUP

Most Davis Cup wins The most wins in the Davis Cup—the men's international team championship—is 31 by the U.S.A. from 1900 to 1995.

Oldest Davis Cup player Yaka-Garonfin Koptigan (Togo) was aged 59 years 147 days on May 27, 2001, when playing against Mauritius.

The world's **oldest tennis player** is José Guadalupe Leal Lemús (Mexico, b. December 13, 1902), who began playing tennis in 1925 and was still playing regularly at the age of 102.

Youngest Davis Cup player Kenny Banzer (Liechtenstein) was 14 years 5 days old on February 16, 2000, when playing against Algeria.

MISCELLANEOUS

Longest competitive singles match Christian Albrecht Barschel and Hauke Daene (both Germany) played a match lasting 25 hr. 25 min. on September 12–13, 2003, at Mölln Tennis Club, Mölln, Germany. The pair played a total of 36 sets.

★**Longest competitive doubles match** The longest competitive doubles tennis match, by one pair playing against all comers, lasted 33 hr. 33 min. 33 sec. and was played by Christian Albrecht Barschel and Hauke

---

TENNIS "GRAND SLAMS"

The term "grand slam" was first used in 1933 to describe winning the four major tennis tournaments of the year:

Australian Open (Melbourne, Australia): inaugurated 1905, hardcourt, January

Tournoi de Roland-Garros (French Open) (Paris, France): inaugurated 1891, red clay, May/June

Wimbledon (London, UK): inaugurated 1877, played on grass, June/July

U.S. Open (New York City, U.S.A.): inaugurated 1881, hardcourt, August/September

---

☆**MOST CLUB CHAMPIONSHIPS WON** The ☆most club championships won by an individual at the same club is 16 (including a record 10 consecutively) by Stuart Foster (UK, pictured) at Leverstock Green Lawn Tennis Club in Hemel Hempsteak, UK, from 1987 to 2004.

Foster also holds records for the ☆most club doubles championships won as a pair, with 17 victories from 1988 to 2004 with partner Graham Fish (UK), and the ☆most mixed doubles won—11—with various partners between 1985 and 2001.

Daene (both Germany), from August 13–15, 2004, at Mölln Tennis Club, Germany.

Longest coaching marathon Butch Heffernan (Australia) coached tennis for 52 hours on November 23–25, 2001, at the Next Generation Club in Brierley Hill, Dudley, West Midlands, UK.

★**Most people bouncing tennis balls on rackets** The most people to bounce tennis balls on tennis rackets simultaneously in one place is 258 at Devonport Tennis Club, Devonport, Tasmania, Australia, on March 11, 2004.

★ YOUNGEST WIMBLEDON WINNERS ★

NAME	COUNTRY	AGE	YEAR
Gentlemen			
Boris Becker	Germany	17 years 227 days	1985
Wilfred Baddely	UK	19 years 174 days	1891
Sidney Wood	U.S.A.	19 years 245 days	1931
Björn Borg	Sweden	20 years 22 days	1976
Ellsworth Vines	U.S.A.	20 years 278 days	1932
Ladies			
Charlotte Dod	UK	15 years 285 days	1887
Martina Hingis	Switzerland	16 years 278 days	1997
Maria Sharapova (*pictured page 536*)	Russia	17 years 75 days	2004
Maureen Connolly	U.S.A.	17 years 292 days	1952
May Sutton	U.S.A.	18 years 286 days	1905

Most tennis balls held in the hand Francisco Peinado Toledo (Spain) held 18 tennis balls in his left hand for 10 seconds at Valencia, Spain, on September 18, 2003.

Oldest ball boy Manny Hershkowitz (U.S.A.) worked on court at the U.S. Open at Flushing Meadow, New York, U.S.A., in September 1999, aged 82.

UNUSUAL SPORTS

Farthest dyno climbing distance In dyno climbing, participants launch from one set of handholds on a climbing wall to a higher set with no intermediate holds. Matt Heason (UK) achieved 8.61 ft. (2.60 m) at the Edge Climbing Centre, Sheffield, UK, on April 20, 2002.

The ☆ **farthest dyno climbing distance by a woman** was by Anne-Laure Chevrier (France), who dyno-ed 6.45 ft. (1.95 m) in Bénodet, France, on August 5, 2004.

★ **Most elephant polo World Championships** The Tiger Top Tuskers (Nepal) have won the championships a record eight times (1983–85, 1987, 1992, 1998, 2000, and 2003).

★ **Fastest 100 m on a spacehopper by a man** Ashrita Furman (U.S.A.) traveled 100 m (328 ft.) on a spacehopper in 30.2 seconds at Flushing Meadow Park, New York City, U.S.A., on November 16, 2004.

★ **Most kabaddi World Cup wins** Inaugurated in 2004, the only kabaddi World Cup contested so far was won by India, who beat Iran 55–27 in the final, played at South Kanara Sports Club, Mumbai, India, on November 21, 2004.

★ **Most consecutive footbag kicks with two footbags** Juha-Matti Rytilahti (Finland) achieved 68 footbag kicks with one foot, using two footbags, at the Turku Fair Center, Turku, Finland, on September 30, 2001.

FASTEST COAL-BAG CARRYING On April 1, 1991, at Gawthorpe, West Yorkshire, UK, David Jones (UK) carried a 110-lb. (50-kg) bag over a 3,322-ft. (1,012.5-m) course in 4 min. 6 sec.—the fastest by a man.

At the 2002 coal-bag carrying championships on April 6, Ruth Clegg (UK) carried a 44-lb. (20-kg) bag over the same distance in 5 min. 4 sec., winning the record of **fastest coal-bag carrying by a woman.**

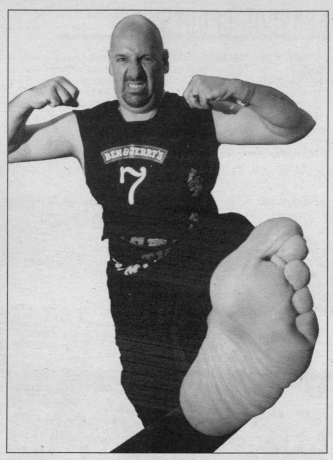

TOE WRESTLING—MOST WORLD CHAMPIONSHIP WINS The toe wrestling World Championships are held annually on the first Saturday in June at Ye Olde Royal Oak, Wetton, Staffordshire, UK. Contestants must push an opponent's foot to the other side of a specially constructed ring called a "toerack" using only their toes. (Mixed matches are not allowed because of the danger of "myxomatoesis.")

In the men's category, Alan Nash (UK) won five championships (1994, 1996–97, 2000, and 2002). Nash, nicknamed "Nasty," also has the honor of being knighted by His Majesty King Leo 1st of Redonda in the West Indies. The record for most toe wrestling World Championships won by a woman is held by Karen Davies (UK), who won a record four titles (1999–2002).

☆ **BOG SNORKELING—MOST CONSECUTIVE WORLD CHAMPIONSHIPS** Two competitors have held the coveted bog snorkeling World Championship title three times in successive years: Steve Griffiths (UK) from 1985 to 1987; and Philip John (UK, pictured) from 2002 to 2004.

☆ **Most entrants at a bog snorkeling World Championships** The bog snorkeling World Championships held on August 30, 2004, at Waen Rhydd peat bog, Llanwrtyd Wells, Powys, UK, saw a record 146 entries.

☆ **Most horseshoe pitching World Championships won** The horseshoe pitching World Championships have historically been played at irregular intervals, but have been held every year since 1946. The record for most titles in the men's category is 10, shared by Ted Allen (U.S.A.) in 1933–40 (competition not held in consecutive years), 1946, 1953, 1955–57, and 1959; and Alan Francis (U.S.A.) in 1989, 1993, 1995–99, 2001, and 2003–04.

★ **Greatest distance rowed on land** Rob Bryant (U.S.A.) rowed 3,280 miles (5,278.5 km) on a specially built land rowing machine. He left Los Angeles, California, U.S.A., on April 2, 1990, and reached Washington, D.C. on July 30, 1990.

★ **Most rotations in table wrestling** Table wrestling involves participants climbing 360° around a table top without touching the ground. The most rotations of a table in one minute is 11 by Chris Sturman (UK) on July 10, 1999.

★ **Fastest underwater archery** The fastest time to complete three circuits of an underwater archery course is 1 min. 21 sec., set by Nicolas Rizzo (France) in Port Leucate, France, on July 23, 2004.

★ **Most crossbred lambs shorn in eight hours** Trevor Bacon (Australia) sheared 471 crossbred lambs—in accordance with World Shearing Record Committee rules—on October 7, 2002, at Walla Brook Farm, Frances, Australia.

★ **Longest game of human table football** A game at Foz do Arelho Beach, Caldas de Rainha, Portugal, on August 12, 2004, was played for 24 hours.

PEA SHOOTING—MOST WORLD CHAMPIONSHIP WINS The pea
shooting World Championships are held every year in Witcham,
Cambridgeshire, UK. The skill is to shoot at a target, the size of a
dartboard and smeared with putty, gaining five points for the inner,
three for the middle, and one for the outer circle, from a distance of 10
ft. 6 in. (3.2 m). The pea shooter should be no longer than 12 in.
(30.48 cm). Mike Fordham (UK) has won seven championships (1977–78,
1981, 1983–85, and 1992). He also holds the record for **most
consecutive pea shooting World Championships**, 1983 to 1985.
David Hollis (UK, pictured) equaled the record (1999–2001) and was also
the youngest world champion, aged just 13 when he first scooped
the title.

What is kiiking?

Kiiking is a sport that originated in Baltic and Scandinavian countries.
The aim is to complete a 360° revolution on an enormous swing. As the
record is based on the length of the shafts for the swing, the longer the
shafts the higher the score.

☆**LONGEST SHAFT USED TO COMPLETE A ROTATION IN KIIKING**
**Andrus Aasamäe (Estonia) used a 23-ft. (7.02-m) shaft to successfully
complete a kiiking rotation in Haapsalu, Estonia, on August 21, 2004.
The women's record is held by Kätlin Kink (Estonia), who used a 19-ft.
5-in. (5.93-m) staff in Palmse, Estonia, on July 19, 2003.**

WATER SPORTS

AQUABIKING

☆ **Most barrel rolls in two minutes** Fred Guerreiro (France) achieved a total of 10 barrel rolls on his aquabike (personal water craft, or PWC) in two minutes for *L'Été De Tous Les Records* at Argeles Gazost, France, on July 15, 2004.

Highest speed Forrest Smith (U.S.A.) achieved a speed of 76.17 mph (122.79 km/h) on a modified Yamaha GP1200R aquabike (PWC) over a measured kilometer in Savannah, Georgia, U.S.A., on July 5, 2002.

CANOEING

Most World and Olympic titles Birgit Fischer (GDR/Germany) won a total of 37 titles from 1979 to 1998: eight Olympic titles and 29 world titles.

Three men have each won a record 13 titles: Gert Fredriksson (Sweden) from 1948 to 1960; Rüdiger Helm (GDR) from 1976 to 1983; and Ivan Patzaichin (Romania) from 1968 to 1984.

Most Olympic gold medals (men) Gert Fredriksson (Sweden) won six gold medals from 1948 to 1960. He added a silver and a bronze for a record eight medals.

Longest race The Canadian Government Centennial Voyageur Canoe Pageant and Race from Rocky Mountain House, Alberta, to the Expo 67 site at Montreal, Quebec, was 3,283 miles (5,283 km). Ten canoes represented Canadian provinces and territories. The winner of the race, which took place from May 24 to September 4, 1967, was the Province of Manitoba canoe *Radisson*.

CANOEING TERMINOLOGY

C: refers to a canoe, a (usually open-decked) boat propelled using a single-blade paddle from a kneeling position (in flat- and white-water canoeing)

K: refers to a kayak, a fully decked boat propelled using a double-blade paddle from a sitting position

The numeral that follows the letter (C4, K2, etc.) designates a one-, two-, or four-man vessel.

★HIGHEST HYDROFOIL JUMP Billy Rossini (U.S.A., pictured) reached a height of 23 ft. (7.01 m) on a hydrofoil at Lake Norman, North Carolina, U.S.A., on August 1, 2004. A hydrofoil consists of a long fin attached beneath a board on which the rider sits in a raised chair. The ★tallest hydrofoil ridden was a 10-ft. 9.1-in. tall (3.28 m) example created by William Blair (UK).

Longest human-powered journey with portages Verlen Kruger and Steven Landick (both U.S.A.) traveled 28,043 miles (45,129 km), starting from Red Rock, Montana, U.S.A., and finishing at Lansing, Michigan, U.S.A., from April 29, 1980 to December 15, 1983. All portages (i.e. carrying the canoe) were human-powered.

Longest waterfall descent Tao Berman (U.S.A.) descended 98.4 ft. (30 m) in 2.4 seconds at the Upper Johnstone Canyon Falls in Banff National Park, Alberta, Canada, on August 23, 1999.

Fastest North Atlantic crossing in a kayak (solo) Peter Bray (UK) crossed the Atlantic by sea kayak, solo and unsupported, in 76 days from June 22 to September 5, 2001.

MOST LIFESAVING AWARDS The greatest number of awards gained by a member of the Royal Life Saving Society is 250 by Eric Deakin of Hightown, Merseyside, UK, from 1954 to 2004.

MOST CONSECUTIVE DAYS SPENT SURFING Dale Webster (U.S.A.) has gone surfing every day since September 2, 1975, passing his 10,407th consecutive day of surfing on February 29, 2004. Webster set himself the condition that "a surf" consists of catching at least three waves to shore each time.

Fastest 100 eskimo rolls

Ray Hudspith (UK) completed 100 eskimo rolls in 3 min. 7.25 sec. at Killingworth Leisure Centre, Tyne and Wear, UK, on March 3, 1991.

★ **Most individual World Championship titles (men)** Vladimir Vala and Jaroslav Slucik (both Slovakia) won four titles at the International Canoe Foundation (ICF) wild-water racing World Championships. They took the C2 events in 1996 and 2000, and two titles in 2004.

MOST OLYMPIC GOLD CANOEING MEDALS (WOMEN) The most golds won by a woman is eight by Birgit Fischer (née Schmidt, GDR/Germany), from 1980 to 2004. She also won four silvers for a record total of 12 medals.

★ Most team World Championship titles (men) Germany has won three titles (K1 in 1996 and C2 in 1996 and 2004) at the ICF World Championships.

☆ Most eskimo rolls in tandem Three teams have performed 26 eskimo rolls in a tandem canoe with paddles in a time of one minute. Bernard Bregeon and Richard Vezzoli (both France) first achieved the feat in Biscarrosse, France, on June 30, 2004. Marc Girardin and Frederic Lascourreges (both France) equaled the record at Argeles Gazost, France, on July 15, 2004. Finally, Yann Hascoet and Emmanuel Baclet (both France) equaled the feat in Bénodet on August 2, 2004. All records were achieved on the set of *L'Été De Tous Les Records*, the French Guinness World Records TV show.

DIVING

Most Olympic medals Klaus Dibiasi (Austria) won five medals for Italy (three gold, two silver) from 1964 to 1976; Gregory Efthimios Louganis (U.S.A.) also won five (four golds, one silver) over the 1976, 1984, and 1988 Games. Two divers have won the high board and springboard doubles at two Games: Patricia Joan McCormick (née Keller, U.S.A.) in 1952 and 1956; and Greg Louganis in 1984 and 1988.

★ Most high-diving World Championships Orlando Duque (Colombia) has won the World High Diving Federation World Championships a record three times—in 2000, 2001, and 2002.

HIGHEST HEADFIRST DIVES Professional divers from La Quebrada (meaning "the break in the rocks") in Acapulco, Mexico, regularly perform headfirst dives from a height of 115 ft. (35 m) into 12 ft. (3.65 m) of water. The base rocks, which project 21 ft. (6.4 m) from the takeoff, require a leap out of 27 ft. (8.22 m).

★**Highest-scored dive** In 2000, during the Cliff-Diving World Championships in Kaunolu, Hawaii, U.S.A., Orlando Duque (Colombia) performed a double back somersault with four twists from a height of 80 ft. (24.40 m). For this dive, he earned a perfect 10 from all seven judges and scored 159.00 points.

WHAT'S THE RECORD FOR THE MOST PEOPLE RIDING ON THE SAME SURFBOARD SIMULTANEOUSLY? FIND OUT ON P. 329

ROWING

Most Olympic gold medals won Steve Redgrave (GB) won five gold medals: coxed fours (1984), coxless pairs (1988, 1992, and 1996), and coxless fours (2000).

Elisabeta Lipa (Romania) won five gold medals from 1984 to 2004, the ★**most women's rowing gold medals won.**

SWIMMING

Farthest distance swum by a 20-strong relay team in 24 hours New Zealand's national relay team swam 113.59 miles (182.807 km) in Lower Hutt, New Zealand, in 24 hours, passing 100 miles (160 km) in 20 hr. 47 min. 13 sec., on December 9–10, 1983.

Fastest time to swim the Channel The official Channel Swimming Association (founded 1927) record is 7 hr. 17 min. by Chad Hundeby (U.S.A.), from Shakespeare Beach, Dover, UK, to Cap Gris-Nez, France, on September 27, 1994.

The **fastest France-to-England time** is 8 hr. 5 min. by Richard Davey (UK) in 1988. The **fastest crossing by a relay team** is 6 hr. 52 min. (England to France) by the U.S. National Swim Team on August 1, 1990. They then completed the **fastest two-way relay** in 14 hr. 18 min.

Largest race in open water The most participants in an open-sea race was 3,070 for The Pier to Pub Swim, Lorne, Victoria, Australia, on January 10, 1998.

Longest ocean swim Susie Maroney (Australia) swam 122 miles (197 km) from Mexico to Cuba—the **longest distance ever swum without flippers in open sea**—in 38 hr. 33 min. She arrived in Cuba on June 1, 1998.

Most World Championship medals won Michael Gross (West Germany) won 13 medals—five gold, five silver, and three bronze—from 1982

☆**OLDEST CHANNEL SWIMMER** George Brunstad (U.S.A., b. August 25, 1934) was 70 years 4 days old when he swam from Dover, UK, to Sangatte, France, in 15 hr. 59 min. on August 29, 2004. The oldest woman to swim the Channel was Susan Fraenkel (South Africa, b. April 22, 1948), aged 46 years 103 days on July 24, 1994, with a time of 12 hr. 5 min.

to 1990. The **most World Championship medals won by a woman** is 10, by Kornelia Ender (GDR, now Germany)—eight gold and two silver in 1973 and 1975.

The **most World Championship medals at a single championship** is seven by Matt Biondi (U.S.A.)—three gold, one silver, three bronze—in 1986. The **most World Championship gold medals won by a man** is eight by Ian Thorpe (Australia) in 1998 and 2001.

Most consecutive olympic gold medals Two swimmers have won the same event three times—Dawn Fraser (Australia), for the 100 m freestyle in 1956, 1960, and 1964; and Krisztina Egerszegi (Hungary), for the 200 m backstroke in 1988, 1992, and 1996.

THE ENGLISH CHANNEL

The English Channel is a named area of the Atlantic Ocean between France and the UK approximately 350 miles (550 km) long. At its narrowest, between Dover (England) and Cap Griz-Nez (France), it measures 21 miles (34 km).

Many swimmers have endeavored to traverse this famous stretch of water. The **first to swim the English Channel from shore to shore (without a life jacket)** was UK merchant navy captain Matthew Webb (1848–83), who swam an estimated 38 miles (61 km) to make the 21-mile (34-km) crossing in 21 hr. 45 min. on August 24–25, 1875.

The **first woman** to succeed was Gertrude Caroline Ederle (U.S.A.), who swam from France to England on August 6, 1926, in the then overall record time of 14 hr. 39 min., earning her a ticker-tape parade on her return to New York City, U.S.A.

WAKEBOARDING

☆**Most wakeboarding World Titles (men)** Darin Shapiro (U.S.A.) has won three men's World Championship titles, in 1999, 2001, and 2002.

The record for the **most women's wakeboarding World Championship titles** is shared between Tara Hamilton (U.S.A.), who won the title in 1998 and 2002, and Meghan Major (U.S.A.), who won in 1999 and 2000.

WATER POLO

☆**Most Olympic wins (men)** Hungary has won the Olympic tournament most often, with eight wins, in 1932, 1936, 1952, 1956, 1964, 1976, 2000, and 2004.

Since women's water polo was introduced at the 2000 Games, the winners have been Australia in 2000 and Italy in 2004.

☆**Most World Championship titles** The first water polo World Championships were held in 1973, and the most wins is three by the USSR, who took the title in 1975, 1982, and 2002 (as Russia).

Since it was introduced in 1986, the women's water polo World Championships have been won twice by Italy, in 1998 and 2001.

Most international water polo goals The greatest number of goals scored by an individual in an international match is 13 by Debbie Handley

★WAKEBOARD—LONGEST RAMP JUMP A wakeboard is a short, broad ski on which a skier is pulled along behind a motorboat. The farthest that anyone has ramp-jumped on a wakeboard is 49.2 ft. (15 m), by Jerome MacQuart (France) on the set of *L'Été De Tous Les Records* in Argeles Gazost, France, on July 14, 2004.

MOST PRO SURFING WORLD CHAMPIONSHIPS (WOMEN) Layne Beachley (Australia) won six ASP (Association of Surfing Professionals) Tour World Championship titles from 1998 to 2003.

for Australia (16) v. Canada (10) at the World Championships in Guayaquil, Ecuador, in 1982.

Longest water polo marathon Rapido 82 Haarlem at the De Planeet pool in Haarlem, the Netherlands, played a water polo marathon lasting 24 hours from April 30 to May 1, 1999.

WATERSKIING (BAREFOOT)

☆**Most World Championships (team)** The team title has been won a total of nine times by the U.S.A. from 1988 to 2004.

Most World Championships (women) Two competitors have won the barefoot World Championship four times each: Kim Lampard (Australia) in 1980, 1982, 1985, and 1986; Jennifer Calleri (U.S.A.) in 1990, 1992, 1994, and 1996.

☆**Oldest barefoot water-skier** George Blair, a.k.a. "Banana George" (U.S.A., b. January 22, 1915), water-skied barefoot on Lake Florence, Winter Haven, Florida, U.S.A., aged 90 years 29 days on February 20, 2005.

☆ **BAREFOOT WATERSKIING WORLD CHAMPION (MEN)** The most titles won by a man is four by Ron Scarpa (U.S.A.), who won in 1992, 1996, 1998, and 2000.

WHITE-WATER RAFTING

Most World Championships (men) The World Rafting Challenge Championship has been held since 1995. Slovenia has won five times from 1995 to 1999.

★ Most World Championships (women) New Zealand has won three times, in 1999, 2000, and 2003.

WINTER SPORTS

BOBSLEDDING

☆ **Most World Championships by a women's team** Since the women's World Championships were introduced in 2000 and debuted at the 2002 Winter Olympic Games, Germany has won the title three times (2000, 2003, and 2004).

Most individual World Championship titles Eugenio Monti (Italy) won 11 titles from 1957 to 1968. He did this by winning eight two-man titles and three four-man titles.

BOBSLEDDING—MOST CRESTA RUN GRAND NATIONAL WINS The most wins in the Grand National (instituted 1885) is eight by the 1948 Olympic champion Nino Bibbia (Italy), 1960–1973; and by Franco Gansser (Switzerland), 1981–1991.

Fastest Cresta Run completion time The Cresta Run course is 3,977 ft. (1,212 m) long with a drop of 514 ft. (157 m). The record—50.09 seconds (average speed 54.13 mph; 87.11 km/h)—was achieved by James Sunley (UK) on February 13, 1999.

Fastest Cresta Run time from the Junction On January 17, 1999, Johannes Badrutt (Switzerland) set a time of 41.02 seconds to travel 2,921 ft. (890 m) on the Cresta Run, starting from the Junction.

CURLING

Largest Bonspiel At the 1988 Bonspiel in Winnipeg, Canada, there were 1,424 teams of four men, a total of 5,696 curlers, using 187 sheets of curling ice. "Bonspiel" means "league game."

CRESTA RUN

The Cresta Run is a hazardously steep and winding channel of ice carved into the natural contours of the Cresta Valley in St. Moritz, Switzerland, each year. The run is 3,977 ft. (1,212 m) long and has a total drop of 514 ft. (157 m). Racers can reach a top speed of 80 mph (129 km/h), and can control their lightweight toboggans by using rakes on their boots as a brake.

There are two starting points on the Cresta Run. The full course is run from the "Top," and only experienced riders are permitted to ride from this point. The other starting point—the "Junction"—is one third of the way down the course.

★ CURLING—MOST WORLD CHAMPIONSHIP MEDALS (INDIVIDUAL)
Dordi Nordby (Norway) won 10 curling medals from 1989 to 2004—two gold, three silver, and five bronze. The ★most medals by a man is nine: Eigil Ramsfjell (Norway) won three gold, two silver, and four bronze medals from 1978 to 1991.

☆ **Most men's World Championship titles** Canada has won the men's World Championships a total of 28 times, from 1959 to 2003.

DOG SLEDDING

Oldest sled dog racing trail The oldest established sled dog trail is the 1,049-mile (1,688-km) Iditarod Trail from Anchorage to Nome, Alaska, U.S.A., which has existed since 1910 and has been the course of an annual race since 1967.

Longest trail The longest race is the 1,243-mile (2,000-km) Berengia Trail from Esso to Markovo, Russia, which started as a 155-mile (250-km) route in April 1990. Now established as an annual event, the fastest time to complete the trail was achieved in 1991 by Pavel Lazarev (Russia) in 10 days 18 hr. 17 min. 56 sec.—an average rate of 5 mph (8 km/h).

☆ CURLING—MOST WORLD CHAMPIONSHIP TITLES (WOMEN) The Canadian women's team has accumulated 13 World Championships in curling (1980, 1984–87, 1989, 1993–94, 1996–97, 2000–01, 2004).

SKATING—FIGURE

Most pairs World Championship titles Irina Rodnina won 10 pairs titles (instituted 1908), four with Aleksey Nikolayevich Ulanov in 1969–72 and six with her husband Aleksandr Gennadyevich Zaitsev (all USSR) in 1973–78.

The **most ice dance titles** (instituted 1952) won is six by Lyudmila Alekseyevna Pakhomova (1946–86) and her husband Aleksandr Georgiyevich Gorshkov (both USSR) in 1970–74 and 1976. The couple also won the first ever Olympic ice dance title in 1976.

Highest marks Donald George Jackson (Canada) scored a total of seven perfect 6.0s in the men's World Championship in Prague, Czechoslovakia (now Czech Republic), in 1962.

Midori Ito (Japan) is the **highest scoring woman** with seven perfect 6.0s awarded at the 1989 figure skating World Championships held in Paris, France.

FIGURE SKATING—MOST WORLD CHAMPIONSHIP TITLES The most World Championship titles by a woman is held by Sonja Henie (Norway), pictured, who won 10 championships from 1927 to 1936.

Ulrich Salchow (Sweden) won 10 individual figure skating world titles in 1901–05 and 1907–11, the most World Championship titles by a man.

Youngest World Champion Tara Lipinski (U.S.A., b. June 10, 1982) was 14 years 286 days old when she won the individual title on March 22, 1997.

SKATING—SPEED

Most World Championship sprint wins by a man Igor Zhelezovskiy (USSR/Belarus) has won six men's sprint overall titles (1985–86, 1989, and 1991–93).

☆ **SPEED SKATING—LOWEST WORLD CHAMPIONSHIP SCORE** The lowest, and therefore best, World Championship speed skating score achieved by a man is 150.478 points by Chad Hedrick (U.S.A.) for the overall title in Hamar, Norway, on February 7–8, 2004. The lowest women's score is 161.479 points, set by Gunda Niemann-Stirnemann (Germany) in Hamar, Norway, on February 6–7, 1999.

Most World Championship titles Two speed skaters have won five titles each: Oscar Mathisen (Norway) won in 1908–09 and 1912–14; Clas Thunberg (Sweden) won in 1923, 1925, 1928–29, and 1931.

WHICH COUNTRY HAS WON THE MOST MEDALS AT THE WINTER OLYMPIC GAMES? FIND OUT ON P. 515

SKIING—ALPINE

Longest race The Inferno in Switzerland stretches over 9.8 miles (15.8 km) from the top of the Schilthorn to Lauterbrunnen.

The **fastest time to complete the course** is 13 min. 53.40 sec. by Urs von Allmen (Switzerland) in 1992. The women's record is 17 min. 8.42 sec. by Christine Sonderegger (Switzerland), also in 1992.

The ☆**greatest number of entries for the race** was 1,611 in 2004.

Most World Cup race wins by a man The World Cup for Alpine events was introduced in 1967. The most individual event wins is 86 (46

SKIING—MOST WORLD CUP WINS IN A SEASON The men's record is held jointly by Ingemar Stenmark (Sweden) with 13 wins in the 1978–79 season and Hermann Maier (Austria, pictured) with 13 wins in the 2000–01 season.

The women's record is held by Vreni Schneider (Switzerland), who won 13 events (and a combined) including all seven slalom events in the 1988–89 season.

giant slalom, 40 slalom from a total of 287 races) by Ingemar Stenmark (Sweden) in 1974–89, including an unprecedented 14 successive giant slalom wins from March 18, 1978, his 22nd birthday, to January 21, 1980.

Most Alpine skiing World Cup race wins by a woman Annemarie Moser (neé Pröll, Austria) achieved a women's record 62 individual event wins (1970–79). She had a record 11 consecutive downhill wins from December 1972 to January 1974 and has also claimed the World Cup overall champion (downhill and slalom events combined) title a record six times since the tour began in 1967.

SKIING—FREESTYLE

Most World Cup titles by a man Eric Laboureix (France) won five titles (1986–88 and 1990–91).

Connie Kissling (Switzerland) won 10 titles from 1983 to 1992, the **most World Cup titles by a woman.**

SKIING (FREESTYLE)—MOST WORLD CHAMPIONSHIP TITLES The first freestyle skiing World Championships were held at Tignes, France, in 1986, with titles awarded in ballet, moguls, aerials, and combined categories. Edgar Grospiron (France) has won a record three titles in moguls (1989 and 1991) and aerials (1995). He has also won an Olympic title, in 1992.

The **most world titles won by a woman** is also three, held by Candice Gilg (France) for moguls in 1993, 1995, and 1997.

Most somersault and twist combination freestyle aerial jumps
Matt Chojnacki (U.S.A.) successfully completed a quadruple-twisting
quadruple backflip at Winter Park Resort, Colorado, U.S.A., on April 4,
2001.

SKIING—NORDIC

Most successful World Champion The first World Nordic Championships were those of the 1924 Winter Olympics in Chamonix, France. The
most titles (including Olympics) won is 17 by Bjørn Dæhlie (Norway,
b. June 19, 1967)—12 individual and five relay, 1991–98. Dæhlie has won a
record 29 medals in total from 1991 to 1999.

Most successful nordic skiing by a woman Yelena Välbe (Russia)
won an unprecedented 10 individual and seven relay titles from 1989 to
1998. With an additional seven medals, her total of 24 is also a record.

Most successful individual in World Championships jumping
The most titles won by a jumper is five by Birger Ruud (Norway) in
1931–32 and 1935–37.

Greatest distance skied in 24 hours (men) The men's record for the
greatest distance traveled in 24 hours by a cross-country skier belongs to
Seppo-Juhani Savolainen (Finland), who covered 258.2 miles (415.5 km) in
Saariselk, Finland, on April 8 9, 1988.

The **greatest distance skied in 24 hours by a woman** is 206.91 miles
(333 km) by Kamila Horakova (Czech Republic) from April 12–13, 2000, at
the Canmore Nordic Center, Alberta, Canada.

Longest race The annual Vasaloppet Race covers a distance of 55.3 miles
(89 km).

The fastest time to complete the race is 3 hr. 48 min. 55 sec., by Bengt
Hassis (Sweden) on March 2, 1986.

SKIING TERMINOLOGY

Aerial = mid-air tricks and jumps, judged on individual merit

Alpine = downhill speed racing

Mogul = a large bump of snow, off which a skier performs jumps or
turns. A patch of bumps is called a "mogul field"

Nordic = cross-country skiing

☆ **LONGEST COMPETITIVE SKIJUMP BY A MAN** Matti Hautamaeki (Finland) successfully landed a skijump measuring 757.8 ft. (231 m) at Planica, Slovenia, on March 23, 2003. Hautamaeki is pictured here competing in the 2002 Winter Olympics in Salt Lake City, U.S.A.

SKIJUMPING

☆ **Longest competitive skijump by a woman** The farthest distance achieved by a female skijumper is 418 ft. 4 in. (127.5 m) and was set by Anette Sagen (Norway) at Oslo, Norway, on March 14, 2004.

☆ **Longest skijump on a dry slope** Veli-Matti Lindstroem (Finland) jumped a distance of 485 ft. 6 in. (148 m) at a dry ski slope at Kuusamo, Finland, on August 4, 2001.

☆ **SNOWBOARDING—MOST WORLD CUP TITLES** Karine Ruby (France) has won an unsurpassed 20 titles: overall (1996–98, 2001–02, and 2003), slalom/parallel slalom (1996–98 and 2002), giant slalom (1995–98 and 2001), snowboard cross (1997, 2001, and 2003–04), and big air (2004). The most men's titles won is six by Mathieu Bozzetto (France): overall (1999–2000) and slalom/parallel slalom (1999–2002).

SNOWBOARDING

☆ **Most World Championship titles** Karine Ruby (France) won a total of seven World Championship titles—the giant slalom in 1996, snowboard cross in 1997, Olympic gold in 1998, giant slalom, parallel slalom, and snowboard cross in 2001, and snowboard cross in 2003.

Highest speed The highest speed recorded by a snowboarder is 125.459 mph (201.907 km/h) by Darren Powell (Australia) at Les Arcs, France, on May 2, 1999.

WHAT WAS THE HIGHEST EVER SCORE IN AN ICE HOCKEY MATCH? FIND OUT ON P. 502

SPORTS REFERENCE

★ ARCHERY—OUTDOOR ★

MEN (RECURVE)	RECORD	NAME & NATIONALITY
FITA Round	1,379	Oh Kyo-moon (South Korea)
90 m	337	Jang Yong-ho (South Korea)
70 m	347	Choi Young-kwang (South Korea)
50 m	351	Kim Kyung-ho (South Korea)
30 m	360/17	Kye Dong-hyun (South Korea)
Team Round	4,074	South Korea (Jang Yong-ho, Choi Young-kwang, Im Dong-hyun)

WOMEN (RECURVE)	RECORD	NAME & NATIONALITY
☆ FITA Round	1,405	Park Sung-hyun (South Korea)
☆ 70 m	351	Park Sung-hyun (South Korea)
☆ 60 m	351	Kim Yu-mi (South Korea)
50 m	350	Park Sung-hyun (South Korea)
☆ 30 m	360/15	Yun Mi-jin (South Korea)
Team Round	4,094	South Korea (Cho Youn-jeong, Kim Soo-nyung, Lee Eun-kyung)

★ INDOOR FIELD EVENTS ★

MEN	RECORD	NAME & NATIONALITY
High jump	7 ft. 11.5 in. (2.43 m)	Javier Sotomayor (Cuba)
Pole vault	20 ft. 2 in. (6.15 m)	Sergei Bubka (Ukraine)
Long jump	28 ft. 10.25 in. (8.79 m)	Carl Lewis (U.S.A.)
Triple jump	58 ft. 6 in. (17.83 m)	Aliecer Urrutia (Cuba)
Shot-put	74 ft. 4.5 in. (22.66 m)	Randy Barnes (U.S.A.)
Heptathlon*	6,476 points	Dan O'Brien (U.S.A.)

WOMEN	RECORD	NAME & NATIONALITY
High jump	6 ft. 9.5 in. (2.07 m)	Heike Henkel (Germany)
☆ Pole vault	16 ft. 1 in. (4.90 m)	Yelena Isinbayeva (Russia)
Long jump	24 ft. 2.25 in. (7.37 m)	Heike Drechsler (GDR)
☆ Triple jump	50 ft. 4.75 in. (15.36 m)	Tatyana Lebedeva (Russia)
Shot-put	73 ft. 10 in. (22.50 m)	Helena Fibingerov (Czechoslovakia)
Pentathlon†	4,991 points	Irina Belova (Russia)

PLACE	DATE
Wonju, South Korea	November 1, 2000
New York City, U.S.A.	June 16, 2003
Hongseong, South Korea	August 20, 2002
Wonju, South Korea	September 1, 1997
Cheongju, South Korea	September 1, 1997
New York City, U.S.A.	July 16, 2003

PLACE	DATE
Cheongju, South Korea	October 10, 2004
Cheongju, South Korea	October 9, 2004
Cheongju, South Korea	August 27, 2004
Yecheon, South Korea	March 12, 2003
Yecheon, South Korea	October 27, 2004
Barcelona, Spain	August 1, 1992

ARCHERY Jang Yong-ho (South Korea) on his way to setting a world record with a score of 337 at 90 m during the 42nd World Archery Outdoor Championships on June 16, 2003.

PLACE	DATE		
Budapest, Hungary	March 4, 1989	*60 m	6.67 sec.
Donets'k, Ukraine	February 21, 1993	Long jump	7.84 m
New York City, U.S.A.	January 27, 1984	Shot-put	16.02 m
Sindelfingen, Germany	March 1, 1997	High jump	2.13 m
Los Angeles, U.S.A.	January 20, 1989	60 m-hurdles	7.85 sec.
Toronto, Canada	March 13–14, 1993	Pole vault	5.20 m
		1,000 m	2 min. 57.96 sec.

PLACE	DATE		
Karlsruhe, Germany	February 9, 1992	†60 m hurdles	8.22 sec.
Madrid, Spain	March 6, 2005	High jump	1.93 m
Vienna, Austria	February 13, 1988	Shot	13.25 m
Budapest, Hungary	March 6, 2004	Long jump	6.67 m
Jablonec, Czechoslovakia	February 19, 1977	800 m	2 min. 10.26 sec.
Berlin, Germany	February 14–15, 1992		

★ OUTDOOR FIELD EVENTS ★

MEN	RECORD	NAME & NATIONALITY
High jump	8 ft. 0.25 in. (2.45 m)	Javier Sotomayor (Cuba)
Pole vault	20 ft. 1.75 in. (6.14 m)	Sergei Bubka (Ukraine)
Long jump	29 ft. 4.5 in. (8.95 m)	Mike Powell (U.S.A.)
Triple jump	60 ft. 0.25 in. (18.29 m)	Jonathan Edwards (GB)
Shot-put	75 ft. 10.25 in. (23.12 m)	Randy Barnes (U.S.A.)
Discus	243 ft. (74.08 m)	Jürgen Schult (GDR)
Hammer	284 ft. 7 in. (86.74 m)	Yuriy Sedykh (USSR)
Javelin	323 ft. 1 in. (98.48 m)	Jan Zelezny (Czech Republic)
Decathlon*	9,026 points	Roman Sebrle (Czech Republic)

WOMEN	RECORD	NAME & NATIONALITY
High jump	6 ft. 10.25 in. (2.09 m)	Stefka Kostadinova (Bulgaria)
☆ Pole vault	16 ft. 1.6 in. (4.92 m)	Yelena Isinbayeva (Russia)
Long jump	24 ft. 8.25 in. (7.52 m)	Galina Chistyakova (USSR)
Triple jump	50 ft. 10.25 in. (15.50 m)	Inessa Kravets (Ukraine)
Shot-put	74 ft. 3 in. (22.63 m)	Natalya Lisovskaya (USSR)
Discus	252 ft. (76.80 m)	Gabriele Reinsch (GDR)
Javelin	234 ft. 8 in. (71.54 m)	Osleidys Menédez (Cuba)
Heptathlon†	7,291 points	Jacqueline Joyner-Kersee (U.S.A.)

**WHAT'S THE FARTHEST DISTANCE ANYONE HAS
EVER ROWED ON LAND? FIND OUT ON P. 539**

PLACE	DATE		
Salamanca, Spain	July 27, 1993	*100 m	10.64 sec.
Sestriere, Italy	July 31, 1994	Long jump	8.11 m
Tokyo, Japan	August 30, 1991	Shot	15.33 m
Gothenburg, Sweden	August 7, 1995	High jump	2.12 m
Los Angeles, U.S.A.	May 20, 1990	400 m	47.79 sec.
Neubrandenburg, Germany	June 6, 1986	110 m hurdles	13.92 sec.
Stuttgart, Germany	August 30, 1986	Discus	47.92 m
Jena, Germany	May 25, 1996	Pole vault	4.80 m
Gotzis, Austria	May 26–27, 2001	Javelin	70.16 m
		1,500 m	4 min. 21.98 sec.

PLACE	DATE		
Rome, Italy	August 30, 1987	†100 m-hurdles	12.69 sec.
Brussels, Belgium	September 3, 2004	High jump	1.86 m
St. Petersburg, Russia	June 1, 1988	Shot-put	15.80 m
Gothenburg, Sweden	August 10, 1995	200 m	22.56 sec.
Moscow, Russia	June 7, 1987	Long jump	7.27 m
Neubrandenburg, Germany	July 9, 1988	Javelin	45.66 m
Rethymno, Greece	July 1, 2001	800 m	2 min. 8.51 sec.
Seoul, South Korea	September 23–24, 1988		

MEN'S 5,000 M Kenenisa Bekele (Ethiopia) celebrates breaking the world 5,000 m record during the Norwich Union Grand Prix at the Birmingham National Indoor Arena (NIA) on February 20, 2004, in Birmingham, UK.

★ INDOOR TRACK EVENTS ★

MEN	TIME	NAME & NATIONALITY
50 m	5.56	Donovan Bailey (Canada)
		Maurice Greene (U.S.A.)
60 m	6.39	Maurice Greene (U.S.A.)
		Maurice Greene (U.S.A.)
200 m	19.92	Frank Fredericks (Namibia)
400 m	44.57	Kerron Clement (U.S.A.)
800 m	1:42.67	Wilson Kipketer (Denmark)
1,000 m	2:14.96	Wilson Kipketer (Denmark)
1,500 m	3:31.18	Hicham El Guerrouj (Morocco)
1 mile	3:48.45	Hicham El Guerrouj (Morocco)
3,000 m	7:24.90	Daniel Komen (Kenya)
5,000 m	12:49.60	Kenenisa Bekele (Ethiopia)
50 m hurdles	6.25	Mark McCoy (Canada)
60 m hurdles	7.30	Colin Jackson (GB)
4 × 200 m relay	1:22.11	Great Britain (Linford Christie, Darren Braithwaite, Ade Mafe, John Regis)
4 × 400 m relay	3:02.83	U.S.A. (Andre Morris, Dameon Johnson, Deon Minor, Milton Campbell)
5,000 m walk	18:07.08	Mikhail Shchennikov (Russia)

WOMEN	TIME	NAME & NATIONALITY
50 m	5.96	Irina Privalova (Russia)
60 m	6.92	Irina Privalova (Russia)
200 m	21.87	Merlene Ottey (Jamaica)
400 m	49.59	Jarmila Kratochvílovà (Czechoslovakia)
800 m	1:55.82	Jolanda Ceplak (Slovenia)
1,000 m	2:30.94	Maria Mutola (Mozambique)
1,500 m	3:59.98	Regina Jacobs (U.S.A.)
1 mile	4:17.14	Doina Melinte (Romania)
3,000 m	8:29.15	Berhane Adere (Ethiopia)
☆5,000 m	14:32.93	Tirunesh Dibaba (Ethiopia)
50 m hurdles	6.58	Cornelia Oschkenat (GDR)
60 m hurdles	7.69	Lyudmila Engquist (Russia)
☆4 × 200 m relay	1:32.41	Russia (Yekaterina Kondratyeva, Irina Khabarova, Yuliva Pechonkina, Julia Gushchina)
☆4 × 400 m relay	3:23.88	Russia (Olesya Krasnomovets, Olga Kotlyarova, Tatyana Levina, Natalya Nazarova)
3,000 m walk	11:40.33	Claudia Iovan (Romania)

WOMEN'S 3,000 M Berhane Adere (Ethiopia) in the 3,000 m women's event, which she completed in 8 min. 29.15 sec. on February 3, 2002, at the International Light Athletic meeting at the Schleyer-Halle in Stuttgart, Germany.

PLACE	DATE
Reno, U.S.A.	February 9, 1996
Los Angeles, U.S.A.	February 3, 1999
Madrid, Spain	February 3, 1998
Atlanta, U.S.A.	March 3, 2001
Lievin, France,	February 18, 1996
Fayetteville, U.S.A.	March 12, 1995
Paris, France	March 9, 1997
Birmingham, UK	February 20, 2000
Stuttgart, Germany	February 2, 1997
Ghent, Belgium	February 12, 1997
Budapest, Hungary	February 6, 1998
Birmingham, UK	February 20, 2004
Kobe, Japan	March 5, 1986
Sindelfingen, Germany	March 6, 1994
Glasgow, UK	March 3, 1991
Maebashi, Japan	March 7, 1999
Moscow, Russia	February 14, 1995

MEN'S 200 M Frank Fredericks (Namibia) pictured after smashing the world record for the 200 m during the Vittel Du Pas Calais meeting in Lievin, France, on February 18, 1996.

PLACE	DATE
Madrid, Spain	February 9, 1995
Madrid, Spain	February 11, 1993
	February 9, 1995
Lievin, France	February 13, 1993
Milan, Italy	March 7, 1982
Vienna, Austria	March 3, 2002
Stockholm, Sweden	February 25, 1999
Boston, U.S.A.	February 2, 2003
East Rutherford, U.S.A.	February 9, 1990
Stuttgart, Germany	February 3, 2002
Boston, U.S.A.	January 29, 2005
Berlin, Germany	February 20, 1988
Chelyabinsk, Russia	February 4, 1993
Glasgow, UK	January 29, 2005
Budapest, Hungary	March 7, 2004
Bucharest, Romania	January 30, 1999

WOMEN'S 200 M Merlene Ottey (Jamaica), holder of the indoor 200 m world record, at the 1996 centennial Olympic Games in Atlanta, Georgia, U.S.A.

★ ATHLETICS—OUTDOOR TRACK EVENTS ★

MEN	TIME	NAME & NATIONALITY
100 m	9.78	Tim Montgomery (U.S.A.)
200 m	19.32	Michael Johnson (U.S.A.)
400 m	43.18	Michael Johnson (U.S.A.)
800 m	1:41.11	Wilson Kipketer (Denmark)
1,000 m	2:11.96	Noah Ngeny (Kenya)
1,500 m	3:26.00	Hicham El Guerrouj (Morocco)
1 mile	3:43.13	Hicham El Guerrouj (Morocco)
2,000 m	4:44.79	Hicham El Guerrouj (Morocco)
3,000 m	7:20.67	Daniel Komen (Kenya)
☆5,000 m	2:37.35	Kenenisa Bekele (Ethiopia)
☆10,000 m	26:20.31	Kenenisa Bekele (Ethiopia)
20,000 m	56:55.60	Arturo Barrios (Mexico, now U.S.A.)
25,000 m	1:13:55.80	Toshihiko Seko (Japan)
30,000 m	1:29:18.80	Toshihiko Seko (Japan)
1 hour	21,101 m	Arturo Barrios (Mexico, now U.S.A.)
110 m hurdles	12.91	Colin Jackson (GB)
400 m hurdles	46.78	Kevin Young (U.S.A.)
☆3,000 m steeplechase	7:53.63	Saif Saaeed Shaheen (Qatar)
4 × 100 m relay	37.40	U.S.A. (Michael Marsh, Leroy Burrell, Dennis Mitchell, Carl Lewis)
		U.S.A. (John Drummond, Jr., Andre Cason, Dennis Mitchell, Leroy Burrell)
4 × 200 m relay	1:18.68	Santa Monica Track Club, U.S.A. (Michael Marsh, Leroy Burrell, Floyd Heard, Carl Lewis)
4 × 400 m relay	2:54.20	U.S.A. (Jerome Young, Antonio Pettigrew, Tyree Washington, Michael Johnson)
4 × 800 m relay	7:03.89	Great Britain (Peter Elliott, Garry Cook, Steve Cram, Sebastian Coe)
4 × 1,500 m relay	14:38.8	West Germany (Thomas Wessinghage, Harald Hudak, Michael Lederer, Karl Fleschen)

WOMEN	TIME	NAME & NATIONALITY
100 m	10.49	Florence Griffith-Joyner (U.S.A.)
200 m	21.34	Florence Griffith-Joyner (U.S.A.)
400 m	47.6	Marita Koch (GDR)
800 m	1:53.28	Jarmila Kratochvílová (Czechoslovakia)
1,000 m	2:28.98	Svetlana Masterkova (Russia)
1,500 m	3:50.46	Qu Yunxia (China)
1 mile	4:12.56	Svetlana Masterkova (Russia)
2,000 m	5:25.36	Sonia O'Sullivan (Ireland)
3,000 m	8:06.11	Wang Junxia (China)
☆5,000 m	14:24.68	Elvan Abeylegesse (Turkey)
10,000 m	29:31.78	Wang Junxia (China)
20,000 m	1:05:26.6	Tegla Loroupe (Kenya)
25,000 m	1:27:05.9	Tegla Loroupe (Kenya)
30,000 m	1:45:50.0	Tegla Loroupe (Kenya)
1 hour	18,340 m	Tegla Loroupe (Kenya)
100 m hurdles	12.21	Yordanka Donkova (Bulgaria)
400 m hurdles	52.34	Yuliya Pechonkina (Russia)

Sports & Games

PLACE	DATE
Paris, France	September 14, 2002
Atlanta, U.S.A.	August 1, 1996
Seville, Spain	August 26, 1999
Cologne, Germany	August 24, 1997
Rieti, Italy	September 5, 1999
Rome, Italy	July 14, 1998
Rome, Italy	July 7, 1999
Berlin, Germany	September 7, 1999
Rieti, Italy	September 1, 1996
Hengelo, Netherlands	May 31, 2004
Ostrava, Czech Republic	June 8, 2004
La Flèche, France	March 30, 1991
Christchurch, New Zealand	March 22, 1981
Christchurch, New Zealand	March 22, 1981
La Flèche, France	March 30, 1991
Stuttgart, Germany	August 20, 1993
Barcelona, Spain	August 6, 1992
Brussels, Belgium	September 3, 2004
Barcelona, Spain	August 8, 1992
Stuttgart, Germany	August 21, 1993
Walnut, U.S.A.	April 17, 1994
New York City, U.S.A.	July 23, 1998
London, UK	August 30, 1982
Cologne, Germany	August 17, 1977

MEN'S 100 M Tim Montgomery (U.S.A.) completes the men's 100 m race in 9.78 seconds on September 14, 2002, at the IAAF Grand-Prix Final in Paris, France.

PLACE	DATE
Indianapolis, U.S.A.	July 16, 1988
Seoul, South Korea	September 29, 1988
Canberra, Australia	October 6, 1985
Munich, Germany	July 26, 1983
Brussels, Belgium	August 23, 1996
Beijing, China	September 11, 1993
Zürich, Switzerland	August 14, 1996
Edinburgh, UK	July 8, 1994
Beijing, China	September 13, 1993
Bergen, Norway	June 11, 2004
Beijing, China	September 8, 1993
Borgholzhausen, Germany	September 3, 2000
Megerkirchen, Germany	September 21, 2002
Warstein, Germany	June 6, 2003
Borgholzhausen, Germany	August 7, 1998
Stara Zagora, Bulgaria	August 20, 1988
Tula, Russia	August 8, 2003

WOMEN'S 5,000 M Elvan Abeylegesse (Turkey) on her way to winning the women's 5,000 m race at the IAAF Bergen Bislett games held on June 11, 2004, in Bergen, Norway.

★ ATHLETICS—OUTDOOR TRACK EVENTS ★

WOMEN	TIME	NAME & NATIONALITY
☆ 3,000 m steeplechase	9:01.59	Gulnara Samitova (Russia)
4 × 100 m relay	41.37	GDR (Silke Gladisch, Sabine Rieger, Ingrid Auerswald, Marlies Göhr)
4 × 200 m relay	1:27.46	United States "Blue" (Latasha Jenkins, LaTasha Colander-Richardson, Nanceen Perry, Marion Jones)
4 × 400 m relay	3:15.17	USSR (Tatyana Ledovskaya, Olga Nazarova, Maria Pinigina, Olga Bryzgina)
4 × 800 m relay	7:50.17	USSR (Nadezhda Olizarenko, Lyubov Gurina, Lyudmila Borisova, Irina Podyalovskaya)

★ ATHLETICS—ROAD RACE ★

MEN	TIME	NAME & NATIONALITY
10 km	27:02	Haile Gebrselassie (Ethiopia)
15 km	41:29	Felix Limo (Kenya)
20 km	56:18	Paul Tergat (Kenya)
Half marathon	59:17	Paul Tergat (Kenya)
☆ 25 km	1:12:45	Paul Kosgei (Kenya)
☆ 30 km	1:28:00	Takayuki Matsumiya (Japan)
Marathon	2:04:55	Paul Tergat (Kenya)
100 km	6:13:33	Takahiro Sunada (Japan)

WOMEN	TIME	NAME & NATIONALITY
10 km	30:21	Paula Radcliffe (UK)
15 km	46:57	Elana Meyer (South Africa)
20 km	1:03:26	Paula Radcliffe (UK)
Half marathon	1:06:44	Elana Meyer (South Africa)
25 km	1:22:31	Naoko Takahashi (Japan)
30 km	1:39:02	Naoko Takahashi (Japan)
Marathon	2:15:25	Paula Radcliffe (UK)
100 km	6:33:11	Tomoe Abe (Japan)

★ ATHLETICS—ULTRA-LONG DISTANCE ★

MEN	TIME/DISTANCE	NAME & NATIONALITY
100 km	6:10:20	Don Ritchie (GB)
☆ 100 miles	11:28:03	Oleg Kharitonov (Russia)
1,000 miles	11 days 13:54:58	Piotr Silikin (Lithuania)
24 hours	188.6 miles (303.5 km)	Yiannis Kouros (Australia)
6 days	635.0 miles (1,022.0 km)	Yiannis Kouros (Greece)

PLACE	DATE
Iraklio, Greece	July 4, 2004
Canberra, Australia	October 6, 1985
Philadelphia, U.S.A.	April 29, 2000
Seoul, South Korea	October 1, 1988
Moscow, Russia	August 5, 1984

PLACE	DATE
Doha, Qatar	December 11, 2002
Nijmegen, Netherlands	November 11, 2001
Milan, Italy	April 4, 1998
Milan, Italy	April 4, 1998
Berlin, Germany	May 9, 2004
Kumamoto, Japan	February 27, 2005
Berlin, Germany	September 28, 2003
Yubetsu, Japan	June 21, 1998

PLACE	DATE
San Juan, Puerto Rico	February 23, 2003
Cape Town, South Africa	November 2, 1991
Bristol, UK	October 6, 2001
Tokyo, Japan	January 15, 1999
Berlin, Germany	September 30, 2001
Berlin, Germany	September 30, 2001
London, UK	April 13, 2003
Yufutsu, Japan	June 25, 2000

WOMEN'S 10 KM
Paula Radcliffe (UK) in training for her record-breaking 10-km run, which she finished in 30 min. 21 sec. in February 2003. She also holds the record for the women's 20 km.

PLACE	DATE
London, UK	October 28, 1978
London, UK	October 2, 2002
Nanango, Australia	March 11–23, 1998
Adelaide, Australia	October 4–5, 1997
New York, U.S.A.	July 2–8, 1984

★ ATHLETICS—ULTRA-LONG DISTANCE ★

WOMEN	TIME/DISTANCE	NAME & NATIONALITY
☆ 100 km	7:14:05	Norimi Sakurai (Japan)
☆ 100 miles	14:25:45	Edit Berces (Hungary)
1,000 miles	13 days 01:54:02	Eleanor Robinson (GB)
☆ 24 hours	155.4 miles (250.1 km)	Edit Berces (Hungary)
6 days	549 miles (883.6 km)	Sandra Barwick (NZ)

★ FREE-DIVING APNEA ★

DEPTH DISCIPLINES	DEPTH	NAME & NATIONALITY
☆ Men—constant weight	337 ft. 10 in. (103 m)	Martin Stepanek (Czech Republic)
☆ Women—constant weight	255 ft. 10 in. (78 m)	Mandy-Rae Cruickshank (Canada)
☆ Men (without fins)—constant weight	262 ft. 5 in. (80 m)	Martin Stepanek (Czech Republic)
☆ Women (without fins)—constant weight	164 ft. (50 m)	Mandy-Rae Cruickshank (Canada)
☆ Men—variable weight	446 ft. 2 in. (136 m)	Martin Stepanek (Czech Republic)
Women—variable weight	400 ft. 3 in. (122 m)	Tanya Streeter (UK)
☆ Men—no limits	561 ft. (171 m)	Loic Leferme (France)
Women—no limits	524 ft. 11 in. (160 m)	Tanya Streeter (U.S.A.)
☆ Men—free immersion	334 ft. 7 in. (102 m)	Martin Stepanek (Czech Republic)
☆ Women—free immersion	242 ft. 9 in. (74 m)	Mandy-Rae Cruickshank (Canada)

DYNAMIC APNEA	DEPTH	NAME & NATIONALITY
Men	656 ft. 1 in. (200 m)	Peter Pedersen (Denmark)
☆ Women	518 ft. 1 in. (158 m)	Johanna Nordblad (Finland)
☆ Men (without fins)	544 ft. 7 in. (166 m)	Stig Aavall Severinsen (Denmark)
☆ Women (without fins)	341 ft. 2 in. (104 m)	Renate De Bruyn (Netherlands)

STATIC APNEA	TIME	NAME & NATIONALITY
☆ Men (without fins, duration)	8 min. 58 sec.	Tom Sietas (Germany)
☆ Women (without fins, duration)	6 min. 31 sec.	Lotta Ericson (Sweden)

★ ROWING ★

MEN	TIME	ROWER(S)/COUNTRY
Single sculls	6:36.33	Marcel Hacker (Germany)
Double sculls	6:04.37	Luka Spik, Iztok Cop (Slovenia)
Quadruple sculls	5:37.68	Italy
Coxless pairs	6:14.27	Matthew Pinsent, James Cracknell (GB)
Coxless fours	5:41.35	Germany
Coxed pairs*	6:42.16	Igor Boraska, Tihomir Frankovic, Milan Razov (Croatia)
Coxed fours*	5:58.96	Germany
☆ Coxed eights	5:19.85	U.S.A.

*Denotes non-Olympic boat classes

PLACE	DATE
Verona, Italy	September 27, 2003
Verona, Italy	September 21–22, 2002
Nanango, Australia	March 11–24, 1998
Verona, Italy	September 21–22, 2002
Campbelltown, Australia	November 18–24, 1990

PLACE	DATE
Spetses Island, Greece	September 10, 2004
Grand Cayman, Cayman Islands	March 21, 2004
Grand Cayman, Cayman Islands	April 9, 2005
Grand Cayman, Cayman Islands	April 8, 2005
Grand Cayman, Cayman Islands	April 14, 2005
Turks and Caicos	July 21, 2003
Nice, France	October 30, 2004
Turks and Caicos	August 17, 2002
Grand Cayman, Cayman Islands	March 23, 2004
Grand Cayman, Cayman Islands	April 11, 2005

PLACE	DATE
Randers, Denmark	July 18, 2003
Limassol, Cyprus	June 14, 2004
Aarhus, Denmark	July 19, 2003
Huy, Belgium	April 25, 2004

MEN'S NO LIMITS Loic Leferme (France) breaks the apnea world record by reaching a depth of 171 m (561 ft.) on October 30, 2004, near Nice, France.

PLACE	DATE
Eindhoven, Netherlands	December 12, 2004
Limassol, Cyprus	June 19, 2004

REGATTA	YEAR
Seville, Spain	2002
St. Catharines, Canada	1999
Indianapolis, U.S.A.	1994
Seville, Spain	2002
Seville, Spain	2002
Indianapolis, U.S.A.	1994
Vienna, Austria	1991
Athens, Greece	2004

MEN'S SINGLE SCULLS Marcel Hacker (Germany) wins the men's single sculls during the Zurich Rowing World Cup event in Munich, Germany, on August 3, 2002.

★ ROWING ★

WOMEN	TIME	ROWER(S)/COUNTRY
Single sculls	7:07.71	Roumiana Neykova (Bulgaria)
Double sculls	6:38.78	Georgina and Caroline Evers-Swindell
Quadruple sculls	6:10.80	Germany
Coxless pairs	6:53.80	Georgeta Andrunache, Viorica Susanu (Romania)
Coxless fours*	6:25.47	Canada
☆ Coxed eights	5:56.55	U.S.A.

MEN (LIGHTWEIGHT)	TIME	ROWER(S)/COUNTRY
Single sculls*	6:47.97	Karsten Nielsen (Denmark)
Double sculls	6:10.80	Elia Luini, Leonardo Pettinari (Italy)
Quadruple sculls*	5:45.18	Italy
Coxless pairs*	6:29.97	Christian Yantani Garces, Miguel Cerda Silva (Chile)
Coxless fours	5:45.60	Denmark
Coxed eights*	5:30.24	Germany

WOMEN (LIGHTWEIGHT)	TIME	ROWER(S)/COUNTRY
Single sculls*	7:15.88	Marit van Eupen (Netherlands)
☆ Double sculls	6:49.90	Sally Newmarch, Amber Halliday (Australia)
Quadruple sculls*	6:29.55	Australia
Coxless pairs*	7:18.32	Eliza Blair, Justine Joyce (Australia)

*Denotes non-Olympic boat classes

★ SPEED SKATING—LONG TRACK ★

MEN	TIME	NAME & NATIONALITY
500 m	34.32	Hiroyasu Shimizu (Japan)
1,000 m	1:07.18	Gerard van Velde (Netherlands)
☆ 1,500 m	1:43.33	Shani Davis (U.S.A.)
☆ 3,000 m	3:39.02	Chad Hendrick (U.S.A.)
5,000 m	6:14.66	Jochem Uytdehaage (Netherlands)
10,000 m	12:58.92	Jochem Uytdehaage (Netherlands)

WOMEN	TIME	NAME & NATIONALITY
500 m	37.22	Catriona LeMay Doan (Canada)
1,000 m	1:13.83	Christine Witty (U.S.A.)
☆ 1,500 m	1:53.87	Cindy Klassen (Canada)
3,000 m	3:57.70	Claudia Pechstein (Germany)
5,000 m	6:46.91	Claudia Pechstein (Germany)

REGATTA	YEAR
Seville, Spain	2002
Seville, Spain	2002
Duisburg, Germany	1996
Seville, Spain	2002
Vienna, Austria	1991
Athens, Greece	2004

REGATTA	YEAR
St. Catharines, Canada	1999
Seville, Spain	2002
Montreal, Canada	1992
Seville, Spain	2002
Lucerne, Switzerland	1999
Montreal, Canada	1992

REGATTA	YEAR
Lucerne, Switzerland	1999
Athens, Greece	2004
Seville, Spain	2002
Aiguebelette, France	1997

WOMEN'S SINGLE SCULLS Roumiana Neykova (Bulgaria) celebrates gold in the single sculls during the FISA Rowing World Championships in Seville, Spain, on September 21, 2002.

PLACE	DATE
Salt Lake City, U.S.A.	March 10, 2001
Salt Lake City, U.S.A.	February 16, 2002
Salt Lake City, U.S.A.	January 9, 2005
Calgary, Canada	March 10, 2005
Salt Lake City, U.S.A.	February 9, 2002
Salt Lake City, U.S.A.	February 22, 2002

PLACE	DATE
Calgary, Canada	December 9, 2001
Salt Lake City, U.S.A.	February 17, 2002
Salt Lake City, U.S.A.	January 9, 2005
Salt Lake City, U.S.A.	February 10, 2002
Salt Lake City, U.S.A.	February 23, 2002

MEN'S 1,000 M SPEED SKATING Gold medalist and new world and Olympic record holder Gerard Van Velde (Netherlands) in the men's 1,000 m speed skating event during the Winter Olympic Games at the Utah Olympic Oval in Salt Lake City, Utah, U.S.A., on February 16, 2002.

WOMEN'S 5,000 M SPEED SKATING
Claudia Pechstein (Germany) skates to victory and a new world record time of 6:46.91 in the women's 5,000 m speed skating event during the Winter Olympic Games at the Utah Olympic Oval in Salt Lake City, Utah, U.S.A., on February 23, 2002.

★ SPEED SKATING—SHORT TRACK ★

MEN	TIME	NAME & NATIONALITY
500 m	41.184	Jean-François Monette (Canada)
1,000 m	1:24.674	Jiajun Li (China)
1,500 m	2:10.639	Ahn Hyun-soo (South Korea)
3,000 m	4:32.646	Ahn Hyun-soo (South Korea)
☆ 5,000 m relay	6:39.990	Canada (Charles Hamelin, Steve Robillard, François-Louis Tremblay, Mathieu Turcotte)

WOMEN	TIME	NAME & NATIONALITY
500 m	43.671	Evgenia Radanova (Bulgaria)
1,000 m	1:30.483	Byun Chun-sa (South Korea)
1,500 m	2:18.861	Jung Eun-ju (South Korea)
3,000 m	5:01.976	Choi Eun-kyung (South Korea)
☆ 3,000 m relay	4:11.742	South Korea (Choi Eun-kyung, Kim Min-jee, Byun Chun-sa, Ko Gi-hyun)

★ LONGEST SPORTS MARATHONS ★

SPORT	TIME	NAME & NATIONALITY
☆ Basketball	30 hr. 12 min.	Beatrice Hoops Basketball Organization (U.S.A.)
Billiards, individual	181 hr. 8 min.	Pierre De Coster (Belgium)
Billiards, pair	45 hr. 10 min.	Arie Hermans and Jeff Fijneman (Netherlands)
☆ Bowling	60 hr. 15 min.	Giancarlo Tolu (Italy)
Bowls, indoor	36 hours	Arnos Bowling Club (UK)
Bowls, outdoor	80 hr. 25 min.	South Grafton Bowling, Sport and Recreation Club (Australia)
Cricket	26 hr. 13 min.	Cricket Club des Ormes (France)
★ Curling	30 hr. 7 min.	Wheat City Curling Club (Canada)
Darts, individual	72 hours	G. Hofstee, A.J. Amerongen and E. Mol (Netherlands)
★ Soccer	25 hr. 35 min.	Trevor McDonald XI and Elstead Village Idiots (UK)
Futsal	25 hr. 10 min.	Ayuntamiento de Almodóvar del Campo (Spain)
Handball	70 hours	HV Mighty/Stevo (Netherlands)
☆ Ice hockey	203 hours	Sudbury Angels (Canada)
Hockey, indoor	24 hours	Mandel Bloomfield AZA (Canada)

MEN'S 10,000 M SPEED SKATING Jochem Uytdehaage (Netherlands) on his way to beating countryman Gianni Romme's world record in 12 min. 58.92 sec. in the men's 10,000 m speed skating race at the Utah Olympic Oval, U.S.A., on February 22, 2002.

PLACE	DATE
Calgary, Canada	October 18, 2003
Bormio, Italy	February 14, 2004
Marquette, U.S.A.	October 24, 2003
Beijing, China	December 7, 2003
Beijing, China	March 13, 2005

PLACE	DATE
Calgary, Canada	October 19, 2001
Budapest, Hungary	February 3, 2002
Beijing, China	January 11, 2004
Calgary, Canada	October 22, 2000
Calgary, Canada	October 19, 2003

PLACE	DATE
Beatrice, U.S.A.	August 6–7, 2004
Kampenhout, Belgium	June 3–10, 2003
Oosterhout, Netherlands	February 12–14, 2004
St. George's Bay, Malta	September 17–19, 2004
Southgate, UK	April 20–21, 2002
South Grafton, Australia	October 1–4, 2004
Dol de Bretagne, France	June 21–22, 2003
Brandon, Canada	March 13–14, 2004
Borculo, Netherlands	April 22–25, 2004
Reading, UK	September 25–26, 2004
Puertollano, Spain	June 28–29, 2003
Tubbergen, Netherlands	August 30–September 2, 2001
Azilda, Canada	April 3–11, 2004
Edmonton, Canada	February 28–29, 2004

★ LONGEST SPORTS MARATHONS ★

SPORT	TIME	NAME & NATIONALITY
Hockey, in-line	24 hours	8K Roller Hockey League (U.S.A.)
★ Hockey, street	30 hours	Conroy Ross Partners (Canada)
Korfball	26 hr. 2 min.	Korfball Club de Vinken (Netherlands)
Netball	54 hr. 15 min.	Castle View School (UK)
Parasailing	24 hr. 10 min.	Berne Persson (Sweden)
★ Pétanque	27 hr. 30 min.	Newcastle Pétanque Club (Australia)
Pool, individual	75 hr. 19 min.	Raf Goossens (Belgium)
☆ Pool, team	144 hours	Bell Hotel (UK)
★ Punching bag	36 hr. 3 min.	Ron Sarchian (U.S.A.)
Rifle shooting, team	26 hours	St. Sebastianus Schützenbruderchaft (Germany)
Skiing	168 hours	Christian Flühr (Germany)
★ Snowboarding	180 hr. 34 min.	Bernhard Mair (Austria)
☆ Softball	55 hr. 11 min.	Ronan's and Burns Blues (Ireland)
Tennis, singles	25 hr. 25 min.	Christian Barschel and Hauke Daene (Germany)
Tennis, doubles	48 hr. 6 min.	Kadzielewski, Siupka, Zatorsk, Milian (Poland)
★ Tennis, doubles, one pair	33 hr. 33 min.	Christian Barschel and Hauke Daene (Germany)
Tennis, individual	52 hours	Butch Heffernan (Australia)
Volleyball	24 hr. 10 min.	Torgau Vocational School (Germany)
Water polo	24 hours	Rapido 82 Haarlem (Netherlands)
Windsurfing	71 hr. 30 min.	Sergiy Naidych (Ukraine)

All of the above records were set using guidelines established after 1998

PLACE	DATE
Eastpointe, U.S.A.	September 13–14, 2002
Edmonton, Canada	September 17–18, 2004
Vinkeveen, Netherlands	May 23–24, 2002
Canvey Island, UK	March 22–24, 2002
Lake Graningesjön, Sweden	July 19–20, 2002
Newcastle, Australia	January 24–25, 2004
Kampenhout, Belgium	February 19–22, 2003
Driffield, UK	August 2–8, 2004
Encino, U.S.A.	June 15–17, 2004
Ettringen, Germany	September 20–21, 2003
Tyrol, Austria	March 8–15, 2003
Bad Kleinkirchheim, Austria	January 9–16, 2004
Dublin, Ireland	April 30–May 2, 2004
Molln, Germany	September 12–13, 2003
Giliwice, Poland	August 30–September 1, 2002
Molln Tennis Club, Germany	August 13–15, 2004
Dudley, UK	November 23–25, 2001
Torgau, Germany	September 30–October 1, 2002
Haarlem, Netherlands	April 30–May 1, 1999
Simerferopol, Ukraine	June 6–9, 2003

MARATHON CRICKET The longest cricket marathon is 26 hr. 13 min., set by Cricket Club des Ormes (France) at Dol de Bretagne, France, on June 21–22, 2003.

★ SHOOTING [ISSF] ★

MEN	SCORE	NAME & NATIONALITY
10 m running target mixed	391	Manfred Kurzer (Germany)
300 m rifle three positions	1,178	Thomas Jerabek (Czech Republic)
300 m rifle prone	600	Harald Stenvaag (Norway)
	600	Bernd Ruecker (Germany)
300 m standard rifle 3×20	589	Trond Kjoell (Norway)
	589	Marcel Buerge (Switzerland)
50 m running target	596	Nicolai Lapin (USSR)
50 m running target mixed	398	Lubos Racansky (Czech Republic)
10 m air pistol	593	Sergei Pyzhianov (USSR)
10 m air rifle	600	Tevarit Majchacheeap (Thailand)
25 m center fire pistol	590	Afanasijs Kuzmins (USSR)
	590	Sergei Pyzhianov (USSR)
	590	Mikhail Nestruev (Russia)
	590	Park Byung-Taek (South Korea)
Double trap	147	Michael Diamond (Australia)
50 m pistol	581	Alexsander Melentiev (USSR)
50 m rifle three positions	1,186	Rajmond Debevec (Slovenia)
50 m rifle prone	600	Numerous competitors have achieved this score
25 m standard pistol	584	Erich Buljung (U.S.A.)
Trap	125	Giovanni Pellielo (Italy)
	125	Ray Ycong (U.S.A.)
	125	Marcello Tittarelli (Italy)
	125	Lance Bade (U.S.A.)
★ 25 m rapid fire pistol	583	Dongming Yang (China)
	583	Emil Milev (Bulgaria)
★ Skeet	124	Vincent Hancock (U.S.A.)

WOMEN	SCORE	NAME & NATIONALITY
10 m running target	391	Wu Xuan (China)
10 m running target mixed	390	Audrey Soquet (France)
300 m rifle three positions	588	Charlotte Jakobsen (Denmark)
300 m rifle prone	597	Marie Enquist (Sweden)
10 m air pistol	393	Svetlana Smirnova (Russia)
10 m air rifle	400	numerous competitors have achieved this score
25 m pistol	594	Diana Iorgova (Bulgaria)
	594	Tao Luna (China)
50 m rifle three positions	592	Vesela Letcheva (Bulgaria)
	592	Shan Hong (China)
50 m rifle prone	597	Marina Bobkova (Russia)
	597	Olga Dovgun (Kazakhstan)
	597	Olga Dovgun (Kazakhstan)
Trap	74	Victoria Chuyko (Ukraine)
★ Skeet	71	Christine Brinker (Germany)
	71	Haley Dunn (U.S.A.)
	71	Cristina Vitali (Italy)
	71	Ning Wei (China)

PLACE	DATE
Pontevedra, Spain	March 14, 2001
Lahti, Finland	July 13, 2002
Moscow, USSR	August 15, 1990
Tolmezzo, Italy	July 31, 1994
Boden, Sweden	July 7, 1995
Lahti, Finland	July 16, 2002
Lahti, Finland	July 25, 1987
Milan, Italy	August 4, 1994
Munich, West Germany	October 13, 1989
Langkawi, Thailand	January 27, 2000
Zagreb, Yugoslavia	July 15, 1989
Moscow, USSR	August 5, 1990
Kouvola, Finland	July 1, 1997
Lahti, Finland	July 14, 2002
Barcelona, Spain	July 19, 1998
Moscow, USSR	July 20, 1980
Munich, West Germany	August 29, 1992
Caracas, Venezuela	August 20, 1983
Nicosia, Sicily, Italy	April 1, 1994
Lahti, Finland	June 9, 1995
Suhl, Germany	June 11, 1996
Barcelona, Spain	July 23, 1998
Changwon, South Korea	April 14, 2005
Ft. Benning, U.S.A.	May 14, 2005
Changwon, South Korea	April 16, 2005

WOMEN'S 300 M SHOOTING— INDIVIDUAL Charlotte Jakobsen (Denmark), holder of the world record in the women's 300 m rifle prone competition, competes at the World Shooting Championships in Lahti, Finland, in 2002. Jakobsen set her world record (594) in the competition and took the gold medal.

PLACE	DATE
Lahti, Finland	July 6, 2002
Lahti, Finland	July 9, 2002
Lahti, Finland	July 12, 2002
Plzen, Czech Republic	July 22, 2003
Munich, Germany	May 23, 1998
Milan, Italy	May 31, 1994
Munich, Germany	August 23, 2002
Munich, Germany	June 15, 1995
Milan, Italy	May 28, 1999
Barcelona, Spain	July 19, 1998
Lahti, Finland	July 4, 2002
Busan, Phillipines	October 4, 2002
Nicosia, Sicily, Italy	July 23, 1998
Changwon, Korea	April 15, 2005
Changwon, Korea	April 15, 2005
Changwon, Korea	April 15, 2005
Changwon, Korea	April 15, 2005

★ SWIMMING—SHORT COURSE ★

MEN	TIME	NAME & NATIONALITY
☆ 50 m freestyle	21.10	Fred Bousquet (France)
☆ 100 m freestyle	46.25	Ian Crocker (U.S.A.)
200 m freestyle	1:41.10	Ian Thorpe (Australia)
400 m freestyle	3:34.58	Grant Hackett (Australia)
800 m freestyle	7:25.28	Grant Hackett (Australia)
1,500 m freestyle	14:10.10	Grant Hackett (Australia)
4 × 50 m freestyle	1:25.55	Netherlands (Mark Veens, Johan Kenkhuis, Gijs Damen, Pieter van den Hoogenband)
4 × 100 m freestyle	3:09.57	Sweden (Johan Nyström, Lars Frolander, Mattias Ohlin, Stefan Nystrand)
4 × 200 m freestyle	6:56.41	Australia (William Kirby, Ian Thorpe, Michael Klim, Grant Hackett)
☆ 50 m butterfly	22.71	Ian Crocker (U.S.A.)
☆ 100 m butterfly	49.07	Ian Crocker (U.S.A.)
200 m butterfly	1:50.73	Frank Esposito (France)
50 m backstroke	23.31	Matthew Welsh (Australia)
☆ 100 m backstroke	50.32	Peter Marshall (U.S.A.)
☆ 200 m backstroke	1:50.52	Aaron Peirsol (U.S.A.)
50 m breaststroke	26.20	Oleg Lissogor (Ukraine)
100 m breaststroke	57.47	Ed Moses (U.S.A.)
200 m breaststroke	2:02.92	Ed Moses (U.S.A.)
☆ 100 m medley	52.51	Roland Schoeman (South Africa)
☆ 200 m medley	1:53.93	George Bovell (Trinidad)
400 m medley	4:02.72	Brian Johns (Canada)
4 × 50 m medley	1:34.46	Germany (Thomas Rupprath, Mark Warnecke, Fabian Freidrich, Carstein Dehmlow)
☆ 4 × 100 m medley	3:25.09	U.S.A. (Aaron Peirsol, Brendan Hansen, Ian Crocker, Jason Lezak)

WOMEN	TIME	NAME & NATIONALITY
50 m freestyle	23.59	Therese Alshammar (Sweden)
100 m freestyle	52.17	Therese Alshammar (Sweden)
200 m freestyle	1:54.04	Lindsay Benko (U.S.A.)
400 m freestyle	3:59.53	Lindsay Benko (U.S.A.)
800 m freestyle	8:13.35	Sachiko Yamada (Japan)
☆ 1,500 m freestyle	15:42.39	Laure Manaudou (France)
4 × 50 m freestyle	1:37.27	U.S.A. (Kara Lynn Joyce, Neka Mabry, Paige Kearns, Andrea Georoff)
4 × 100 m freestyle	3:34.55	China (Le Jingyi, Na Chao, Shan Ying, Nian Yin)
4 × 200 m freestyle	7:46.30	China (Xu Yanvei, Zhu Yingven, Tang Jingzhi, Yang Yu)
50 m butterfly	25.36	Anne-Karin Kammerling (Sweden)
100 m butterfly	56.34	Natalie Coughlin (U.S.A.)
200 m butterfly	2:04.04	Yu Yang (China)
50 m backstroke	26.83	Hui Li (China)
100 m backstroke	56.71	Natalie Coughlin (U.S.A.)
200 m backstroke	2:03.62	Natalie Coughlin (U.S.A.)

PLACE	DATE
New York City, U.S.A.	March 25, 2004
New York City, U.S.A.	March 27, 2004
Berlin, Germany	February 6, 2000
Sydney, Australia	July 18, 2002
Perth, Australia	August 3, 2001
Perth, Australia	August 7, 2001
Dublin, Ireland	December 14, 2003
Athens, Greece	March 16, 2000
Perth, Australia	August 7, 2001
Indianapolis, U.S.A.	October 10, 2004
New York City, U.S.A.	March 26, 2004
Antibes, France	December 8, 2002
Melbourne, Australia	September 2, 2002
New York City, U.S.A.	March 26, 2004
Indianapolis, U.S.A.	October 11, 2004
Berlin, Germany	January 26, 2002
Stockholm, Sweden	January 23, 2002
Berlin, Germany	January 17, 2004
Stockholm, Sweden	January 18, 2005
New York City, U.S.A.	March 25, 2004
Victoria, Canada	February 21, 2003
Dublin, Ireland	December 11, 2003
Indianapolis, U.S.A.	October 11, 2004

MEN'S 50 M BUTTERFLY Ian Crocker (U.S.A.) takes the lead in the qualifying heat for the men's 50 m butterfly during the FINA World Swimming Championships on October 9, 2004 in Indianapolis, U.S.A. He went on to win the event the following day.

PLACE	DATE
Athens, Greece	March 18, 2000
Athens, Greece	March 17, 2000
Moscow, Russia	April 7, 2002
Berlin, Germany	January 26, 2003
Nishinomya-shi, Japan	January 24, 2004
La Roche sur Yon, France	November 9, 2004
Texas, U.S.A.	March 18, 2004
Gothenburg, Sweden	April 19, 1997
Moscow, Russia	April 3, 2002
Stockholm, Sweden	January 25, 2001
New York, U.S.A.	November 22, 2002
Berlin, Germany	January 18, 2004
Shanghai, China	December 2, 2001
New York City, U.S.A.	November 23, 2002
New York City, U.S.A.	November 27, 2001

WOMEN'S 4 × 100 M FREESTYLE Australian team members Petria Thomas (left), Lisbeth Lenton (center), and Alice Mills (right) cheer their teammate Jodie Henry on their way to winning gold in the women's 4 × 100 m long-course freestyle relay final on August 14, 2004 during the Summer Olympic Games in Athens, Greece.

★ SWIMMING—SHORT COURSE ★

MEN	TIME	NAME & NATIONALITY
50 m breaststroke	29.96	Emma Igelstrom (Sweden)
☆ 100 m breaststroke	1:04.79	Tara Kirk (U.S.A.)
200 m breaststroke	2:17.75	Leisel Jones (Australia)
100 m medley	58.80	Natalie Coughlin (U.S.A.)
200 m medley	2:07.79	Allison Wagner (U.S.A.)
400 m medley	4:27.83	Yana Klochkova (Ukraine)
4 × 50 m medley	1:48.31	Sweden (Therese Alshammar, Emma Igelström, Anna-Karin Kammerling, Johanna Sjöberg)
☆ 4 × 100 m medley	3:54.95	Australia (Sophie Edington, Brooke Hanson Jessica Schipper, Lisbeth Lenton)

★ SWIMMING—LONG COURSE [50-M POOL] ★

MEN	TIME	NAME & NATIONALITY
50 m freestyle	21.64	Alexander Popov (Russia)
100 m freestyle	47.84	Pieter van den Hoogenband (Netherlands)
200 m freestyle	1:44.06	Ian Thorpe (Australia)
400 m freestyle	3:40.08	Ian Thorpe (Australia)
800 m freestyle	7:39.16	Ian Thorpe (Australia)
1,500 m freestyle	14:34.56	Grant Hackett (Australia)
☆ 4 × 100 m freestyle relay	3:13.17	South Africa (Roland Schoeman, Lydon Ferns, Darian Townsend, Ryk Neethling)
4 × 200 m freestyle relay	7:04.66	Australia (Grant Hackett, Michael Klim, William Kirby, Ian Thorpe)
☆ 50 m butterfly	23.30	Ian Crocker (U.S.A.)
☆ 100 m butterfly	50.76	Ian Crocker (U.S.A.)
☆ 200 m butterfly	1:53.93	Michael Phelps (U.S.A.)
☆ 50 m backstroke	24.80	Thomas Rupprath (Germany)
☆ 100 m backstroke	53.45	Aaron Peirsol (U.S.A.)
☆ 200 m backstroke	1:54.74	Aaron Peirsol (U.S.A.)
50 m breaststroke	27.18	Oleg Lisogor (Ukraine)
☆ 100 m breaststroke	59.30	Brendan Hansen (U.S.A.)
☆ 200 m breaststroke	2:09.04	Brendan Hansen (U.S.A.)
200 m medley	1:55.94	Michael Phelps (U.S.A.)
☆ 400 m medley	4:08.26	Michael Phelps (U.S.A.)
☆ 4 × 100 m medley relay	3:30.68	U.S.A. (Aaron Peirsol, Brendon Hanson, Ian Crocker, Jason Lezak)

WOMEN	TIME	NAME & NATIONALITY
50 m freestyle	24.13	Inge de Bruijn (Netherlands)
☆ 100 m freestyle	53.52	Jodie Henry (Australia)
200 m freestyle	1:56.64	Franziska van Almsick (Germany)
400 m freestyle	4:03.85	Janet Evans (U.S.A.)
800 m freestyle	8:16.22	Janet Evans (U.S.A.)
1,500 m freestyle	15:52.10	Janet Evans (U.S.A.)

PLACE	DATE
Moscow, Russia	April 4, 2002
Texas, U.S.A.	March 19, 2004
Melbourne, Australia	November 29, 2003
New York City, U.S.A.	November 23, 2003
Palma de Mallorca, Spain	December 5, 1993
Paris, France	January 19, 2002
Valencia, Spain	December 16, 2000
Indianapolis, U.S.A.	October 9, 2004

PLACE	DATE
Moscow, Russia	June 16, 2000
Sydney, Australia	September 19, 2000
Fukuoka, Japan	July 25, 2001
Manchester, UK	July 30, 2002
Fukuoka, Japan	July 24, 2001
Fukuoka, Japan	July 29, 2001
Athens, Greece	August 15, 2004
Fukuoka, Japan	July 27, 2001
Austin, U.S.A.	February 29, 2004
Long Beach, U.S.A.	July 13, 2004
Barcelona, Spain	July 22, 2003
Barcelona, Spain	July 27, 2003
Athens, Greece	August 21, 2004
Long Beach, U.S.A.	July 12, 2004
Berlin, Germany	August 2, 2002
Long Beach, U.S.A.	July 8, 2004
Long Beach, U.S.A.	July 11, 2004
Maryland, U.S.A.	August 9, 2003
Athens, Greece	August 14, 2004
Athens, Greece	August 21, 2004

MEN'S 200 M BACKSTROKE Aaron Peirsol (U.S.A.) swims to victory in the men's 200 m at the 2004 U.S. Olympic Team Trials in Long Beach, California, U.S.A., on July 12, 2004.

PLACE	DATE
Sydney, Australia	September 22, 2000
Athens, Greece	August 18, 2004
Berlin, Germany	August 3, 2002
Seoul, South Korea	September 22, 1988
Tokyo, Japan	August 20, 1989
Orlando, U.S.A.	March 26, 1988

★ SWIMMING—LONG COURSE [50-M POOL] ★

WOMEN	TIME	NAME & NATIONALITY
☆ 4 × 100 m freestyle relay	3:35.94	Australia (Alice Mills, Lisbeth Lenton, Petria Thomas, Jodie Henry)
☆ 4 × 200 m freestyle relay	7:53.42	U.S.A. (Natalie Coughlin, Carly Piper, Dana Vollmer, Kaitlin Sandeno)
50 m butterfly	25.57	Anna-Karin Kammerling (Sweden)
100 m butterfly	56.61	Inge de Bruijn (Netherlands)
200 m butterfly	2:05.78	Otylia Jedrejczak (Poland)
50 m backstroke	28.25	Sandra Voelker (Germany)
100 m backstroke	59.58	Natalie Coughlin (U.S.A.)
200 m backstroke	2:06.62	Krisztina Egerszegi (Hungary)
50 m breaststroke	30.57	Zoe Baker (UK)
100 m breaststroke	1:06.37	Jones Liesel (Australia)
☆ 200 m breaststroke	2:22.44	Amanda Beard (U.S.A.)
200 m medley	2:09.72	Wu Yanyan (China)
400 m medley	4:33.59	Yana Klochkova (Ukraine)
☆ 4 × 100 m medley relay	3:57.32	Australia (Giaan Rooney, Leisel Jones, Petria Thomas, Jodie Henry)

★ WATERSKIING ★

MEN	RECORD	NAME & NATIONALITY
Slalom	1 buoy/9.75-m line	Jeff Rogers (U.S.A.)
		Andy Mapple (GB)
		Jamie Beauchesne (U.S.A.)
Tricks	12,320 points	Nicolas Le Forestier (France)
Ski fly	298 ft. 10 in. (91.1 m)	Jaret Llewellyn (Canada)
Jump	235 ft. 9 in. (71.9 m)	Jimmy Siemers (U.S.A.)
Overall	2,818.01 points	Jaret Llewellyn (Canada)

WOMEN	RECORD	NAME & NATIONALITY
Slalom	1 buoy/10.25-m line	Kristi Overton Johnson (U.S.A.)
Tricks	8,630 points	Tawn Larsen Hahn (U.S.A.)
Ski fly	227 ft. 7 in. (69.4 m)	Elena Milakova (Russia)
Jump	186 ft. (56.6 m)	Elena Milakova (Russia)
☆ Overall	2,903.43 points	Clementine Lucine (France)

★ WATERSKIING—BAREFOOT ★

MEN	RECORD	NAME & NATIONALITY
Jump	89.8 ft. (27.4 m)	David Small (GB)
Slalom	20.5 crossings of wake in 15 sec.	Brian Fuchs (U.S.A.)
Tricks	9,550 points	David Small (GB)

WOMEN	RECORD	NAME & NATIONALITY
Jump	67.58 ft. (20.6 m)	Nadine de Villiers (South Africa)
Slalom	17.0 crossings of wake in 15 sec.	Nadine de Villiers (South Africa)
Tricks	4,400 points	Nadine de Villiers (South Africa)

PLACE	DATE
Athens, Greece	August 14, 2004
Athens, Greece	August 18, 2004
Berlin, Germany	July 31, 2000
Sydney, Australia	September 17, 2000
Berlin, Germany	August 2, 2002
Berlin, Germany	June 17, 2000
Fort Lauderdale, U.S.A.	August 13, 2002
Athens, Greece	August 25, 1991
Manchester, UK	July 30, 2002
Barcelona, Spain	July 21, 2003
Long Beach, U.S.A.	July 12, 2004
Shanghai, China	October 17, 1997
Sydney, Australia	September 16, 2000
Athens, Greece	August 21, 2004

WOMEN'S 4 × 200 M FREESTYLE
Carly Piper (left), Natalie Coughlin (center), and Dana Vollmer (right) of the U.S. women's 4 × 200 m long-course freestyle relay team celebrate their victory after winning the gold medal at the Olympic Games in Athens, Greece, on August 18, 2004. Kaitlin Sandeno, the fourth member of the team, is out of shot.

PLACE	DATE
Charleston, U.S.A.	August 31, 1997
Miami, U.S.A.	October 4, 1998
Charleston, U.S.A.	July 6, 2003
Chaugey, France	July 13, 2003
Orlando, U.S.A.	May 4, 2000
Lago Santa Fe, U.S.A.	August 10, 2003
Seffner, U.S.A.	September 29, 2002

PLACE	DATE
West Palm Beach, U.S.A.	September 14, 1996
Wilmington, U.S.A.	July 11, 1999
Pine Mountain, U.S.A.	May 26, 2002
Rio Linda, U.S.A.	July 27, 2002
Mauzac, France	August 8, 2004

PLACE	DATE
New South Wales, Australia	February 8, 2004
New South Wales, Australia	April 1994
New South Wales, Australia	February 5, 2004

PLACE	DATE
Roodeplaat Dam, South Africa	March 4, 2000
Wolwekrans, South Africa	January 5, 2001
Wolwekrans, South Africa	January 5, 2001

★ WEIGHT LIFTING WORLD RECORDS ★

MEN	CATEGORY	WEIGHT LIFTED	NAME & NATIONALITY
56 kg	Clean & jerk	168 kg	Halil Mutlu (Turkey)
	Snatch	138.5 kg	Halil Mutlu (Turkey)
	Total	305.0 kg	Halil Mutlu (Turkey)
62 kg	Clean & jerk	182.5 kg	Maosheng Le (China)
	Snatch	153 kg	Zhiyong Shi (China)
	Total	325 kg	World Standard*
69 kg	Clean & jerk	197.5 kg	Guozheng Zhang (China)
	Snatch	165 kg	Georgi Markov (Bulgaria)
	Total	357.5 kg	Galabin Boevski (Bulgaria)
77 kg	Clean & jerk	218 kg	Oleg Perepetchenov (Russia)
☆	Snatch	173.5 kg	Sergey Filimonov (Kazakhstan)
	Total	377.5 kg	Plamen Zhelyazkov (Bulgaria)
85 kg	Clean & jerk	218 kg	Zhang Yong (China)
	Snatch	182.5 kg	Andrei Ribakov (Bulgaria)
	Total	395 kg	World Standard*
94 kg	Clean & jerk	232.5 kg	Szymon Kolecki (Poland)
	Snatch	188 kg	Akakios Kakiashvilis (Greece)
	Total	417 kg	World Standard*
105 kg	Clean & jerk	242 kg	World Standard*
	Snatch	198.5 kg	Marcin Dolega (Poland)
	Total	440 kg	World Standard*
☆ +105 kg	Clean & jerk	263.5 kg	Hossein Rezazadeh (Iran)
	Snatch	213.0 kg	Hossein Rezazadeh (Iran)
	Total	472.5 kg	Hossein Rezazadeh (Iran)

WOMEN	CATEGORY	WEIGHT LIFTED	NAME & NATIONALITY
48 kg	Clean & jerk	116.5 kg	Zhuo Li (China)
☆	Snatch	97.5 kg	Nurcan Taylan (Turkey)
☆	Total	210 kg	Nurcan Taylan (Turkey)
53 kg	Clean & jerk	127.5 kg	Xueju Li (China)
	Snatch	102.5 kg	Ri Song Hui (North Korea)
	Total	225 kg	Yang Xia (China)
58 kg	Clean & jerk	133 kg	Caiyan Sun (China)
	Snatch	110 kg	Li Wang (China)
	Total	240 kg	Li Wang (China)
63 kg	Clean & jerk	138 kg	Natalia Skakun (Ukraine)
☆	Snatch	115 kg	Anna Batsiushka (Belarus)
	Total	247.5 kg	Xia Liu (China)
☆ 69 kg	Clean & jerk	153 kg	Chunhong Liu (China)
☆	Snatch	122.5 kg	Chunhong Liu (China)
☆	Total	275 kg	Chunhong Liu (China)
75 kg	Clean & jerk	152.5 kg	Ruiping Sun (China)
☆	Snatch	125 kg	Natalia Zaboloynaia (Russia)
	☆ Total	272.5 kg	Natalia Zaboloynaia (Russia)
+75 kg	Clean & jerk	182.5 kg	Gonghong Tang (China)
	Snatch	137.5 kg	Meiyuan Ding (China)
☆	Total	305 kg	Gonghong Tang (China)

*From January 1, 1998, the International Weightlifting Federation (IWF) introduced modified body weight categories, thereby making the then world records redundant. This is the new listing with the world standards for the new body weight categories. Results achieved at IWF-approved competitions

PLACE	DATE
Trencin, Slovakia	April 24, 2001
Antalya, Turkey	November 4, 2001
Sydney, Australia	September 16, 2000
Busan, Korea	October 2, 2002
Izmir, Turkey	June 28, 2002
Qinhuangdao, China	September 11, 2003
Sydney, Australia	September 20, 2000
Athens, Greece	November 24, 1999
Trencin, Slovakia	April 27, 2001
Almaty, Kazakhstan	April 9, 2004
Doha, Qatar	March 27, 2002
Tel Aviv, Israel	April 25, 1998
Havirov, Czech Republic	June 2, 2002
Sofia, Bulgaria	April 29, 2000
Athens, Greece	November 27, 1999
Havirov, Czech Republic	June 4, 2002
Athens, Greece	August 25, 2004
Qinhuangdao, China	September 14, 2003
Sydney, Australia	September 26, 2000

WEIGHT LIFTING MEN'S +105 KG CLEAN AND JERK Hossein Rezazadeh (Iran) celebrates his gold medal in the men's superheavyweight +105 kg Olympic weight lifting competition in Athens, Greece, on August 25, 2004. Rezazadeh won the gold medal with a world-record-breaking display in the clean and jerk of 263.5 kg, beating his own previous record of 263 kg.

PLACE	DATE
Qinhuangdao, China	September 10, 2003
Athens, Greece	August 14, 2004
Athens, Greece	August 14, 2004
Busan, South Korea	November 20, 2002
Warsaw, Poland	October 1, 2002
Sydney, Australia	September 18, 2000
Izmir, Turkey	June 28, 2002
Bali, Indonesia	August 10, 2003
Bali, Indonesia	August 10, 2003
Vancouver, Canada	November 18, 2003
Athens, Greece	August 18, 2004
Qinhuangdao, China	September 12, 2003
Athens, Greece	August 19, 2004
Athens, Greece	August 19, 2004
Athens, Greece	August 19, 2004
Busan, South Korea	October 7, 2002
Athens, Greece	August 20, 2004
Athens, Greece	August 20, 2004
Athens, Greece	August 21, 2004
Vancouver, Canada	November 21, 2003
Athens, Greece	August 21, 2004

WEIGHT LIFTING—MEN'S 56 KG Halil Mutlu (Turkey) in action while winning the gold medal in the 56 kg snatch at the Sydney Convention and Exhibition Centre during the 2000 Olympic Games in Sydney, Australia. He currently holds all records in the category.

exceeding the world standards by 0.5 kg for snatch or clean and jerk, or by 2.5 kg for the total, will be recognized as world records.

★ X GAMES—WINTER ★

MEN	MEDALS	HOLDER & NATIONALITY
★ Overall	10	Barrett Christy (U.S.A.)
★ Skiing (overall)	8	Jon Olsson (Sweden)
★ Snowboard (overall)	10	Barrett Christy (U.S.A.)
★ Snocross	7	Blair Morgan (Canada)
★ Ultracross	3	Peter Lind (Sweden) and Xavier de le Rue (France)
★ Moto X	2	Tommy Clowers, Mike Jones, Mike Metzger, Caleb Wyatt (all U.S.A.)

★ X GAMES—SUMMER ★

DISCIPLINE	MEDALS	HOLDER & NATIONALITY
★ Overall	18	Dave Mirra (U.S.A.)
★ Bike stunt	18	Dave Mirra (U.S.A.)
★ Moto X	9	Brian Deegan (U.S.A.)
★ Skateboard	16	Tony Hawk (U.S.A.)
★ Aggressive in-line skate	8	Fabiola da Silva (Brazil)
★ Wakeboard	6	Darin Shapiro (U.S.A.)

☆ **LONGEST SKATEBOARD RAMP JUMP** Professional skateboarder Danny Way (USA) performed a 79-ft. (24-m) 360° air on his Megaramp at X Games X in Los Angeles, California, USA, on August 8, 2004. He also holds the record for the ☆ highest skateboard air off a quarter-pipe, with a 23-ft. 6-in. (7.1-m) method air performed off a 27-ft. (8.2-m) pipe at Point X Camp near Aguanga, California, USA, on June 19, 2003. *For more X Games records, see the special feature on p. 337.*

★ **AGGRESSIVE IN-LINE SKATING** Fabiola da Silva (Brazil)—holder of the most in-line skating medals record—performs at the launch of the X Games Xperience at Disney's California Adventure at Disneyland on July 1, 2003, in Anaheim, California, U.S.A.

★ **MOTO X** Brian Deegan (U.S.A.) has won an unsurpassed nine medals in Moto X. He is pictured left riding in the first round of the Moto X Freestyle event in the ESPN X Games VIII on August 15, 2002, at First Union Center in Philadelphia, Pennsylvania, U.S.A.

INDEX

This year's index is organized into two parts: by subject and by superlative. **Bold** entries in the subject index indicate a main entry on a topic, and entries in CAPS indicate an entire chapter. Neither index lists personal names.

SUBJECT

21st Century Tower, Dubai, UAE, 334

31-legged races, 57

A

Abdul Aziz, 396, 397
Abyss Live, 144
Academy Awards, 298–303
acid rain, 196–197, 199
actors and actresses
   ageing, 14
   movies, 298–303
   theater, 353–358
   TV, 307–317
   see also movies & movie stars
Admiral Nakhimov, 146
adoptions, 21
advertising rates (TV), 314, 315
aerobatics, 429
aerogel, 229
AFL (Australian Football League), 452–453, 454
age (living things), youngest and oldest
   actors, 14, 301–302, 307
   authors, 280
   bacteria, 183
   ball boys, 536
   bank robbers, 265
   barefoot water skiers, 549
   BASE jumpers, 16
   birds, 170
   chelonians, 171
   composers, xxviii
   drivers, 17, 509, 511
   elephants, 155
   heads of state, 261–263
   mothers, 17
   parachute jumpers, 433
   pea shooting world champions, 540
   pets, 100–101
   pinnipeds, 163–164
   prime ministers, 259
   rugby internationals, 523

   siblings, 17
   swimmers, 547
   tennis players, 534, 535
   theater producers, 356
   X Games athletes, xxvii, 339
aggressive inline skating, 337, 339
air (extreme sports maneuver), 337, 588
air hockey, 47
air sickness bags, 110
air sports, 429–434
   banzai skydiving, 67
air travel *see* flights
Airborne Laser (ABL), 407
aircraft, 398–402, 403, 404, 405
   circumnavigation, 41–43
   pulled by hand, 45
   recoveries, 143
airlines, 250–253; air sickness bags, 110;
   tags, 112
airports, 251; control towers, 333
airships, 402
Akashi-Kaikyo bridge, Japan, 421
albinos, 18
alcohol
   beer festivals, 258
   nebulae, 210
   racing alcohol, 503
   shot (liquor) slam, 109
   tastings & toasts, 258
alphabets, 284, 287
Amazon (river), 127
amphibians, 151–152
amphibious ships, 405
Angkor Watt, Cambodia, 417–418
Anik F2, 217
animal & saddle sports, 438–443
animals
   magic show appearances, 367
   pets, 97–106
   zoos, 154–157
   see also specific groups (e.g., dogs) &
      groups of animals (e.g., mammals)
animation, 295, 296, 303, 311, 312
Antarctica, 124, 125, 133, 137, 140
   treks and crossings, 14, 37–39
ants, 91
Apollo missions, 211, 212, 213, 215, 275
appendixes, 10
aquabikes (personal water crafts, PWCs), 32, 58, 542
Arabian Tower, 335
Aral Sea, 199
archery, 525–526; underwater, 539
arches, 122, 334
archipelagoes, 140
Arctic tern, 168

P

SUPERLATIVES

serving: female prime minister, 261; head
of state, 259; prisoner in solitary
confinement, 264; professional
computer gaming referee, 370
spinning a basketball on one finger, 471
standing motionless, 66
stop-motion feature film, 305–306
surviving medical patients, 7–11
suspension for an on-court incident
(basketball), 468
table tennis rally, 520
tennis coaching marathons, 535
tennis matches, 534–535
theatrical runs, 356
unbeaten soccer premiership run, 493
with bullet in head, 11

Loudest
animal sound, 165
human noises, 60–61, 63

Lowest
birthrate, 239
budget expenditure, 263
Championships score, 554
clouds, 132
death rate, 240
death-dive escape, 368
elapsed time in a funny car, 503
fertility rates, 241
golf scores, 496–497
selling singles (music), 322
suicide rates, 241
temperatures, 133
vocal notes, 348

Most
accurate kilogram, 231
acidic rain, 196–197
active volcano, 131
advanced: battlefield simulator, 372;
planetarium projector, 233
cold-resistant animal, 151
complex character in a computer game,
370
complicated wristwatch, 268
contaminated lake, 197
distant: image of Earth, 203; landing by
spacecraft, 203
durable: cell (mobile) phone number, 216;
space station, 211–212
fuel-efficient car, 381
heavily armed space station, 212
intelligent handgun, 409
polluted town, 197
prolific: quick-change illusion artist,
363–364; stuntman, 303–304;
composer (theater), 354–355
reflective body in the solar system, 206
sensitive nose for a land mammal, 157
spherical man-made objects, 228
sports titles won *see specific sports in
subject index*
succinct word, 288
time spent in space, 214

Most dangerous
ant, 91; bee, 91; pinniped, 164; plants,
187–188; poisonous plant, 187

Most expensive
art and sculpture, 275–276, 278, 279
computer game development, 372
food and drink, 79, 80, 82, 83
insect, 96
magic show, 368
motorcycle, 386, 387
music video, 348
objects of desire, 267–271
popstar clothing, 348
soccer player, 492
stage productions, 354, 355, 357
theater admission prices, 294
TV advertisement, 314
TV documentary series, 313
vehicle registration, 384

Most (number)
100-km races (lifetime), 449
abundant animal, 149
action gamers on a single server, 371
albums signed consecutively, 346
aquabike (personal water craft, PWC)
barrel rolls, 542
bananas snapped, 106
beer mats flipped, 61–62
Big Macs consumed, 107
blood: donated, 11; transfused, 12
BMX gyrator spins, 485
body piercings in one session, 86
bones broken in a lifetime, 305
bras unhooked (with one hand), 61
bridal bouquets caught, 242
bridesmaids, 239
bullwhip cracks, 62
casinos played in 24 hours, 69
cell (mobile) phone subscribers, 215
characters played by one actor, 355
chess moves in a game, 69
click sounds in a language, 288
clothespins clipped on a face, 21, 61
commercials starring a company founder,
315
common language, 286
common language sound, 288
competitors in a sack race, 76–77
conquests of Mount Everest, 36
consecutive bog snorkeling World
Championship wins, 539
consecutive footbag kicks with two bags,
537
consecutive holes-in-one, 497
consecutive multicoin rolls, 367
consecutive passes in beach volleyball,
462
consecutive soccer passes, xxix
consecutive wins on a game show, 311
consonants in a language, 288
countries to compete in the Olympic
Games, 515

ACHNOWLEDGMENTS

The 2006 book team would like to thank the following people for their help during the production of this year's edition:

Laura Baker; Laura Barrett; Jim Booth; Nicky Boxall; James Bradley; Nadine Causey; Ann Collins; Sam Fay; Marco Frigatti; Lisa Gibbs; Simon Gold; Nick Hanbridge; James Herbert; Mary Hill; Sam Knights; Peter Laker; Joyce Lee; Anthony Liu; Simon McKeown; Laura McTurk; Rob Molloy; Yeung Poon; Christopher Reinke; Alistair Richards; David Roberts; Paul Rouse; Nicola Savage; Malcolm Smith; Nicola Shanks; Amanda Sprague; Ryan Tunstall; Nicholas Watson; Kate White.

The team also wishes to give special thanks to the following individuals and organizations:

Faisa Abdi; Ernest Adams; Dr. Leslie Aiello; Stan Allen; Roy Allon; Dr. Martyn Amos; Jorgen Vaaben Andersen; David Anderson; Anritsu; Aqua Hotel South Beach Miami; Lance Armstrong; Vic Armstrong; Augie; Aussie Man & Van; Ron Baalke; John Bain; Bank of England; Dr. Peter Barham; BBC; BBC Wildlife Magazine; Capt. Alan Bean; Guenter Bechly; Thomas Blackthorne; Chris Bishop; Richard Boatfield; Jim Booth; Dr. Richard Bourgerie; Professor John Brown Bernie Barker; BP; Laura Bradley; Sir Richard Branson; British Academy of Film & Television Arts; British Antarctic Survey; British Board of Film Classification; British Museum; British National Space Centre; Tim Brostom; BT; Cambridge University; Caida; Caltech; Dr. Robert Carney; Cassella CEL, Inc.; Alan Cassidy; Dr. Kenneth Catania; Michael Motsa, British High Commission, Swaziland; CERN; Dr. Hubert Chanson; Professor Phil Charles; Charlotte Street Hotel; Franklin Chang-Diaz; Edd China; Christie's; CIA World Fact Book; Cinderella May A Holly Grey; Isabelle Clark; Admiral Roy Clare; Richard Clark; CMR/TNS Media Intelligence; Competitive Media Reporting/TNS Media; Kathleen Conroy; David Copperfield; Dr. Mike Coughlan; Warren Cowan; Dr. Paul Craddock; Neil Cresswell; Professor Mike Cruise; Jack Cruwys-Finnigan; Dr. Pam Dalton; Davy's at Regent's Place; Elaine Davidson; Professor Kris Davidson; Dr. Ashley Davies; Jim DeMerritt; Dr. David Dilcher; Discovery News; Martin Dodge; Tracy Eberts; *The Economist;* Lourdes Edlin; Dr. Joan Edwards; EETimes; Brad Ekman; Dr. Farouk El-Baz; Elysium; Dr. John Emsley; Louis Epstein; Dr. Cynan Ellis-Evans; Exeter University; Xiaohui Fan; Adam Fenton; Keo Films; Sarah Finney; Forbes; Brian Ford; Steve Fossett; Arran Frood; Tim Furniss; Drew Gardner; Michael Galbe; Martin Gedny; Geographical Magazine; Geological Society of London; Dr. Richard Ghail; Mauricio Giuliani; Stephanie Gordon; Donald Gorske; Dr. Robert Angus Buchanan; Professor John Guest; Dr. Jim Gunson; Mary Hanson; Andy Harris; Colin Hart; Fiona Hartley;

Russell Harrington; Harvard-Smithsonian Center for Astrophysics; David Hasselhoff; Tony Hawk; Jeff Hecht; Stuart Hendry; Mark Higgins; Dr. Paul Hillyard; Ron Hildebrant; His Majesty King Mswati III of Swaziland; Shannon Holt; Dr. David Horne; Graham Hudson; Paul Hughes; Amanda Hunter; David Huxley; Intel; Intelligence; International Energy Agency; International Jugglers' Association; Imperial College London; Institute of Nanotechnology; Steve Irwin; Professor Steve Jones; Iggy Jovanovic; JoAnn Kaeding; Emily Kao; Judy Katz; David Keys; Dr. Nichol Keith; Taig Khris; Paul Kieve; Professor Joseph Kirschvink; Jamie & Ryan Knowles; Sir John Kreb; Panama J. Kubecka; Lancaster University; Dr. Rolf Landua; Dr. Roger Launius; Alain Leger; John Lee; Tony Lloyd; Kate Long; Los Alamos National Laboratories; Robert Loss; Mr. & Mrs. Michel Lotito (Mr. Mangetout); Louisiana State University; Dr. Karl Lyons; Ranald Mackechnie; Klaus Madengruber; R. Aidan Martin, Director—ReefQuest Centre for Shark Research; Ludivine Maitre; Simone Mangaroo; Professor Giles Marion; Lockheed Martin; Brian Marşden; Jenny Marshall; Dr. Jim Marshall; Dave McAleer; McDonald's Family Restaurant, Mont Fort, Dallas, Texas; Matthew McGrory; Paul McKain; Dr. Alan McNaught; The Met Office; Erin Mick; Microsoft; Lauren Miller; Lucy Millington; Andy Milroy; Robert Milton; Edgar Mitchell; Dr. Sir Patrick Moore; Professor Jon Morse; Derek Musso; Munich Re; Martin Munt; Michael Murphy; National Academy of Sciences; National Federation of Window Cleaners; National Geographic; Natural History Museum; National Physical Laboratory; National Maritime Museum; National Science Foundation; NASA; the Nelson; NetNames; Ted Nield; NOAA; Barry Norman; NT gaming clan; Nua.com; Oracle; Oxford University; Alan Paige; Ed Parsons; Stephen & Morag Paskins; Conoco Phillips; PPARC; Qantas; Qinetiq; Professor Sir Martin Rees; Regional Planetary Image Facility, University College London; Brian Reinert; Greg Rice; John Rice; Ian Ridpath; Dr. Mervyn Rose; Cory Ross; Sally Roth; Royal Astronomical Society; Royal Geographical Society with the Institute of British Geographers; Royal Horticultural Society's *Dictionary of Gardening;* The Royal Institution; Royal Philips Electronics; Royal Society of Chemistry; Rutherford Appleton Laboratory; Ryan Sampson; Amy Saunders; Franz Schreiber; Score on Lincoln, Ali Scrivens; The Science Museum, London; Search Engine Watch; Istvan Sebestyen; Dr. Paul Selden; Prof. Dick Selley; Jordi Serra; SETI Institute; Kit Shah; Kiran Shah; Chris Sheedy; Dr. Seth Shostak; Schumacher West Palm Beach; Dr. Martin Siegert; Siemens; Sotheby's; Speed Stacks Inc.; Lara Speicher; Stapleford Airport; Dirk Steiner; Natalie Stormer; Danny Sullivan; SuperHire; Sword Swallowers Association International; Greg Swift; Carolyn Syangbo; Sydney Kingsford Smith Airport; Charlie Taylor; Telegeography; Gary Thuerk; Heather Tinsley; T J Graphics; Garry Turner; Twin Galaxies; UK Planetary Forum; Professor Martin Uman; United Nations; University of Bath; University of Birmingham; University of Boston; University of Colorado; University of Dundee; University of Florida; University of Greenwich; University of Hertfordshire; University of Oklahoma; University of Southampton; Emily Voigt; Juhani Virola; Ryan Wallace; Dr. David

Wark; Professor Kevin Warwick; Bryony Watts; Danny Way; Isabel Way; Andy Weintraub; James Withers; Richard Winter; Dr. Richard Wiseman; Greg Wood; World Bank; World Flying Disc Federation; World Footbag Association; World Meteorological Organisation; Professor Joshua Wurman; Dr. David Wynn-Williams; www.nationmaster.com; Robert Young.

PICTURE CREDITS

xi–xiii US: © Ranald Mackechnie/GWR; Andy Catterall/ HIT Entertainment Ltd;
GWR (3)

xiv–xvi: c/o Fox Broadcasting(5); c/o Mike Howard; c/o Seven Network Australia (2)

xvii–xviii: © ITV (3); © Drew Gardner/GWR; c/o L'Été de Tous Les Records (2); Rob
Molloy

xx–xxii: Taylor Herring/GWR (2); c/o Deira City Centre shopping mall; Julian
Camilleri

xxi–xxiii: Andy Roberts; c/o Rocketbuster Boots; Laura Barrett

xxv–xxvi: National Geographic Kids; Nickelodeon Australia (3)

xxviii: c/o Adám Lórincz

3, 4: Empics; c/o Coffey family

5, 7: Getty Images; Gamma

8–10: Paul Hughes/GWR; c/o John Prestwich; c/o Alexander Stone (2)

10–12: c/o Kolyo Tanev Kolov (2); c/o Brett House

13: © Drew Gardner/GWR (3)

14–16: c/o Flossie Bennett; Ana Venegas; c/o Beverly Allen

18–19: © Drew Gardner/GWR; c/o Flaherty family (2)

18, 20: c/o Laura Shelley; c/o Caroline Cargado; Jay L. Clendenin/Polaris

22: © Drew Gardner/GWR

1, 23–27: © Ranald Makechnie/GWR; Alamy; © Drew Gardner/GWR; c/o Radhakant
Bajpai; Alamy; Corbis; Alamy; c/o Tribhuwan and Triloki Yadav; c/o Daniel Valdes

27: © Ranald Mackechnie/GWR

31, 32: c/o Rick Hansen; Corbis

33, 34: c/o David Dyson; c/o David Abrutat

36: c/o Rainer Zietlow & Ronald Bormann; Corbis

38, 39: c/o Matty McNair; c/o Tina Sjógren

40: Corbis; Getty Images

40, 42: Getty Images (2)

43: © Ranald Mackechnie/GWR

45, 46: Getty Images; © David Anderson/GWR

47, 48: c/o Ricki Lake Show; c/o Heart Health Hop

50: © Drew Gardner/GWR

51–53: Getty Images; © Paul Hughes/GWR; c/o Sentosa Leisure Management

54, 55: c/o Brian Spotts; c/o Maverick Marketing & Communications

55, 56: Empics/PA; © Paul Hughes/GWR; Reuters

58, 59: c/o East Lansing High School; Benny Schmidt

60, 61: © Drew Gardner/GWR; © Fotostudio Huber André/GWR

62–64: Paul Hughes/GWR; c/o Deafblind UK; Jonny Greene/GWR

62, 65: c/o Gary Duschl; © Paul Hughes/GWR; © Ranald Mackechnie/GWR

66, 68: © Ranald Mackechnie/GWR; © Drew Gardner/GWR

69, 72: Rex Features; © Paul Hughes/GWR (2)

70, 71: c/o Great East Asia Surveyors & Consultants Co. Ltd; © Paul Hughes/GWR;
c/o Domino Day 2004

74–76: c/o Chinese YMCA; Empics/AP; © Paul Hughes/GWR

76–78: © Paul Hughes/GWR (2); c/o Youlia Bereznitskiaia

79, 80: Getty Images; Brad Barket/GWR

81, 82: c/o Pretoria University; Jeff Day/Splash News

84–90: Rex Features (2); Science Photo Library; c/o Cindy Jackson (2); Rex
Features; c/o Kam Ma; © Ranald Mackechnie/GWR; © Drew Gardner/GWR; Alamy;
Corbis; c/o Fulvia Celica Siguas Sandoval; Corbis

91–97: Natural History Museum Picture Library; Science Photo Library; Corbis (3);
OSF; Science Photo Library; Corbis (2); NHPA; Corbis

29, 97–105: c/o Igor Kvetko; c/o Marina Merne; © Matthew Pontin/GWR; c/o Paulette
Keller; Rex Features; © Drew Gardner/GWR; Corinna Atkinson; c/o Cathy Smith;

c/o Mokumoku Tedsukuri Farm; c/o Bill Pierfert; c/o Waymon and Margaret Nipper;
© Drew Gardner/GWR

107, 108:	© Drew Gardner/GWR; c/o Salil Wilson (3); © Paul Hughes/GWR
110, 111:	c/o Anita Cash; c/o Henry Shelford
113–115:	© Drew Gardner/GWR; c/o Kevin Cook; Zuma Press; Will & Deni McIntyre/Photo Researchers, Inc.; © Paul Hughes/GWR
142:	Getty Images
120, 121:	NASA; Corbis
121, 122:	Getty Images; Corbis
123, 125:	Corbis; BAS/EPICA
126, 127:	Corbis; Jacques Descloitres, MODIS Land Rapid Response Team, NASA/GSFC
128, 129:	Science Photo Library; National Geographic Images
131:	USGS × 3
133–135:	National Geographic Images; Getty Images
136, 137:	Corbis (2)
139, 140:	Science Photo Library (2); Corbis
141, 142:	Science Photo Library; Cliff Tan; Ian Bull
145:	Brad Seibel; Getty Images
146, 147:	c/o JAMSTEC; SeaPics
149, 151:	Ardea; Getty Images
150, 152:	SeaPics; Ardea
153–156:	Taylor Herring/GWR; Reuters; c/o Chengdu Research Base; Barcroft Media
158, 159:	Alamy; c/o Vanderbilt Education
161:	Alamy
163, 164:	Corbis; SeaPics
165, 166:	OSF; SeaPics
167–169:	OSF; c/o Steve Bird/Birdseekers
169, 170:	OSF (2)
171–173:	Rex Features; Getty Images; Corbis
173, 174:	Corbis; Topham Picturepoint
176, 179:	Science Photo Library; c/o Dr. Neil Clark
178, 180,	
181:	Science Photo Library; c/o The Heyuan Museum; Corbis
182, 183:	Science Photo Library (2)
184, 185:	Empics/AP; Corbis
187, 188:	OSF (2)
189, 190:	Corbis; OSF
192, 193:	c/o Norm Craven; c/o Scott Robb
194:	Forest Service, an agency of DARD Northern Ireland
197:	Getty
198, 199:	Corbis; USGS Eros Data Center, based on data provided by the Landsat Science team (3); c/o Senna Tree Company
204, 205:	NASA/LMSAL; NASA/JPL; ESA/NASA/University of Arizona; NASA/JSC/Cornell; Science Photo Library
204, 205:	NASA/JPL/SSI
207, 208:	ESA/NASA, the AVO project and Paolo Padovani; ESA
209, 210:	NASA/ESA and The Hubble Heritage Team (STScI/AURA); NASA, ESA and H.E. Bond (STScI) (5)
212, 213:	Corbis; Getty Images
213:	Corbis; Getty Images
216, 217:	c/o Complan Medien GmbH; Getty Images
218, 219:	NASA-HQ-GRIN; c/o Arecibo
220, 222:	DefCon Wi-Fi Shootout; TNO TPD
221–223:	c/o Gary Thuerk; Test image for the PICA project from CCETT in France (2); Getty Images; c/o Martin Dodge/www.cybergeography.com
224–226:	© Paul Hughes/GWR; EFDA-JET (2); Corbis; c/o Edison International
228, 229:	Don Harley; NASA-KSC; c/o Cornell University
230, 231:	NASA; Getty Images

232, 233: UC Berkeley; OQO
234, 235: NASA; ASIMO Honda (3)
256: Getty Images
239, 240: c/o Christa Rasanayagam; c/o Suresh Arulanantham
242, 243: c/o Tadao & Minoru Watanabe; Getty Images
245, 246: Corbis (2)
247, 248: Corbis (2)
250, 251: Getty Images; Alamy
252, 253: c/o Maurizio Giuliano; Alamy
254, 255: Getty Images; Paul Hughes/GWR; c/o Fellsmere Frog Leg Festival
257, 258: Corbis; Rex Features
260: Getty Images (3)
261, 262: Getty Images (2)
264, 265: Corbis; Empics
266: Corbis
269, 270: Getty Images; c/o Ran Gorenstein
270, 271: Christie's Images; Empics/AP
276, 277: c/o Michael Carmichael; c/o Bev Kirk
278, 279: © Succession Picasso/ DACS 2005; c/o Universal Press Syndicate; c/o Maesa Elephant Camp (2)
281, 282: c/o Bon Prix; Rex Features
283, 284: Alamy; © Rankin
285: Getty Images
287, 288: Colleen Manassa; Corbis
290, 291: NewsPix; Alamy
292, 293: Getty Images; c/o Cinema Dei Piccoli
295: Corbis
296, 297: Rex Features/Photograph from the motion picture "Shrek 2" TM & © 2004 DreamWorks L.L..C. and PDI, reprinted with permission by DreamWorks Animation; Rex Features; Getty Images (2); Rex Features (3); The Ronald Grant Archive
299, 300: c/o Sony (3); Getty Images
302: Getty Images
303, 304: THE POLAR EXPRESS © 2004 Warner Bros. Entertainment Inc. All Rights Reserved; © Ranald Mackechnie/GWR
305, 306: Empics/AP; © Ranald Mackechnie/GWR; Moviestore Collection
307, 308: Getty Images; © Ranald Mackechnie/GWR
309, 310: Rex Features (2); Getty Images; Rex Features (3); Getty Images (2)
313, 314: © BBC Archive; Getty Images
315, 316: Corbis; © BBC Archive (2); Jonny Greene/Taylor Herring; Getty Images
317, 318: Getty Images; Comic Relief UK
320, 321: Courtesy of Apple (2); Archos; Getty Images
322–324: Getty Images (3)
324, 325: Getty Images (3)
326–331: c/o Laura Hughes; c/o Truly Nolen; c/o Mike Stephenson; c/o Foundation Skateboards; © Drew Gardner/GWR; Rex Features; c/o HARIBO GmbH & Co KG; Discovery Channel BIG!; Getty Images
332–336: Corbis; c/o Residents of Bethel; Empics/AP; Getty Images; Getty Images; c/o 101 Tower; Building Illustrations by Cliff Tan
338–343: Buzz Pictures; Getty Images (2); Action Plus (2); Buzz Pictures; Getty Images (3)
344, 345: Getty Images (2)
346, 347: c/o Yahir Othón Parra; Getty Images
350: c/o The Grand Boys; c/o George Barbar
351, 352: Getty Images
353, 354: Rex Features; Cylla von Tiedemann © Kevin Wallace Ltd. 2005
356, 357: Getty Images (3)
357, 360: c/o Cirque du Soleil; © Paul Hughes/GWR; Rick Diamond/Cirque de Soleil (2)
361, 362: c/o Paul-Erik Lillholm; © Ranald Mackechnie/GWR

364–368: Royal Mail (2); Christie's Images; Showtime 2003; Corbis; Ramon Torra; c/o Gaillup Extreme Productions

370, 371: © 2001–2005 Lionhead Studios Limited All Rights Reserved; c/o David Storey

377, 378: Namco; Rockstar Games (2); Courtesy of Computer History Museum; *Dragon's Lair* creators: Don Bluth, Rick Dyer, Gary Goldman and John Pomeroy © Bluth Group LTD.

377, 378: c/o MAN TAKRAF Fórdertechnik GmbH; c/o Jonathan Reeves (2)

375,

379–380: c/o Autostadt GmbH (2); c/o Stephen McGill

381: c/o Koenigsegg CCR; c/o Team FANCY CAROL-NOK

382–384: c/o Ken O'Hara; Corbis; c/o International 7300 CTX

386, 387: c/o MTT; c/o Roger LeBlanc

388, 389: Getty Images; c/o Bobby Root

391: c/o Great Southern Railway; Corbis

390–393: Corbis; c/o Holloman High Speed Test Track

394: Getty Images

395, 397: Reuters (2)

401: AirTeamImages.com; The Flight Collection; Jan Lidestrand

400–402: Corbis

404, 405: Richard Hunt; U.S. Navy

404, 405: Defence Picture Library; Corbis

406, 407: Getty Images (2); c/o Lockheed Martin

408, 409: c/o APOPO; Corbis

410–413: © Paul Hughes/GWR; c/o Angus Robson (9)

415–417: Getty Images; Corbis; Alamy

418, 421: c/o Sportschallengers; Corbis

419: Corbis

420, 422: Corbis (2)

422, 423: Mollison Communications/Luna Park Melbourne; c/o The Holy Land Experience

424, 425: c/o Kristin Siebeneicher PR; Corbis

429–431: c/o The Echo Trust; Corbis

432–433: c/o Paraclub Flevo; c/o Thomas S. Nielsen; c/o Jay Stokes

434–435: Getty Images (2)

436–438: Getty Images (3)

439, 441: c/o Mad Cow Entertainment P/L (5); Getty Images

442, 443: Getty Images (2)

444, 445: Getty Images (2)

446, 447: Getty Images (2)

448, 449: Getty Images (2)

450, 451: Getty Images (2)

453, 455: Getty Images; Newspix

454, 456: Getty Images; Empics

458, 459: Getty Images; Corbis

460, 461: Empics; Reuters; Getty Images

463, 464: Getty Images; c/o Joe Pfeiffer

465, 466: Getty Images (2)

468, 469: NBA/Getty Images (2)

470, 471: NBA/Getty Images; Getty Images

472, 473: Empics; Getty Images; c/o Mongolian Wrestling Tournament; Corbis

474, 477: Getty Images (2)

476, 480: Getty Images (2)

481, 483: Getty Images (2)

484, 485: Getty Images (2)

486, 487: c/o Eric Kirchner and Patrick Herresthal; c/o Mission Hills

488, 490: Getty Images

490, 491: Empics; Getty Images

493, 494: Empics; Getty Images

STOP PRESS

Driving to the highest altitude by car Matthias Jeschke (Germany) drove a Toyota Land Cruiser 90 to an altitude of 20,860 ft. (6,358 m) on the slopes of the volcano Ojos del Salado on the Chile-Argentina border on March 4, 2005.

Largest military air show The annual Royal International Air Tattoo at RAF Fairford, Gloucestershire, UK, is the world's largest in terms of participating aircraft. An average of 350 static and flying aircraft attend each year, with a record total of 535 aircraft at the 2003 show.

Longest marriage—living couple Percy and Florence Arrowsmith (both UK) celebrated 80 years of marriage on June 1, 2005. They are also the **oldest living married couple,** with an aggregate age of 205 years 293 days.

Most concerts by a symphony orchestra The New York Philharmonic (U.S.A.) has played 14,000 concerts over the last 162 years. The orchestra's archive has the first performance on December 7, 1842, and the 14,000th on December 18, 2004.

Largest company mascot Duracell Latin America created a giant version of the Duracell Bunny measuring 40 ft. 2 in. (12.6 m) tall. The mas-

LARGEST ELVIS GATHERING A record total of 77 Elvis impersonators gathered at Selfridges' London store, UK, on April 17, 2005, to sing "Viva Las Vegas." Each Elvis wore an appropriate outfit from a period of the King's career, including GI uniforms and jump suits.

HIGHEST BOX OFFICE GROSS—OPENING DAY *Star Wars: Episode III—Revenge of the Sith* (U.S.A., 2005) took a record $50,013,859 on its opening day in the U.S.A. on May 19, 2005, from a total of 3,661 cinemas. The movie was also given the ☆**largest print run** of any film in history, with 9,000, and the ☆**largest simultaneous premier,** opening in 115 countries.

cot was completed and measured in Los Angeles, California, U.S.A., on April 20, 2005.

Highest attendance for a baseball franchise The highest cumulative attendance for a baseball franchise is 165,770,718 by the Los Angeles Dodgers (U.S.A.) between 1901 and 2004.

MOST PEOPLE INSIDE A SOAP BUBBLE Fan Yang (Canada) blew a soap bubble large enough to enclose 18 adults—all no shorter than 5 ft. (1.52 m) tall—at the Toys "R" Us store in Times Square, New York City, U.S.A., on March 19, 2005.

Largest bank robbery The largest bank robbery was an estimated £26.5 million ($51.46 million) stolen from the Northern Bank, Belfast, UK, between December 19, and December 20, 2004.

LONGEST DOG EARS
Tigger the bloodhound—owned by Bryan and Christina Flessner of St. Joseph, Illinois, U.S.A.—has ears measuring 13.75 in. (34.9 cm) and 13.5 in. (34.2 cm) for his right and left ears respectively.